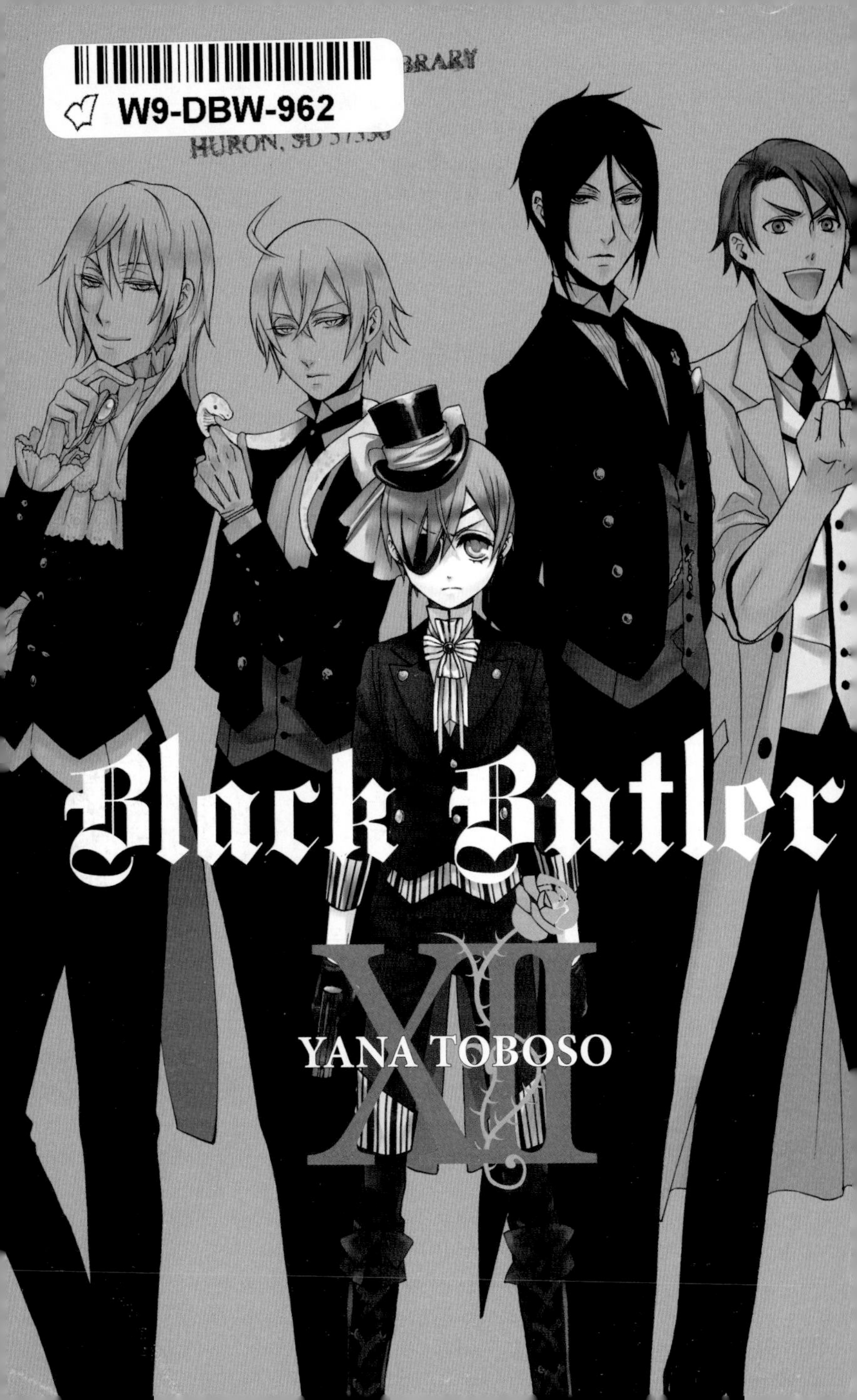
Black Butler
XII
YANA TOBOSO

Contents

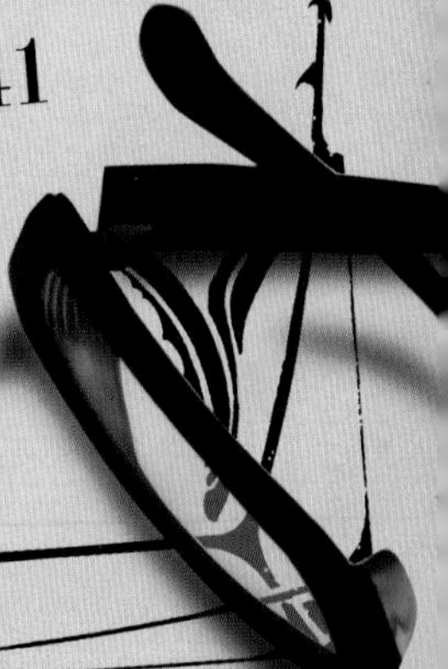

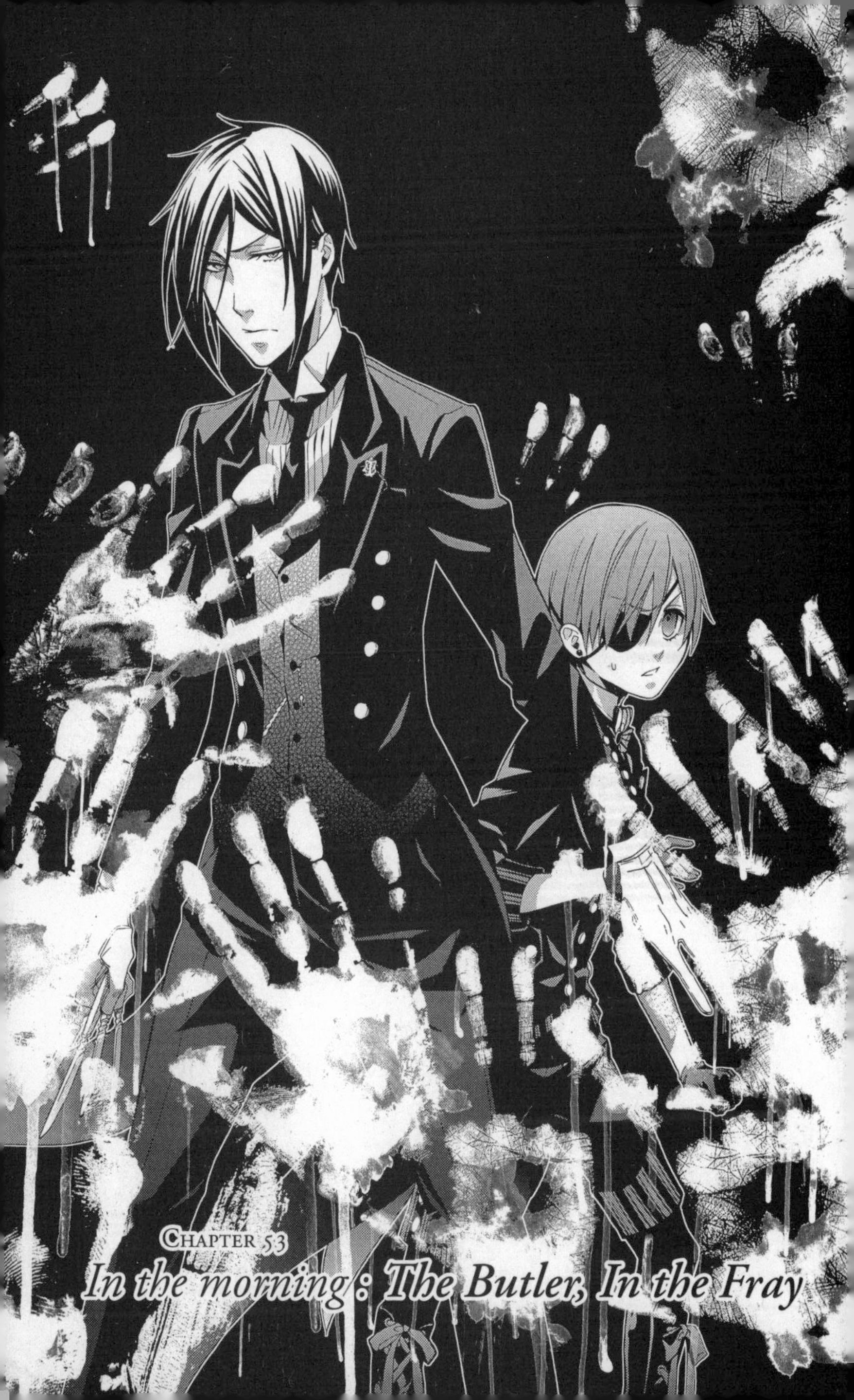
Chapter 53
In the morning : The Butler, In the Fray

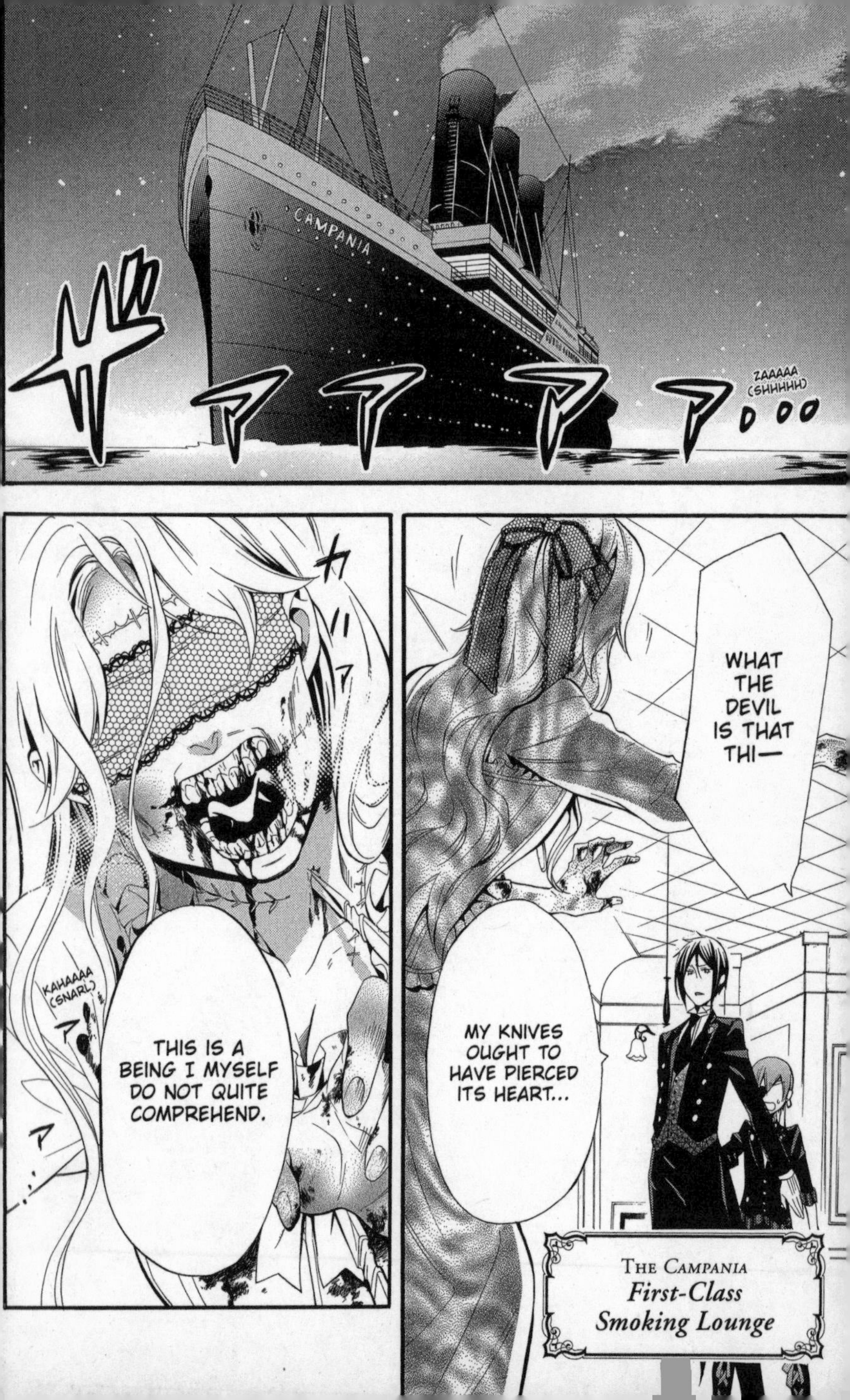
ZAAAAA (SHHHHH)
WHAT THE DEVIL IS THAT THI—
MY KNIVES OUGHT TO HAVE PIERCED ITS HEART...
THE CAMPANIA First-Class Smoking Lounge
KAHAAAA (SNARL)
THIS IS A BEING I MYSELF DO NOT QUITE COMPREHEND.

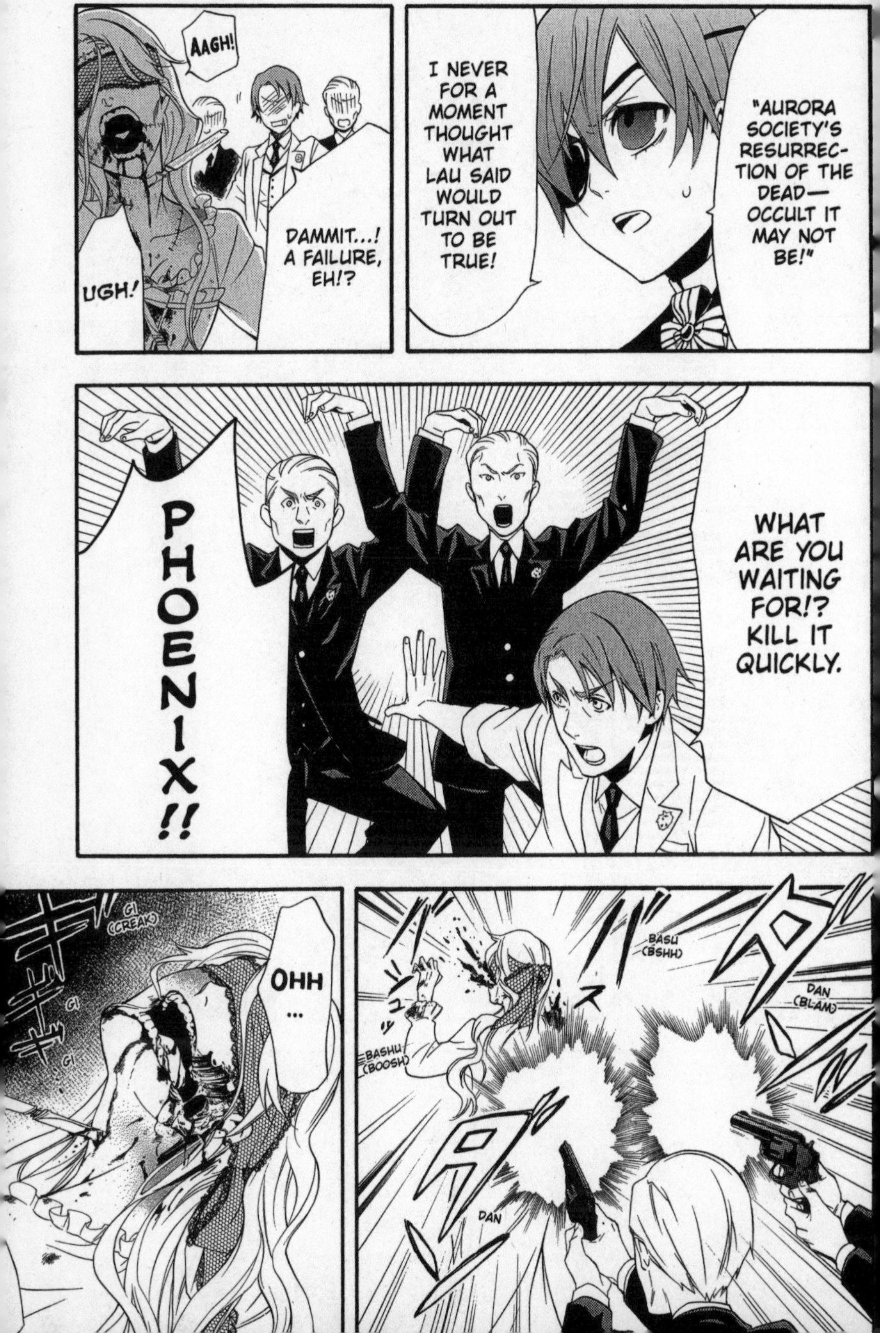
"AURORA SOCIETY'S RESURRECTION OF THE DEAD— OCCULT IT MAY NOT BE!"
I NEVER FOR A MOMENT THOUGHT WHAT LAU SAID WOULD TURN OUT TO BE TRUE!
AAGH!
DAMMIT...! A FAILURE, EH!?
UGH!
WHAT ARE YOU WAITING FOR!? KILL IT QUICKLY.
PHOENIX!!
BASU (BSHH)
DAN (BLAM)
BASHU (BOOSH)
DAN
GI (CREAK)
GI
GI
OHH...

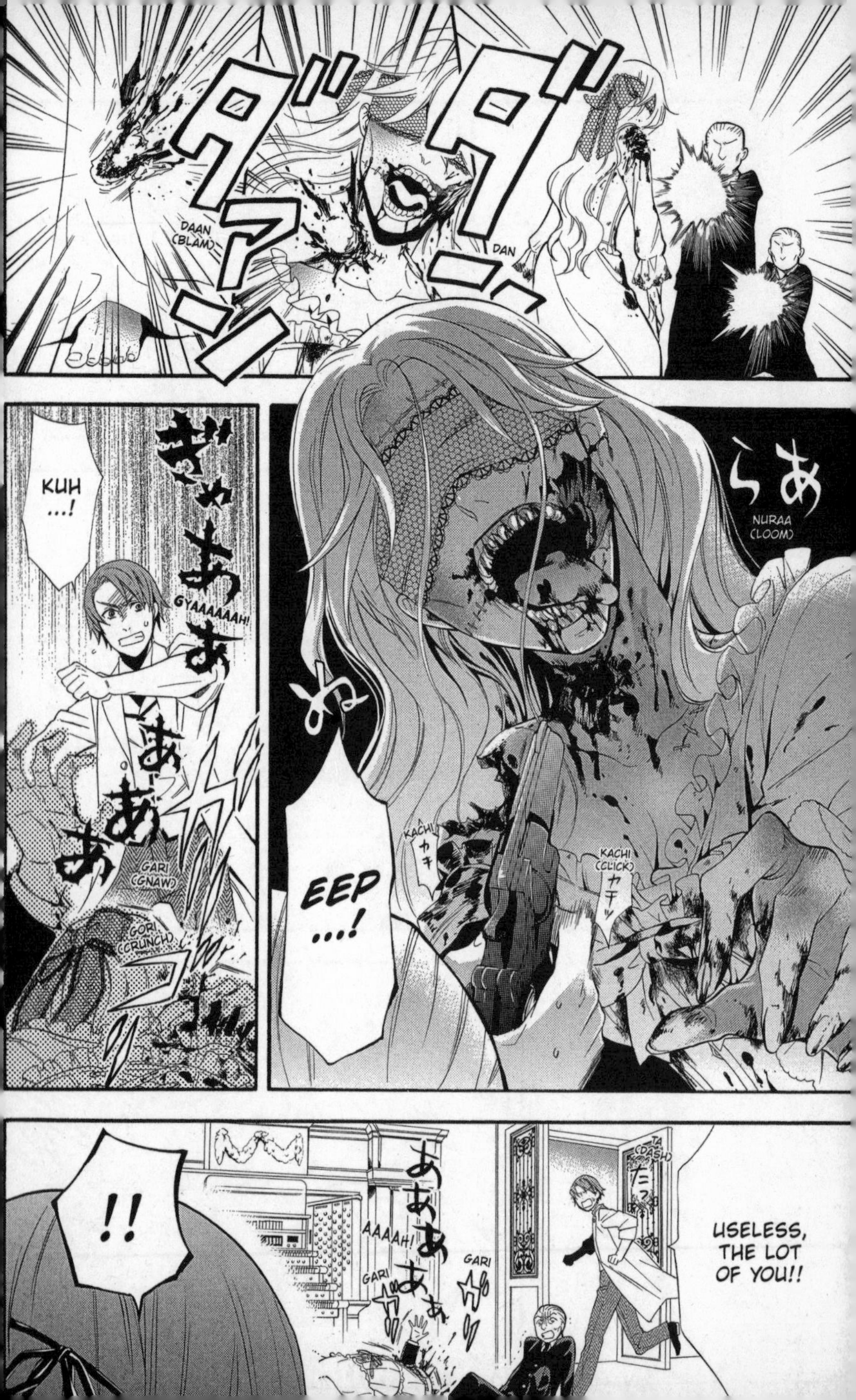
DAN
DAAN (BLAM)
NURAA (LOOM)
KACHI (CLICK)
KACHI
EEP ...!
KUH ...!
GYAAAAAAH!
GARI (GNAW)
GORI (CRUNCH)
USELESS, THE LOT OF YOU!!
TA (DASH)
GARI
AAAAH!
GARI
!!

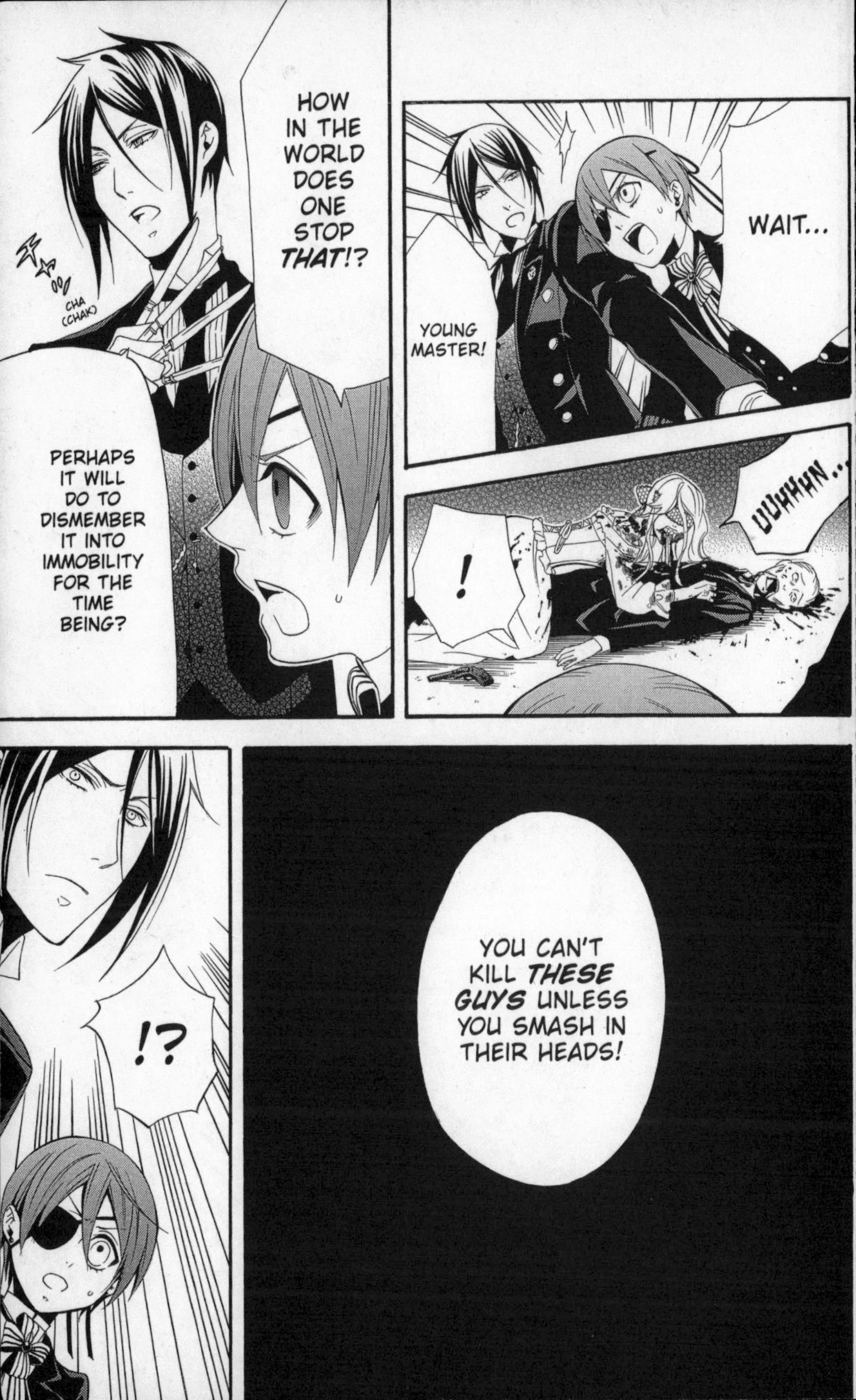
WAIT...
YOUNG MASTER!
UUHHHN...
!
HOW IN THE WORLD DOES ONE STOP *THAT*!?
CHA (CHAK)
PERHAPS IT WILL DO TO DISMEMBER IT INTO IMMOBILITY FOR THE TIME BEING?
YOU CAN'T KILL *THESE GUYS* UNLESS YOU SMASH IN THEIR HEADS!
!?

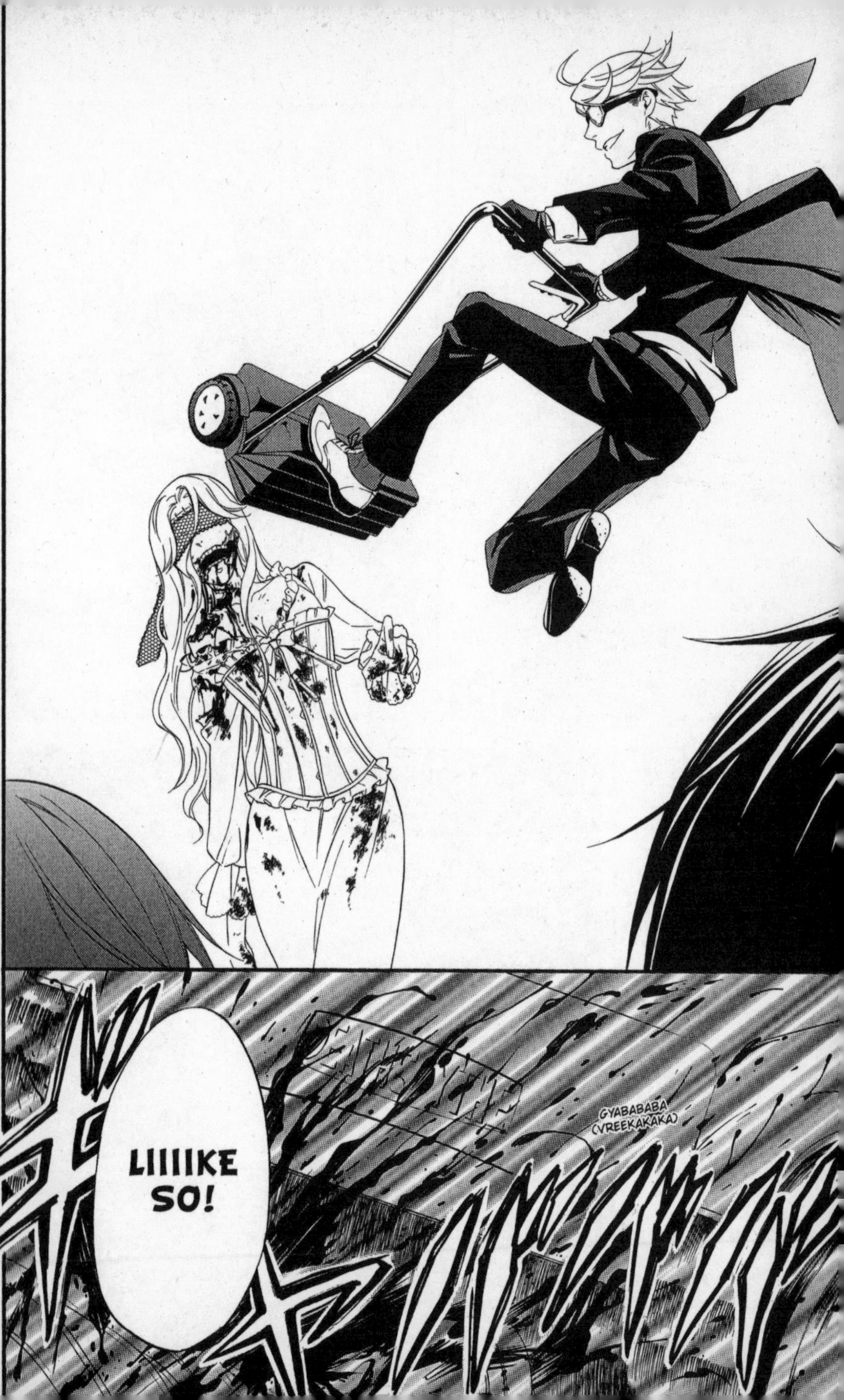
GYABABABA
(VREEKAKAKA)
LIIIKE SO!

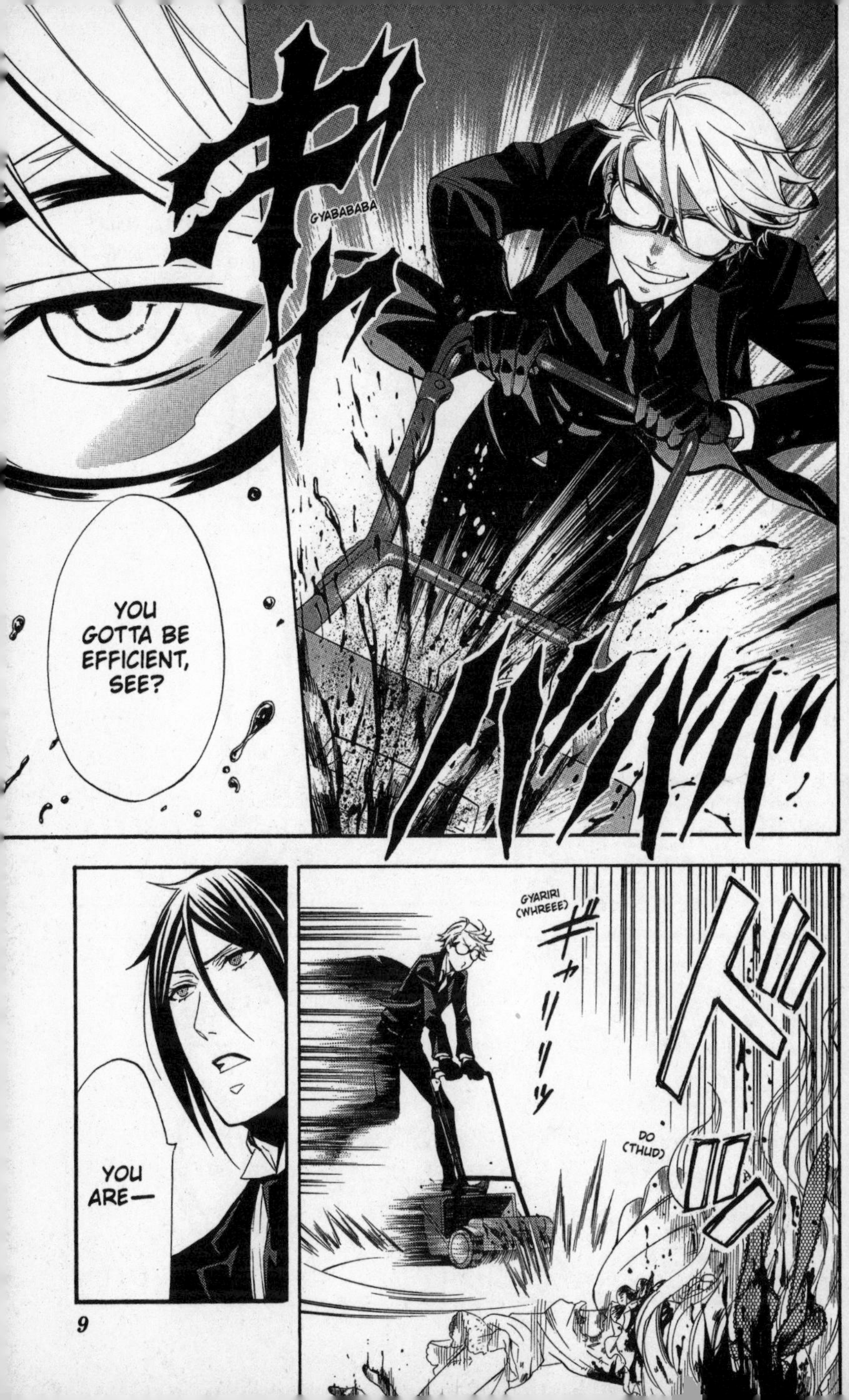
GYABABABA
YOU GOTTA BE EFFICIENT, SEE?
GYARIRI (WHREEE)
DO (THUD)
YOU ARE—

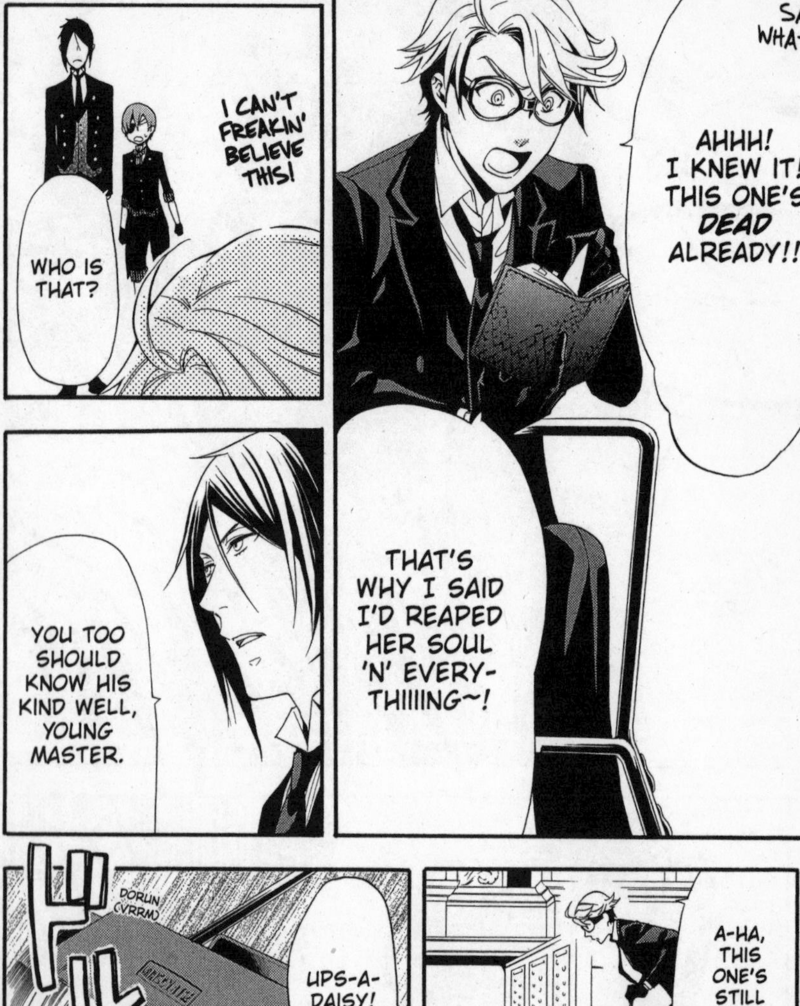
SAY WHAT!?
AHHH! I KNEW IT! THIS ONE'S *DEAD* ALREADY!!
THAT'S WHY I SAID I'D REAPED HER SOUL 'N' EVERY-THIIIING~!
I CAN'T FREAKIN' BELIEVE THIS!
WHO IS THAT?
YOU TOO SHOULD KNOW HIS KIND WELL, YOUNG MASTER.
A-HA, THIS ONE'S STILL GOT A SOUL.
ヒョイッ
HYOI (LEAP)
UPS-A-DAISY!
DORUN (VRRM)

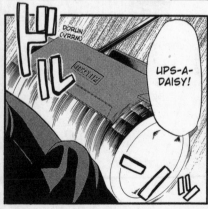

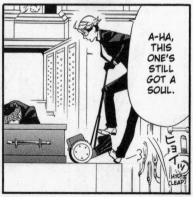

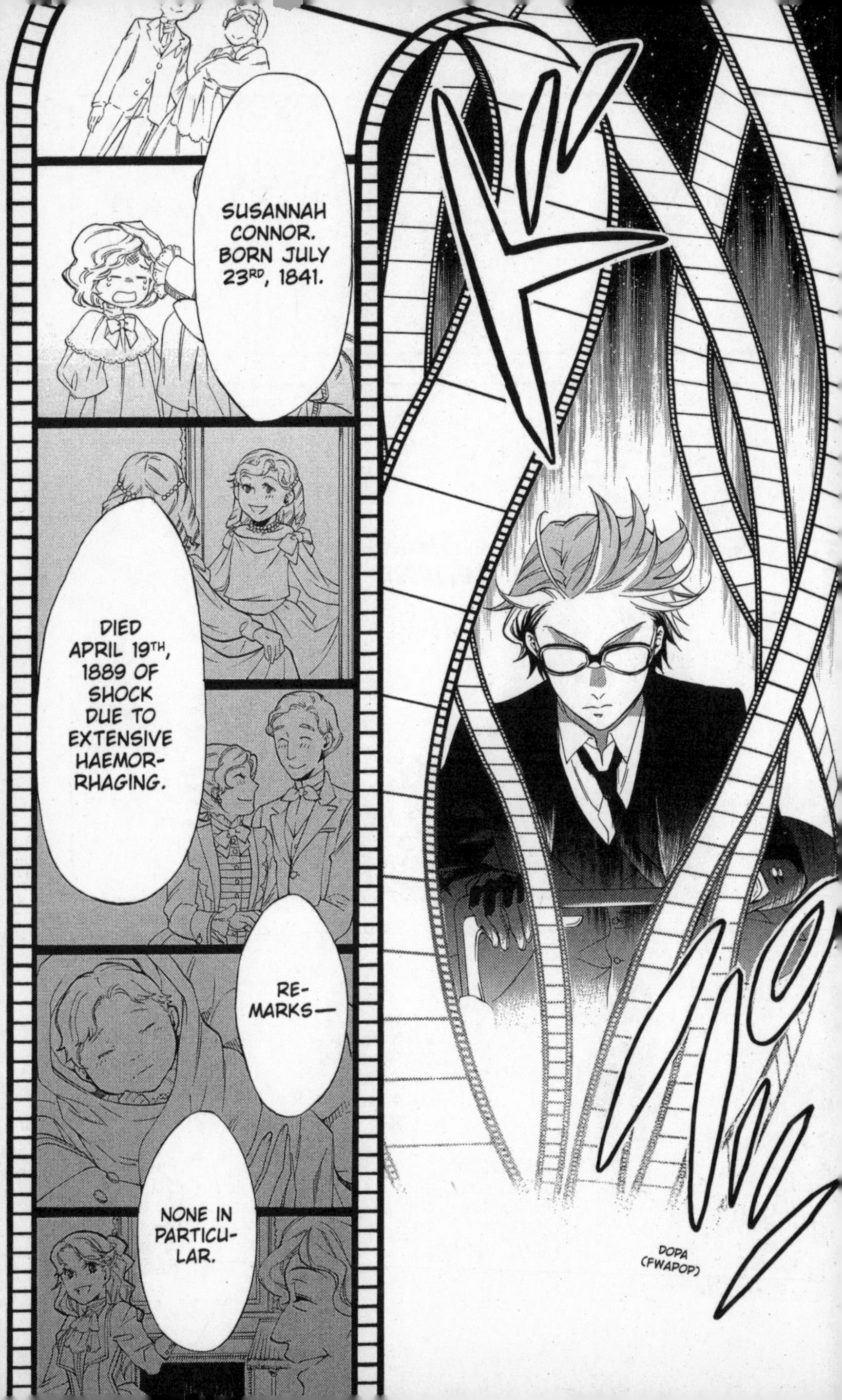
DOPA (FWAPOP)
SUSANNAH CONNOR. BORN JULY 23RD, 1841.
DIED APRIL 19TH, 1889 OF SHOCK DUE TO EXTENSIVE HAEMOR-RHAGING.
RE-MARKS—
NONE IN PARTICU-LAR.

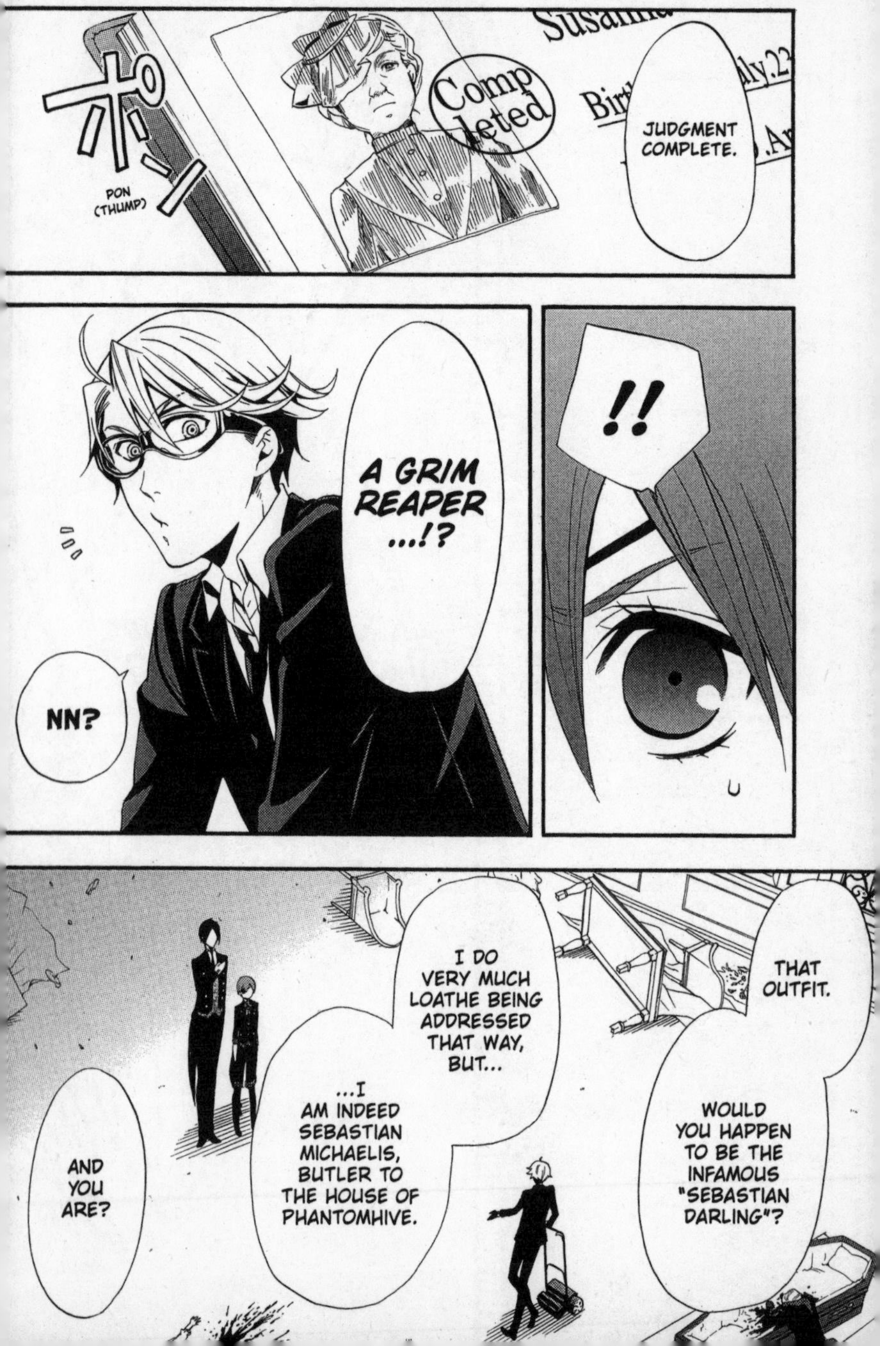
Completed
JUDGMENT COMPLETE.
ポーン
PON (THUMP)
!!
A GRIM REAPER ...!?
NN?
THAT OUTFIT.
WOULD YOU HAPPEN TO BE THE INFAMOUS "SEBASTIAN DARLING"?
I DO VERY MUCH LOATHE BEING ADDRESSED THAT WAY, BUT...
...I AM INDEED SEBASTIAN MICHAELIS, BUTLER TO THE HOUSE OF PHANTOMHIVE.
AND YOU ARE?

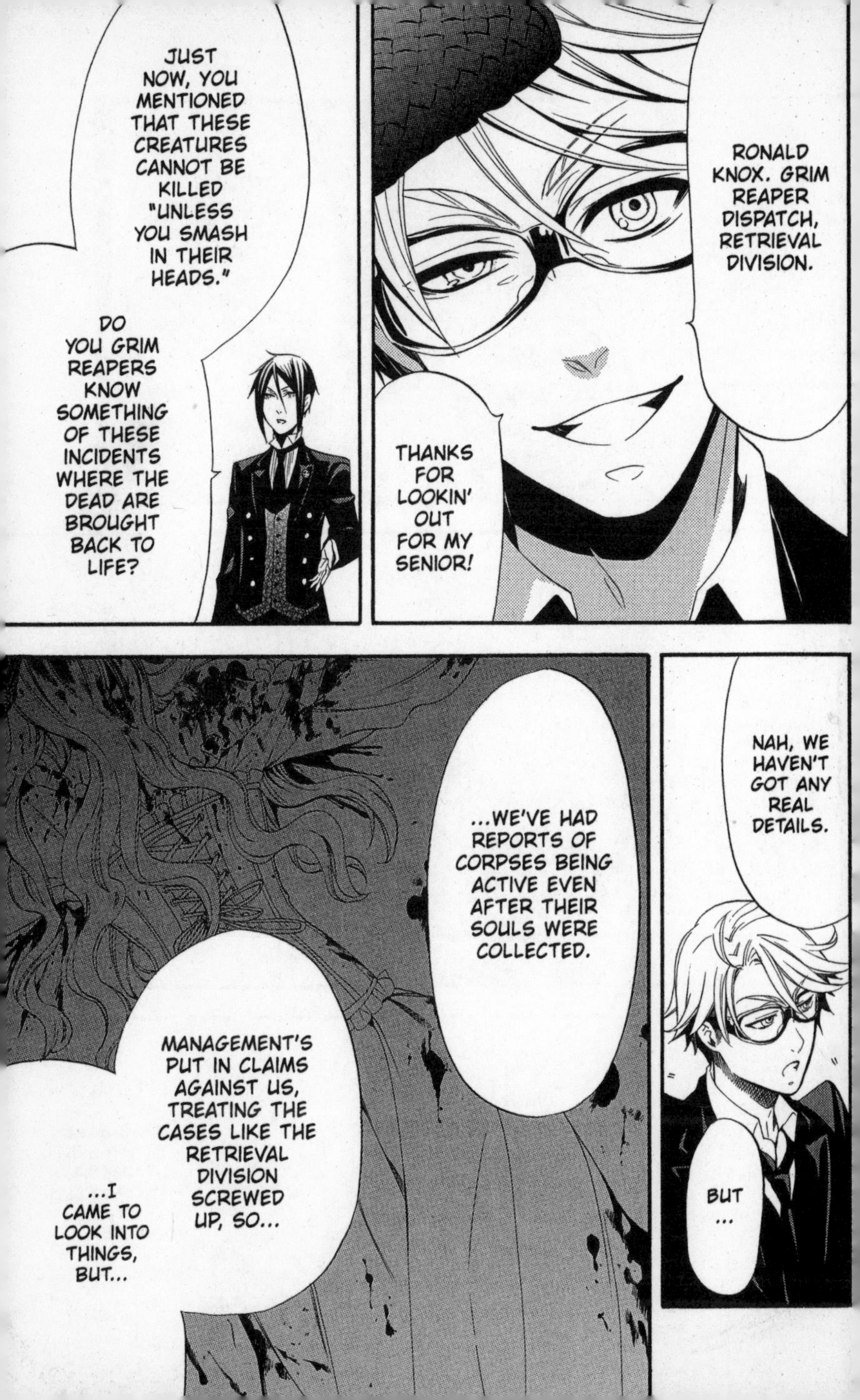
RONALD KNOX. GRIM REAPER DISPATCH, RETRIEVAL DIVISION.
THANKS FOR LOOKIN' OUT FOR MY SENIOR!
JUST NOW, YOU MENTIONED THAT THESE CREATURES CANNOT BE KILLED "UNLESS YOU SMASH IN THEIR HEADS."
DO YOU GRIM REAPERS KNOW SOMETHING OF THESE INCIDENTS WHERE THE DEAD ARE BROUGHT BACK TO LIFE?
NAH, WE HAVEN'T GOT ANY REAL DETAILS.
BUT...
...WE'VE HAD REPORTS OF CORPSES BEING ACTIVE EVEN AFTER THEIR SOULS WERE COLLECTED.
MANAGEMENT'S PUT IN CLAIMS AGAINST US, TREATING THE CASES LIKE THE RETRIEVAL DIVISION SCREWED UP, SO...
...I CAME TO LOOK INTO THINGS, BUT...

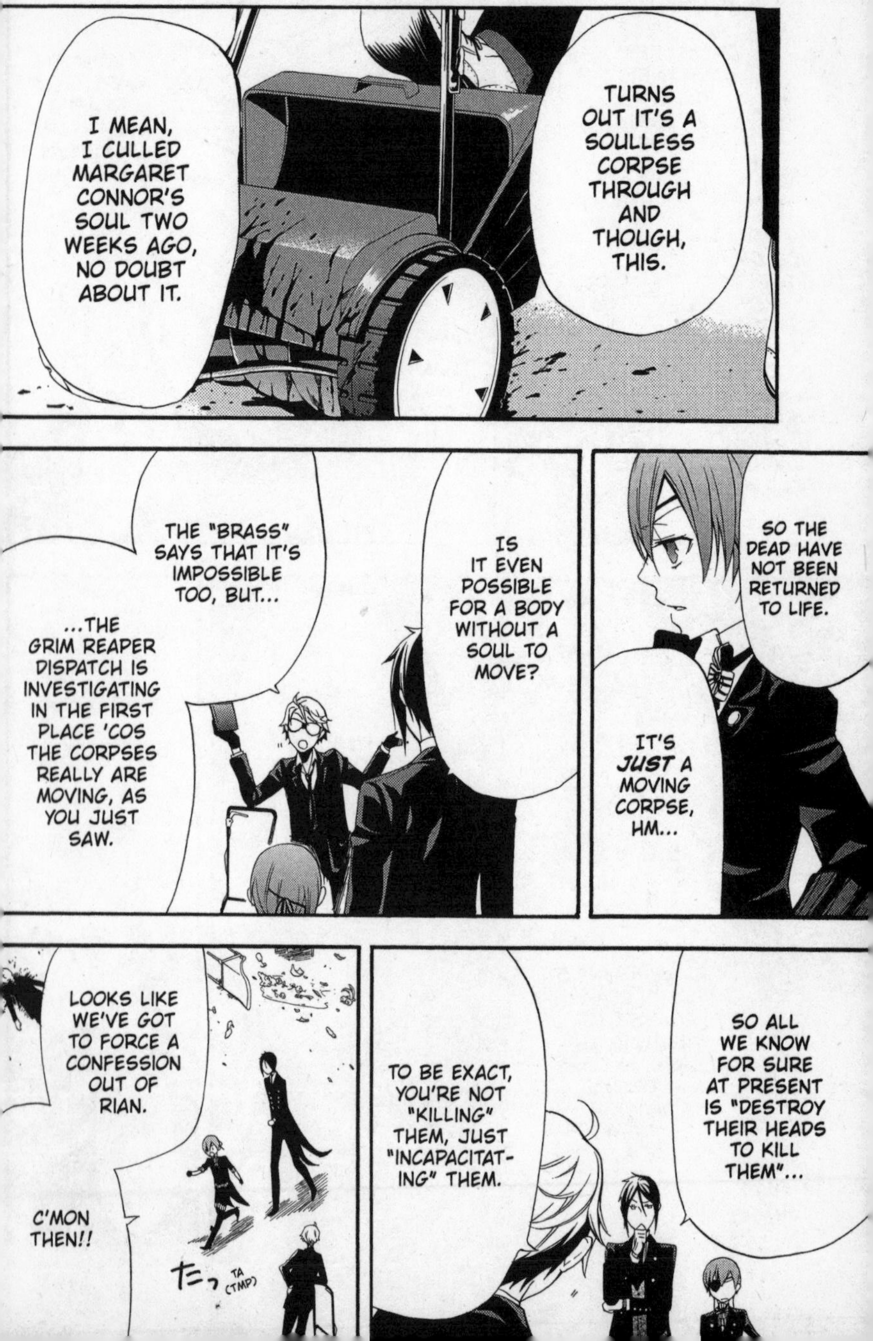
TURNS OUT IT'S A SOULLESS CORPSE THROUGH AND THOUGH, THIS.
I MEAN, I CULLED MARGARET CONNOR'S SOUL TWO WEEKS AGO, NO DOUBT ABOUT IT.
SO THE DEAD HAVE NOT BEEN RETURNED TO LIFE.
IT'S *JUST* A MOVING CORPSE, HM...
IS IT EVEN POSSIBLE FOR A BODY WITHOUT A SOUL TO MOVE?
THE "BRASS" SAYS THAT IT'S IMPOSSIBLE TOO, BUT...
...THE GRIM REAPER DISPATCH IS INVESTIGATING IN THE FIRST PLACE 'COS THE CORPSES REALLY ARE MOVING, AS YOU JUST SAW.
SO ALL WE KNOW FOR SURE AT PRESENT IS "DESTROY THEIR HEADS TO KILL THEM"...
TO BE EXACT, YOU'RE NOT "KILLING" THEM, JUST "INCAPACITATING" THEM.
LOOKS LIKE WE'VE GOT TO FORCE A CONFESSION OUT OF RIAN.
C'MON THEN!!
たっ TA (TMP)

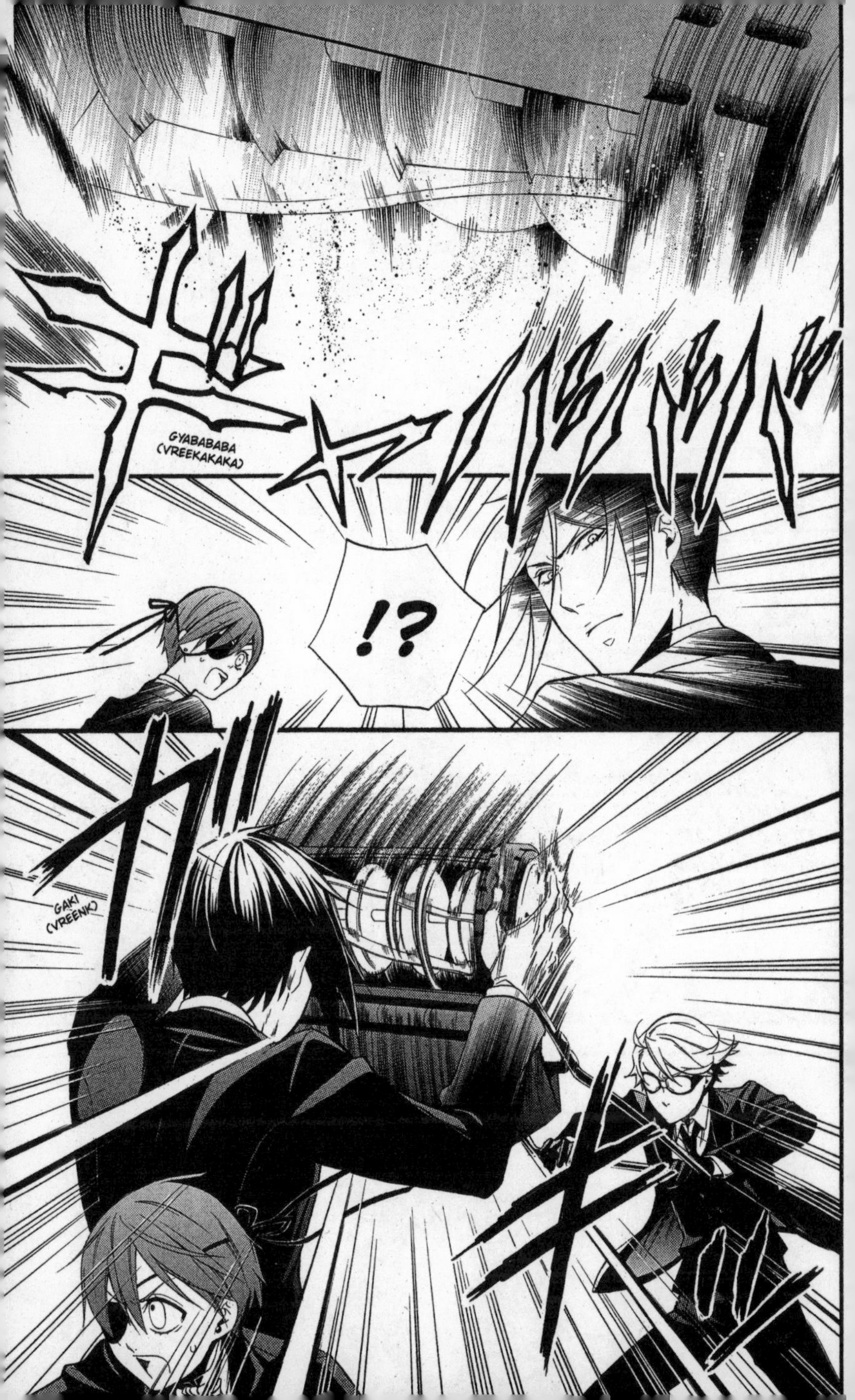
GYABABABA (VREEKAKAKA)
!?
GAKI (VREENK)

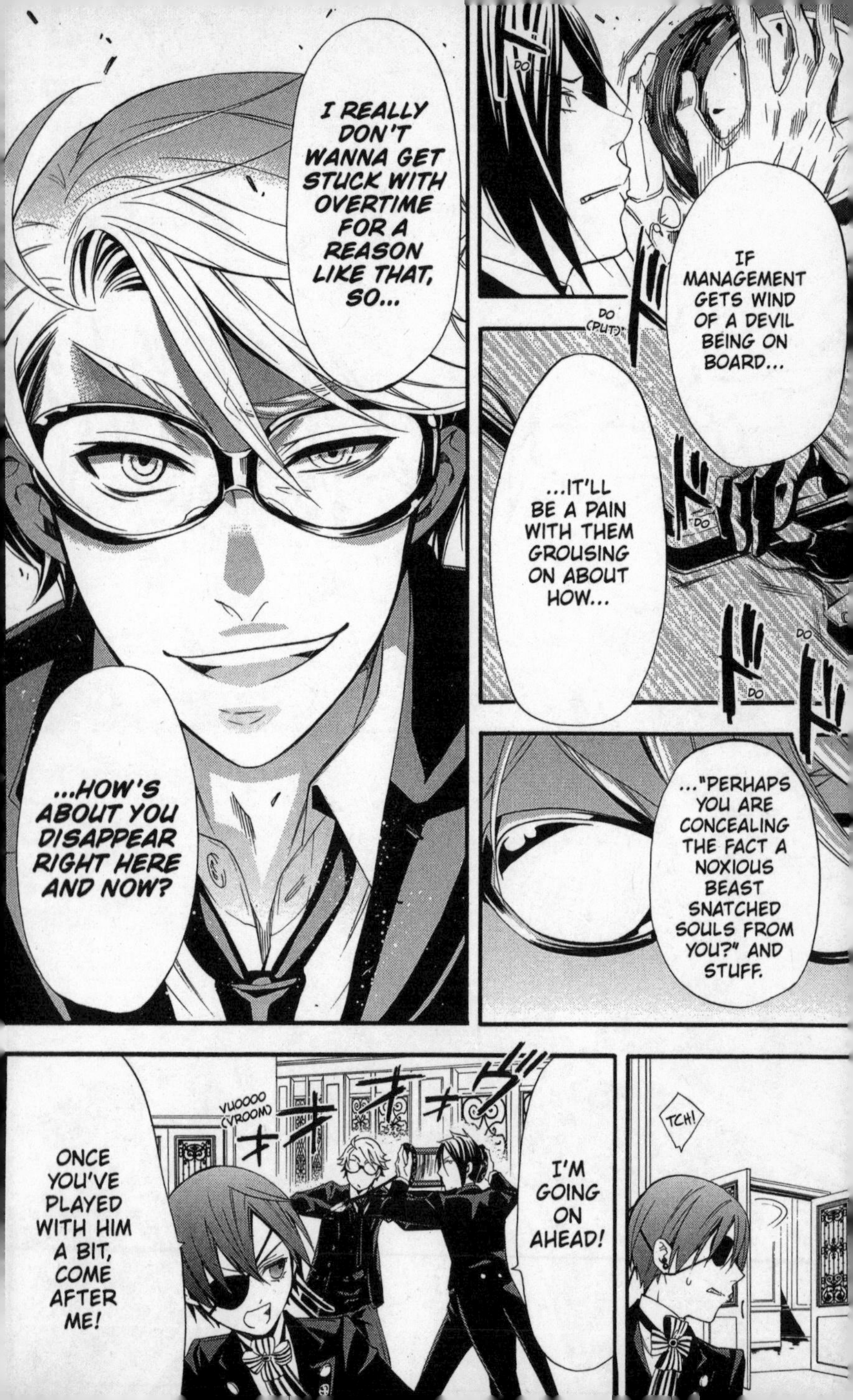
DO
IF MANAGEMENT GETS WIND OF A DEVIL BEING ON BOARD...
DO (PUT)
...IT'LL BE A PAIN WITH THEM GROUSING ON ABOUT HOW...
DO
DO
DO
..."PERHAPS YOU ARE CONCEALING THE FACT A NOXIOUS BEAST SNATCHED SOULS FROM YOU?" AND STUFF.
I REALLY DON'T WANNA GET STUCK WITH OVERTIME FOR A REASON LIKE THAT, SO...
...HOW'S ABOUT YOU DISAPPEAR RIGHT HERE AND NOW?
TCH!
VUOOOO (VROOM)
I'M GOING ON AHEAD!
ONCE YOU'VE PLAYED WITH HIM A BIT, COME AFTER ME!

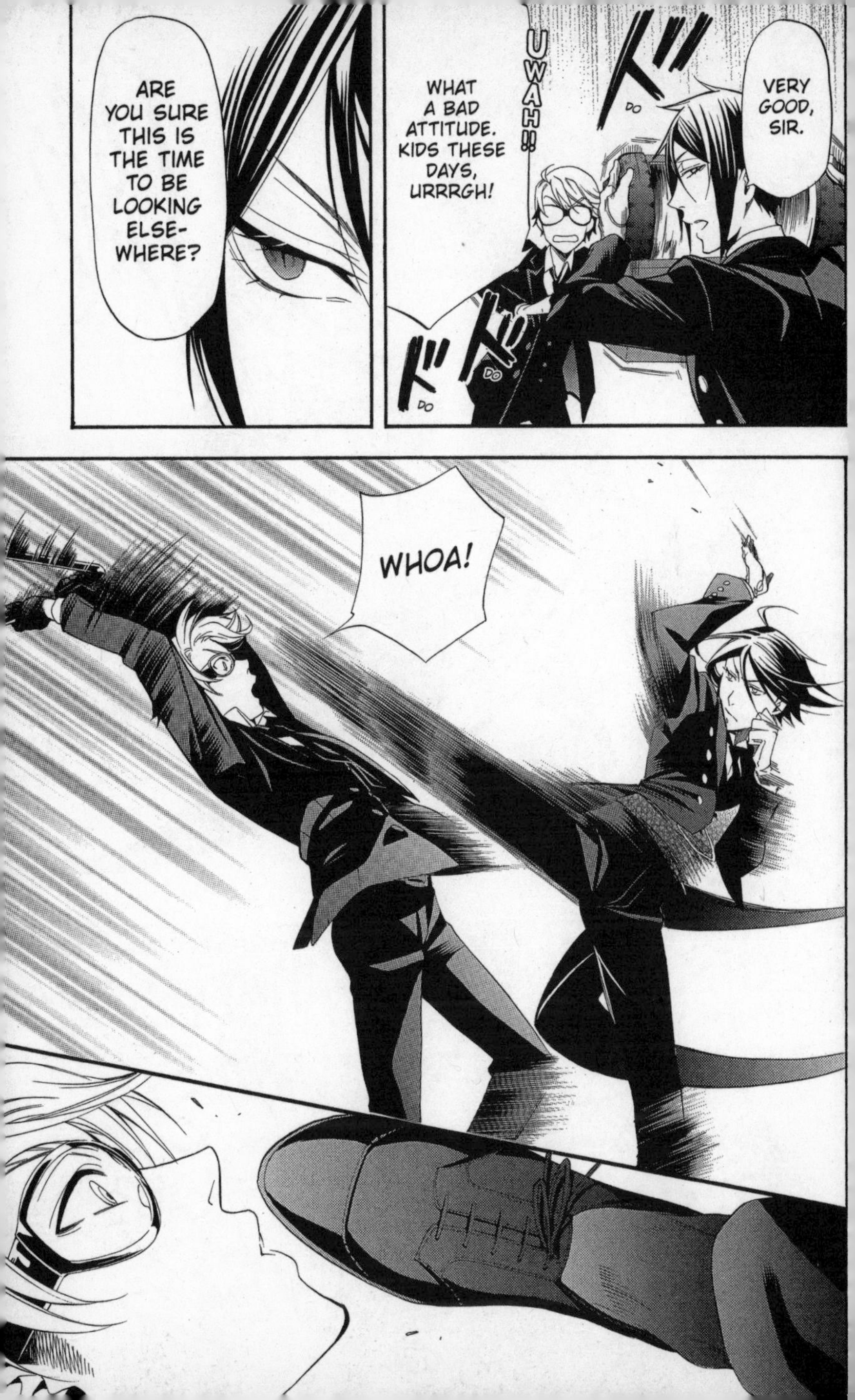
VERY GOOD, SIR.
ド
DO
UWAH!!
WHAT A BAD ATTITUDE. KIDS THESE DAYS, URRRGH!
ドド
DO
DO
ARE YOU SURE THIS IS THE TIME TO BE LOOKING ELSE-WHERE?
WHOA!

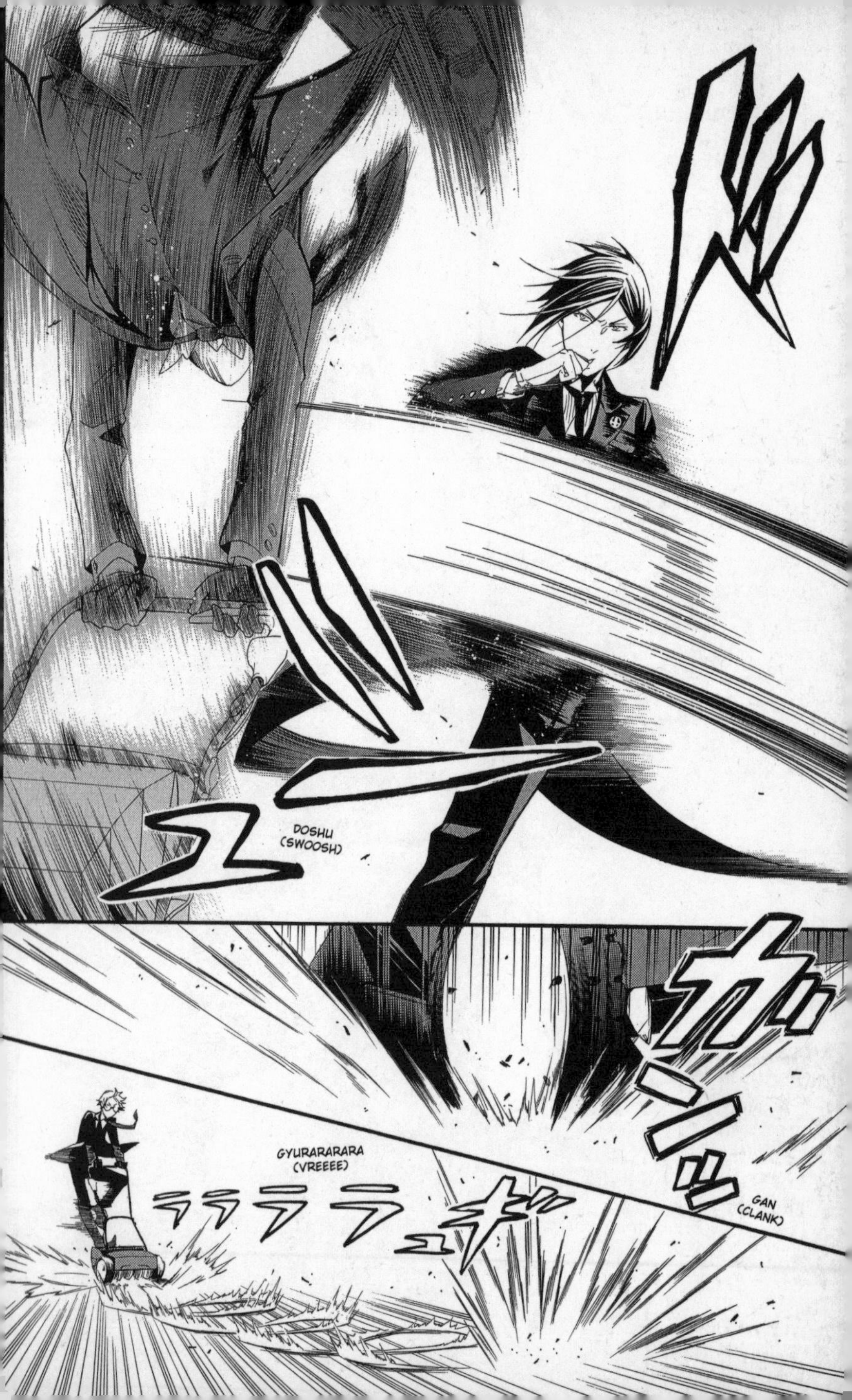
DOSHU
(SWOOSH)
GAN
(CLANK)
GYURARARARA
(VREEEE)

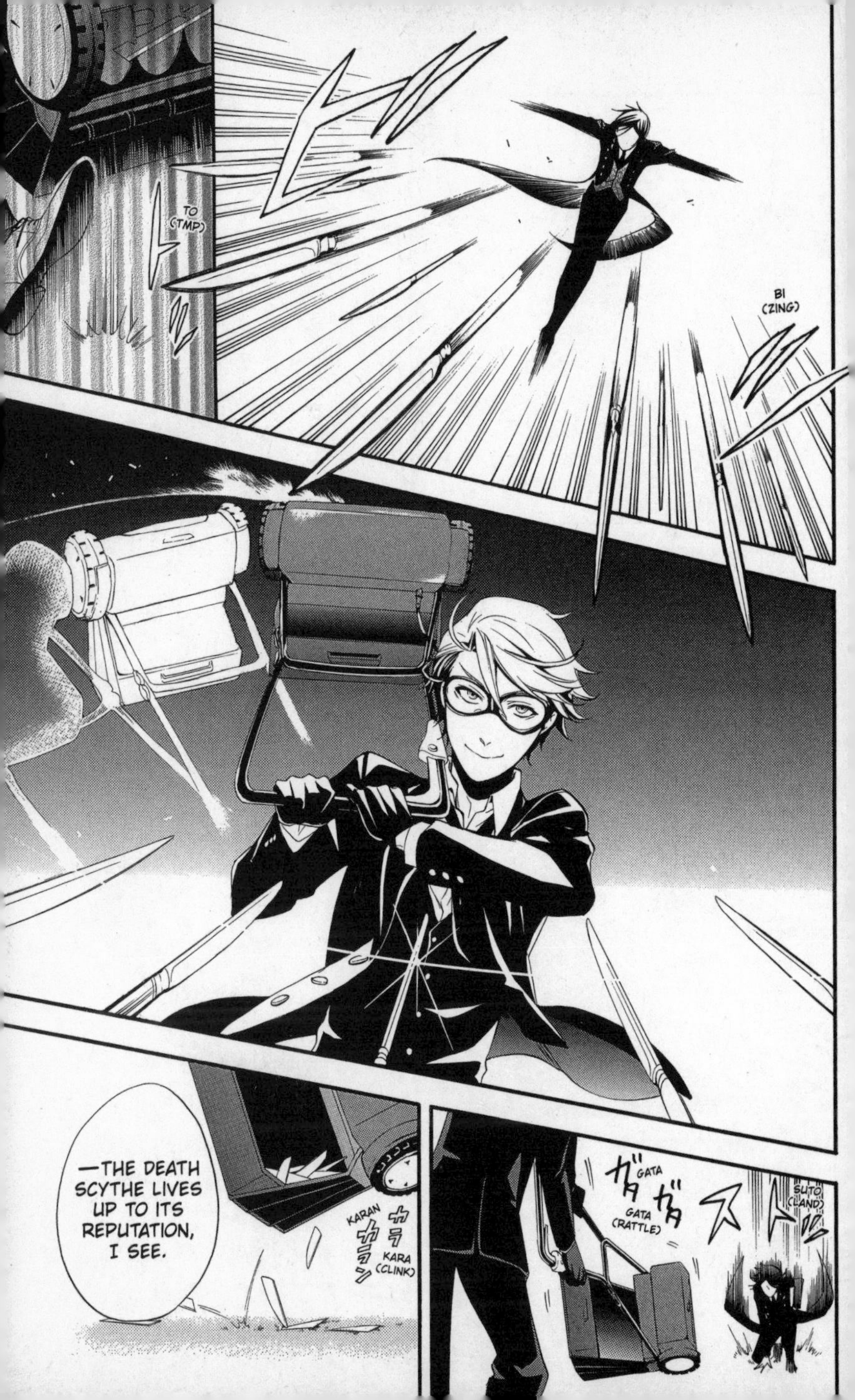
BI (ZING)
TO (TMP)
SUTO (LAND)
GATA GATA (RATTLE)
—THE DEATH SCYTHE LIVES UP TO ITS REPUTATION, I SEE.
KARAN KARA (CLINK)

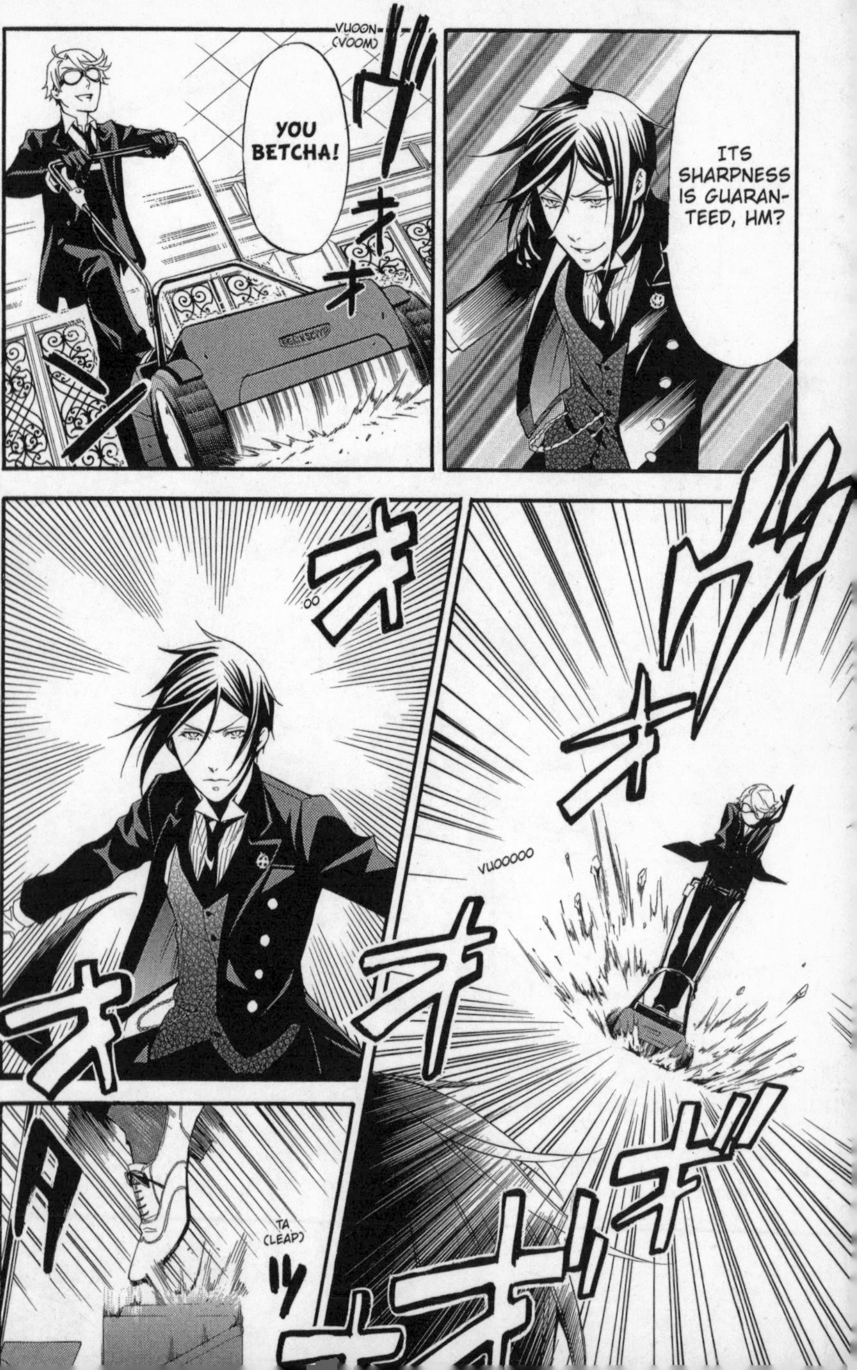
ITS SHARPNESS IS GUARAN-TEED, HM?
VUOON- (VOOM)
YOU BETCHA!
VUOOOOO
TA (LEAP)

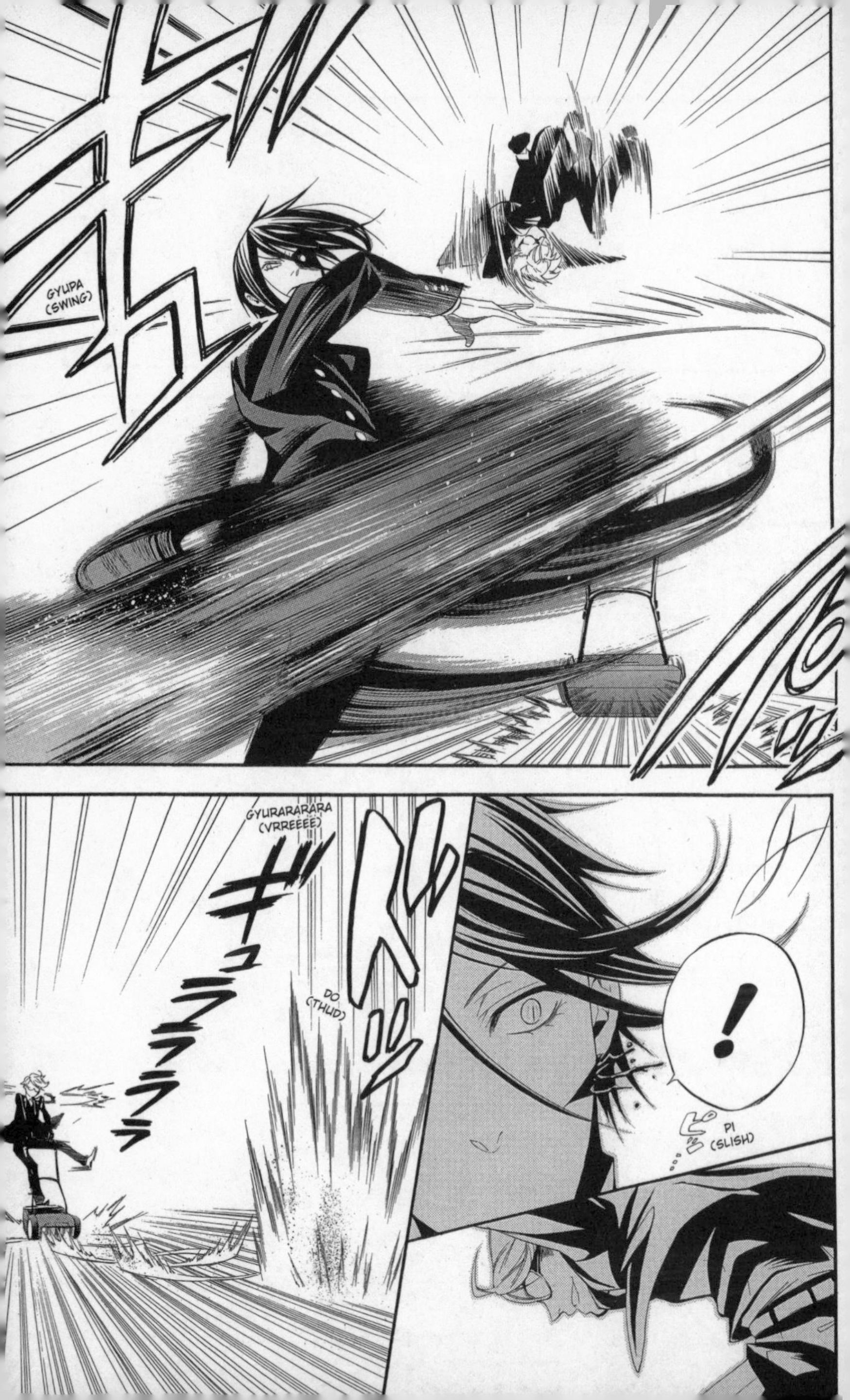

GYUPA (SWING)
!
PI (SLISH)
GYURARARARA (VRREEEE)
DO (THUD)

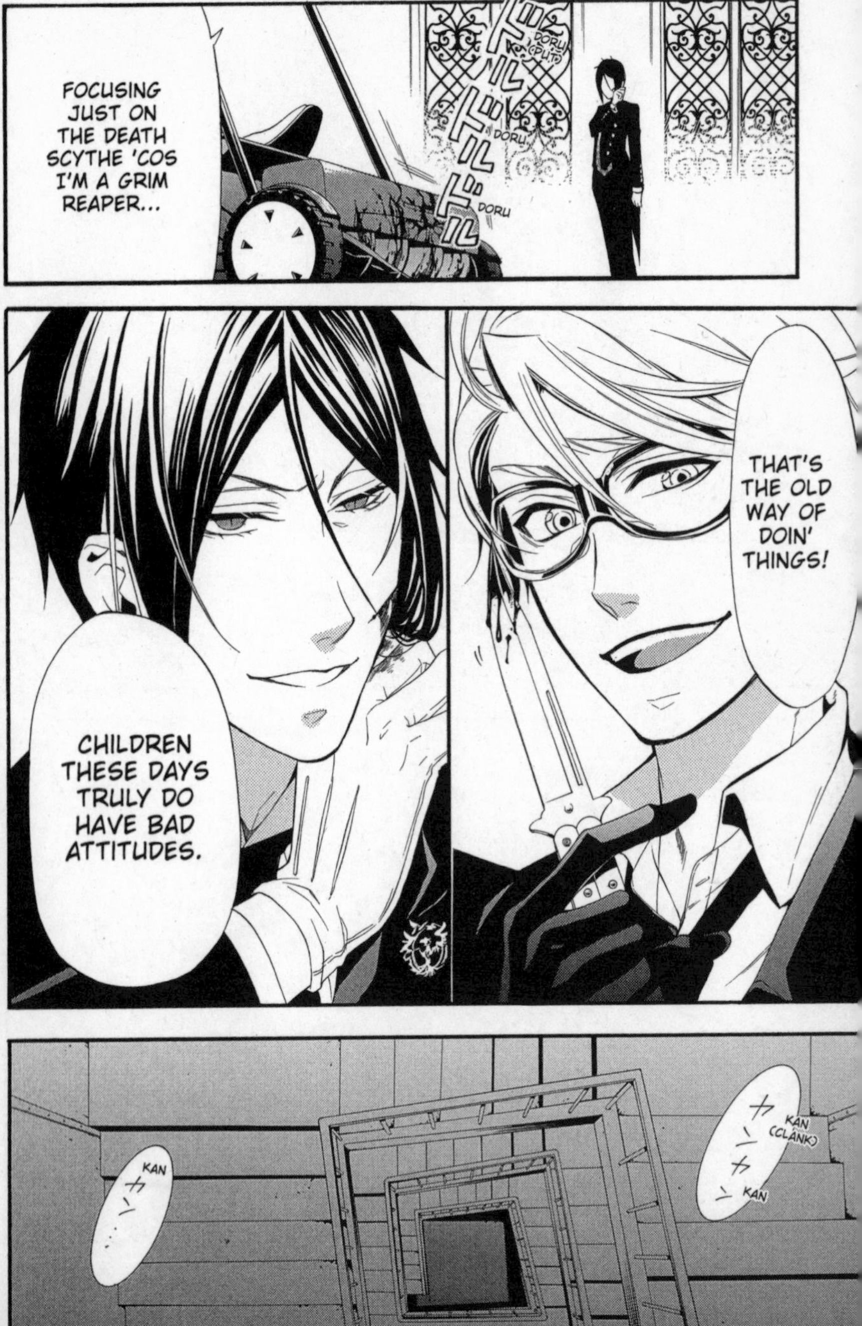
DORU (PUTT)
DORU
DORU
FOCUSING JUST ON THE DEATH SCYTHE 'COS I'M A GRIM REAPER...
THAT'S THE OLD WAY OF DOIN' THINGS!
CHILDREN THESE DAYS TRULY DO HAVE BAD ATTITUDES.
KAN (CLANK)
KAN
KAN

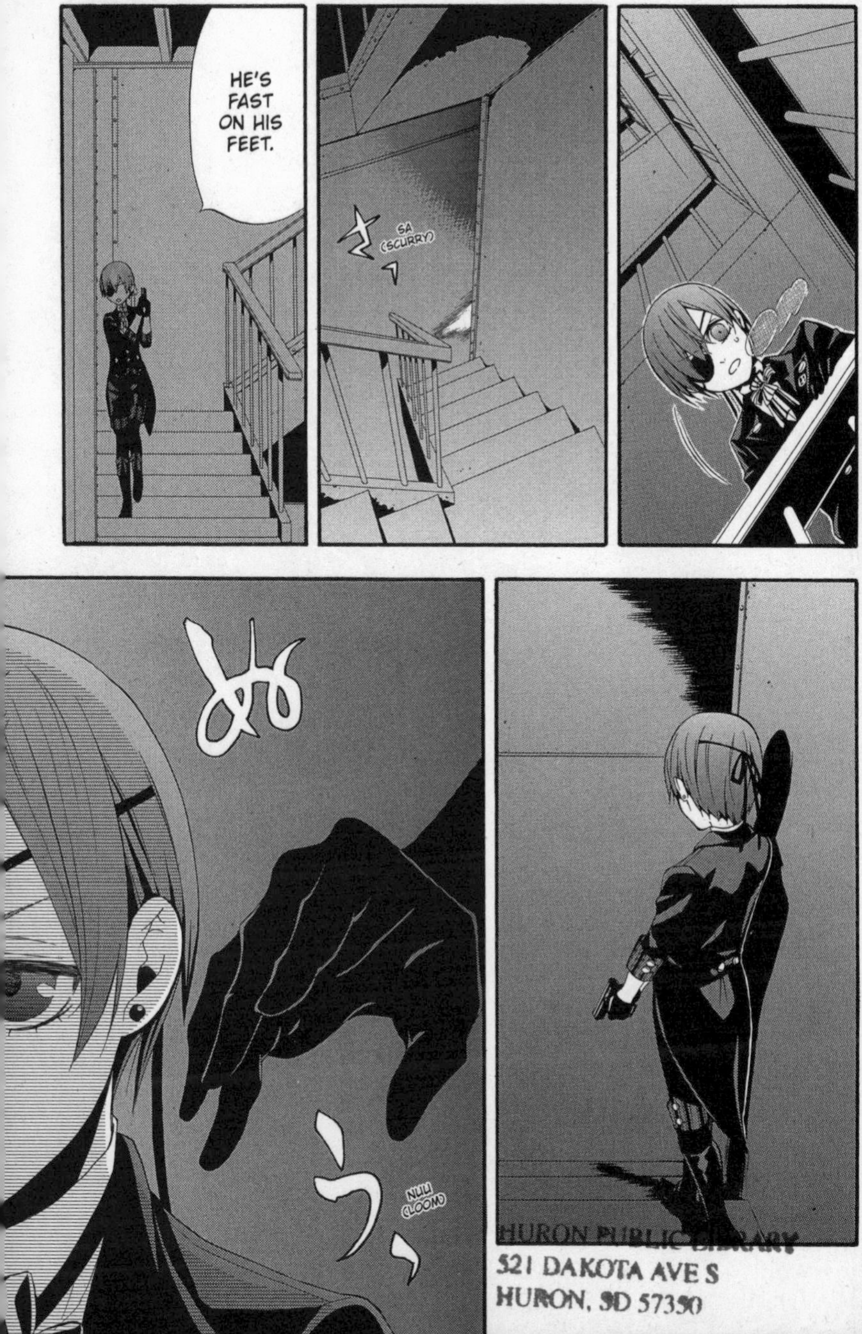
SA (SCURRY)
HE'S FAST ON HIS FEET.
NUU (LOOM)

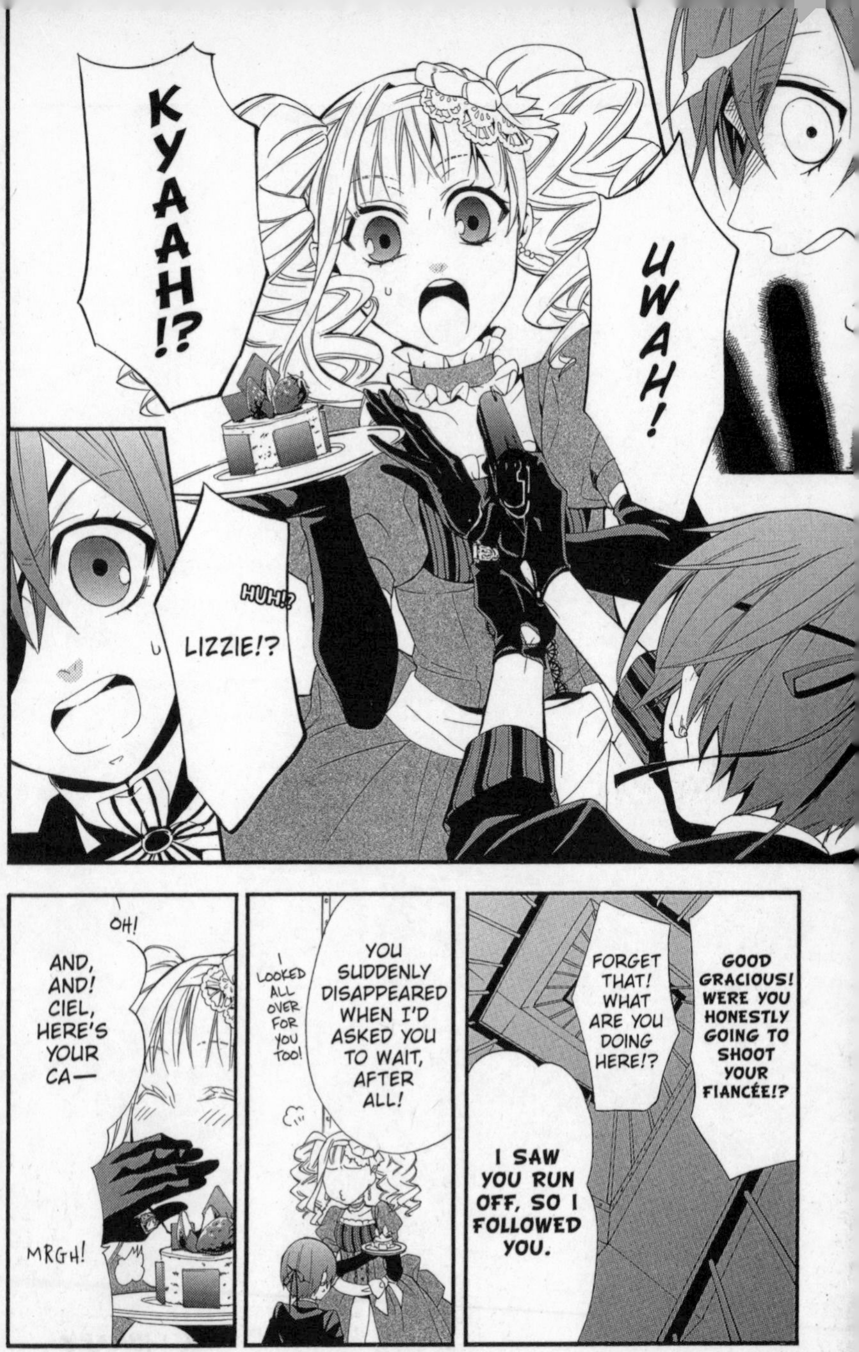
UWAH!
KYAAH!?
HUH!?
LIZZIE!?
GOOD GRACIOUS! WERE YOU HONESTLY GOING TO SHOOT YOUR FIANCÉE!?
FORGET THAT! WHAT ARE YOU DOING HERE!?
I SAW YOU RUN OFF, SO I FOLLOWED YOU.
YOU SUDDENLY DISAPPEARED WHEN I'D ASKED YOU TO WAIT, AFTER ALL!
I LOOKED ALL OVER FOR YOU TOO!
OH!
AND, AND! CIEL, HERE'S YOUR CA—
MRGH!

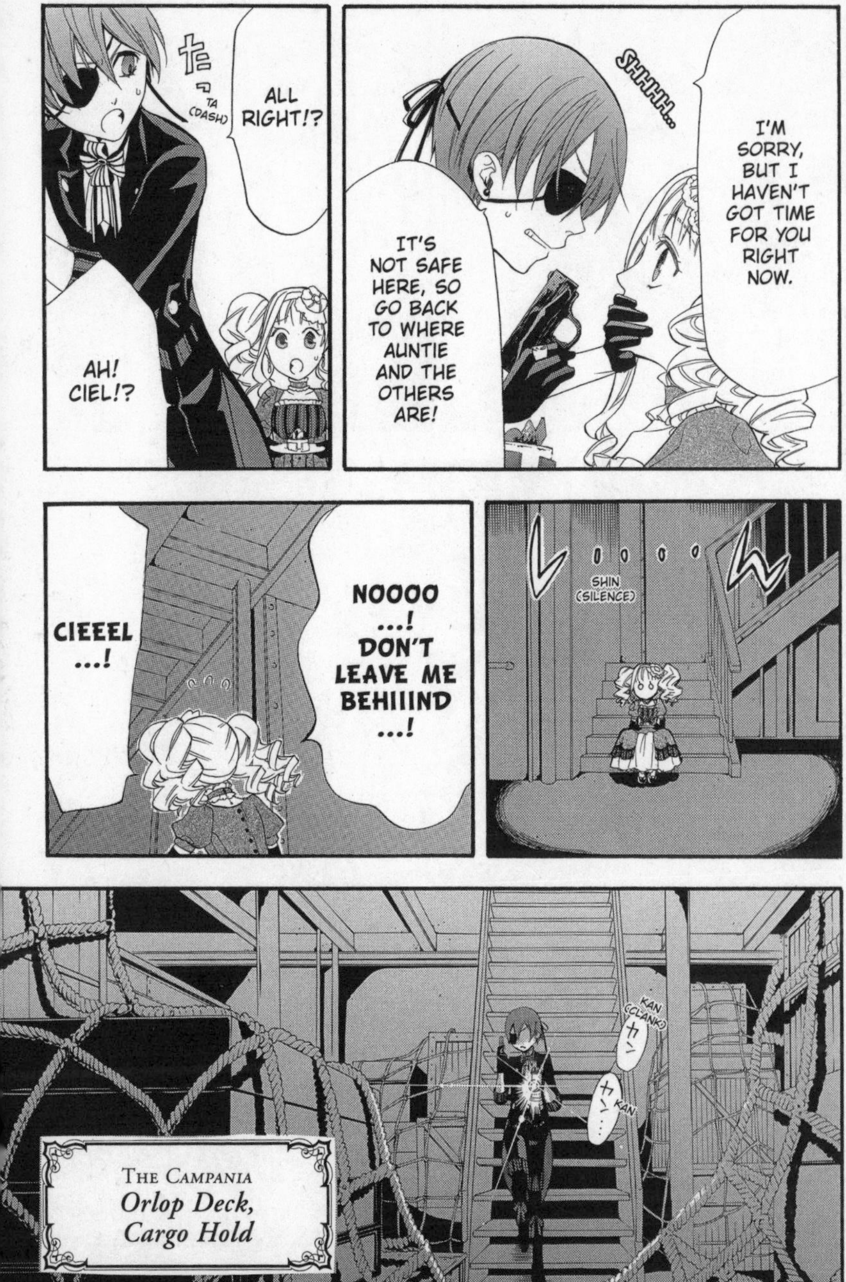
SHHHH...
I'M SORRY, BUT I HAVEN'T GOT TIME FOR YOU RIGHT NOW.
IT'S NOT SAFE HERE, SO GO BACK TO WHERE AUNTIE AND THE OTHERS ARE!
TA (DASH)
ALL RIGHT!?
AH! CIEL!?
SHIN (SILENCE)
NOOOO ...! DON'T LEAVE ME BEHIIIND ...!
CIEEEL ...!
KAN (CLANK)
KAN
THE CAMPANIA
Orlop Deck, Cargo Hold

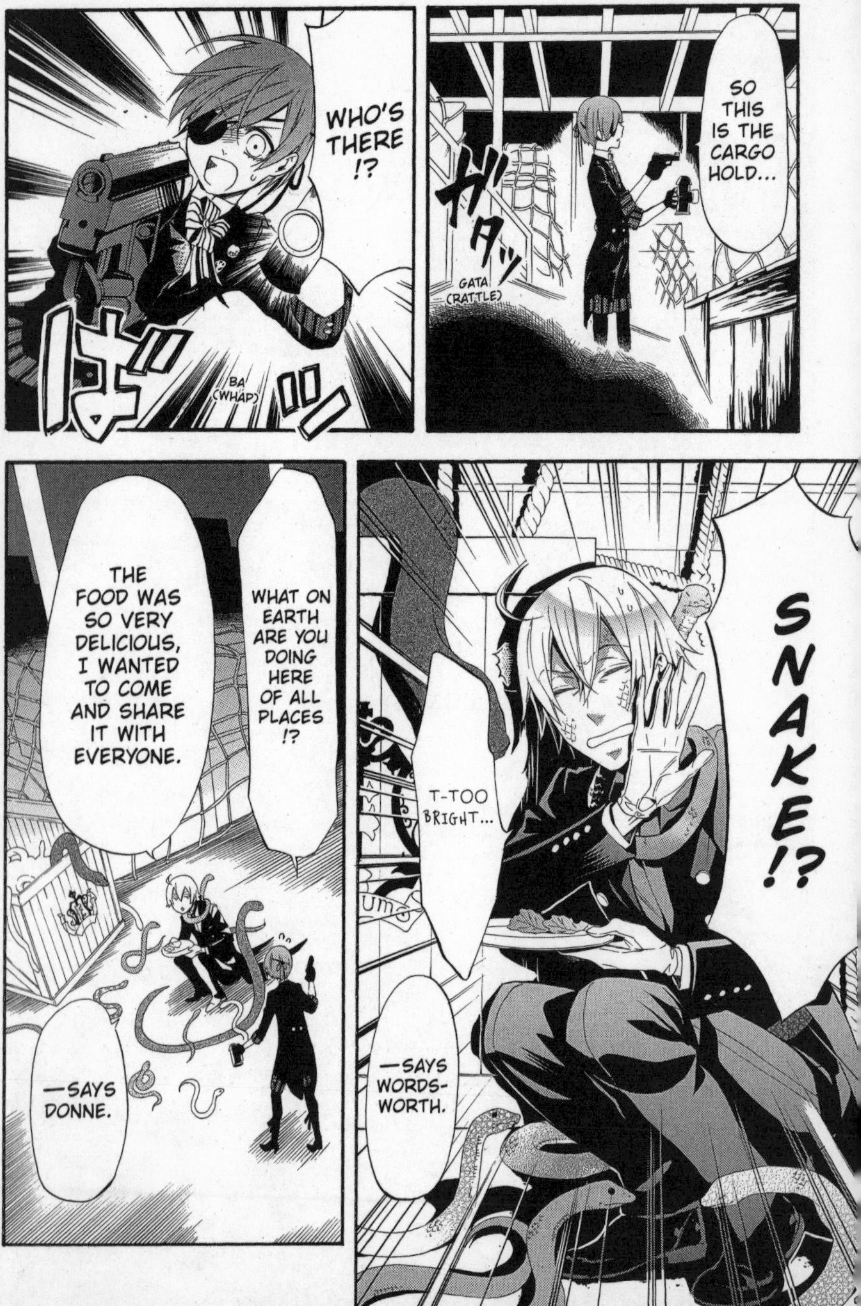
SO THIS IS THE CARGO HOLD...
GATA (RATTLE)
WHO'S THERE!?
BA (WHAP)
SNAKE!?
T-TOO BRIGHT...
—SAYS WORDS-WORTH.
WHAT ON EARTH ARE YOU DOING HERE OF ALL PLACES!?
THE FOOD WAS SO VERY DELICIOUS, I WANTED TO COME AND SHARE IT WITH EVERYONE.
—SAYS DONNE.

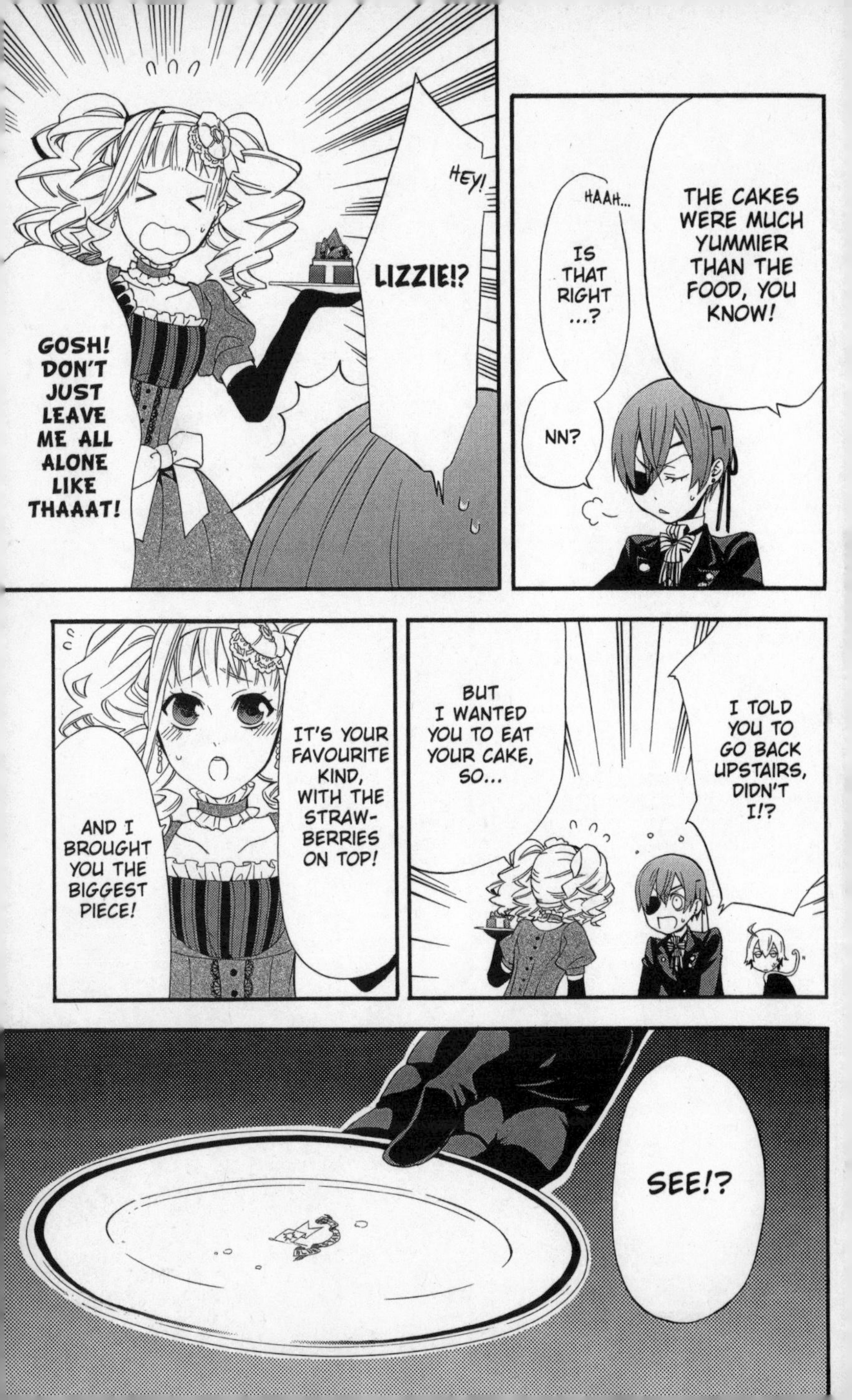
THE CAKES WERE MUCH YUMMIER THAN THE FOOD, YOU KNOW!
HAAH... IS THAT RIGHT ...?
NN?
HEY!
LIZZIE!?
GOSH! DON'T JUST LEAVE ME ALL ALONE LIKE THAAAT!
I TOLD YOU TO GO BACK UPSTAIRS, DIDN'T I!?
BUT I WANTED YOU TO EAT YOUR CAKE, SO...
IT'S YOUR FAVOURITE KIND, WITH THE STRAW-BERRIES ON TOP!
AND I BROUGHT YOU THE BIGGEST PIECE!
SEE!?

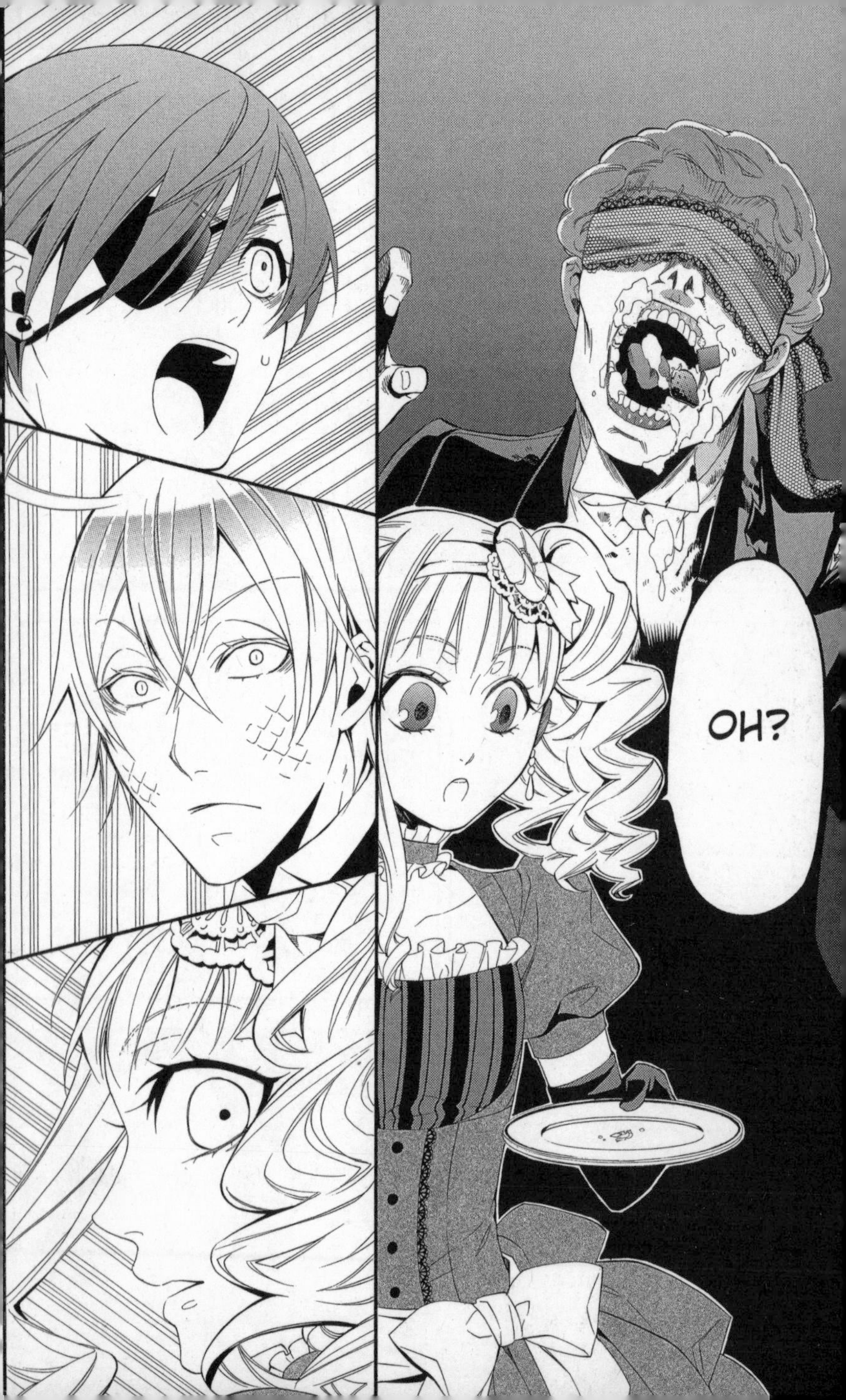
OH?

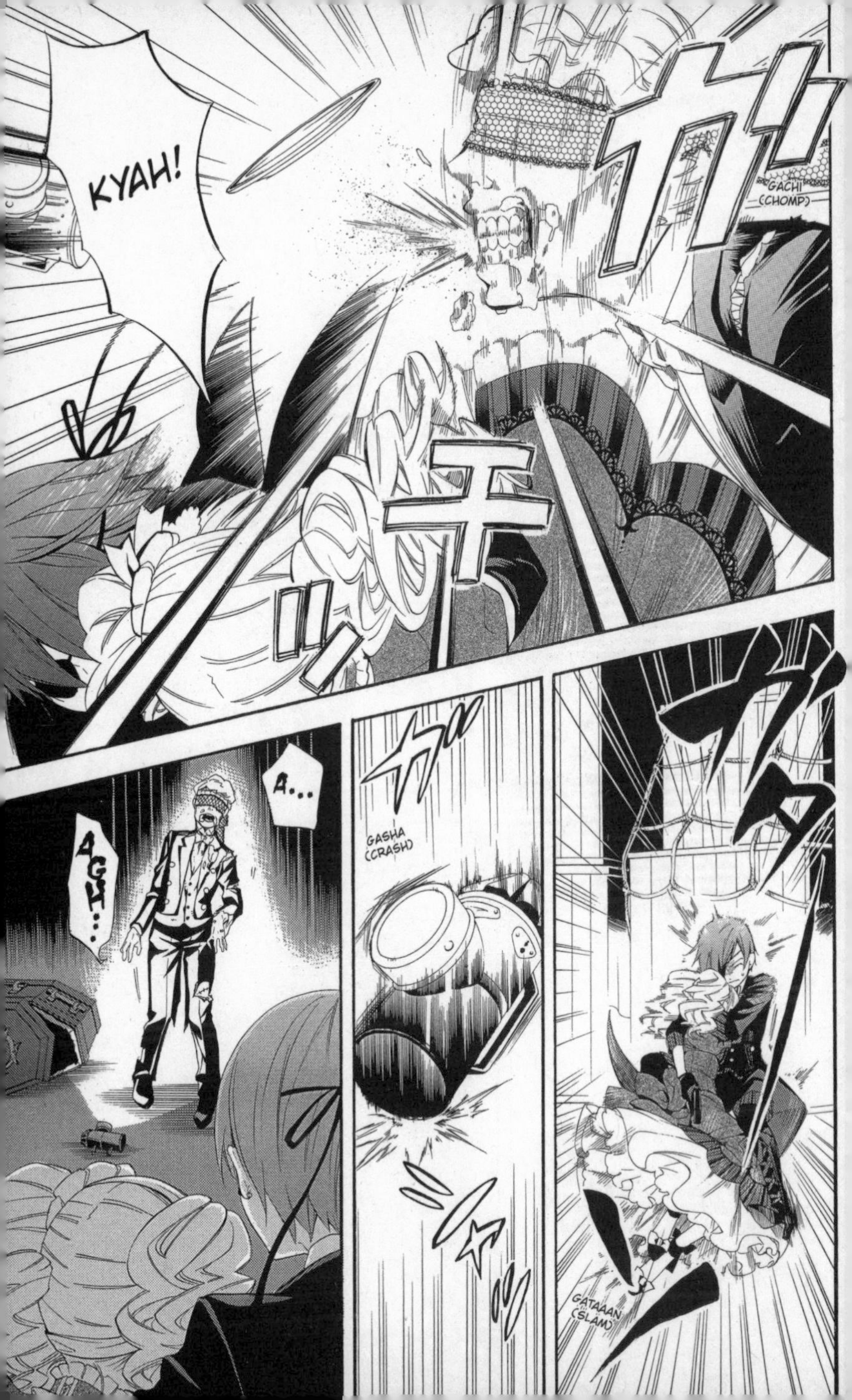
GACHI (CHOMP)
KYAH!
GATAAAN (SLAM)
GASHA (CRASH)
A...
AGH...

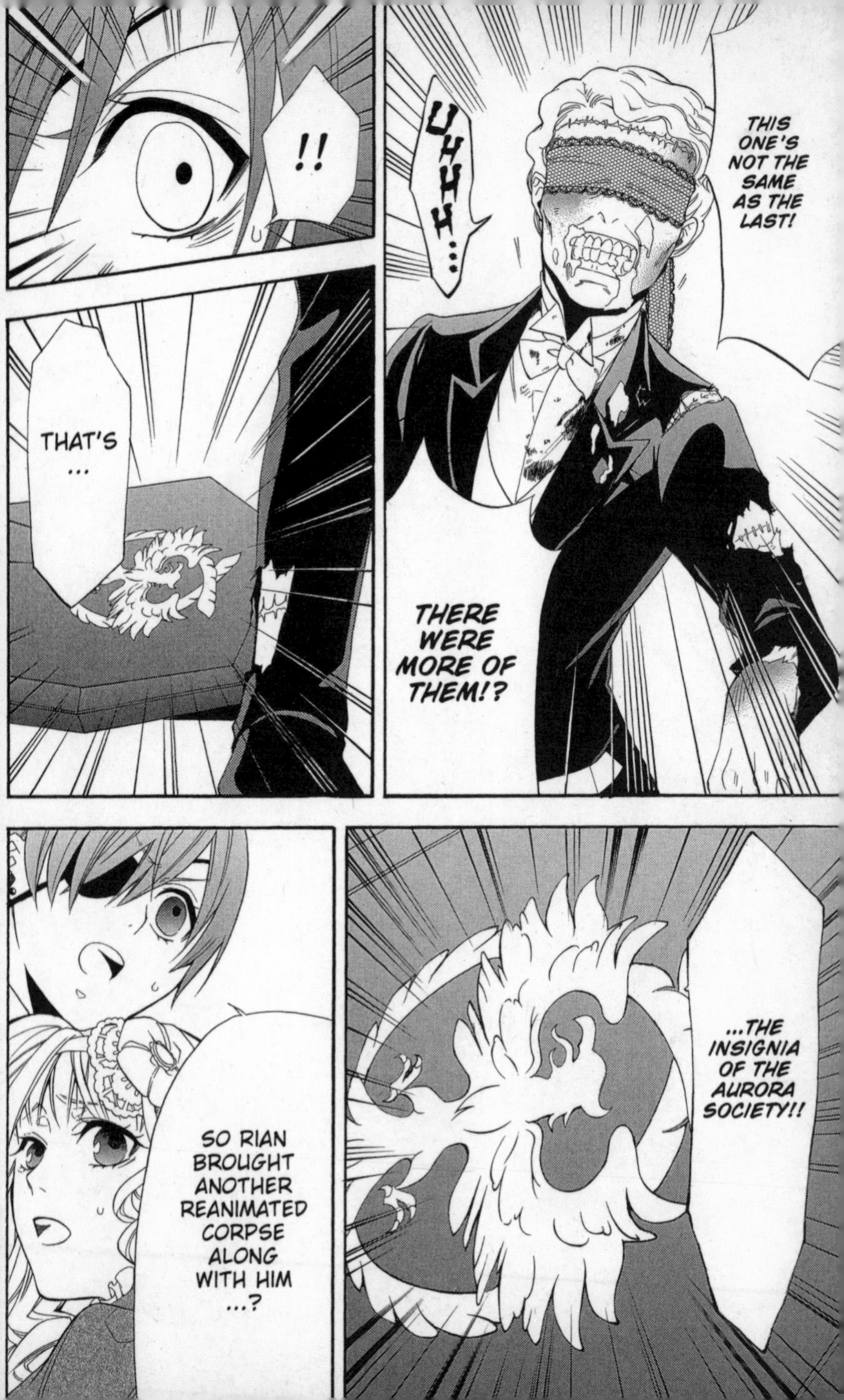
THIS ONE'S NOT THE SAME AS THE LAST!
UHHH...
THERE WERE MORE OF THEM!?
!!
THAT'S ...
...THE INSIGNIA OF THE AURORA SOCIETY!!
SO RIAN BROUGHT ANOTHER REANIMATED CORPSE ALONG WITH HIM ...?

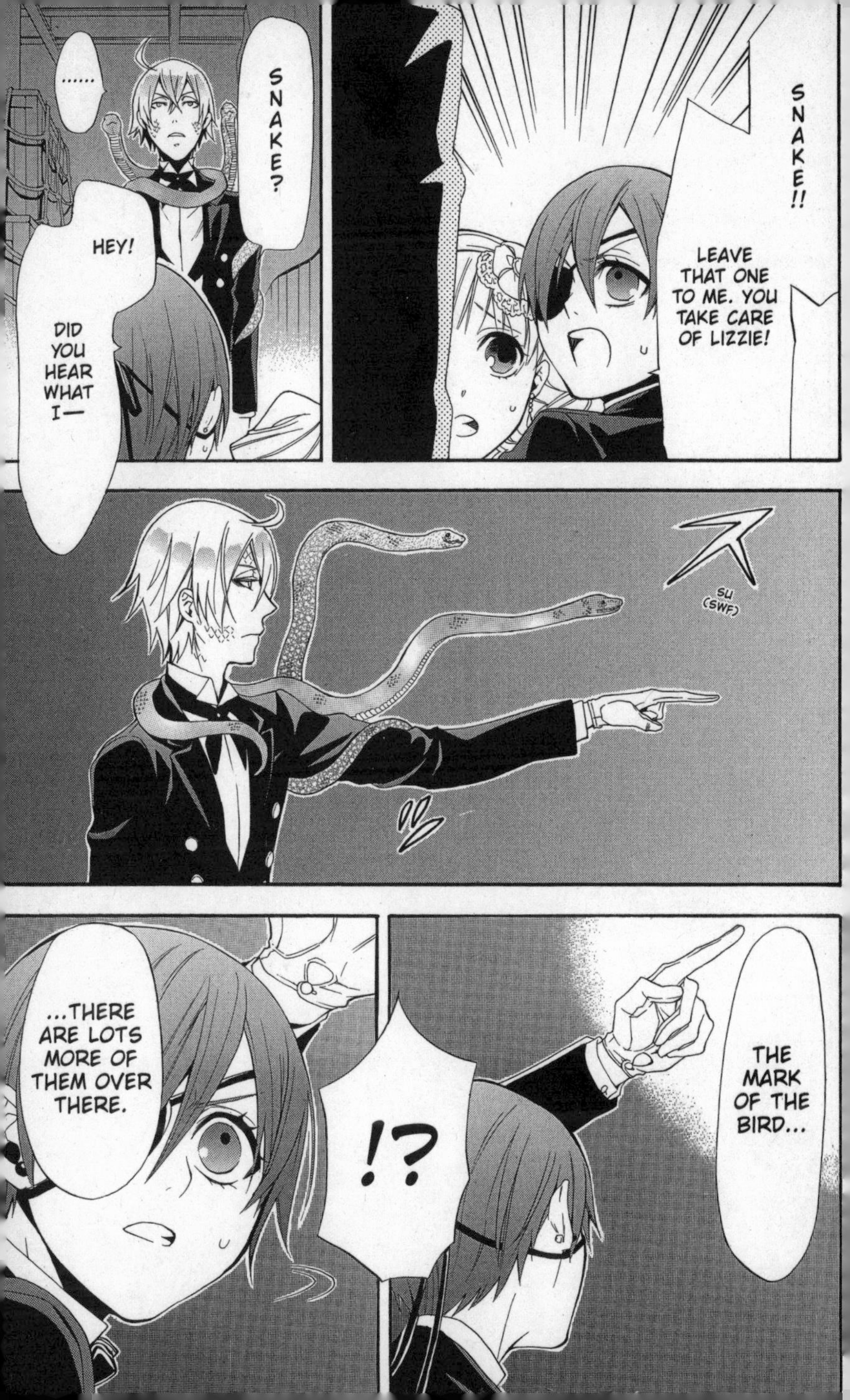
SNAKE!!
LEAVE THAT ONE TO ME. YOU TAKE CARE OF LIZZIE!
SNAKE?
......
HEY!
DID YOU HEAR WHAT I—
SU (SWF)
THE MARK OF THE BIRD...
!?
...THERE ARE LOTS MORE OF THEM OVER THERE.

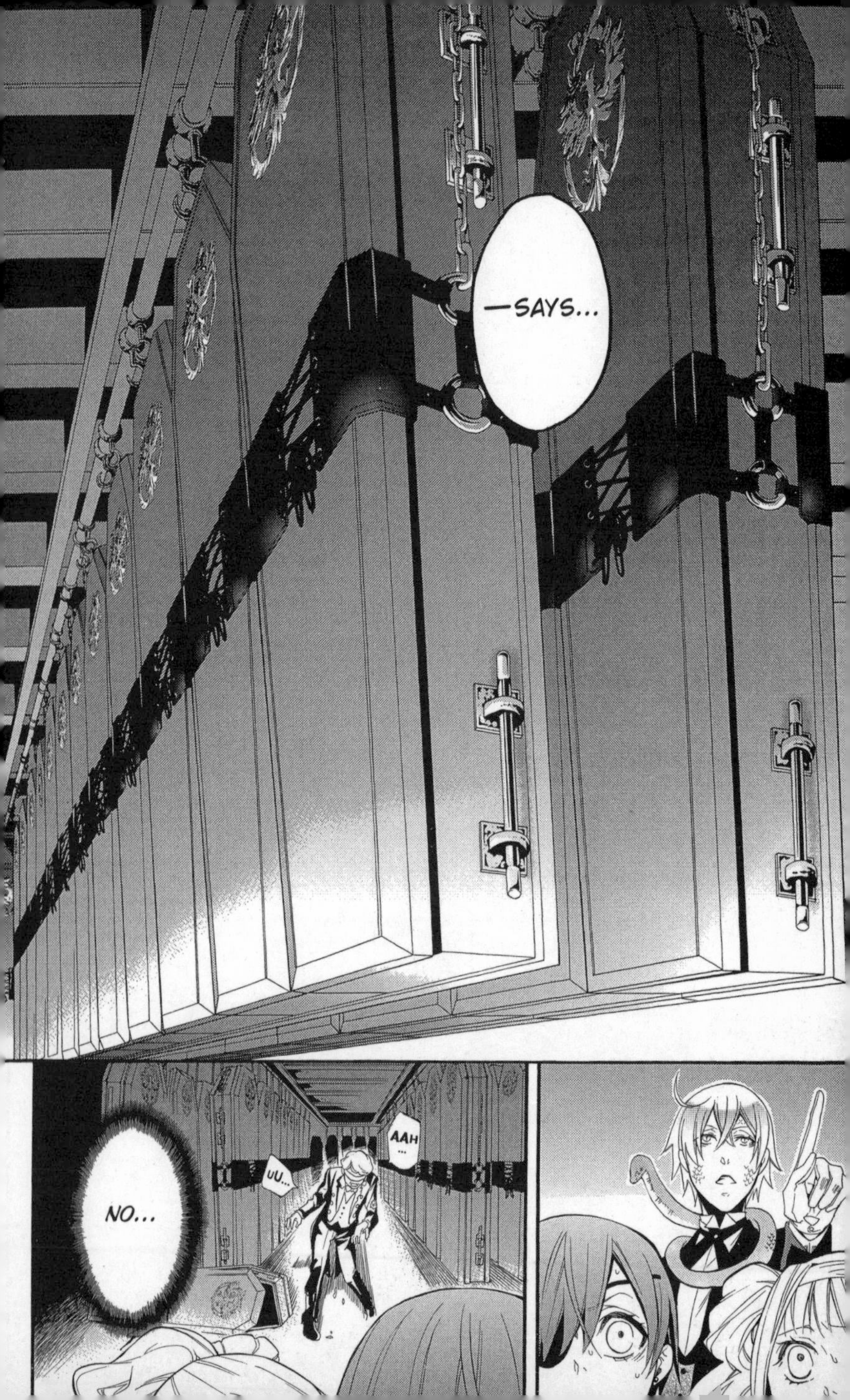
—SAYS...
AAH...
UU...
NO...

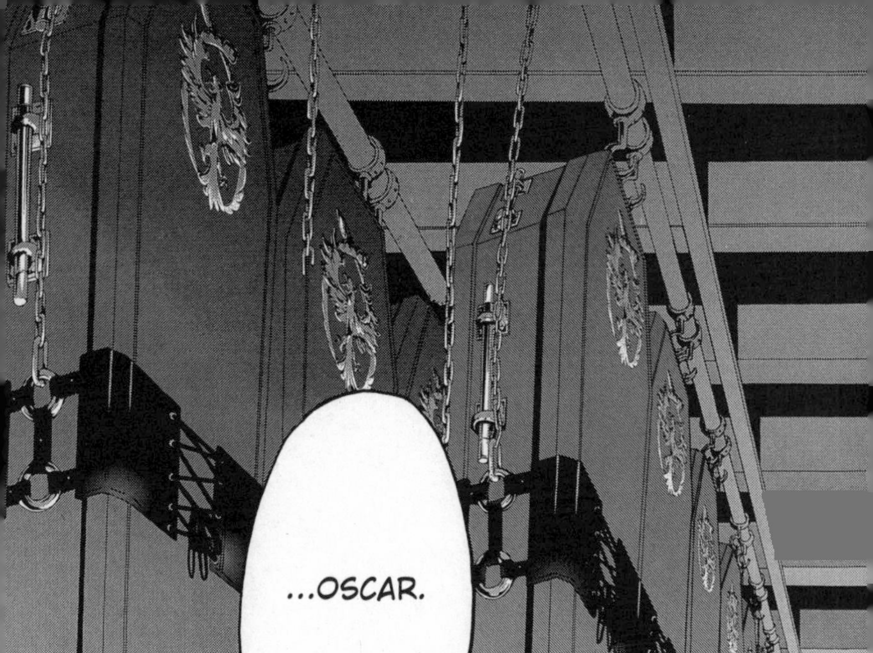
...OSCAR.
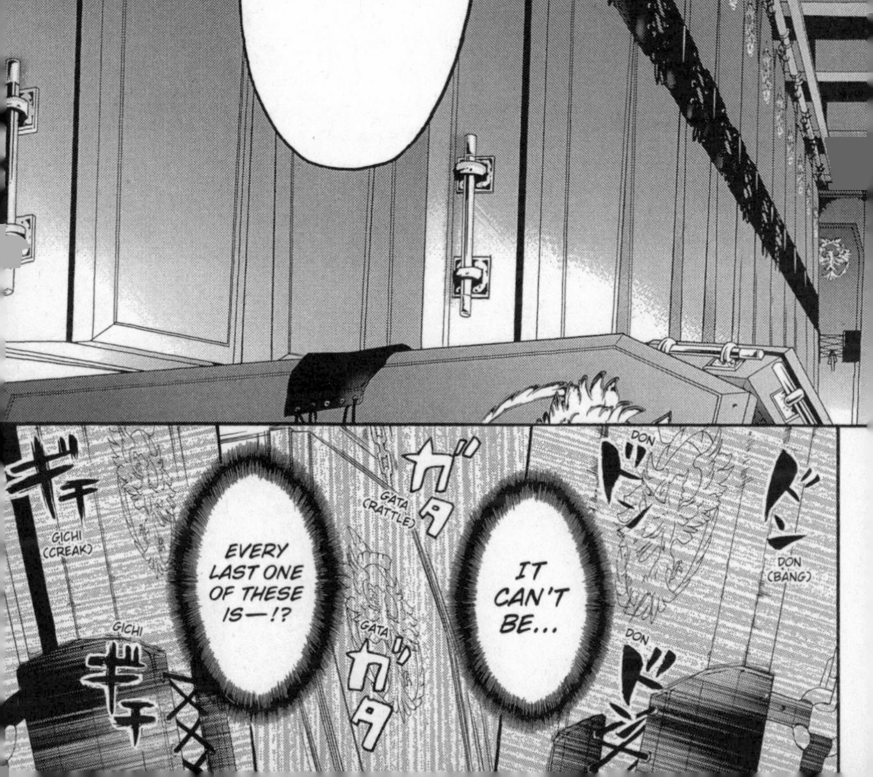
DON
DON (BANG)
DON
IT CAN'T BE...
GATA (RATTLE)
GATA
EVERY LAST ONE OF THESE IS—!?
GICHI (CREAK)
GICHI

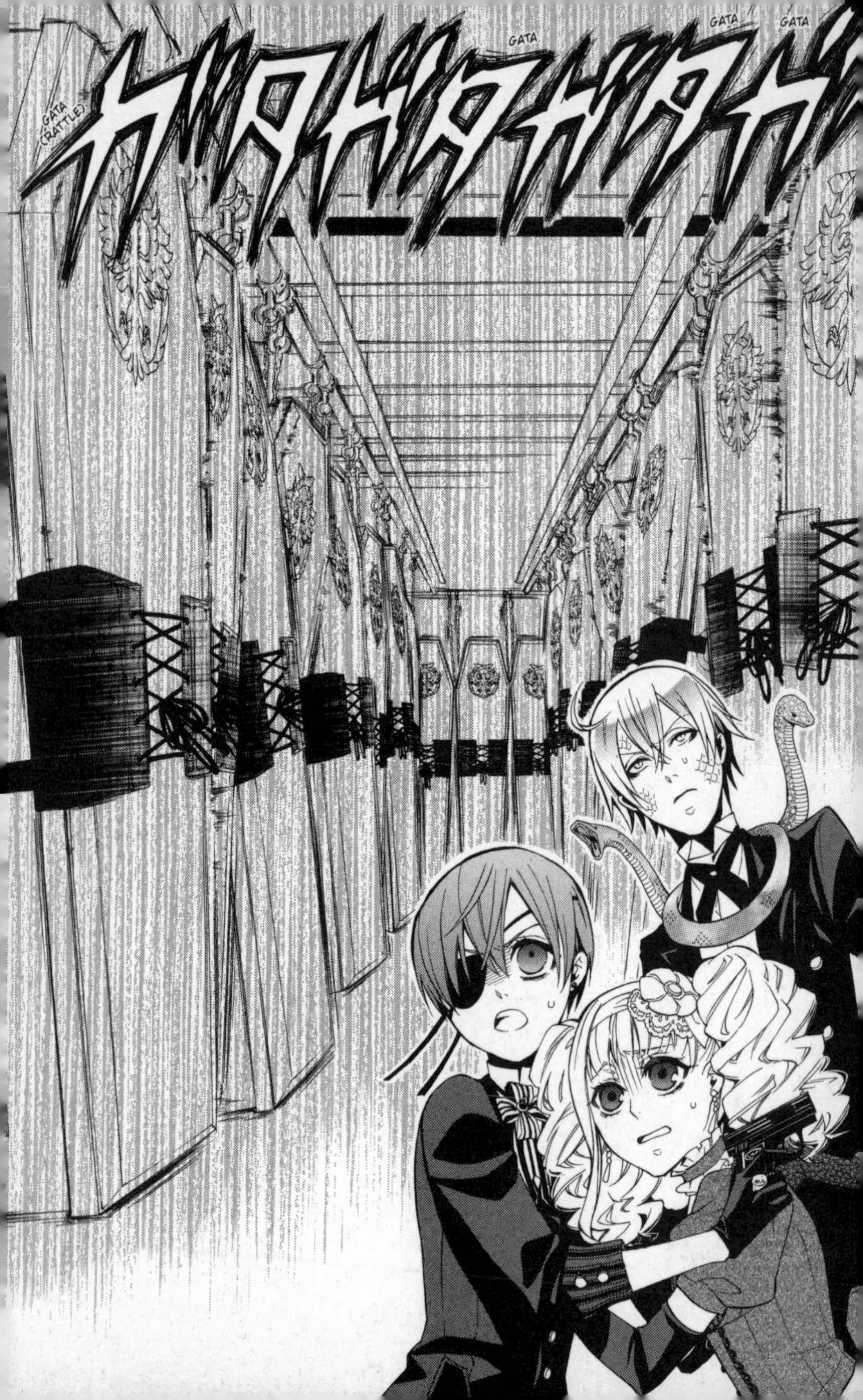
GATA
GATA
GATA
GATA (RATTLE)

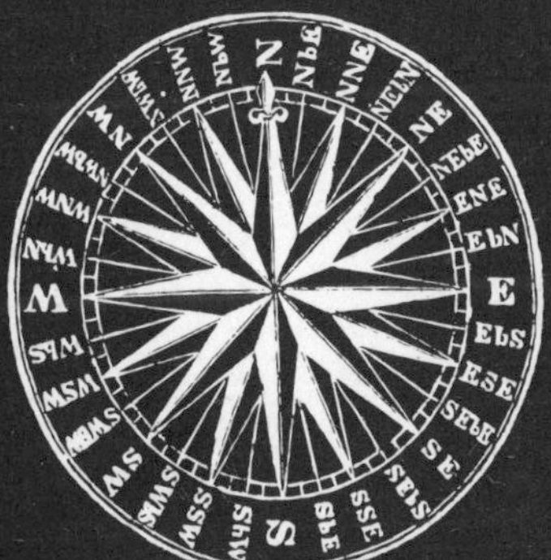
N
NbE
NNE
NEbN
NE
NEbE
ENE
EbN
E
EbS
ESE
SEbE
SE
SEbS
SSE
SbE
S
SbW
SSW
SWbS
SW
SWbW
WSW
WbS
W
WbN
WNW
NWbW
NW
NWbN
NNW
NbW

Black Butler

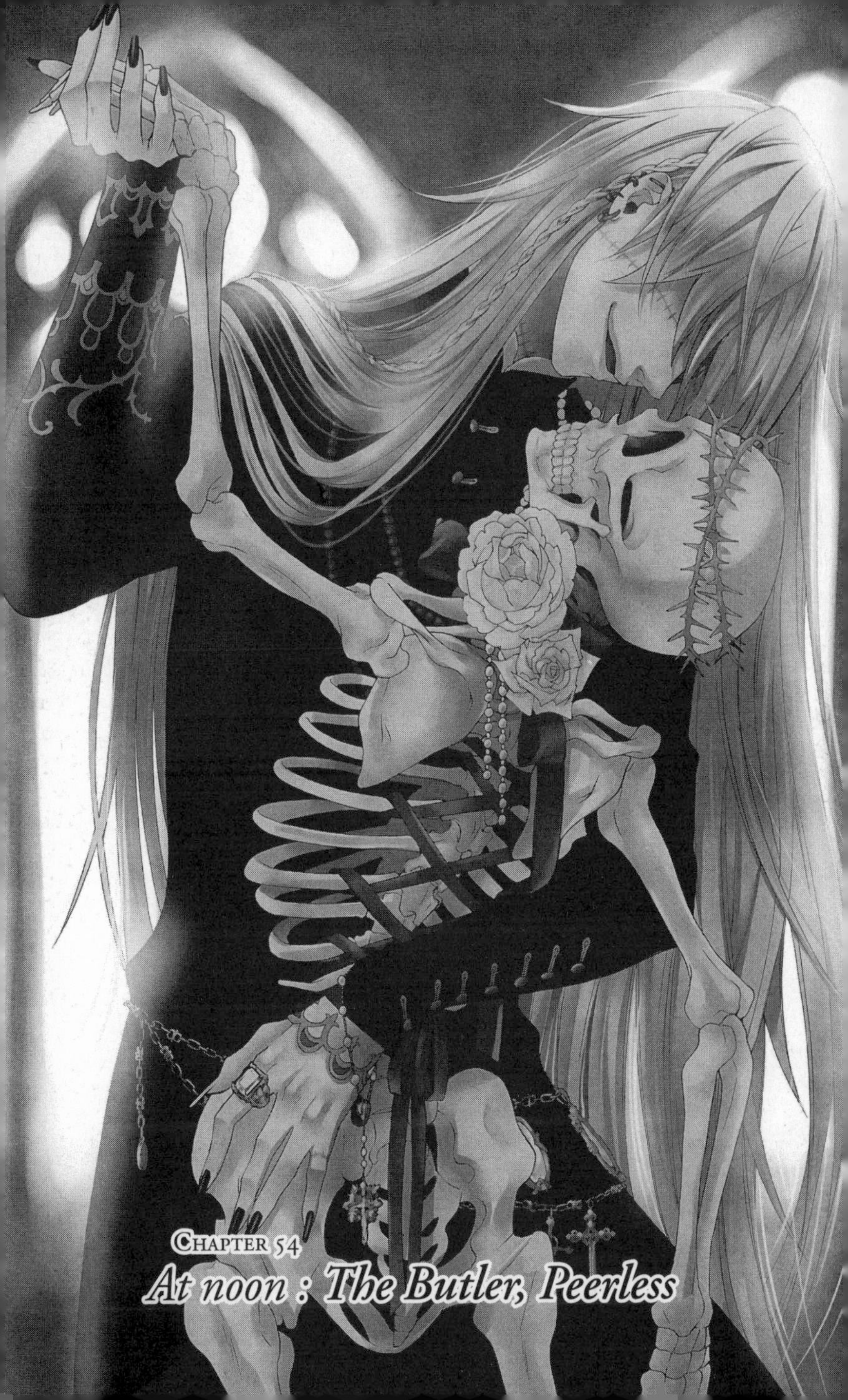
CHAPTER 54
At noon : The Butler, Peerless

Black Butler

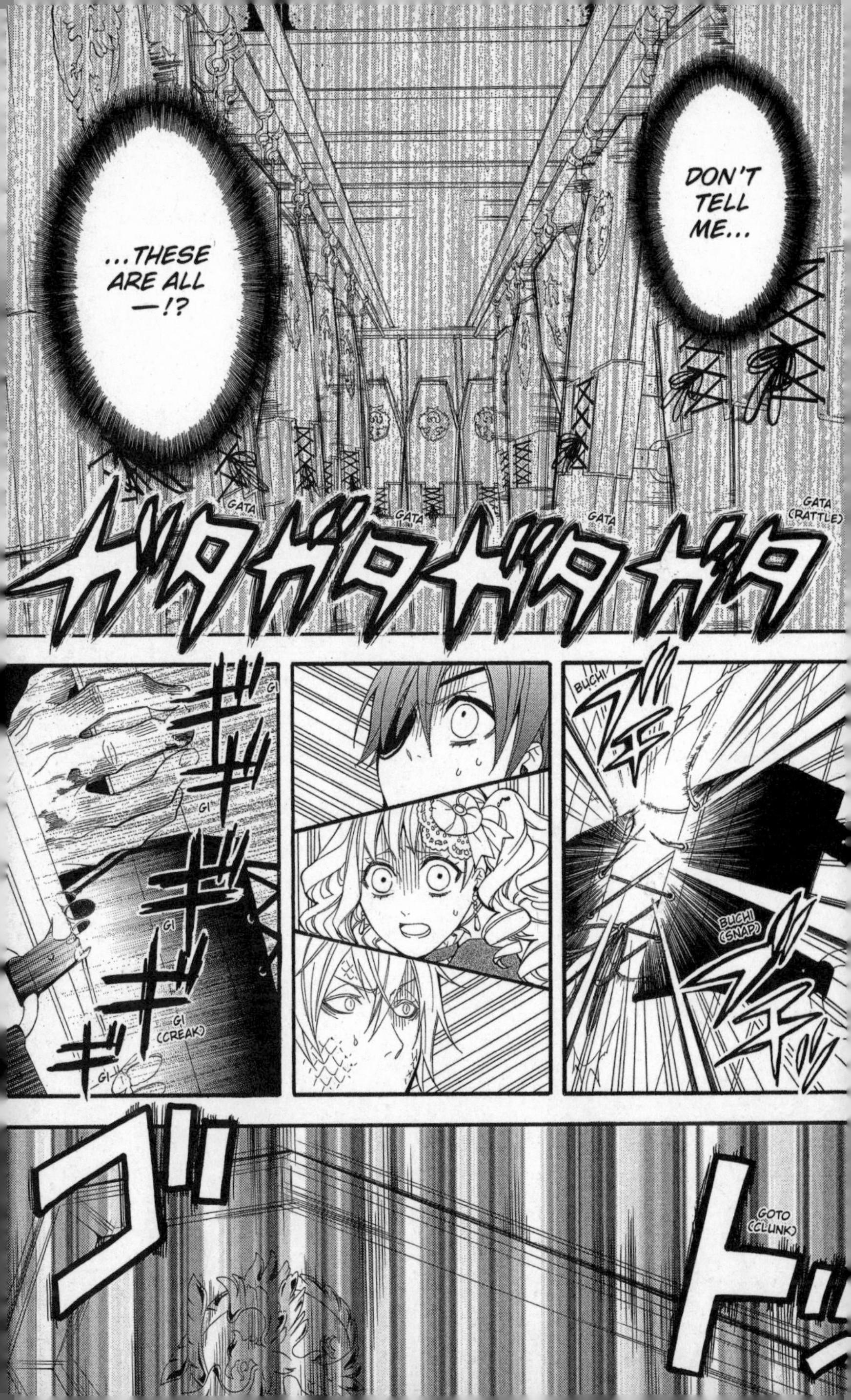
DON'T TELL ME...
...THESE ARE ALL —!?
GATA (RATTLE)
GATA
GATA
GATA
BUCHI
BUCHI (SNAP)
GI
GI
GI
GI (CREAK)
GI
GOTO (CLUNK)

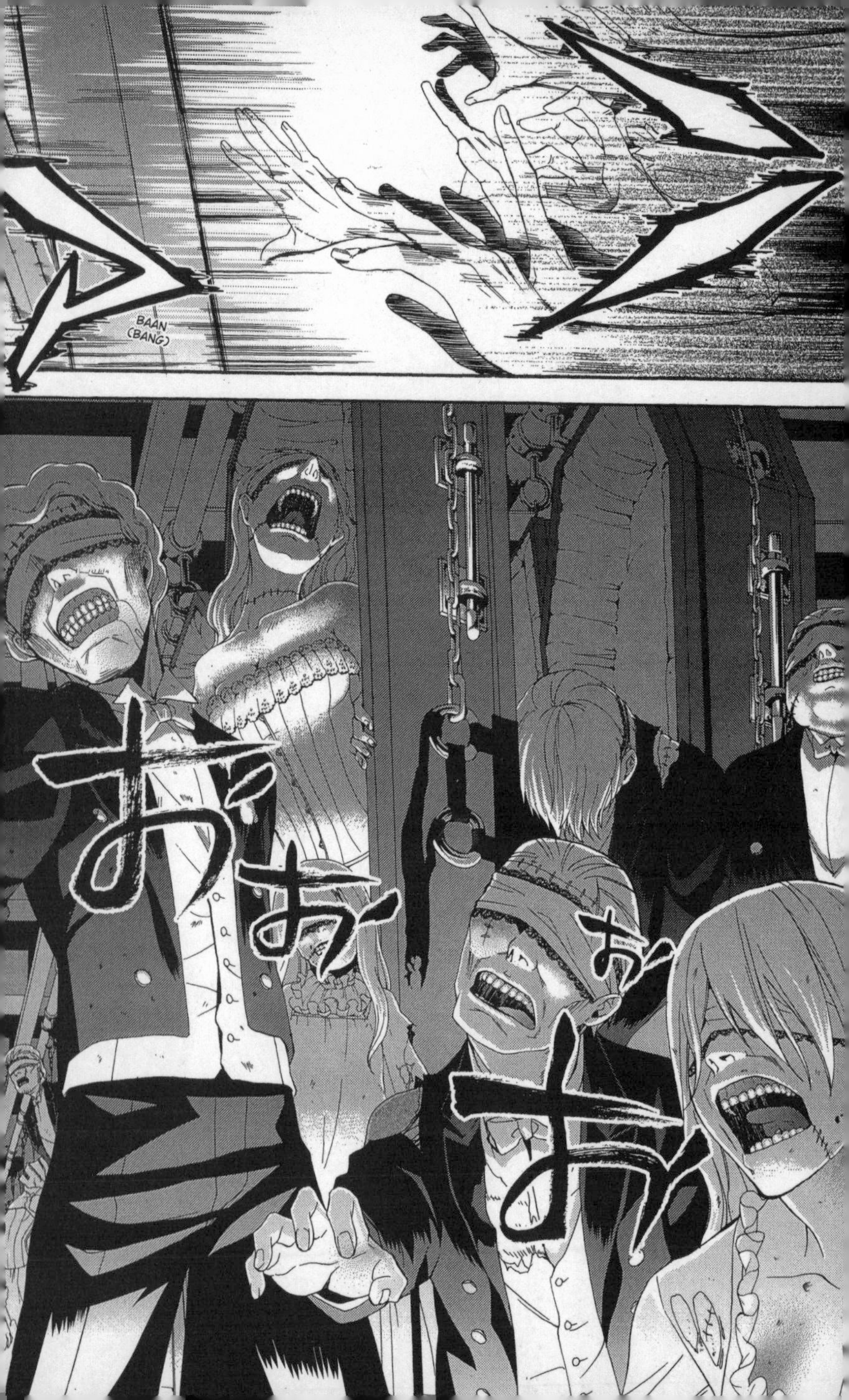
BAAN
(BANG)

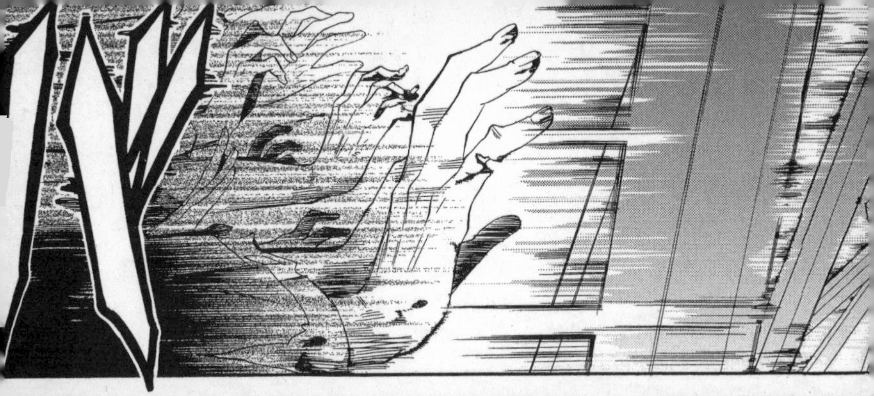

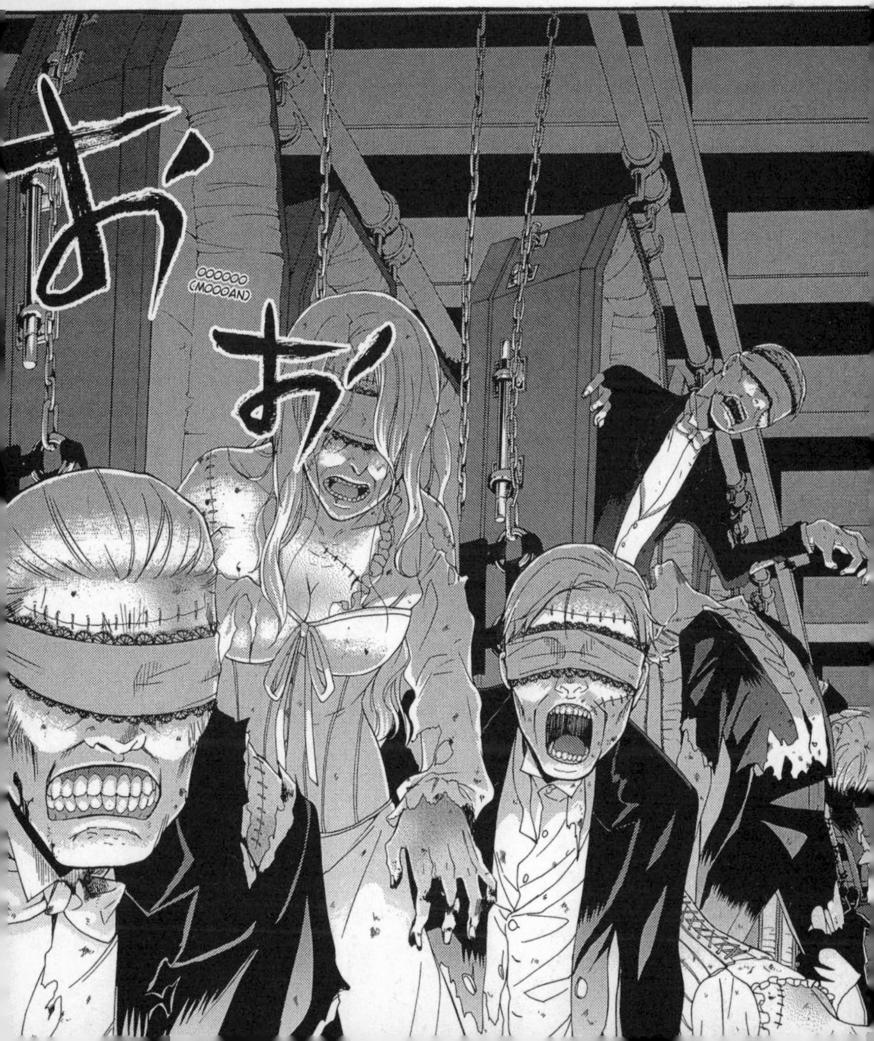
おお
OOOOOO
(MOOOAN)

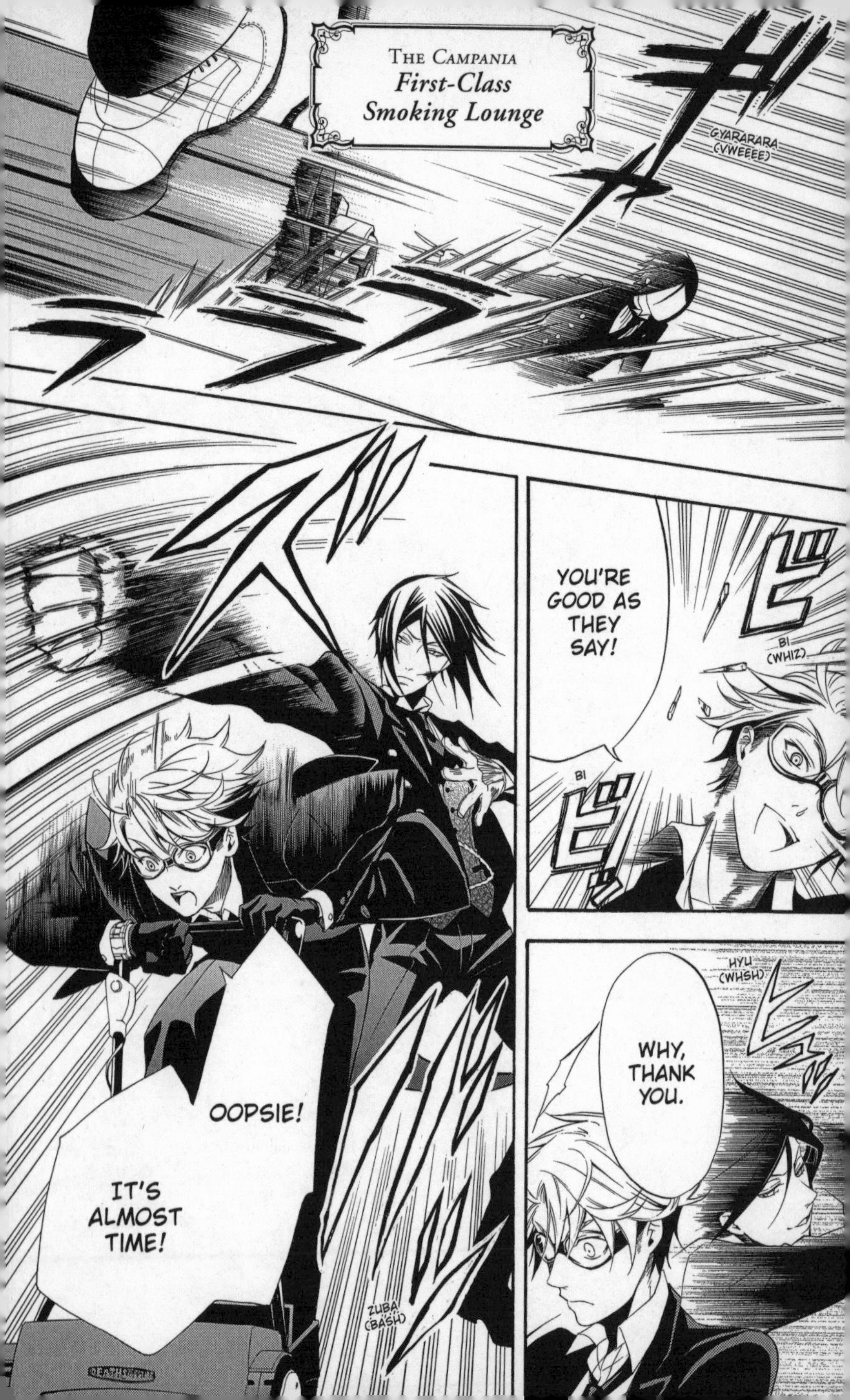
The Campania
First-Class
Smoking Lounge
GYARARARA
(VWEEEE)
YOU'RE GOOD AS THEY SAY!
BI
(WHIZ)
BI
HYU
(WHSH)
WHY, THANK YOU.
OOPSIE!
IT'S ALMOST TIME!
ZUBA
(BASH)

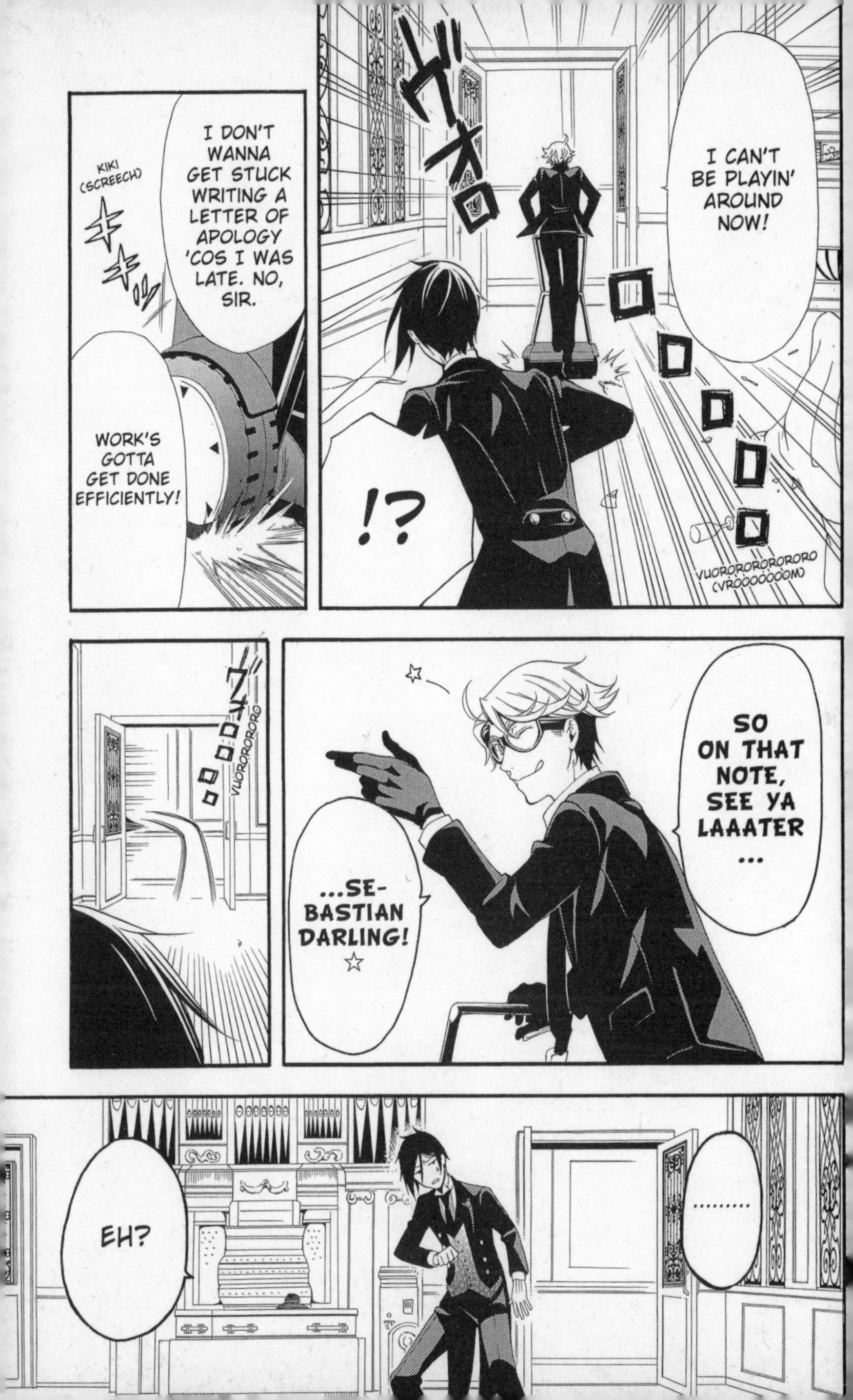

I CAN'T BE PLAYIN' AROUND NOW!
!?
VUORORORORORO (VROOOOOOOM)
I DON'T WANNA GET STUCK WRITING A LETTER OF APOLOGY 'COS I WAS LATE. NO, SIR.
KIKI (SCREECH)
WORK'S GOTTA GET DONE EFFICIENTLY!
SO ON THAT NOTE, SEE YA LAAATER ...
...SE-BASTIAN DARLING! ☆
VUORORORO
....
EH?

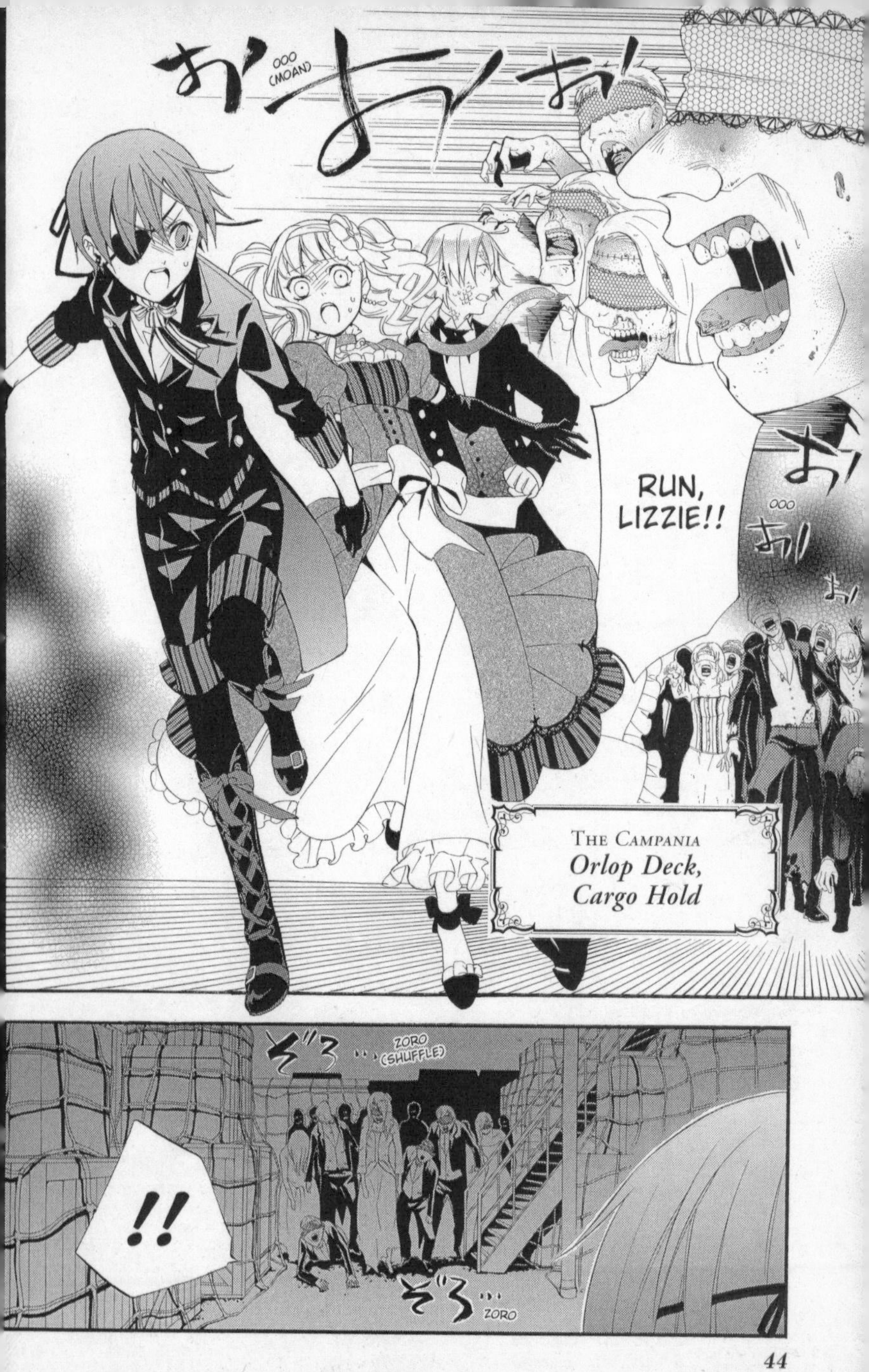
OOO (MOAN)
RUN, LIZZIE!!
OOO
THE CAMPANIA
Orlop Deck, Cargo Hold
ZORO (SHUFFLE)
!!
ZORO

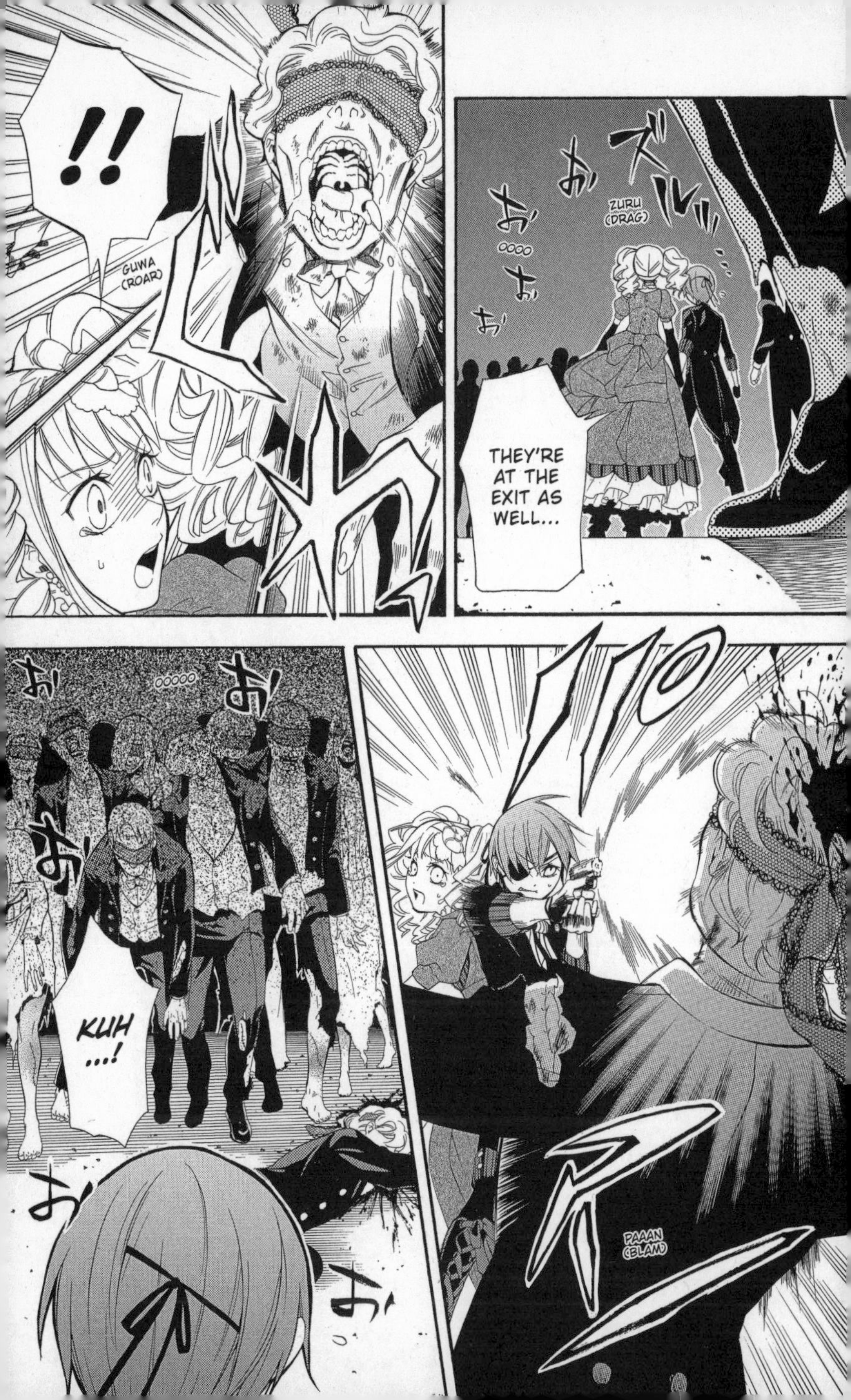

ZURU (DRAG)
OOOO
THEY'RE AT THE EXIT AS WELL...
!!
GUWA (ROAR)
PAAAN (BLAM)
OOOOO
KUH ...!

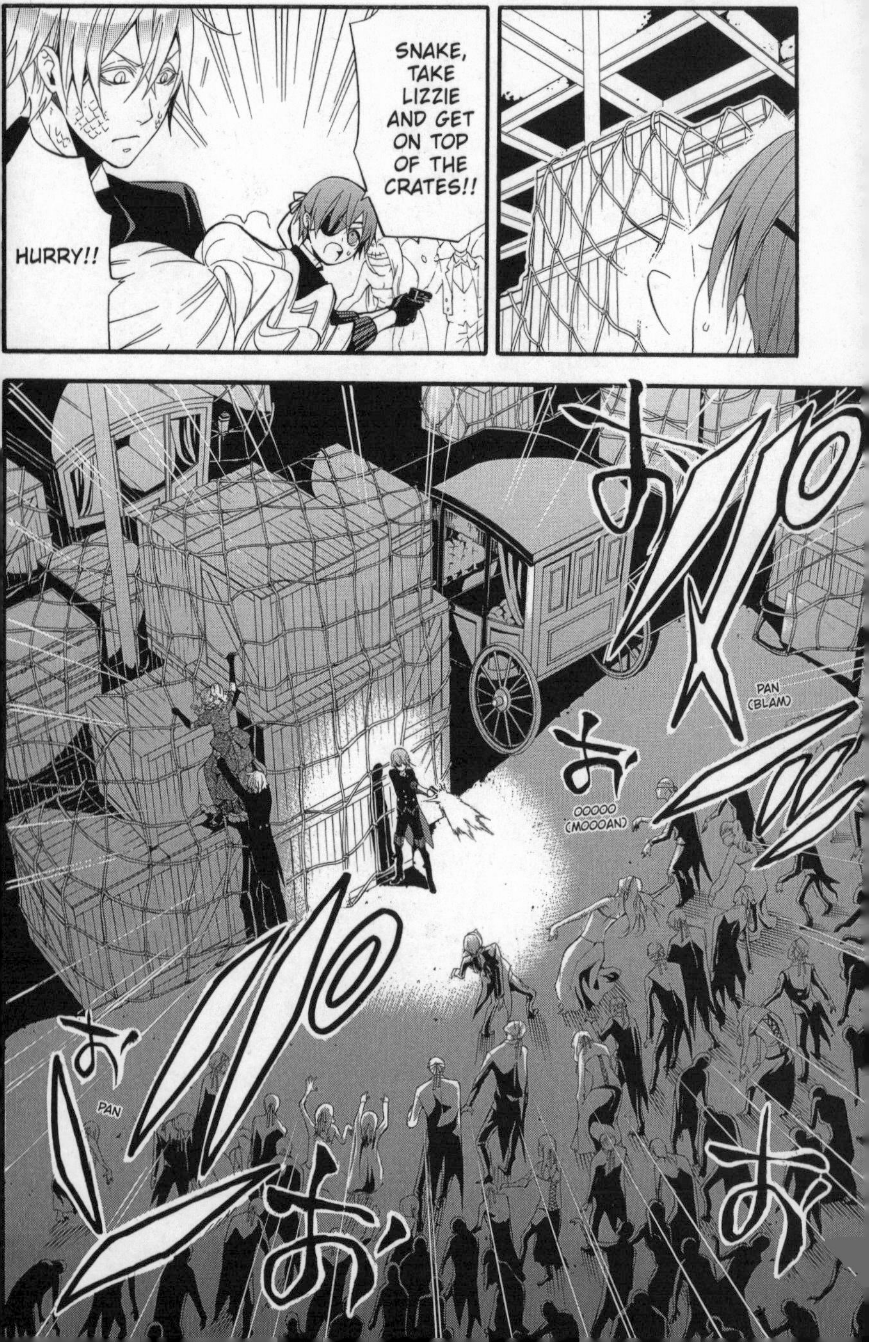
SNAKE, TAKE LIZZIE AND GET ON TOP OF THE CRATES!!
HURRY!!
PAN (BLAM)
OOOOO (MOOOAN)
PAN

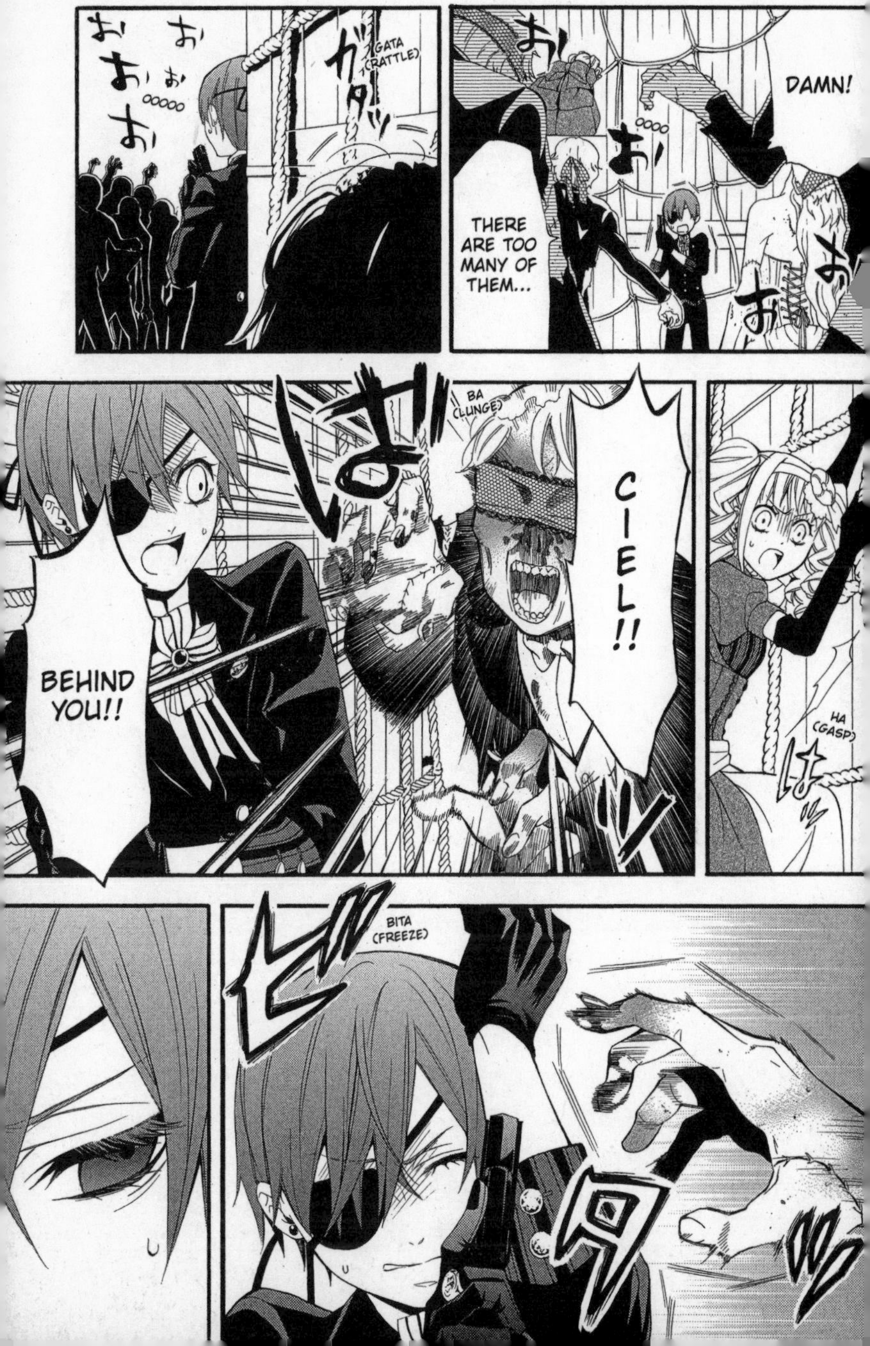
DAMN!
OOOO
THERE ARE TOO MANY OF THEM...
GATA (RATTLE)
OOOOO
HA (GASP)
CIEL!!
BA (LUNGE)
BEHIND YOU!!
BITA (FREEZE)

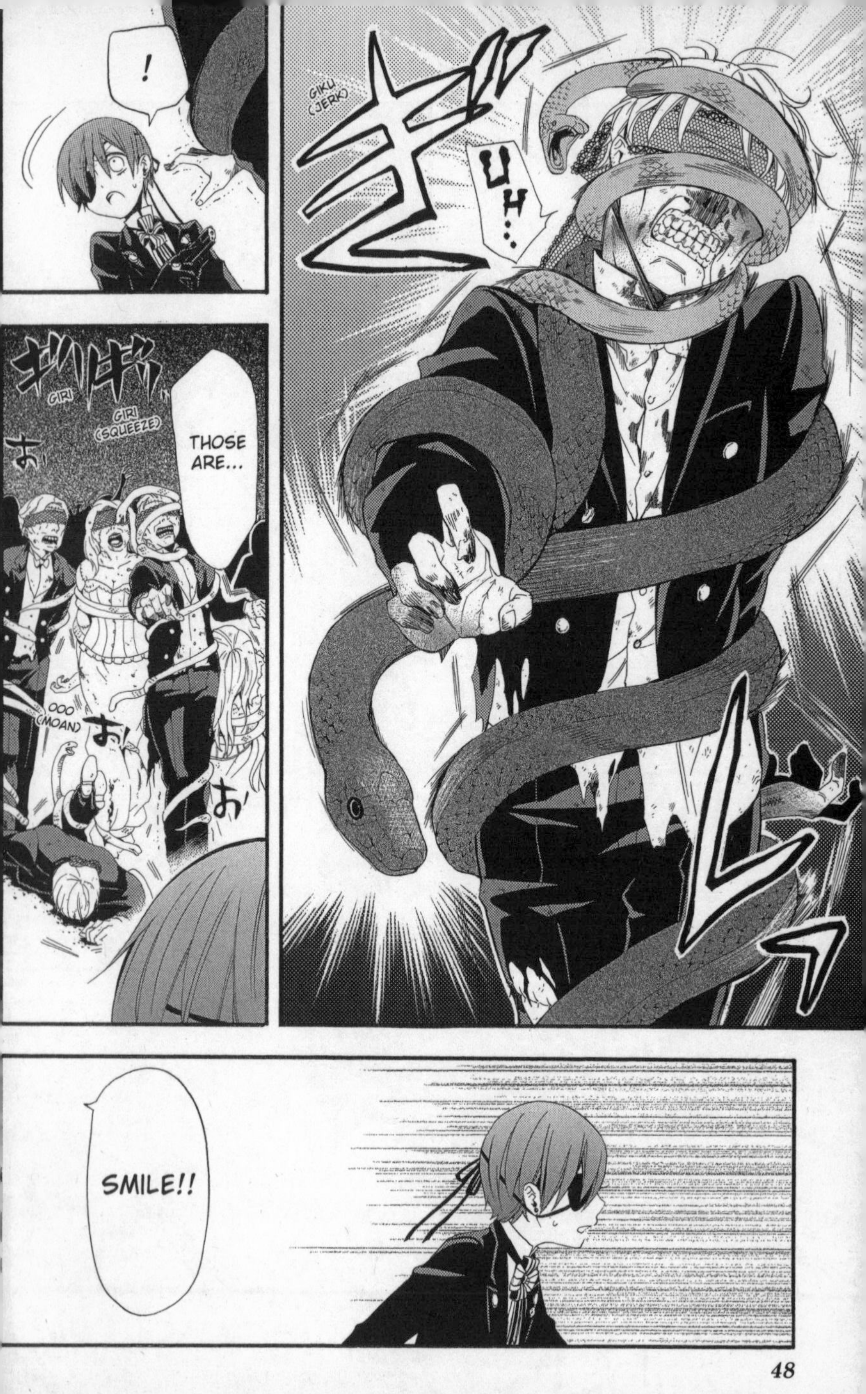
GIKU (JERK)
UH...
!
GIRI
GIRI (SQUEEZE)
THOSE ARE...
OOO (MOAN)
SMILE!!

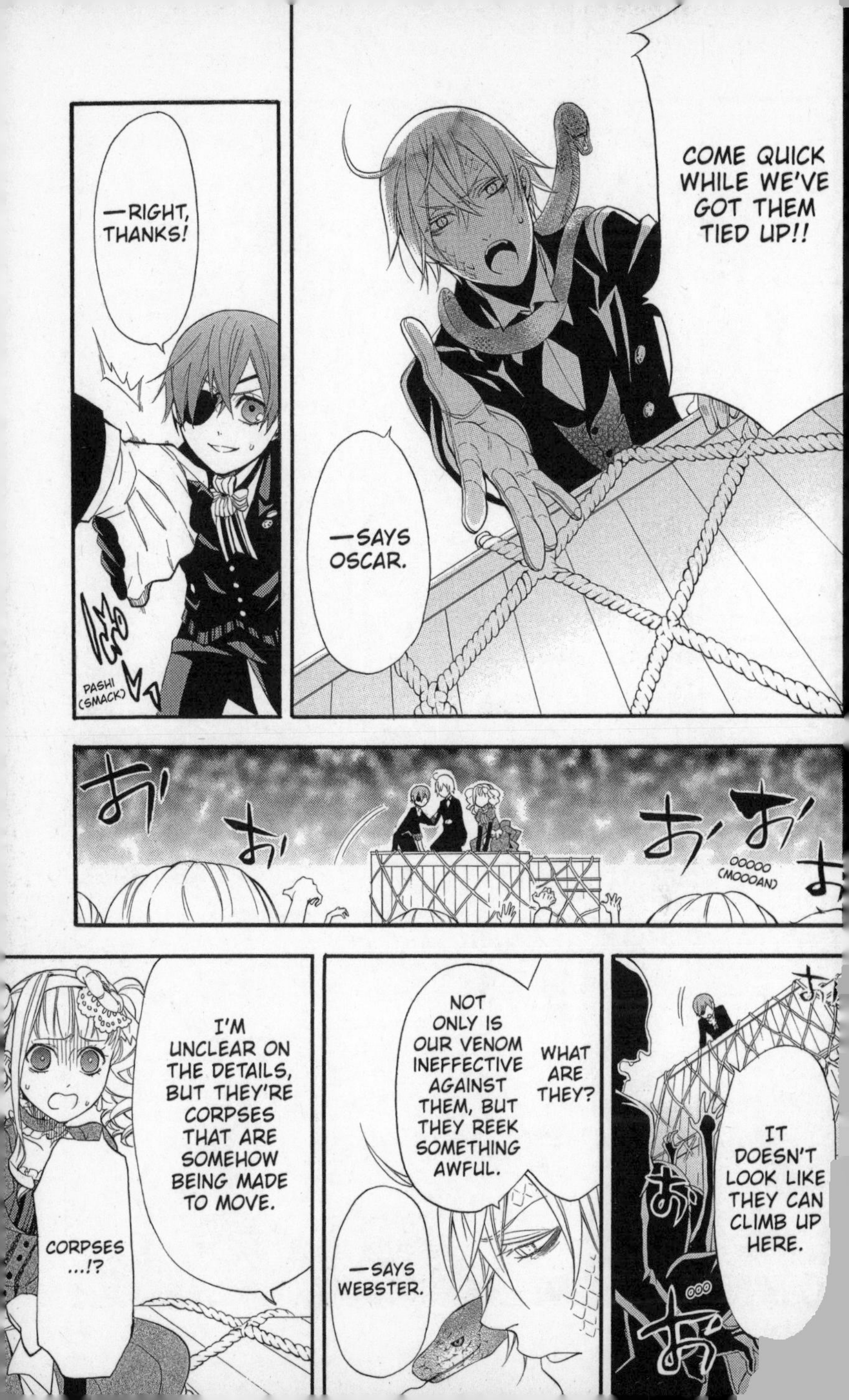
COME QUICK WHILE WE'VE GOT THEM TIED UP!!
—SAYS OSCAR.
—RIGHT, THANKS!
PASHI (SMACK)
OOOOO (MOOOAN)
IT DOESN'T LOOK LIKE THEY CAN CLIMB UP HERE.
WHAT ARE THEY?
NOT ONLY IS OUR VENOM INEFFECTIVE AGAINST THEM, BUT THEY REEK SOMETHING AWFUL.
—SAYS WEBSTER.
I'M UNCLEAR ON THE DETAILS, BUT THEY'RE CORPSES THAT ARE SOMEHOW BEING MADE TO MOVE.
CORPSES ...!?

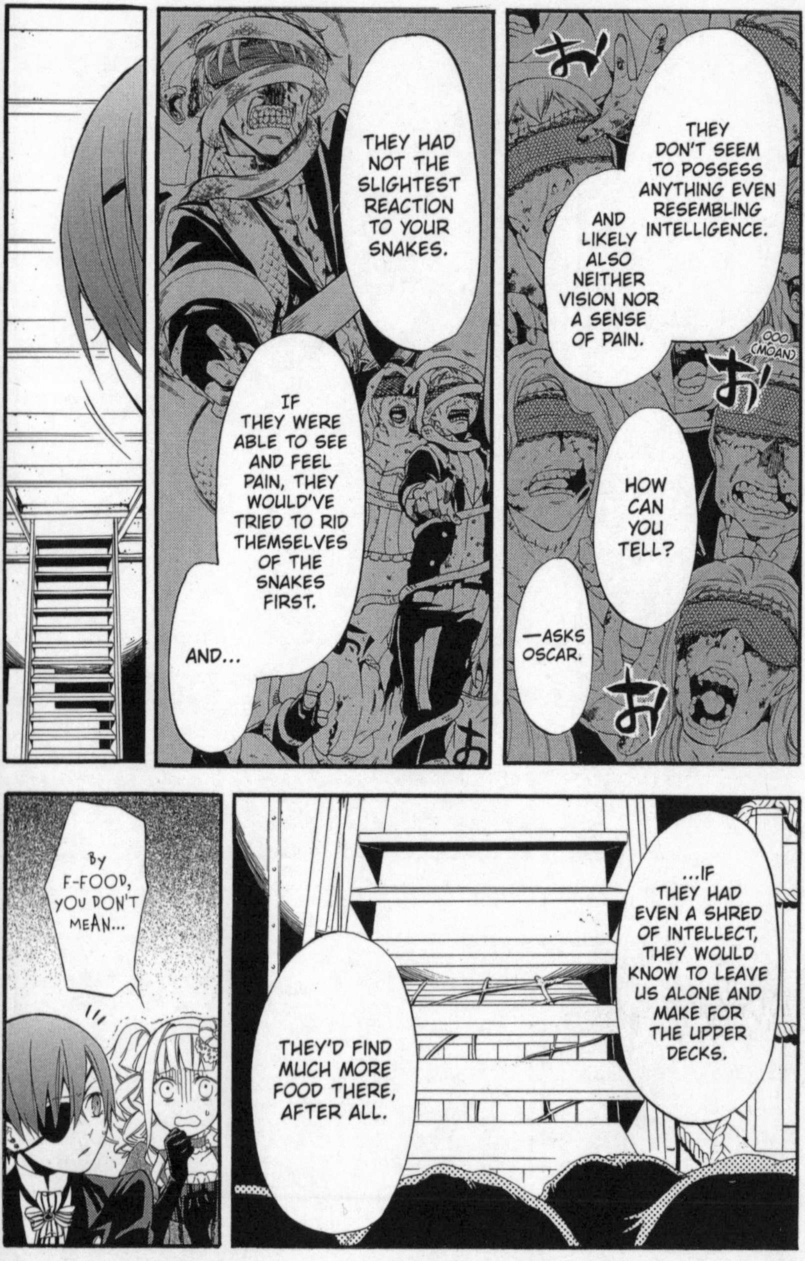
THEY DON'T SEEM TO POSSESS ANYTHING EVEN RESEMBLING INTELLIGENCE.
AND LIKELY ALSO NEITHER VISION NOR A SENSE OF PAIN.
OOO (MOAN)
HOW CAN YOU TELL?
—ASKS OSCAR.
THEY HAD NOT THE SLIGHTEST REACTION TO YOUR SNAKES.
IF THEY WERE ABLE TO SEE AND FEEL PAIN, THEY WOULD'VE TRIED TO RID THEMSELVES OF THE SNAKES FIRST.
AND...
...IF THEY HAD EVEN A SHRED OF INTELLECT, THEY WOULD KNOW TO LEAVE US ALONE AND MAKE FOR THE UPPER DECKS.
THEY'D FIND MUCH MORE FOOD THERE, AFTER ALL.
By F-FOOD, YOU DON'T MEAN...

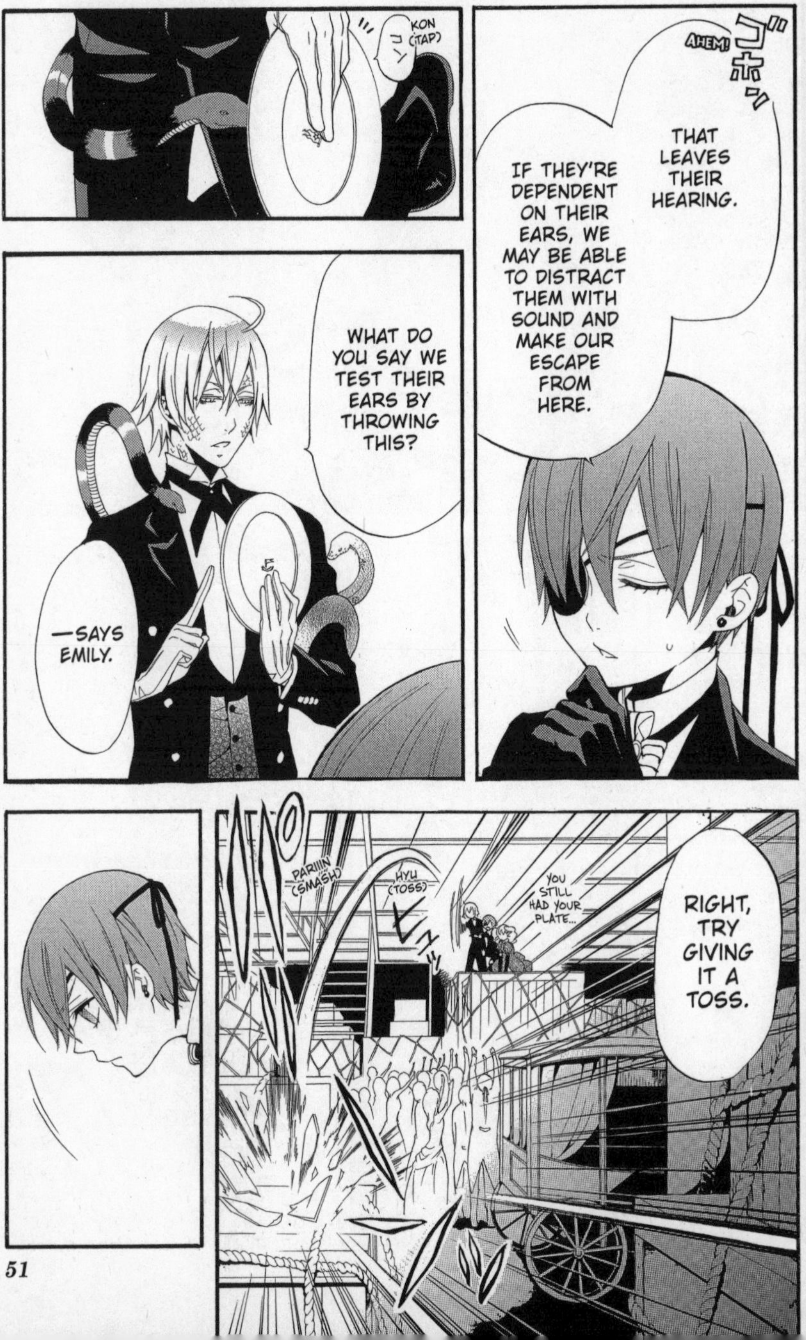
AHEM!
THAT LEAVES THEIR HEARING.
IF THEY'RE DEPENDENT ON THEIR EARS, WE MAY BE ABLE TO DISTRACT THEM WITH SOUND AND MAKE OUR ESCAPE FROM HERE.
KON (TAP)
WHAT DO YOU SAY WE TEST THEIR EARS BY THROWING THIS?
—SAYS EMILY.
RIGHT, TRY GIVING IT A TOSS.
HYU (TOSS)
YOU STILL HAD YOUR PLATE...
PARIIIN (SMASH)

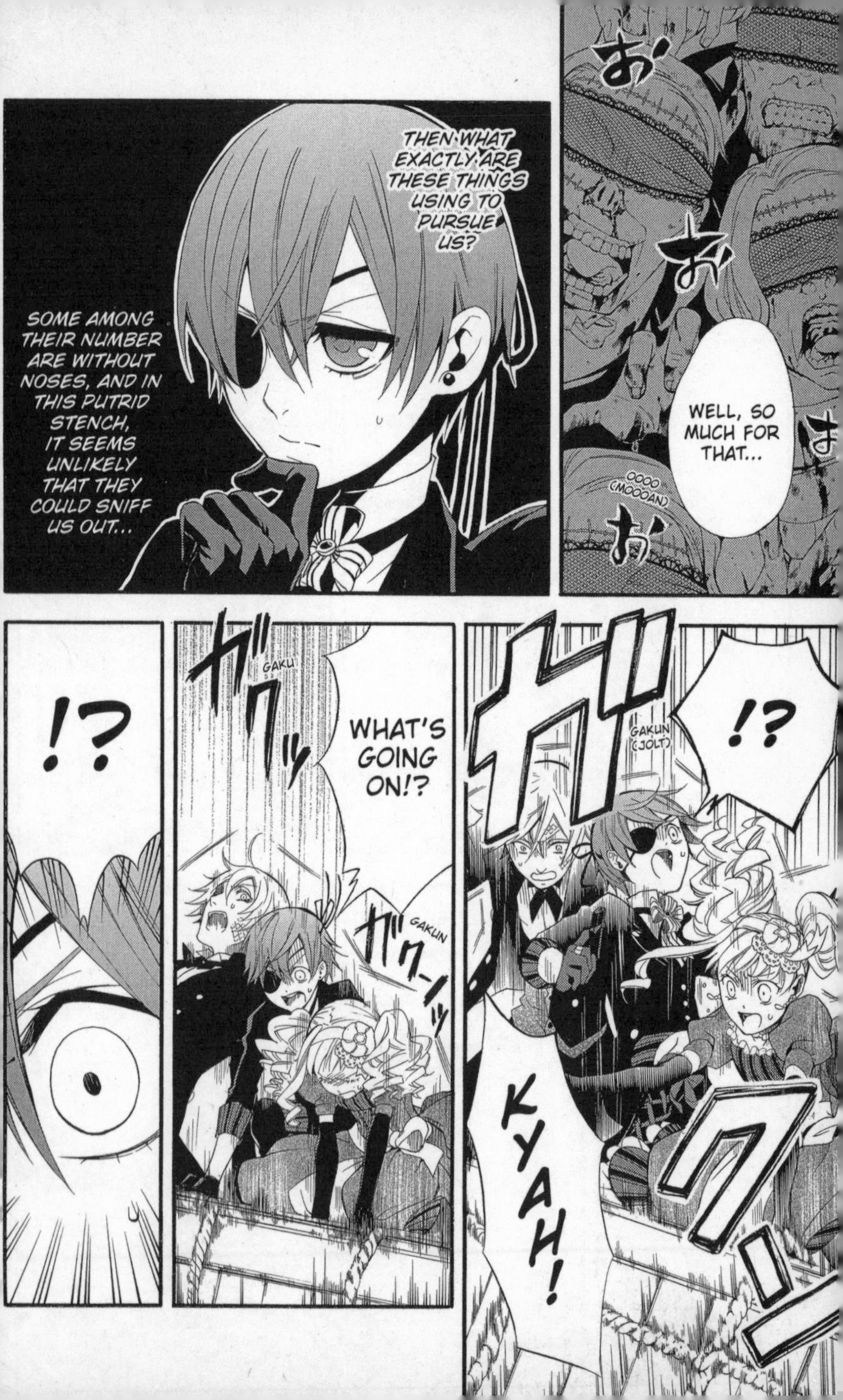
WELL, SO MUCH FOR THAT...
OOOO (MOOOAN)
THEN WHAT EXACTLY ARE THESE THINGS USING TO PURSUE US?
SOME AMONG THEIR NUMBER ARE WITHOUT NOSES, AND IN THIS PUTRID STENCH, IT SEEMS UNLIKELY THAT THEY COULD SNIFF US OUT...
!?
GAKUN (JOLT)
KYAH!
GAKU
WHAT'S GOING ON!?
GAKUN
!?

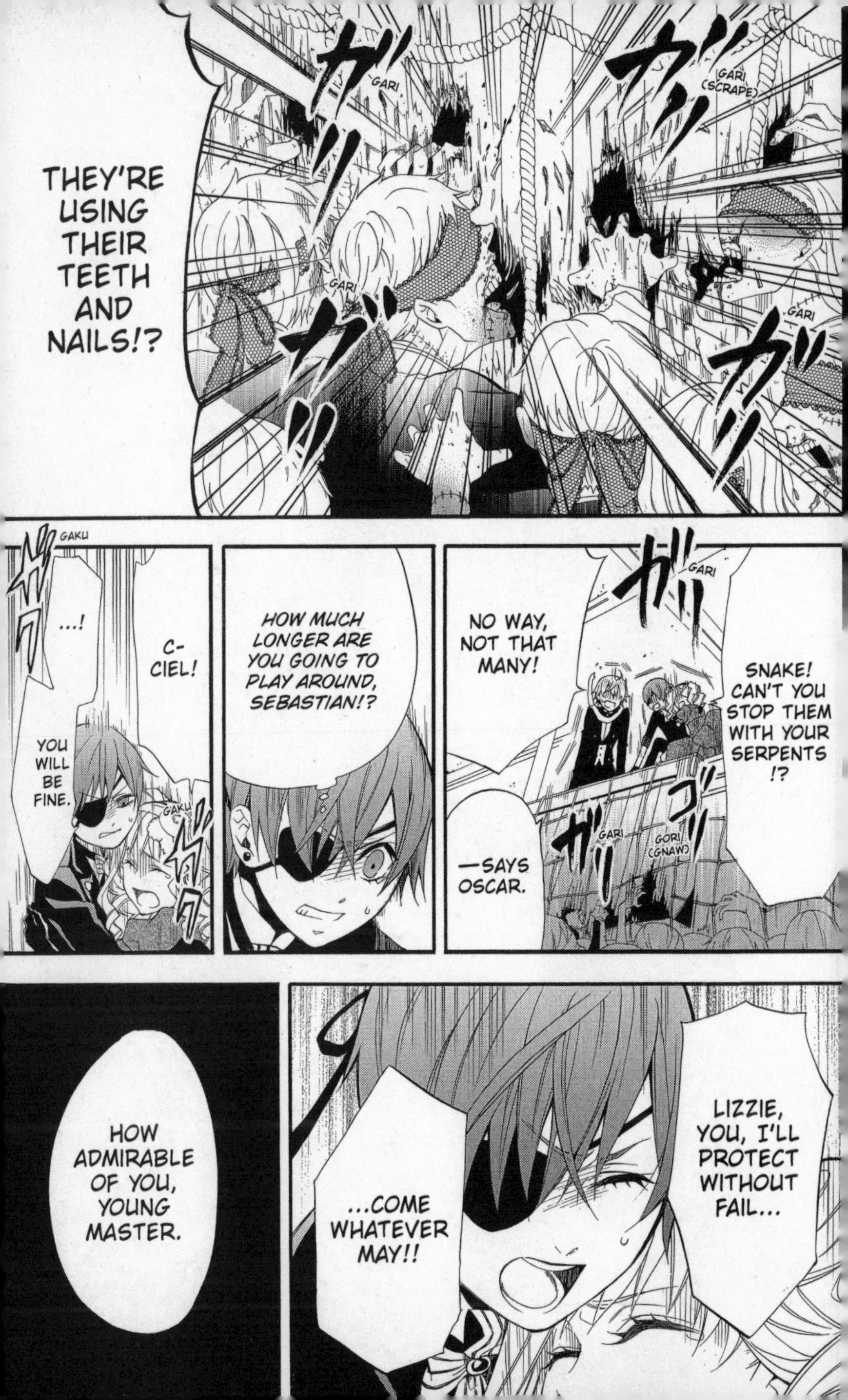
GARI (SCRAPE)
GARI
THEY'RE USING THEIR TEETH AND NAILS!?
GARI
GARI
GARI
SNAKE! CAN'T YOU STOP THEM WITH YOUR SERPENTS!?
NO WAY, NOT THAT MANY!
GORI (GNAW)
GARI
—SAYS OSCAR.
HOW MUCH LONGER ARE YOU GOING TO PLAY AROUND, SEBASTIAN!?
GAKU
...!
C-CIEL!
YOU WILL BE FINE.
GAKU
LIZZIE, YOU, I'LL PROTECT WITHOUT FAIL...
...COME WHATEVER MAY!!
HOW ADMIRABLE OF YOU, YOUNG MASTER.

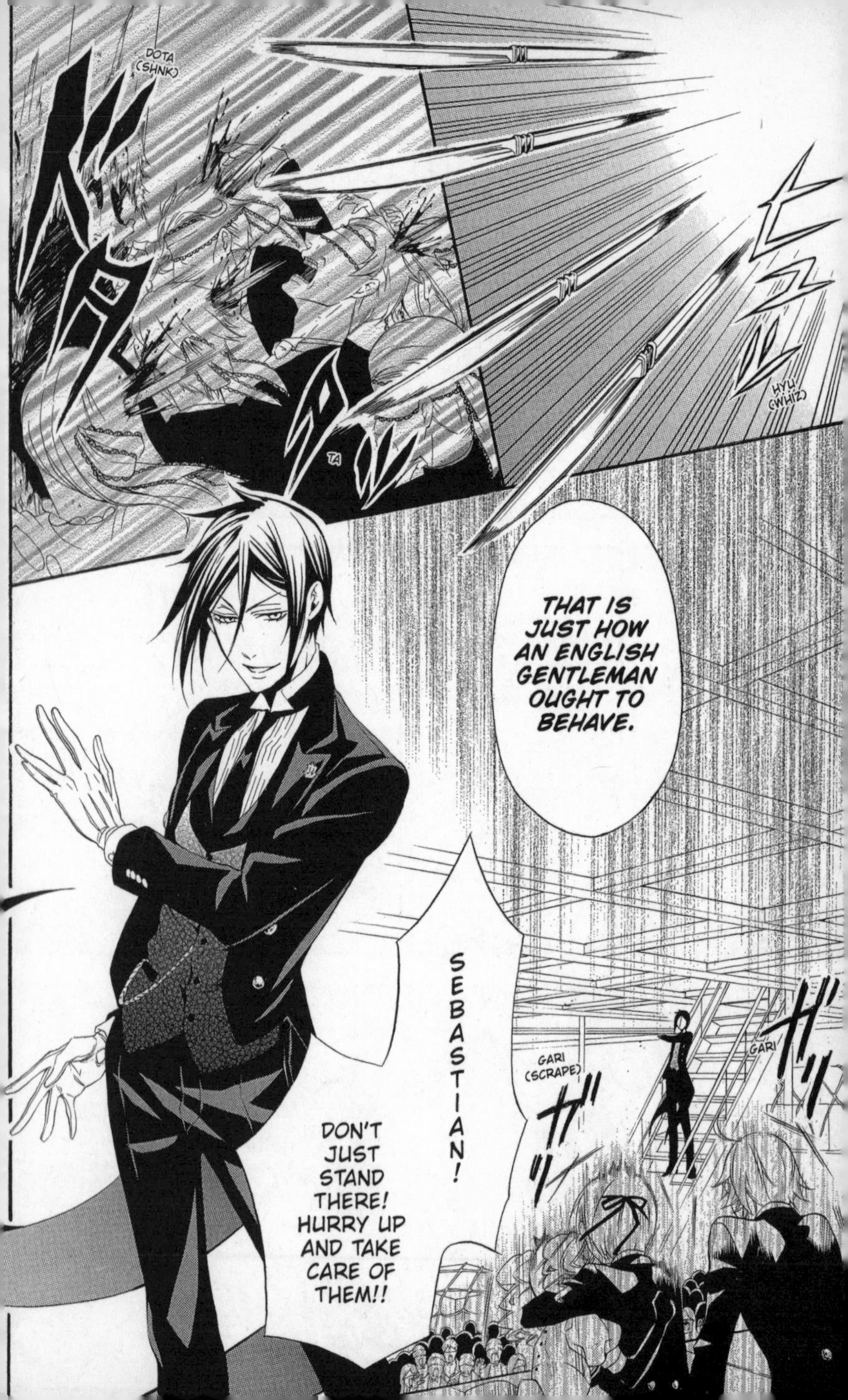
HYU (WHIZ)
TA
DOTA (SHNK)
THAT IS JUST HOW AN ENGLISH GENTLEMAN OUGHT TO BEHAVE.
SEBASTIAN!
GARI
GARI (SCRAPE)
DON'T JUST STAND THERE! HURRY UP AND TAKE CARE OF THEM!!

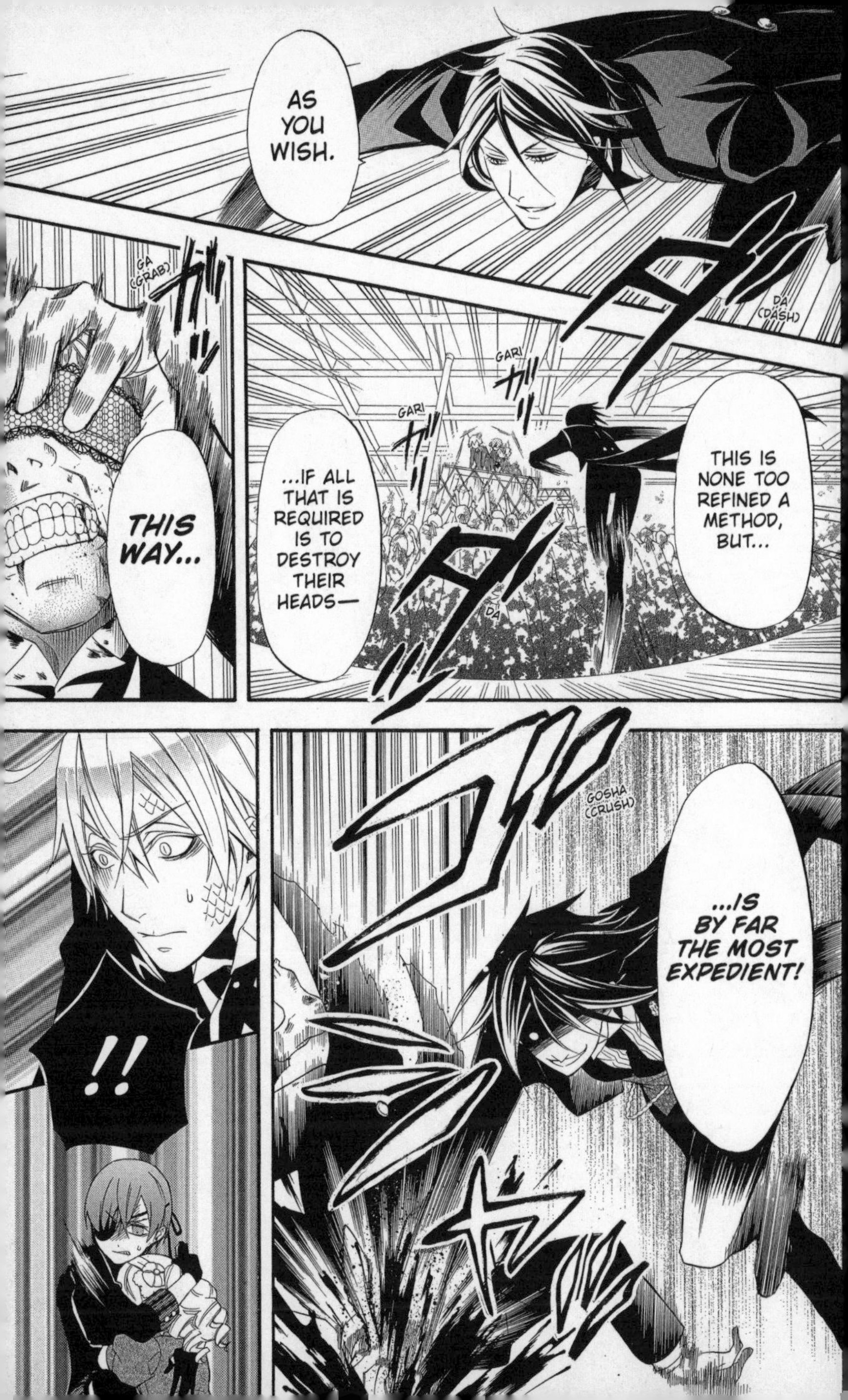
AS YOU WISH.
DA (DASH)
THIS IS NONE TOO REFINED A METHOD, BUT...
GARI
GARI
...IF ALL THAT IS REQUIRED IS TO DESTROY THEIR HEADS—
DA
GA (GRAB)
THIS WAY...
GOSHA (CRUSH)
...IS BY FAR THE MOST EXPEDIENT!
!!

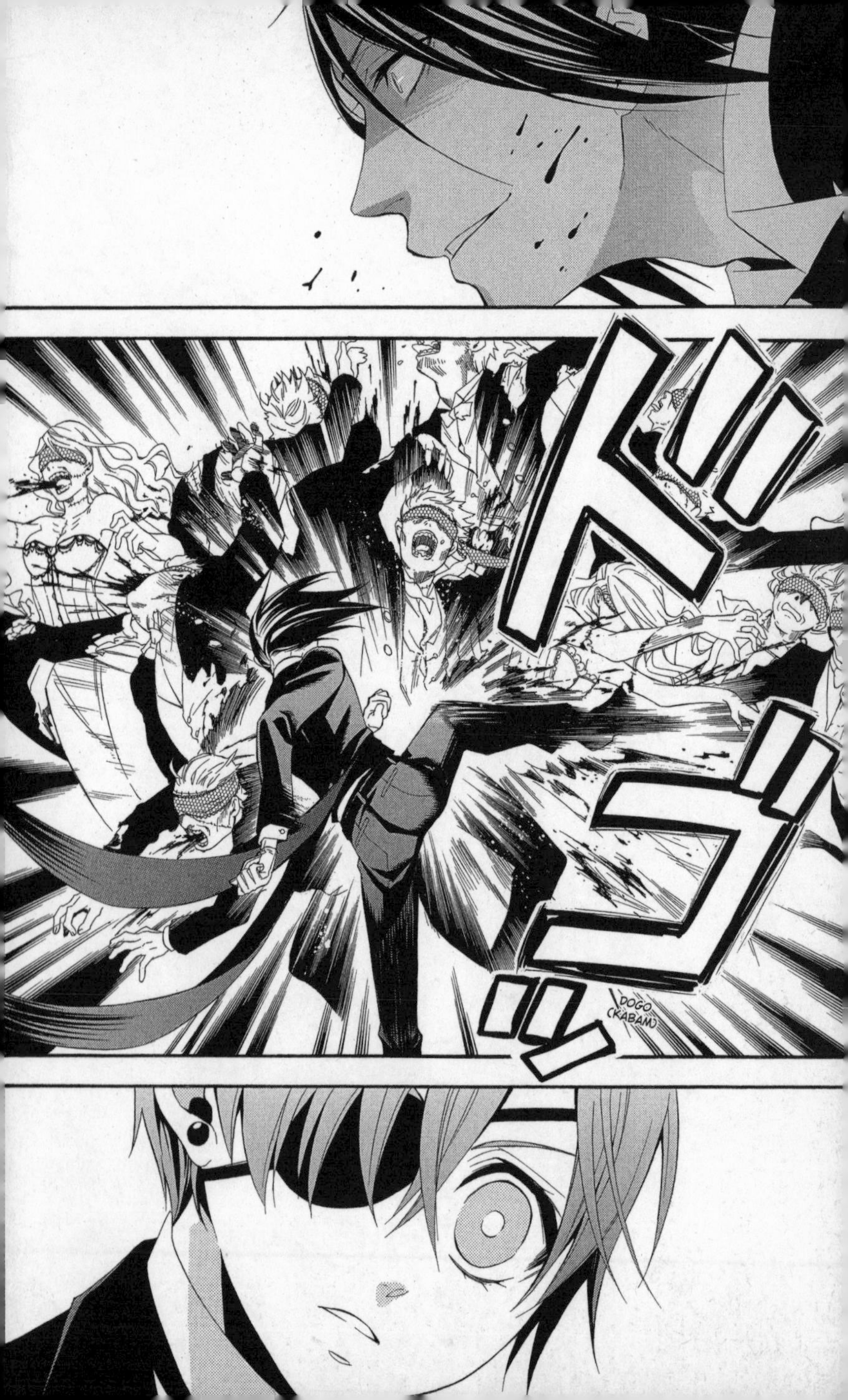
DOGO
(KABAM)

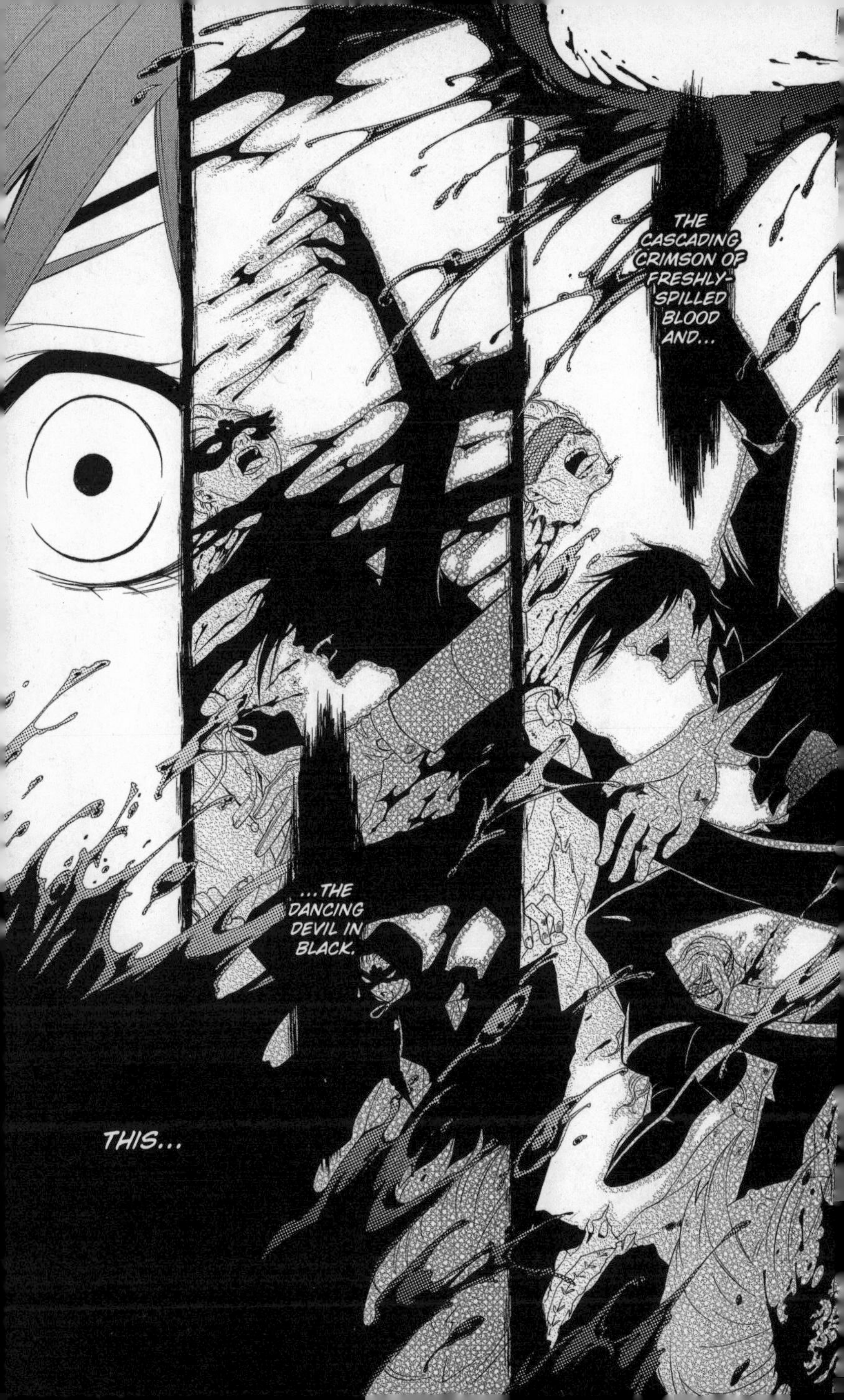
THE CASCADING CRIMSON OF FRESHLY-SPILLED BLOOD AND...
...THE DANCING DEVIL IN BLACK.
THIS...

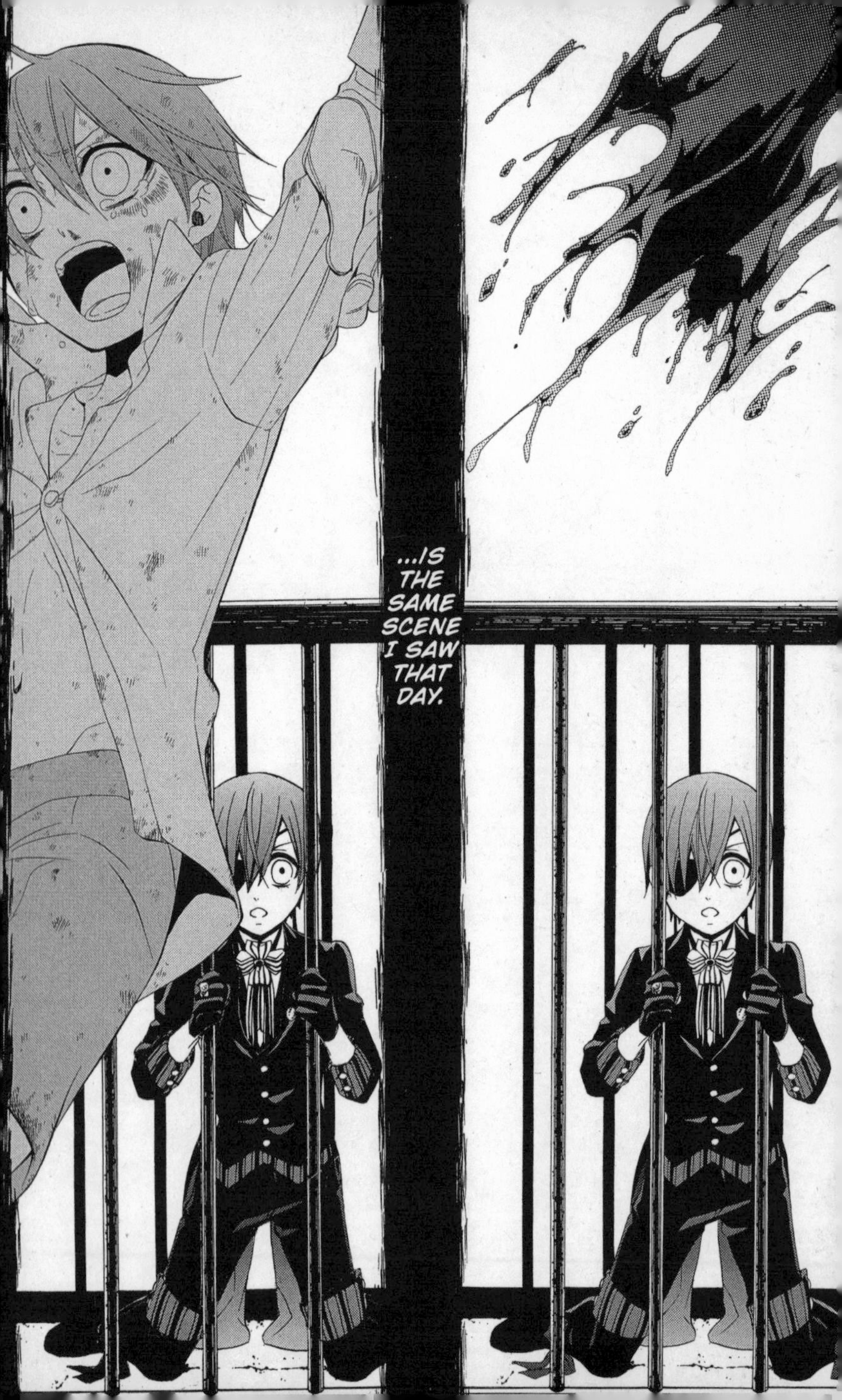
...IS THE SAME SCENE I SAW THAT DAY.

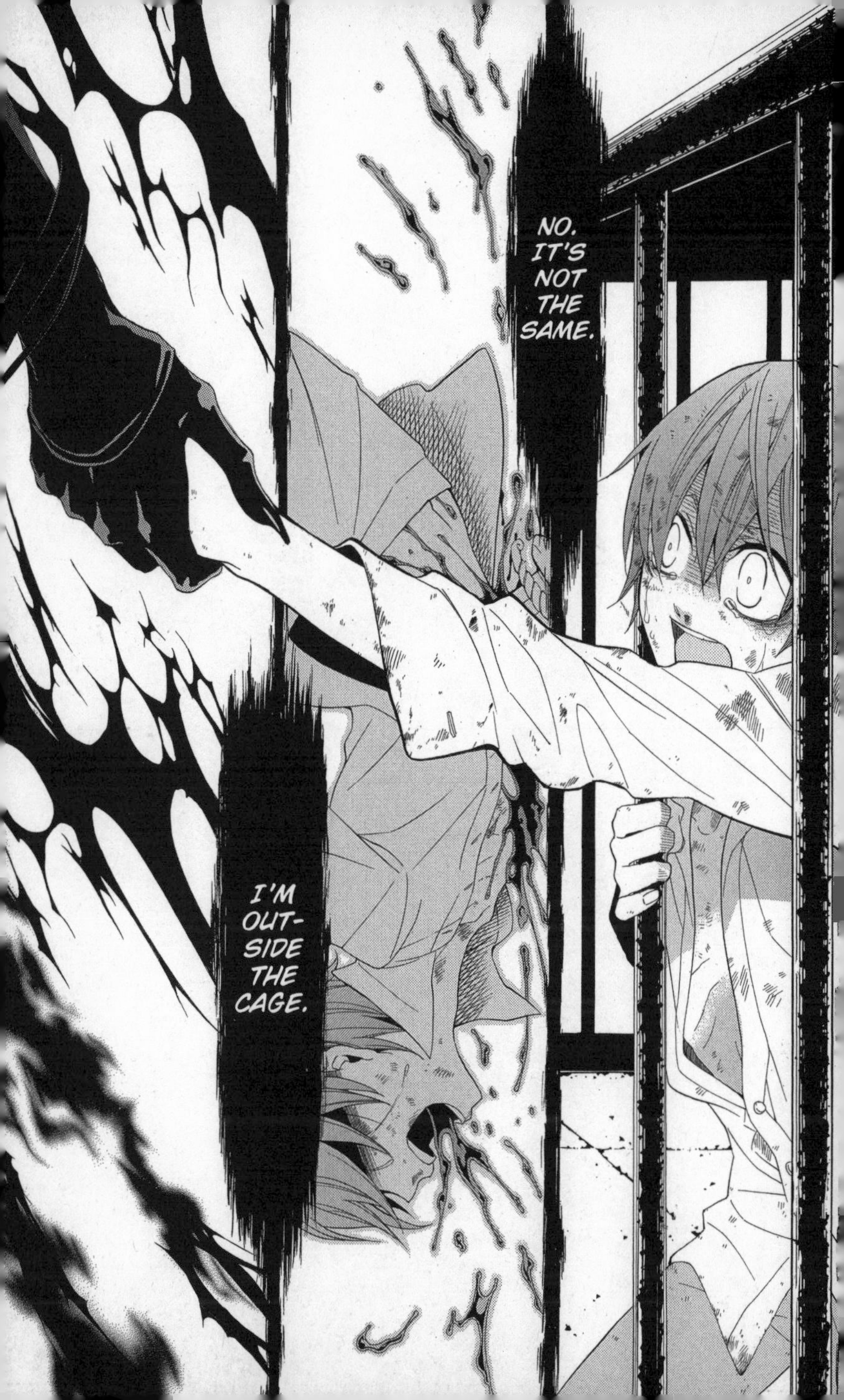
NO. IT'S NOT THE SAME.
I'M OUT-SIDE THE CAGE.

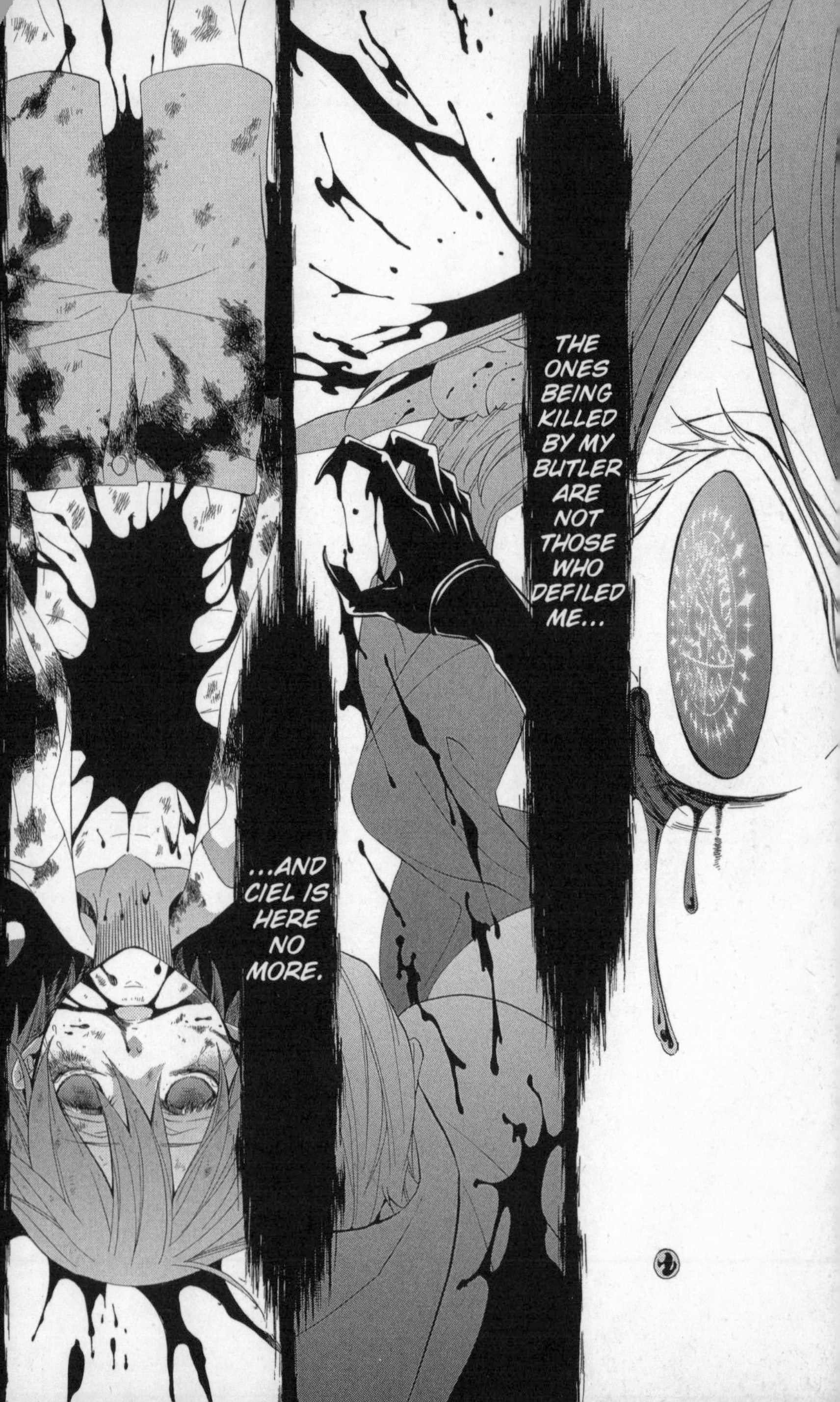
THE ONES BEING KILLED BY MY BUTLER ARE NOT THOSE WHO DEFILED ME...
...AND CIEL IS HERE NO MORE.

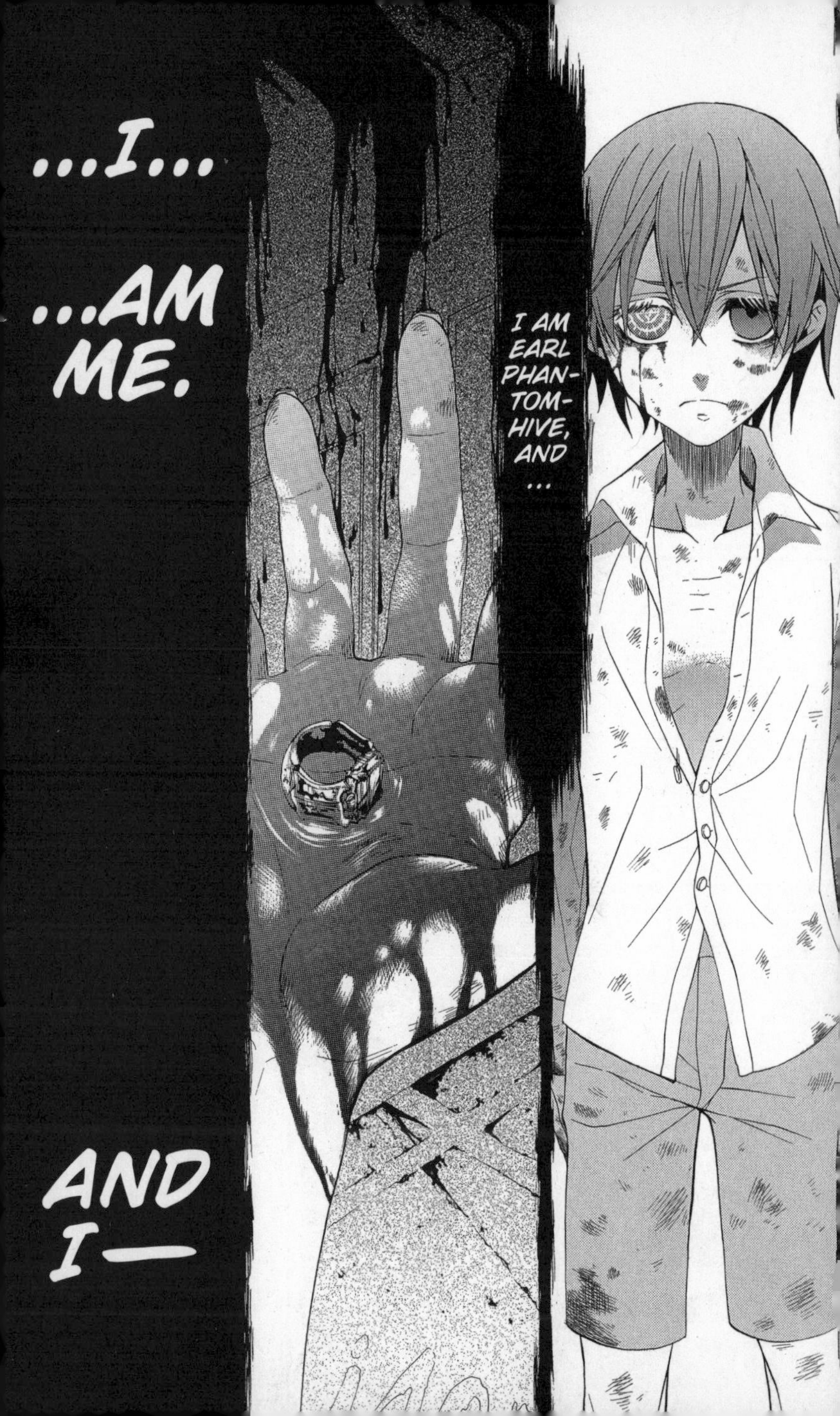
I AM EARL PHAN-TOM-HIVE, AND ...
...I...
...AM ME.
AND I—

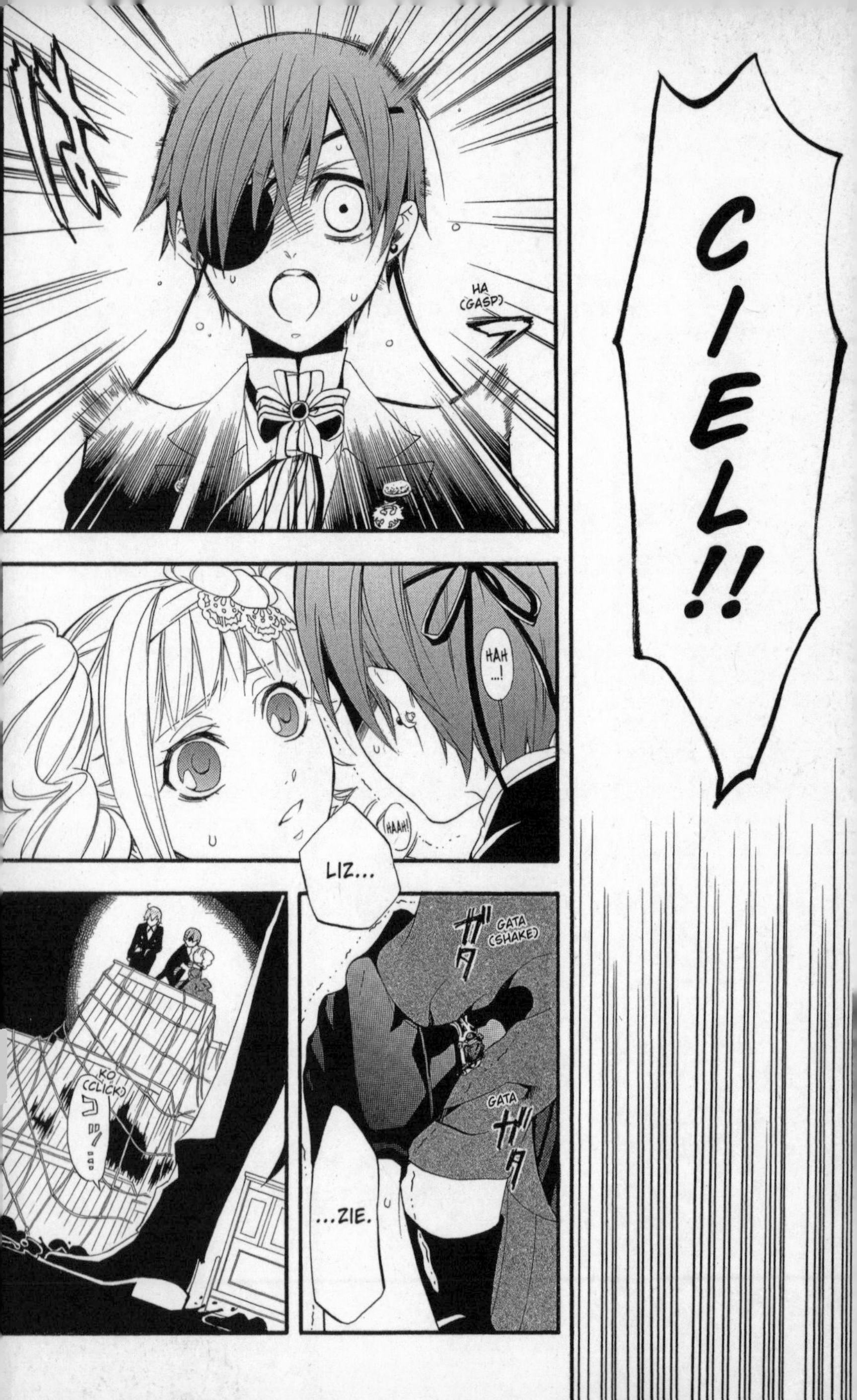
CIEL!!
HA (GASP)
HAH ...!
HAAH!
LIZ...
GATA (SHAKE)
GATA
...ZIE.
KO (CLICK)

ALL DONE, YOUNG MASTER.

IS SOMETHING WRONG?

HAH!

HAAH!

HERE, PLEASE LET ME HELP YOU.

NOW.

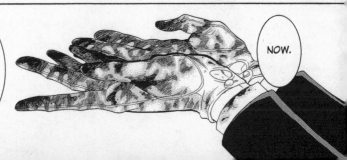

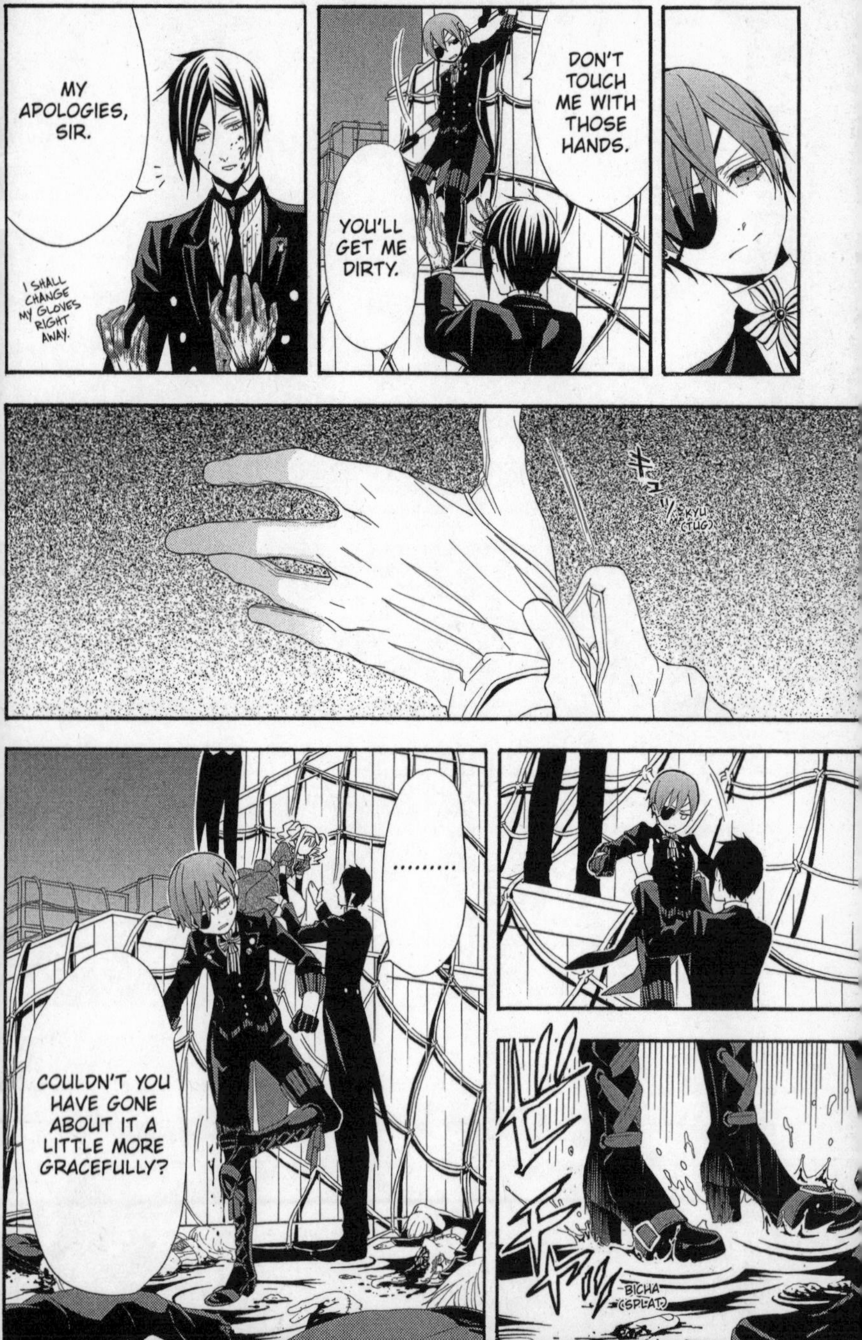
DON'T TOUCH ME WITH THOSE HANDS.
YOU'LL GET ME DIRTY.
MY APOLOGIES, SIR.
I SHALL CHANGE MY GLOVES RIGHT AWAY.
KYU (TUG)
BICHA (SPLAT)
....
COULDN'T YOU HAVE GONE ABOUT IT A LITTLE MORE GRACEFULLY?

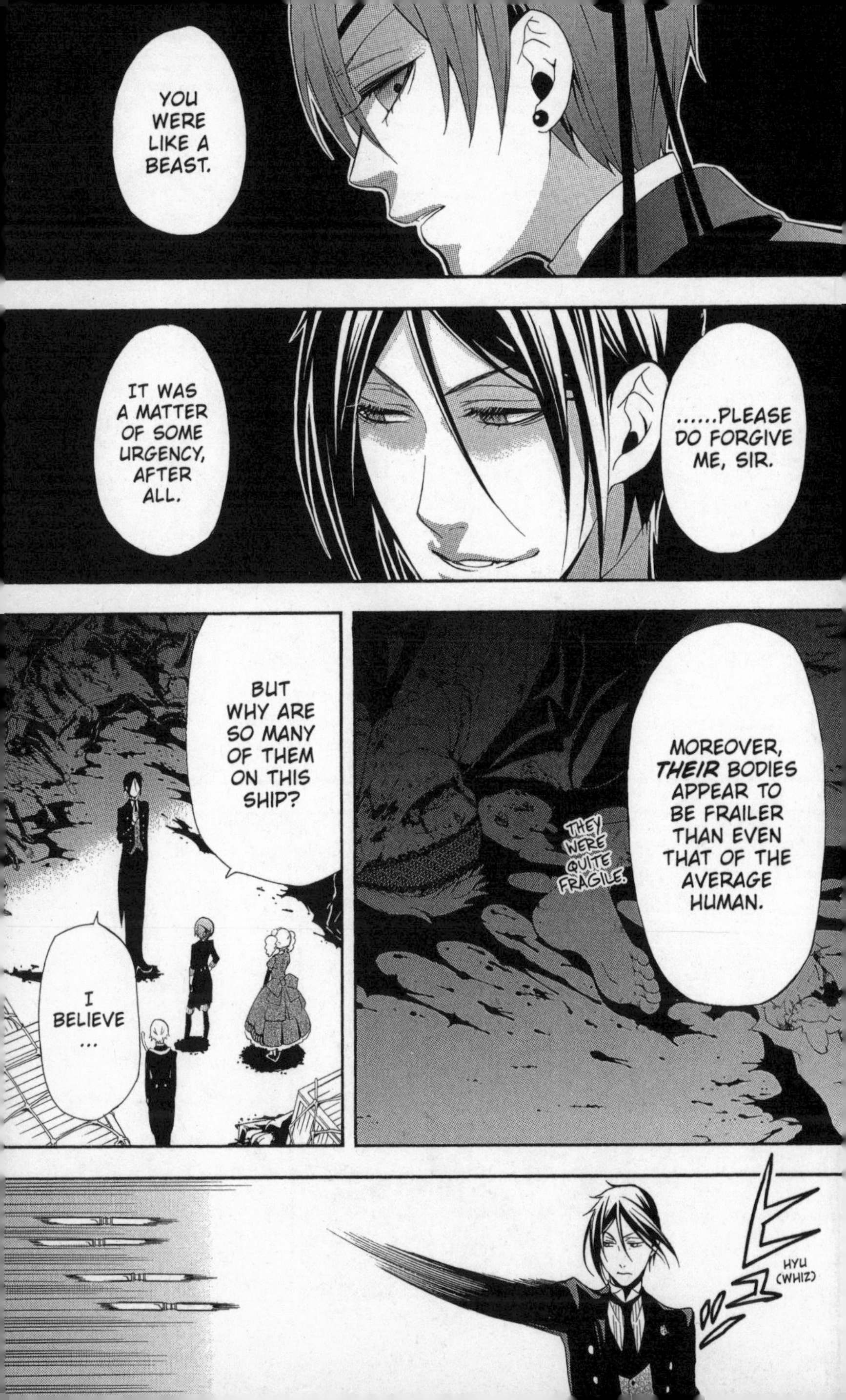
YOU WERE LIKE A BEAST.
......PLEASE DO FORGIVE ME, SIR.
IT WAS A MATTER OF SOME URGENCY, AFTER ALL.
MOREOVER, THEIR BODIES APPEAR TO BE FRAILER THAN EVEN THAT OF THE AVERAGE HUMAN.
THEY WERE QUITE FRAGILE.
BUT WHY ARE SO MANY OF THEM ON THIS SHIP?
I BELIEVE ...
HYU (WHIZ)

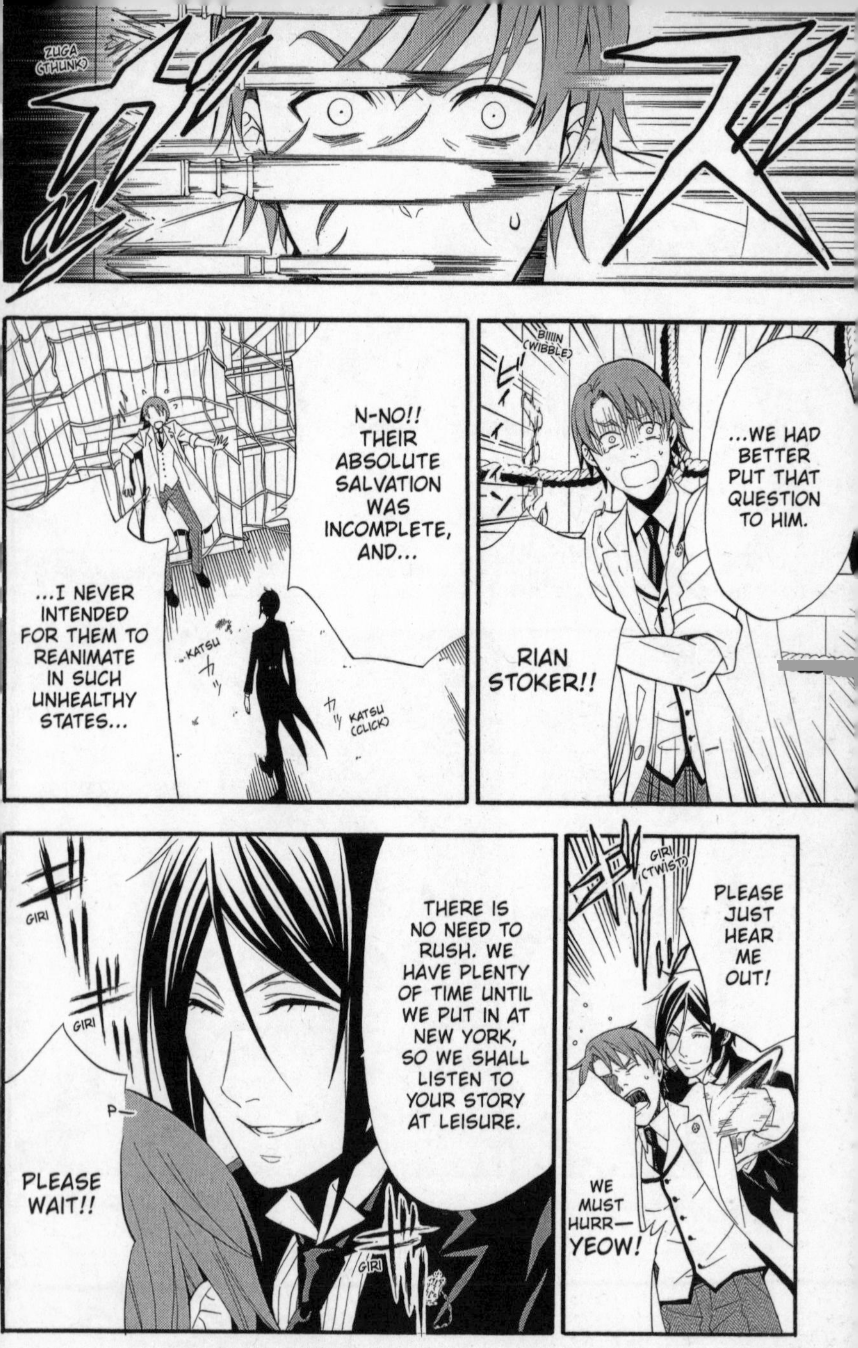
ZUGA (THUNK)
BIIIIN (WIBBLE)
...WE HAD BETTER PUT THAT QUESTION TO HIM.
RIAN STOKER!!
N-NO!! THEIR ABSOLUTE SALVATION WAS INCOMPLETE, AND...
...I NEVER INTENDED FOR THEM TO REANIMATE IN SUCH UNHEALTHY STATES...
KATSU
KATSU (CLICK)
GIRI (TWIST)
PLEASE JUST HEAR ME OUT!
WE MUST HURR—YEOW!
THERE IS NO NEED TO RUSH. WE HAVE PLENTY OF TIME UNTIL WE PUT IN AT NEW YORK, SO WE SHALL LISTEN TO YOUR STORY AT LEISURE.
GIRI
GIRI
P—
PLEASE WAIT!!
GIRI

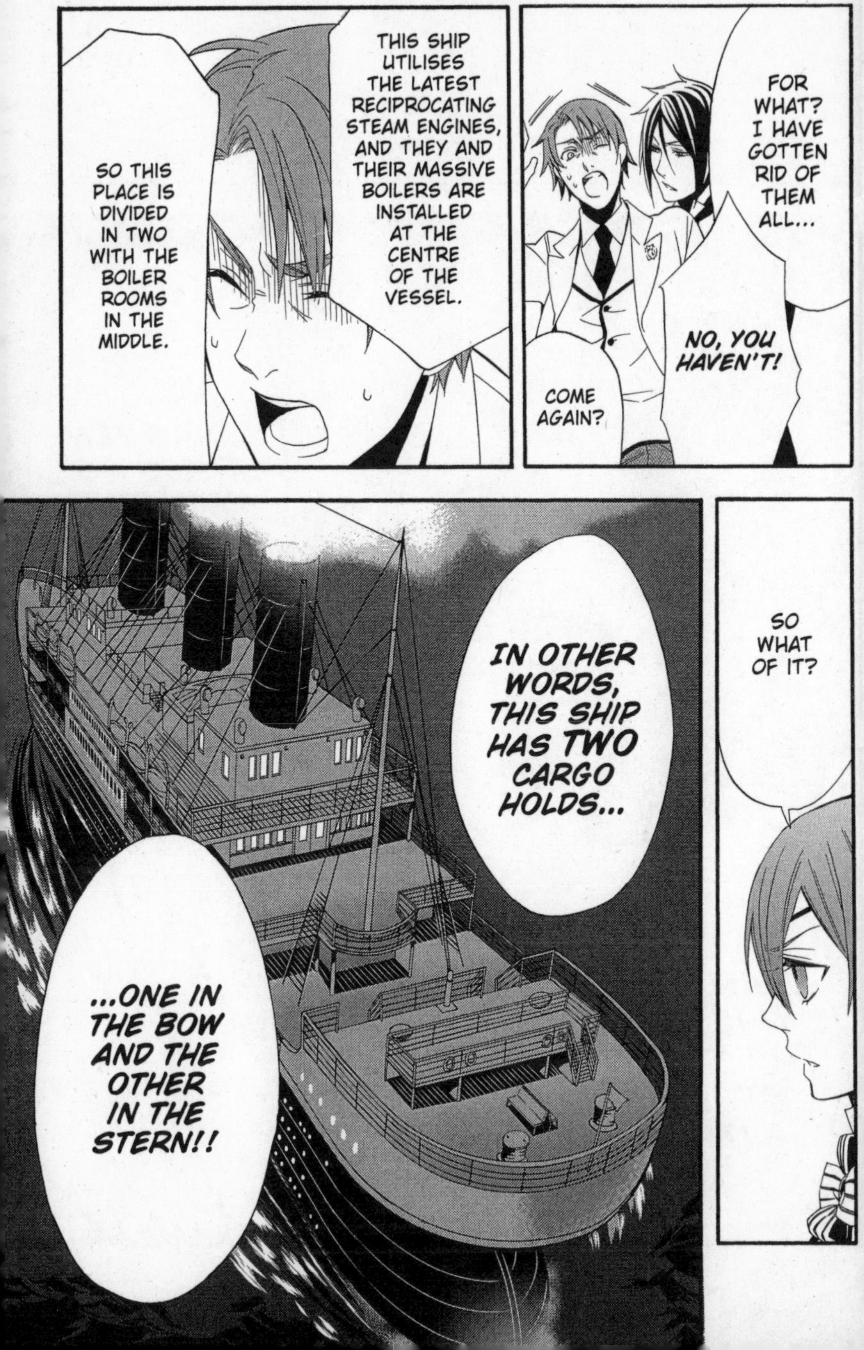
FOR WHAT? I HAVE GOTTEN RID OF THEM ALL...
NO, YOU HAVEN'T!
COME AGAIN?
THIS SHIP UTILISES THE LATEST RECIPROCATING STEAM ENGINES, AND THEY AND THEIR MASSIVE BOILERS ARE INSTALLED AT THE CENTRE OF THE VESSEL.
SO THIS PLACE IS DIVIDED IN TWO WITH THE BOILER ROOMS IN THE MIDDLE.
SO WHAT OF IT?
IN OTHER WORDS, THIS SHIP HAS TWO CARGO HOLDS...
...ONE IN THE BOW AND THE OTHER IN THE STERN!!

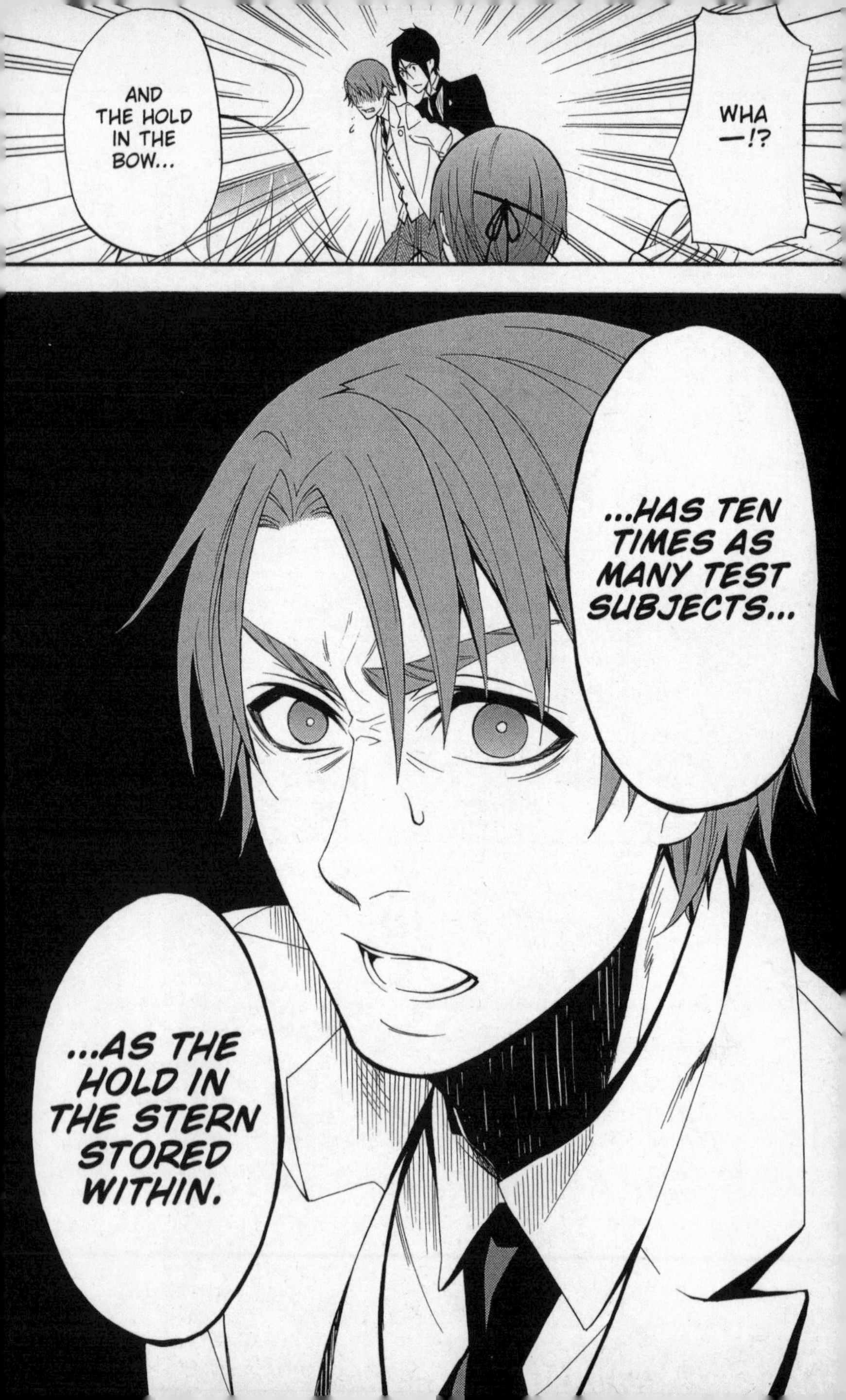
WHA—!?
AND THE HOLD IN THE BOW...
...HAS TEN TIMES AS MANY TEST SUBJECTS...
...AS THE HOLD IN THE STERN STORED WITHIN.

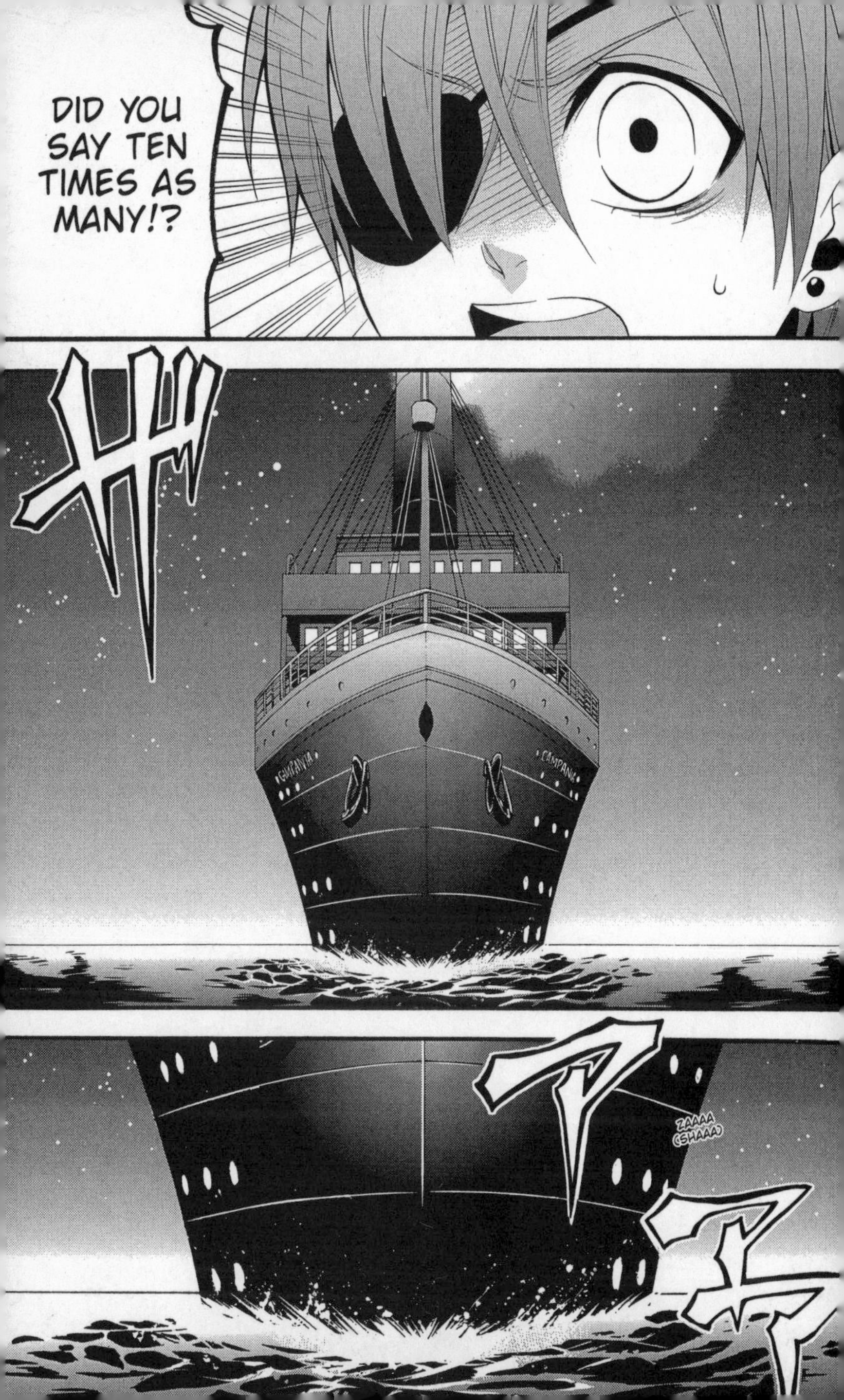
DID YOU SAY TEN TIMES AS MANY!?
ZAAAA (SHAAA)

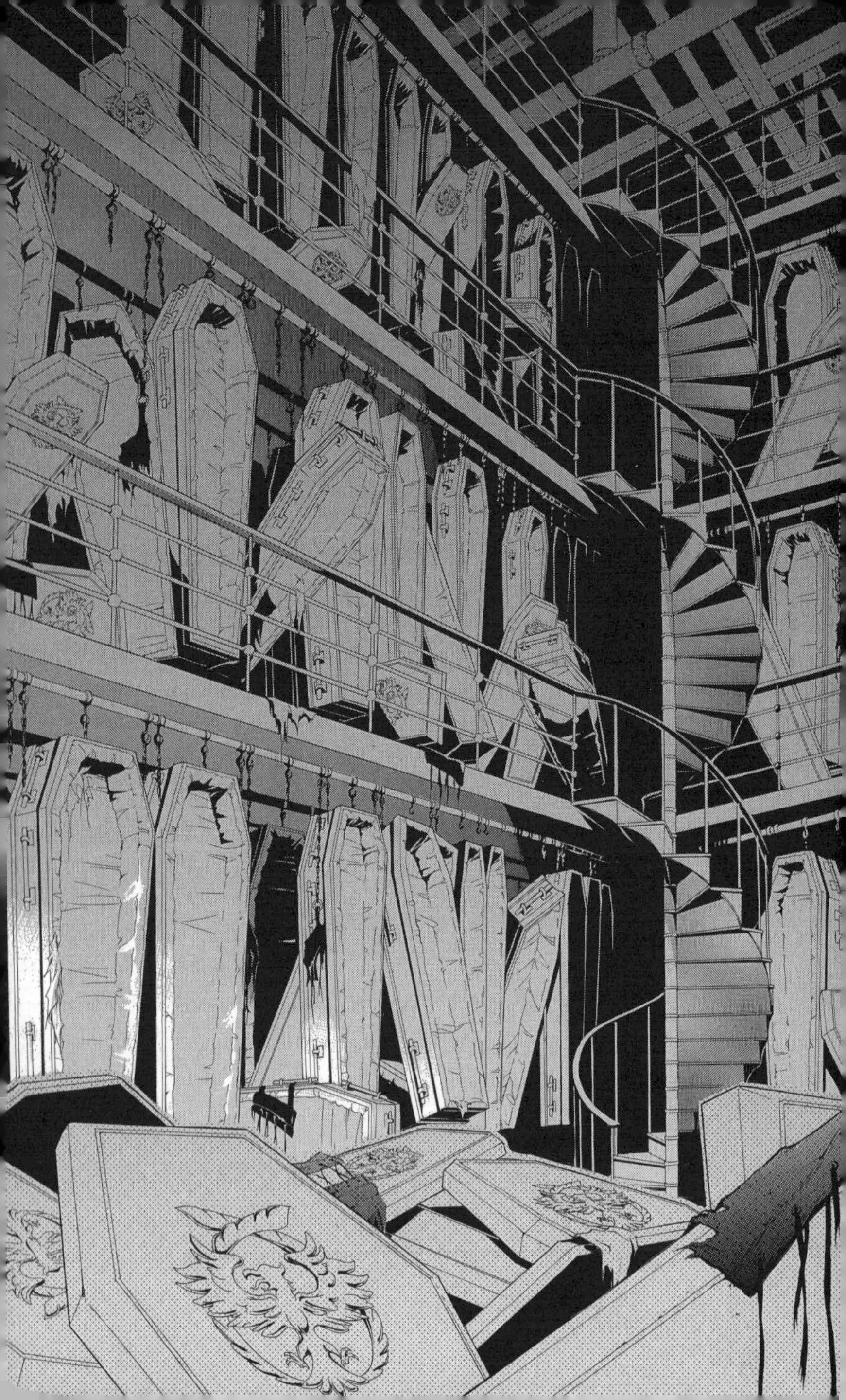

Black Butler

Chapter 55

In the afternoon : The Butler, In Vain

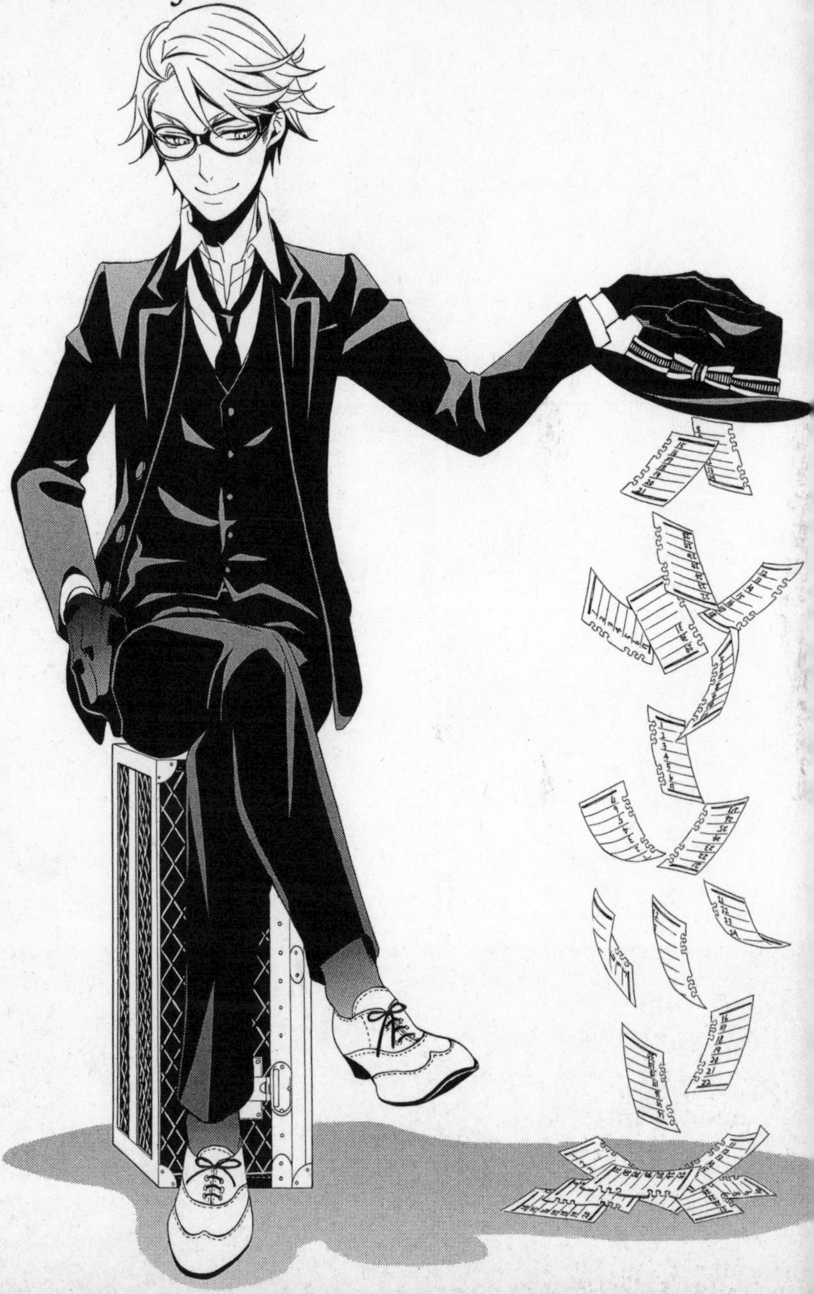

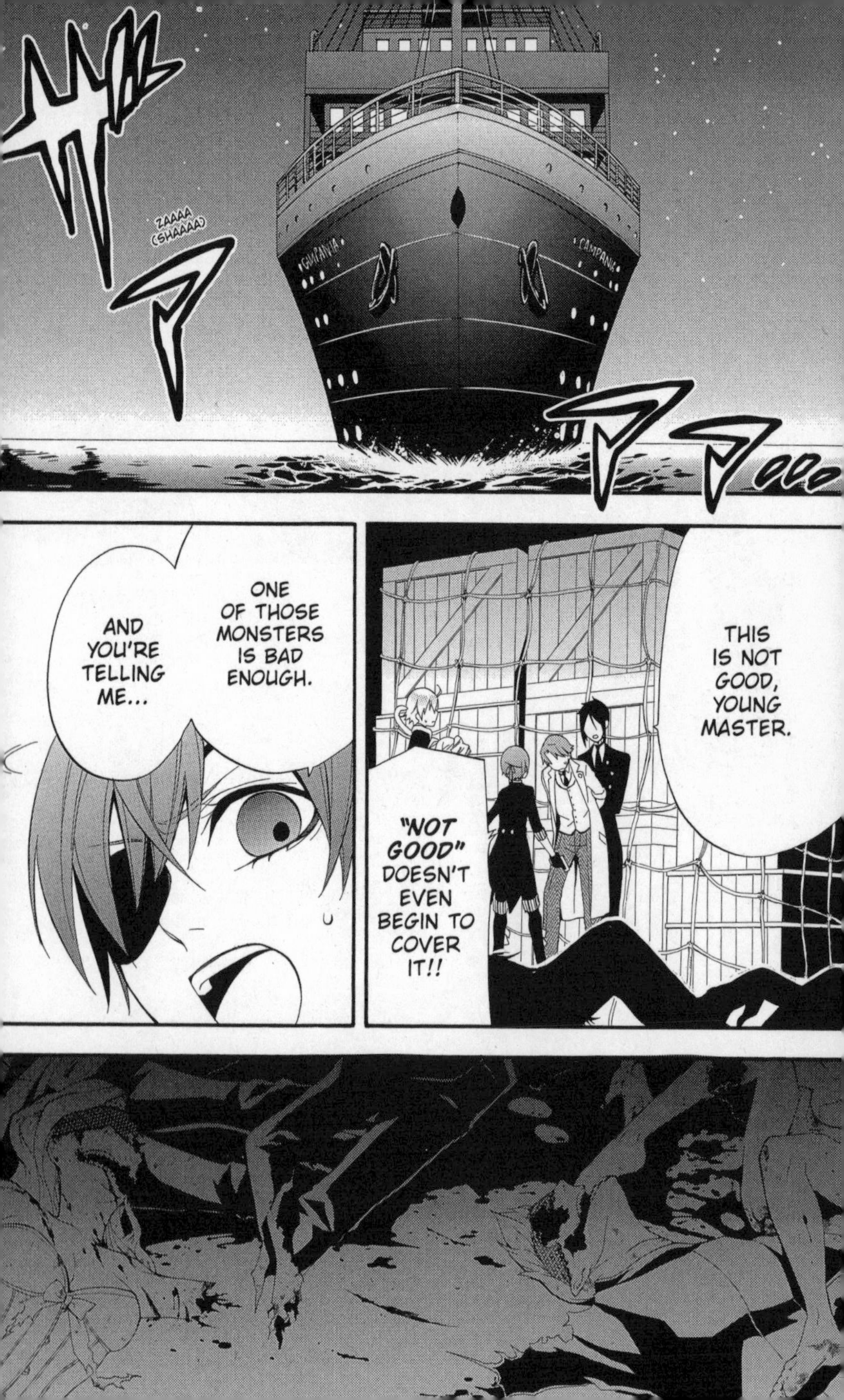
ZAAAA (SHAAAA)
CAMPANIA
CAMPANIA
THIS IS NOT GOOD, YOUNG MASTER.
"NOT GOOD" DOESN'T EVEN BEGIN TO COVER IT!!
ONE OF THOSE MONSTERS IS BAD ENOUGH.
AND YOU'RE TELLING ME...

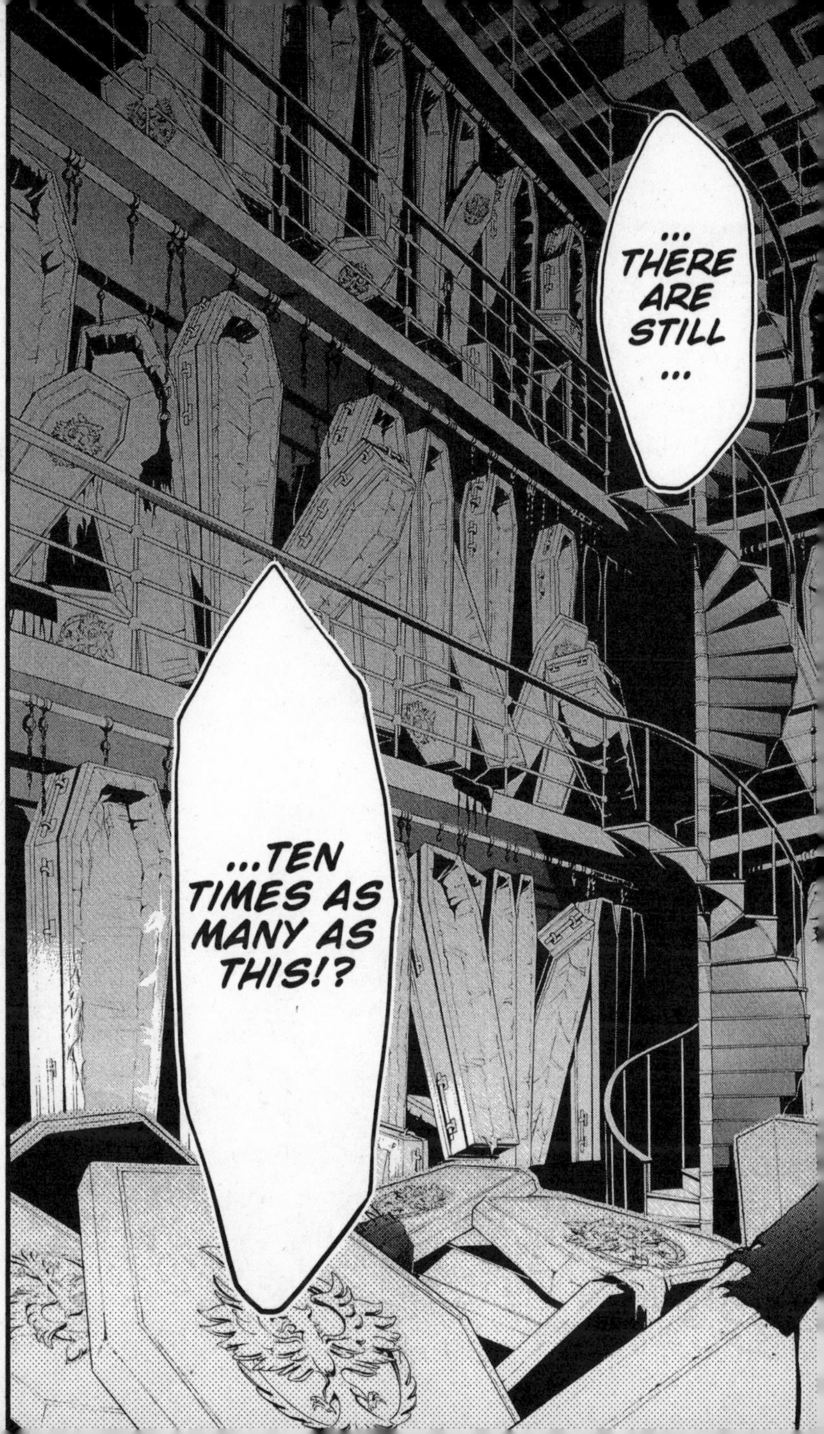
...THERE ARE STILL ...
...TEN TIMES AS MANY AS THIS!?

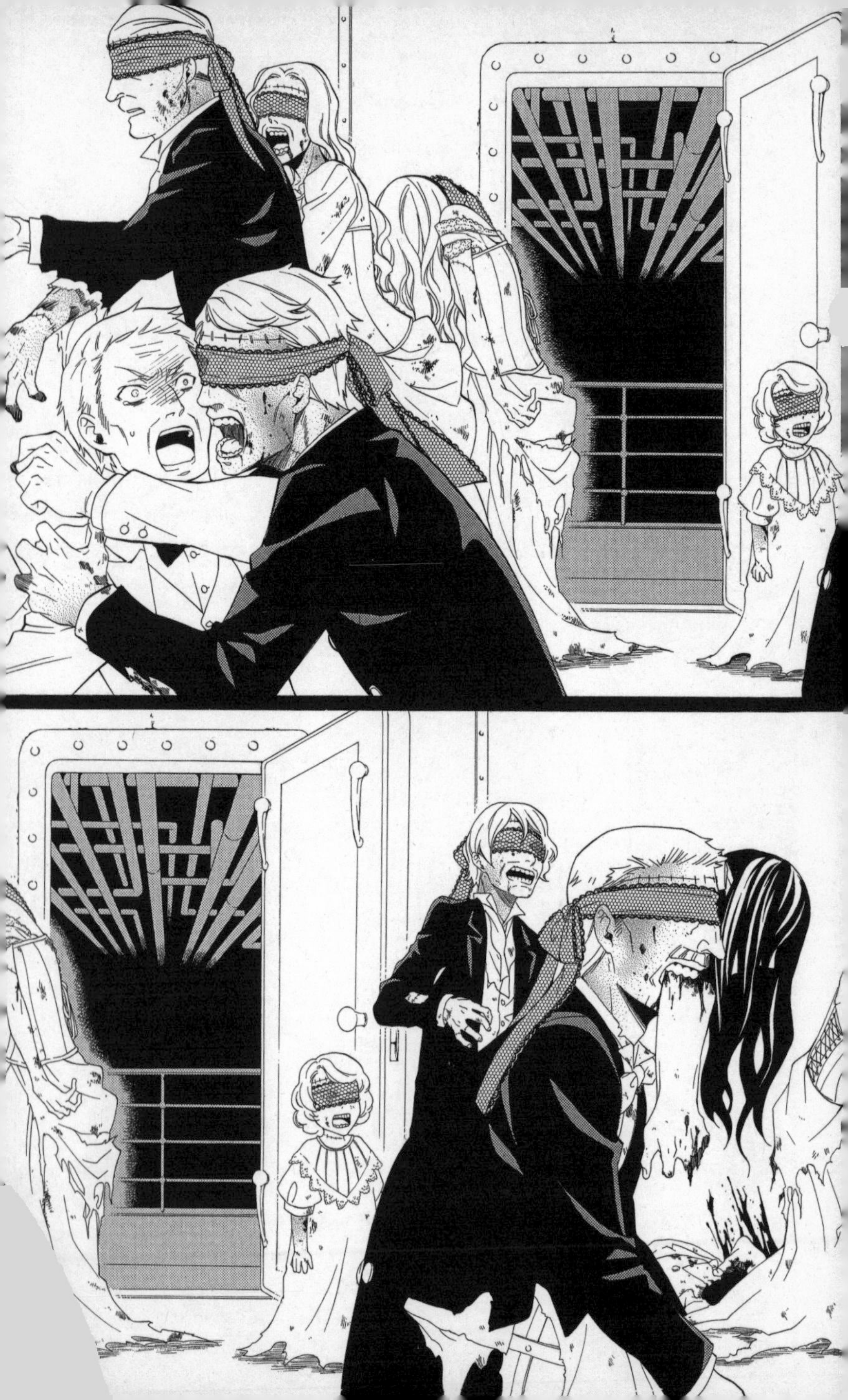

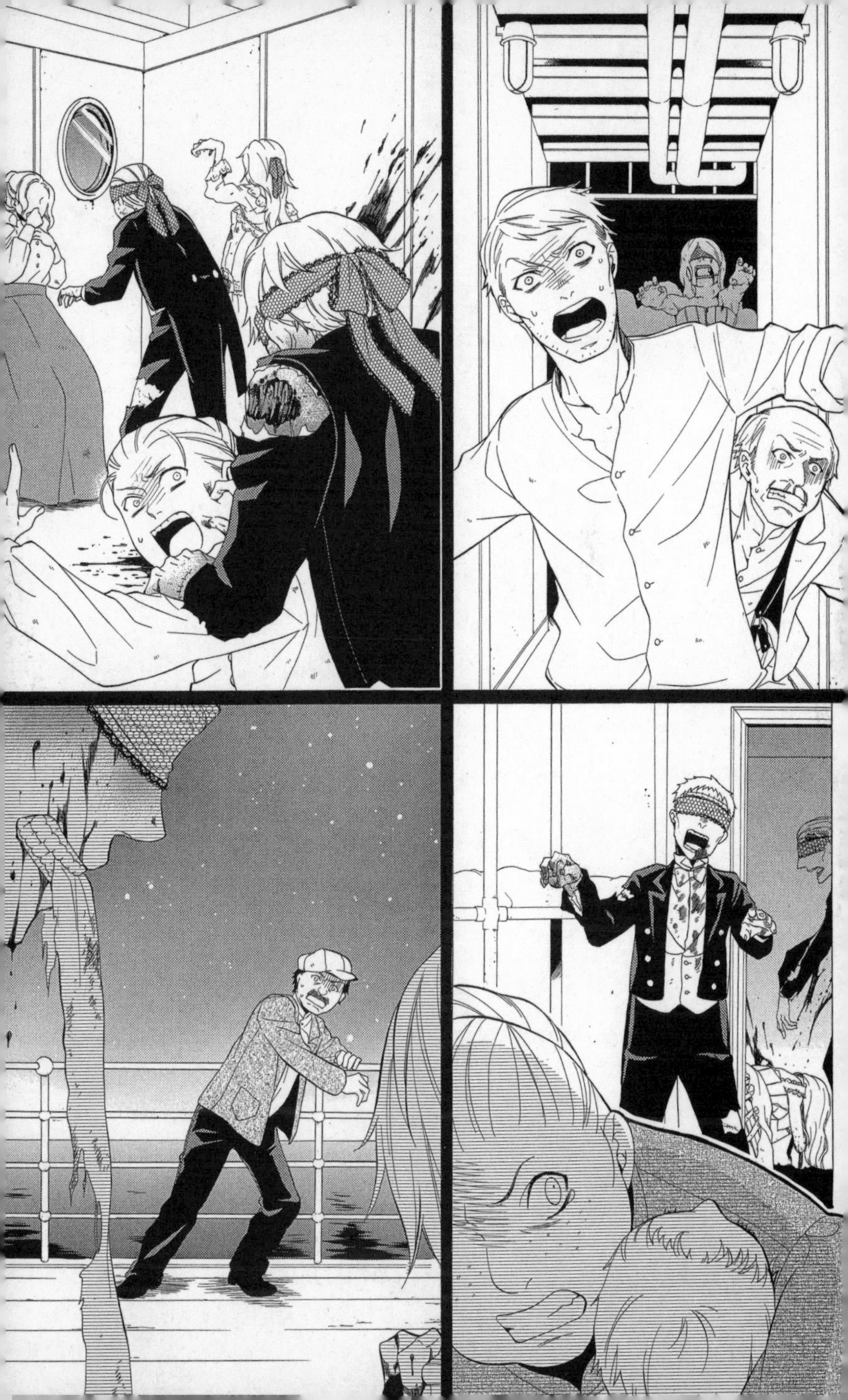

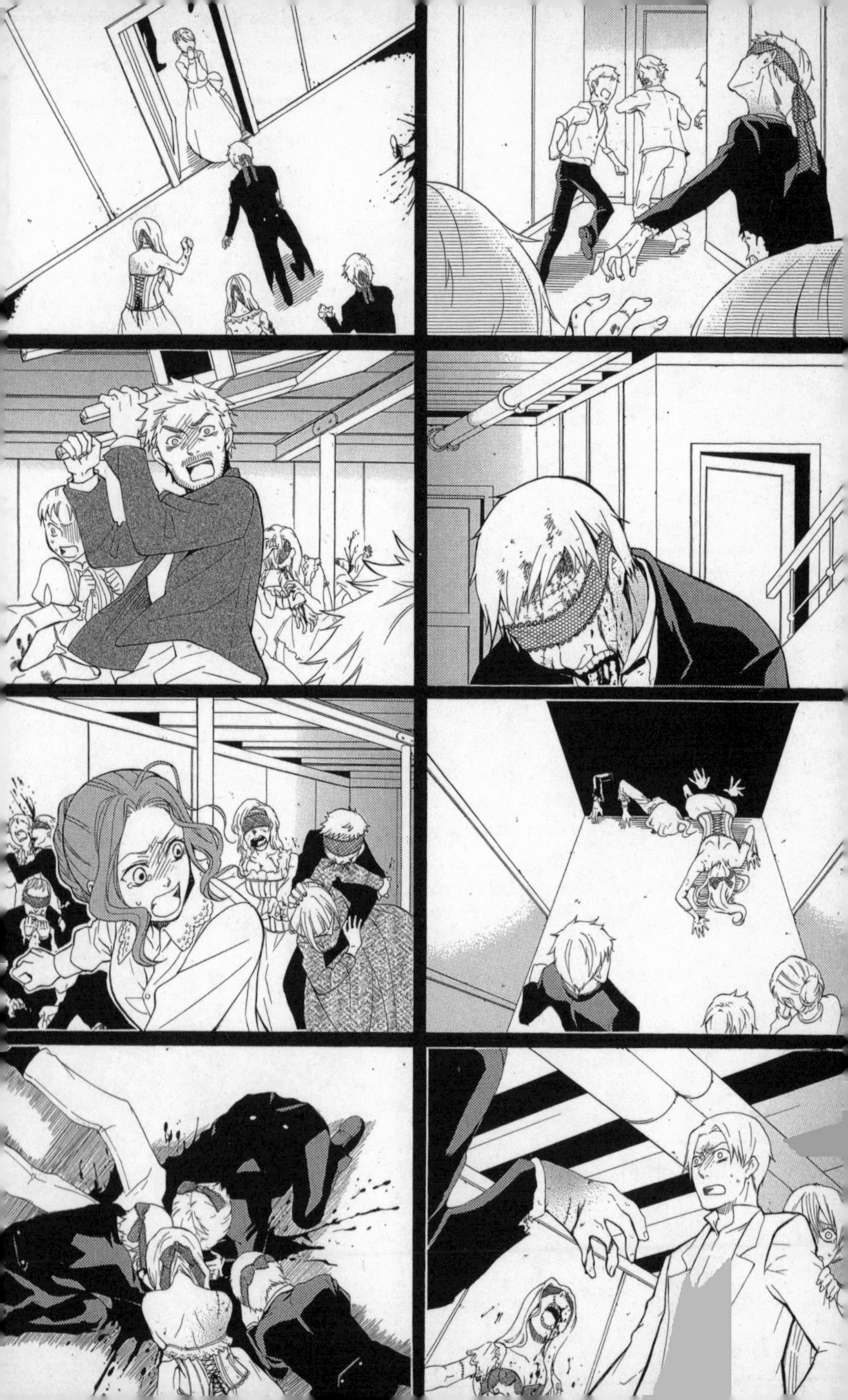

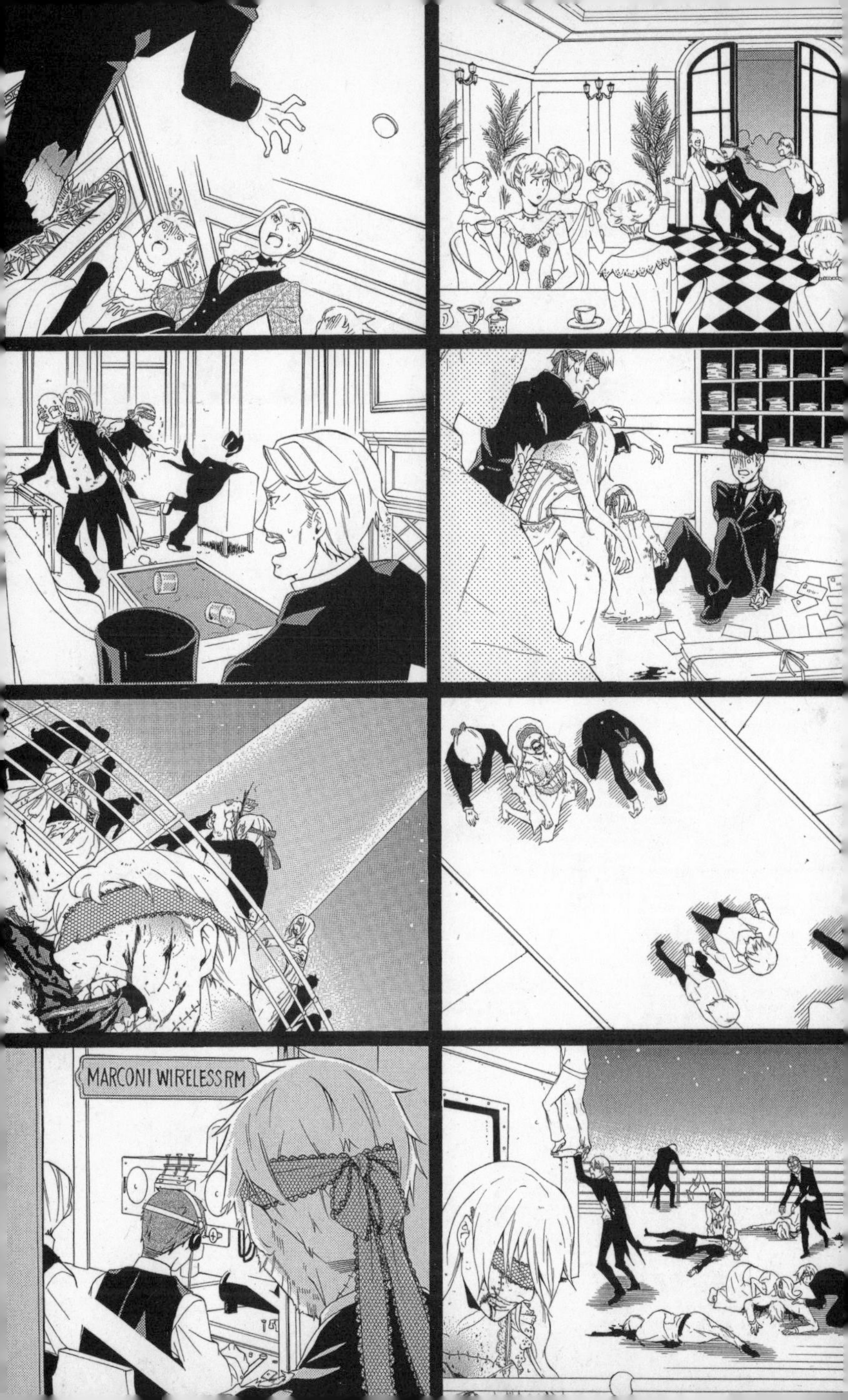
MARCONI WIRELESS RM

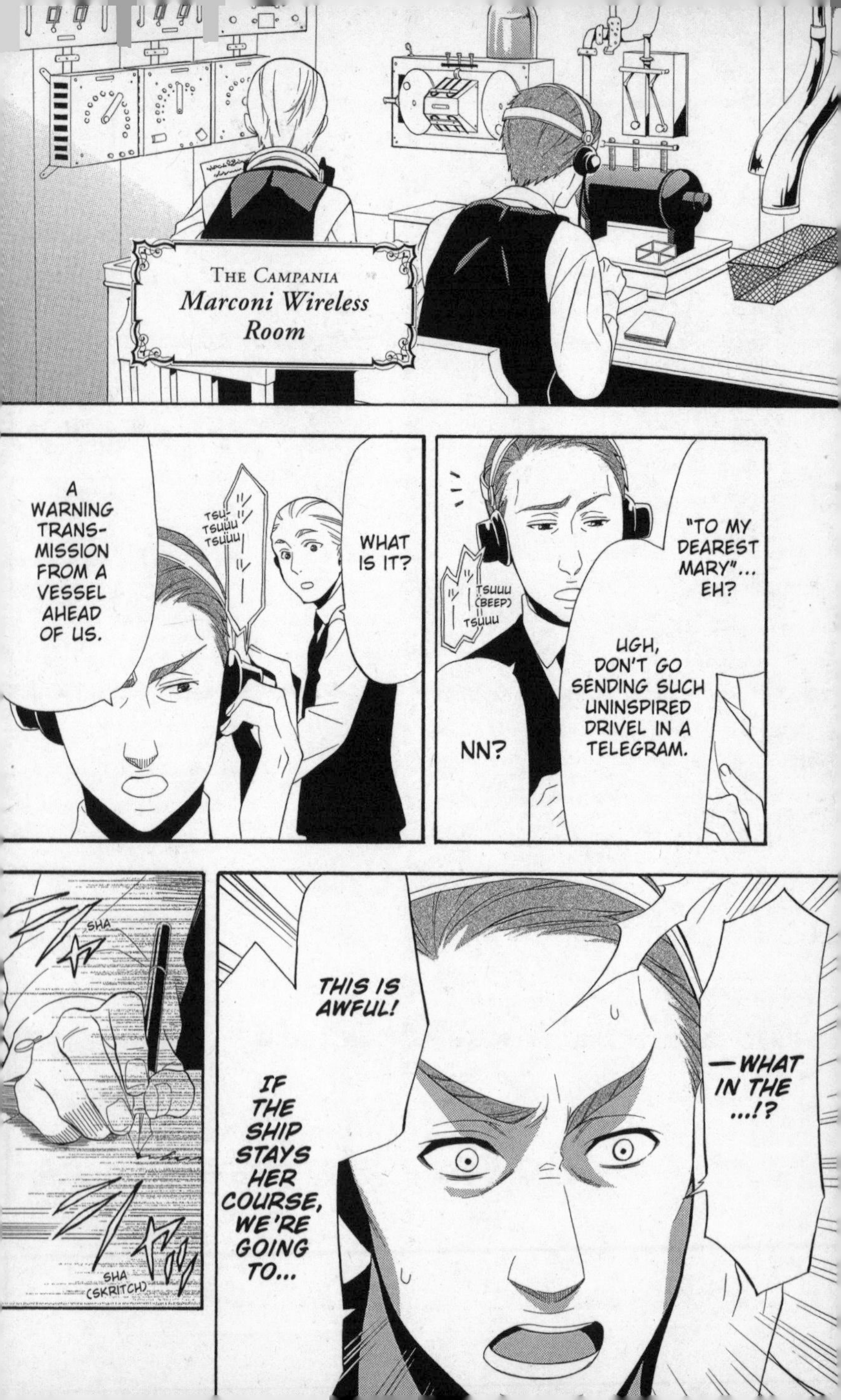
THE CAMPANIA
Marconi Wireless Room
"TO MY DEAREST MARY"... EH?
TSUUU (BEEP) TSUUU
UGH, DON'T GO SENDING SUCH UNINSPIRED DRIVEL IN A TELEGRAM.
NN?
WHAT IS IT?
TSU- TSUUU TSUUU
A WARNING TRANSMISSION FROM A VESSEL AHEAD OF US.
—WHAT IN THE ...!?
THIS IS AWFUL!
IF THE SHIP STAYS HER COURSE, WE'RE GOING TO...
SHA
SHA (SKRITCH)

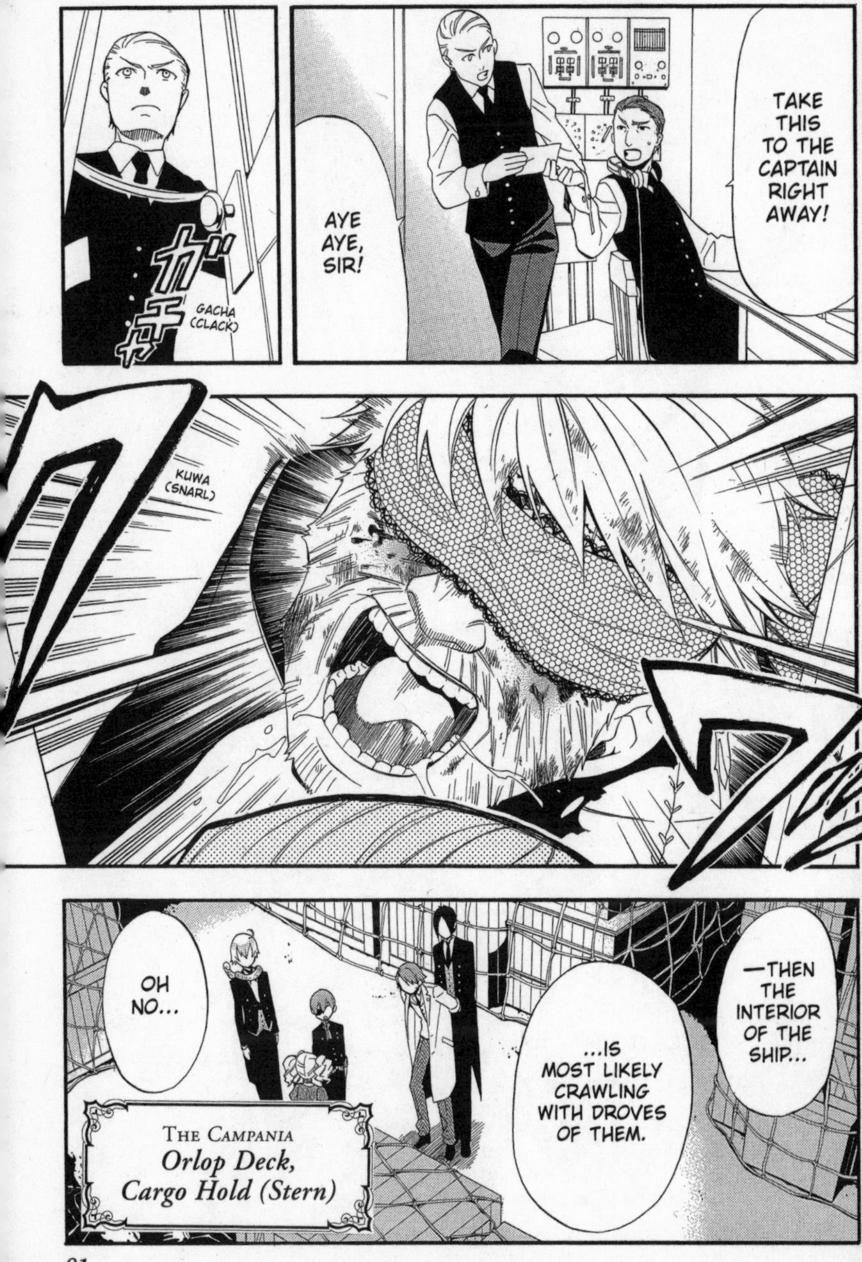
TAKE THIS TO THE CAPTAIN RIGHT AWAY!
AYE AYE, SIR!
GACHA (CLACK)
KUWA (SNARL)
—THEN THE INTERIOR OF THE SHIP...
...IS MOST LIKELY CRAWLING WITH DROVES OF THEM.
OH NO...
THE CAMPANIA
Orlop Deck, Cargo Hold (Stern)

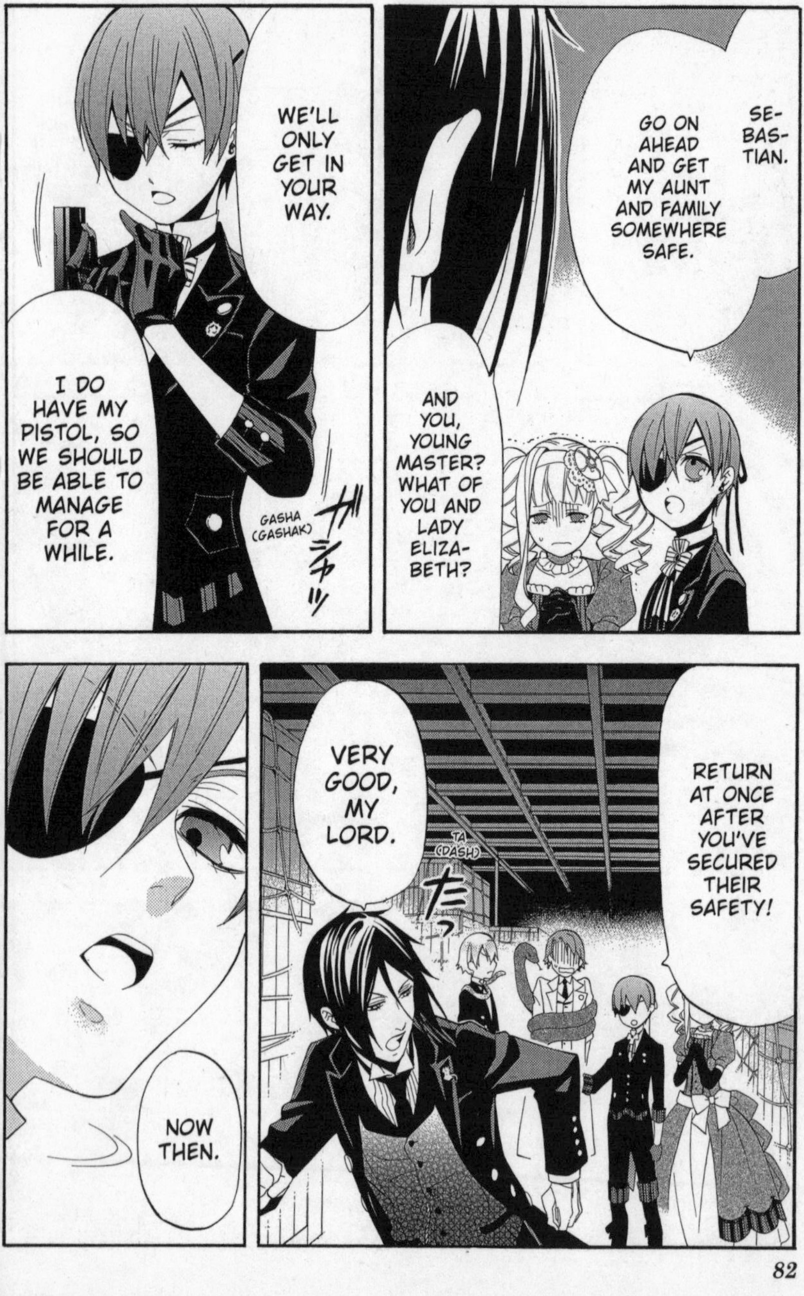
SE-BAS-TIAN.
GO ON AHEAD AND GET MY AUNT AND FAMILY SOMEWHERE SAFE.
AND YOU, YOUNG MASTER? WHAT OF YOU AND LADY ELIZA-BETH?
WE'LL ONLY GET IN YOUR WAY.
GASHA (GASHAK)
I DO HAVE MY PISTOL, SO WE SHOULD BE ABLE TO MANAGE FOR A WHILE.
RETURN AT ONCE AFTER YOU'VE SECURED THEIR SAFETY!
VERY GOOD, MY LORD.
TA (DASH)
NOW THEN.

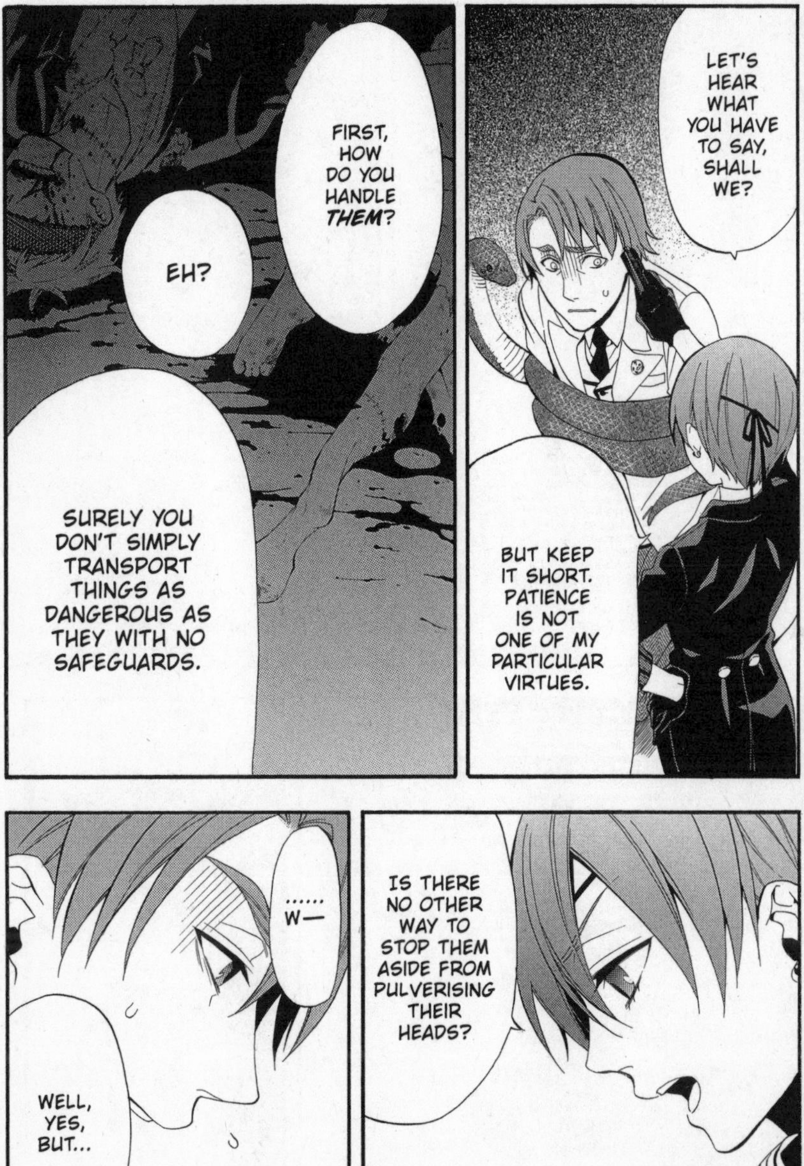
LET'S HEAR WHAT YOU HAVE TO SAY, SHALL WE?
BUT KEEP IT SHORT. PATIENCE IS NOT ONE OF MY PARTICULAR VIRTUES.
FIRST, HOW DO YOU HANDLE *THEM*?
EH?
SURELY YOU DON'T SIMPLY TRANSPORT THINGS AS DANGEROUS AS THEY WITH NO SAFEGUARDS.
IS THERE NO OTHER WAY TO STOP THEM ASIDE FROM PULVERISING THEIR HEADS?
...... W—
WELL, YES, BUT...

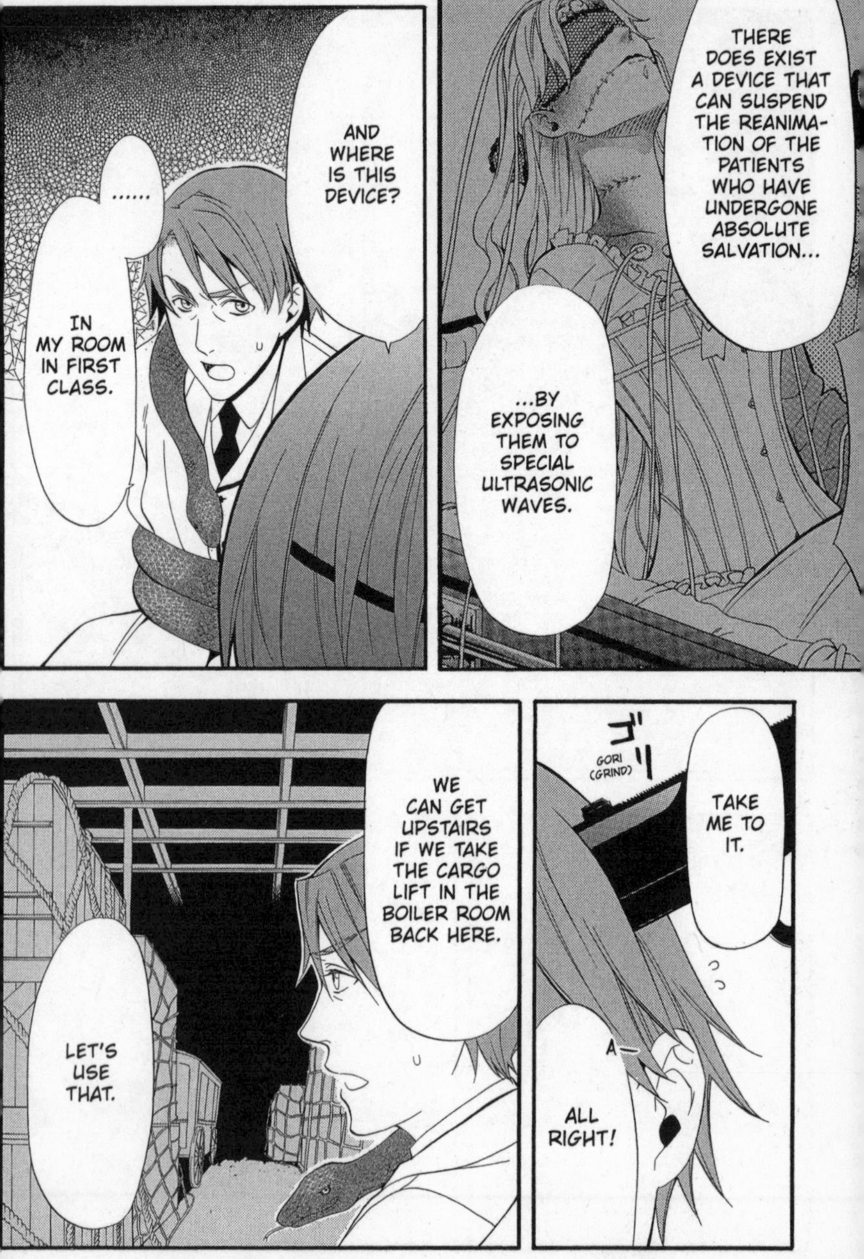
THERE DOES EXIST A DEVICE THAT CAN SUSPEND THE REANIMATION OF THE PATIENTS WHO HAVE UNDERGONE ABSOLUTE SALVATION...
...BY EXPOSING THEM TO SPECIAL ULTRASONIC WAVES.
AND WHERE IS THIS DEVICE?
......
IN MY ROOM IN FIRST CLASS.
ゴリ
GORI (GRIND)
TAKE ME TO IT.
A—
ALL RIGHT!
WE CAN GET UPSTAIRS IF WE TAKE THE CARGO LIFT IN THE BOILER ROOM BACK HERE.
LET'S USE THAT.

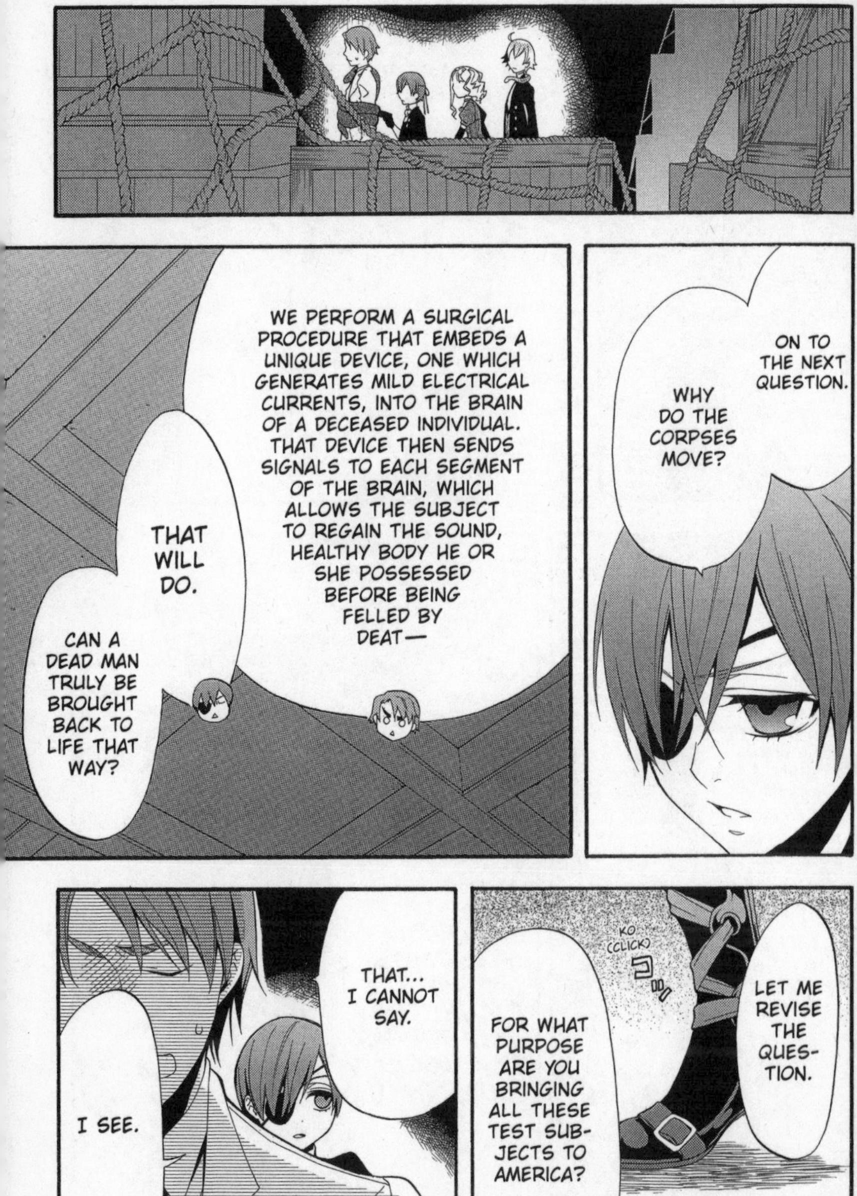
ON TO THE NEXT QUESTION.
WHY DO THE CORPSES MOVE?
WE PERFORM A SURGICAL PROCEDURE THAT EMBEDS A UNIQUE DEVICE, ONE WHICH GENERATES MILD ELECTRICAL CURRENTS, INTO THE BRAIN OF A DECEASED INDIVIDUAL. THAT DEVICE THEN SENDS SIGNALS TO EACH SEGMENT OF THE BRAIN, WHICH ALLOWS THE SUBJECT TO REGAIN THE SOUND, HEALTHY BODY HE OR SHE POSSESSED BEFORE BEING FELLED BY DEAT—
THAT WILL DO.
CAN A DEAD MAN TRULY BE BROUGHT BACK TO LIFE THAT WAY?
LET ME REVISE THE QUES-TION.
KO (CLICK)
FOR WHAT PURPOSE ARE YOU BRINGING ALL THESE TEST SUB-JECTS TO AMERICA?
THAT... I CANNOT SAY.
I SEE.

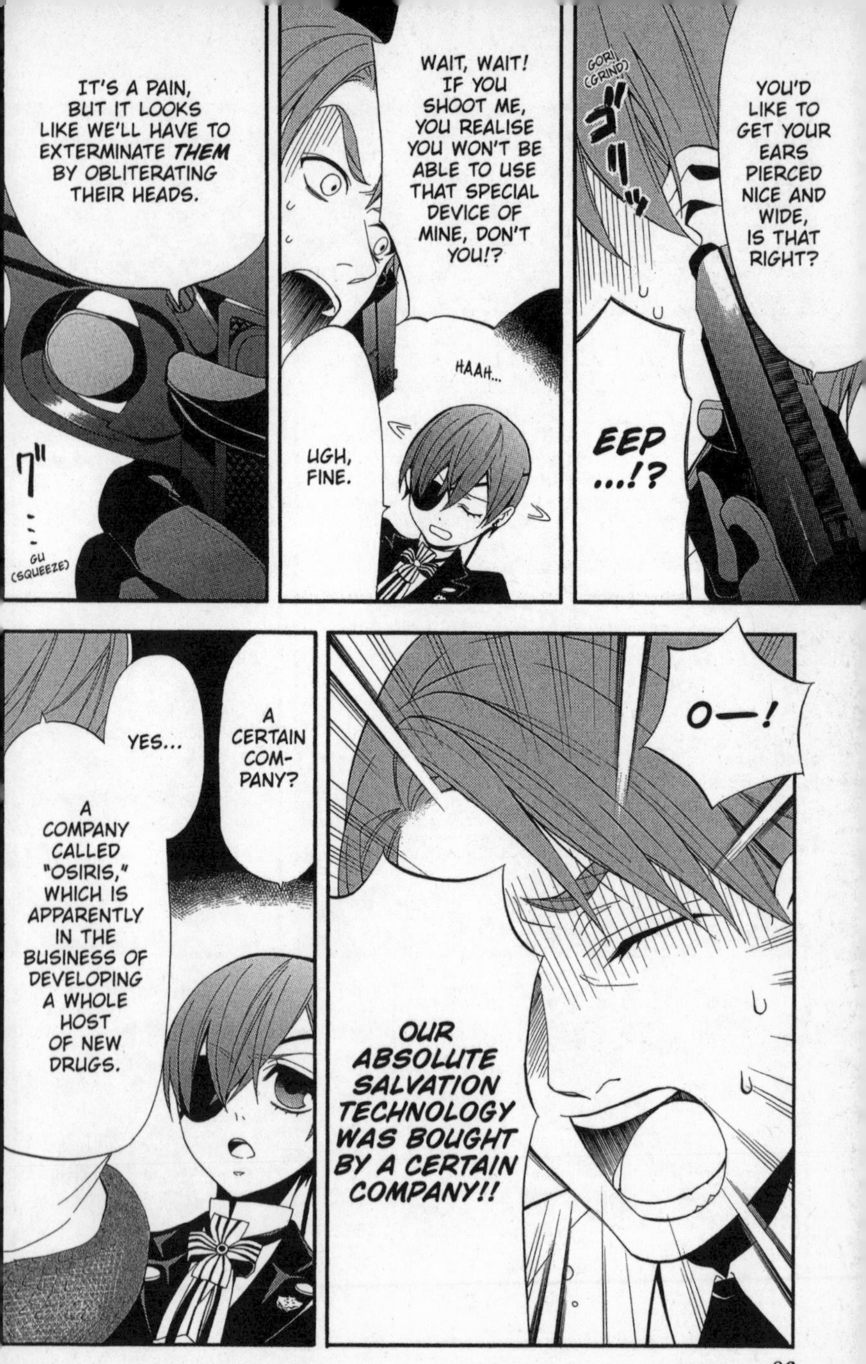
YOU'D LIKE TO GET YOUR EARS PIERCED NICE AND WIDE, IS THAT RIGHT?
GORI (GRIND)
EEP ...!?
WAIT, WAIT! IF YOU SHOOT ME, YOU REALISE YOU WON'T BE ABLE TO USE THAT SPECIAL DEVICE OF MINE, DON'T YOU!?
HAAH...
UGH, FINE.
IT'S A PAIN, BUT IT LOOKS LIKE WE'LL HAVE TO EXTERMINATE *THEM* BY OBLITERATING THEIR HEADS.
GU (SQUEEZE)
O—!
OUR ABSOLUTE SALVATION TECHNOLOGY WAS BOUGHT BY A CERTAIN COMPANY!!
A CERTAIN COMPANY?
YES...
A COMPANY CALLED "OSIRIS," WHICH IS APPARENTLY IN THE BUSINESS OF DEVELOPING A WHOLE HOST OF NEW DRUGS.

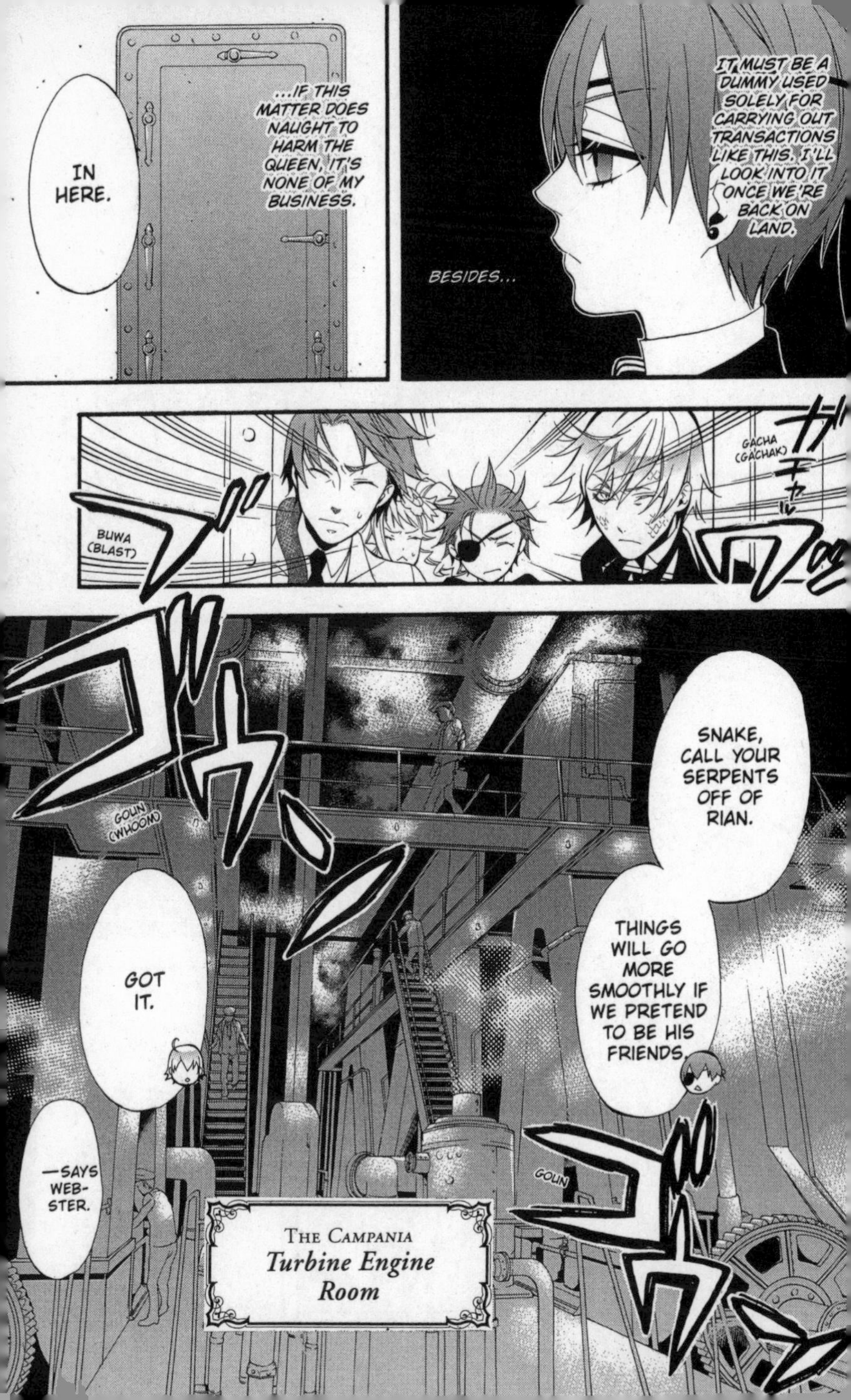

IT MUST BE A DUMMY USED SOLELY FOR CARRYING OUT TRANSACTIONS LIKE THIS. I'LL LOOK INTO IT ONCE WE'RE BACK ON LAND.
BESIDES...
...IF THIS MATTER DOES NAUGHT TO HARM THE QUEEN, IT'S NONE OF MY BUSINESS.
IN HERE.
GACHA (GACHAK)
BUWA (BLAST)
SNAKE, CALL YOUR SERPENTS OFF OF RIAN.
THINGS WILL GO MORE SMOOTHLY IF WE PRETEND TO BE HIS FRIENDS.
GOUN (WHOOM)
GOT IT.
GOUN
—SAYS WEB-STER.
THE CAMPANIA
Turbine Engine Room

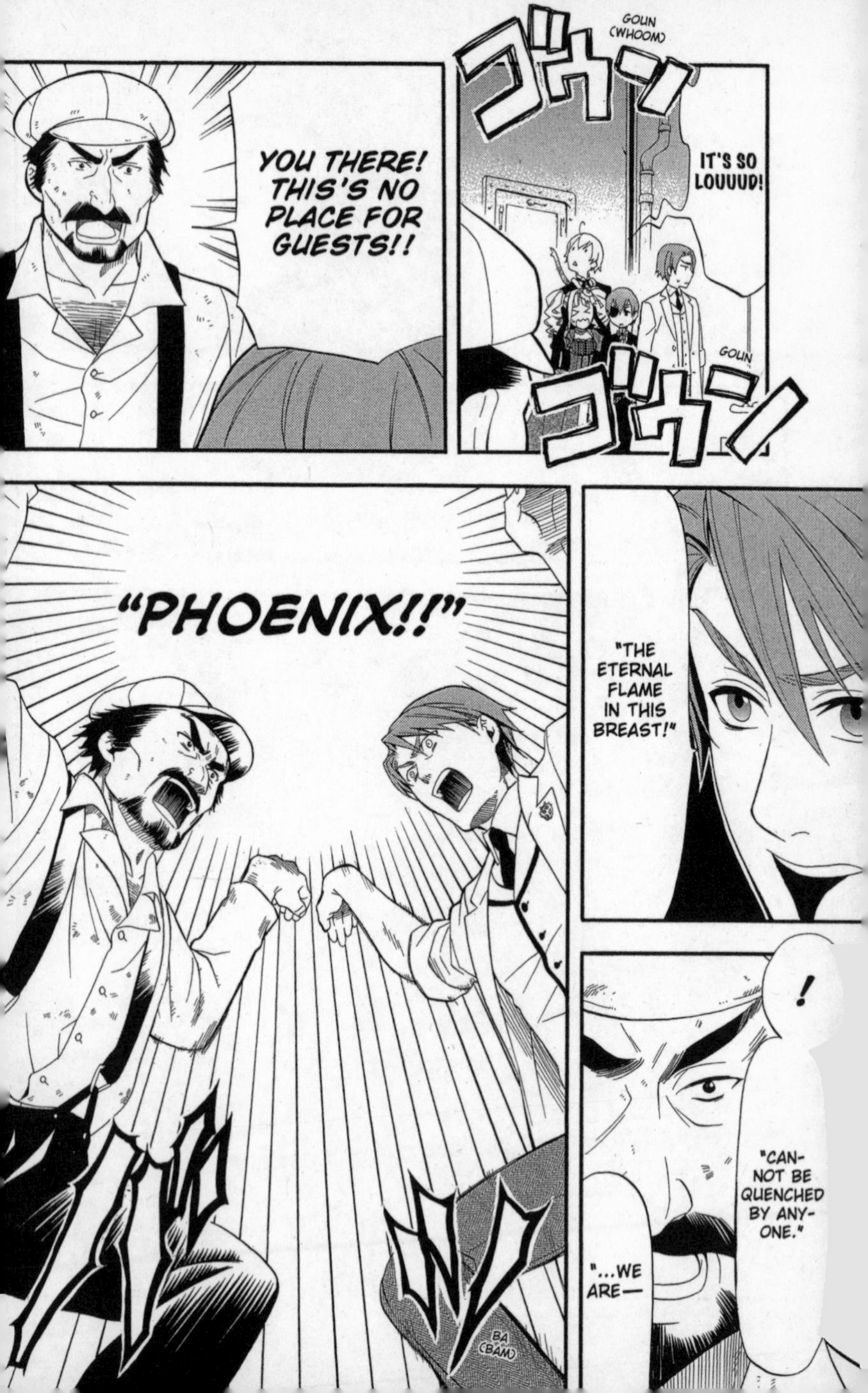
GOUN (WHOOM)
IT'S SO LOUUUD!
GOUN
YOU THERE! THIS'S NO PLACE FOR GUESTS!!
"THE ETERNAL FLAME IN THIS BREAST!"
!
"CAN-NOT BE QUENCHED BY ANY-ONE."
"...WE ARE—
"PHOENIX!!"
BA (BAM)

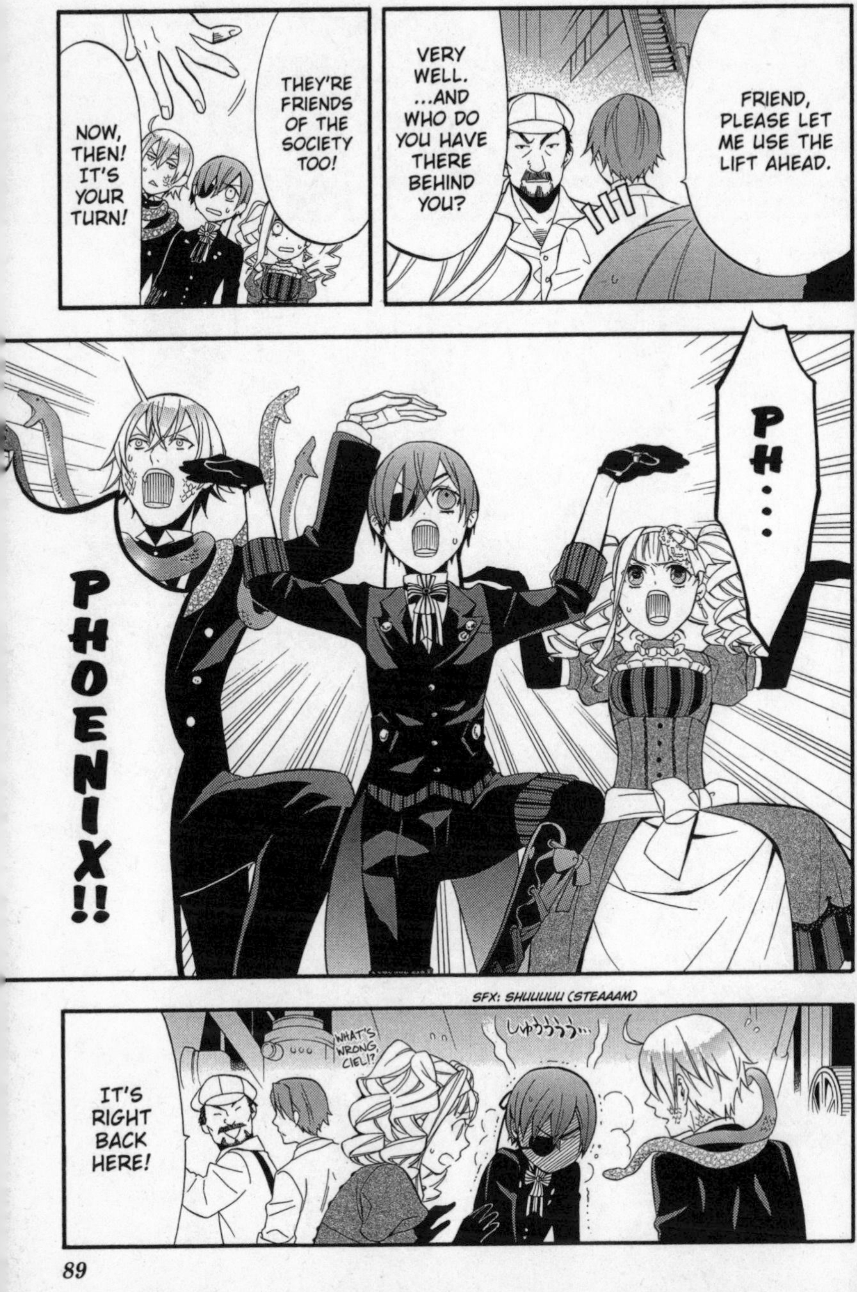
FRIEND, PLEASE LET ME USE THE LIFT AHEAD.
VERY WELL. ...AND WHO DO YOU HAVE THERE BEHIND YOU?
THEY'RE FRIENDS OF THE SOCIETY TOO!
NOW, THEN! IT'S YOUR TURN!
PH...
PHOENIX!!
SFX: SHUUUUU (STEAAAM)
しゅううう…
WHAT'S WRONG, CIEL!?
IT'S RIGHT BACK HERE!

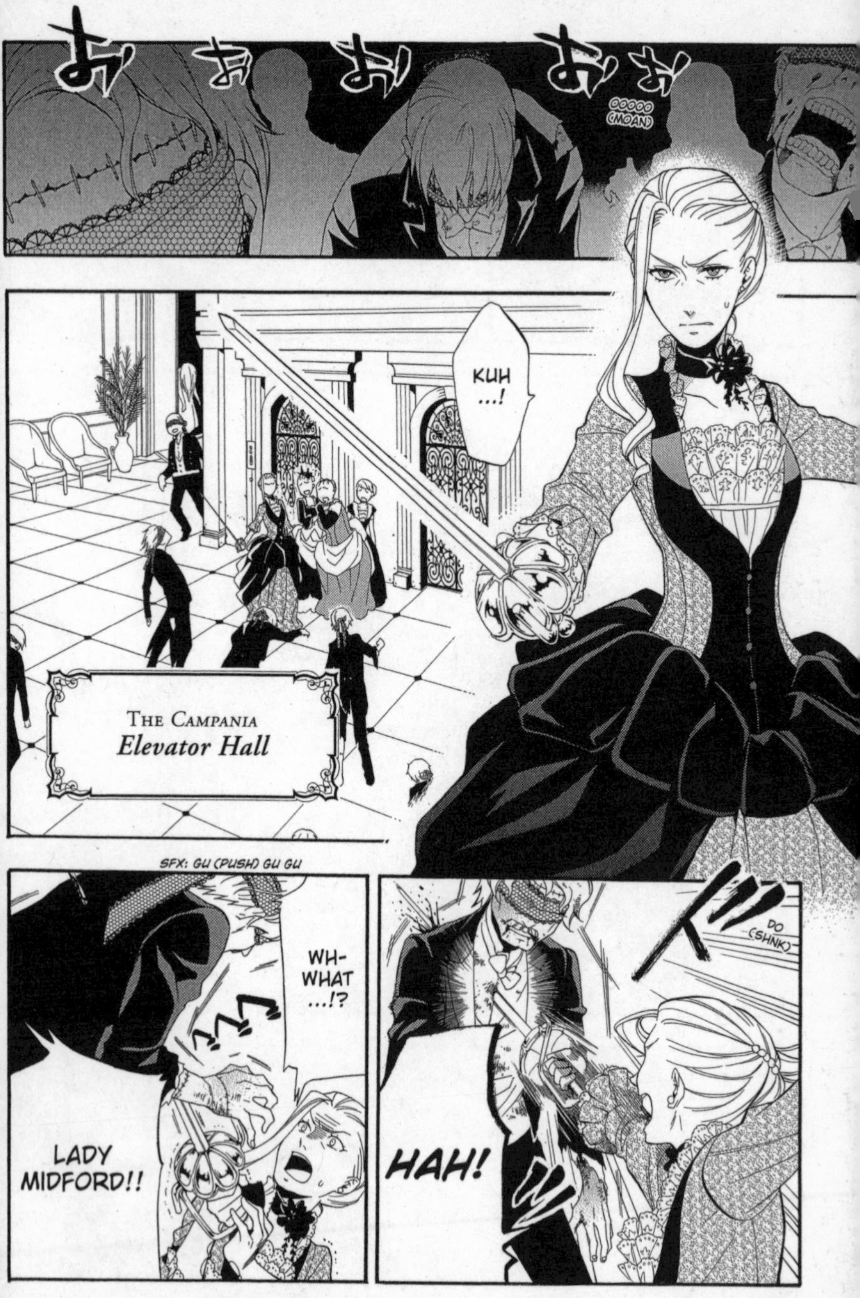
おぉお
おぉ
OOOOO (MOAN)
KUH ...!
THE CAMPANIA
Elevator Hall
SFX: GU (PUSH) GU GU
DO (SHNK)
HAH!
WH- WHAT ...!?
LADY MIDFORD!!

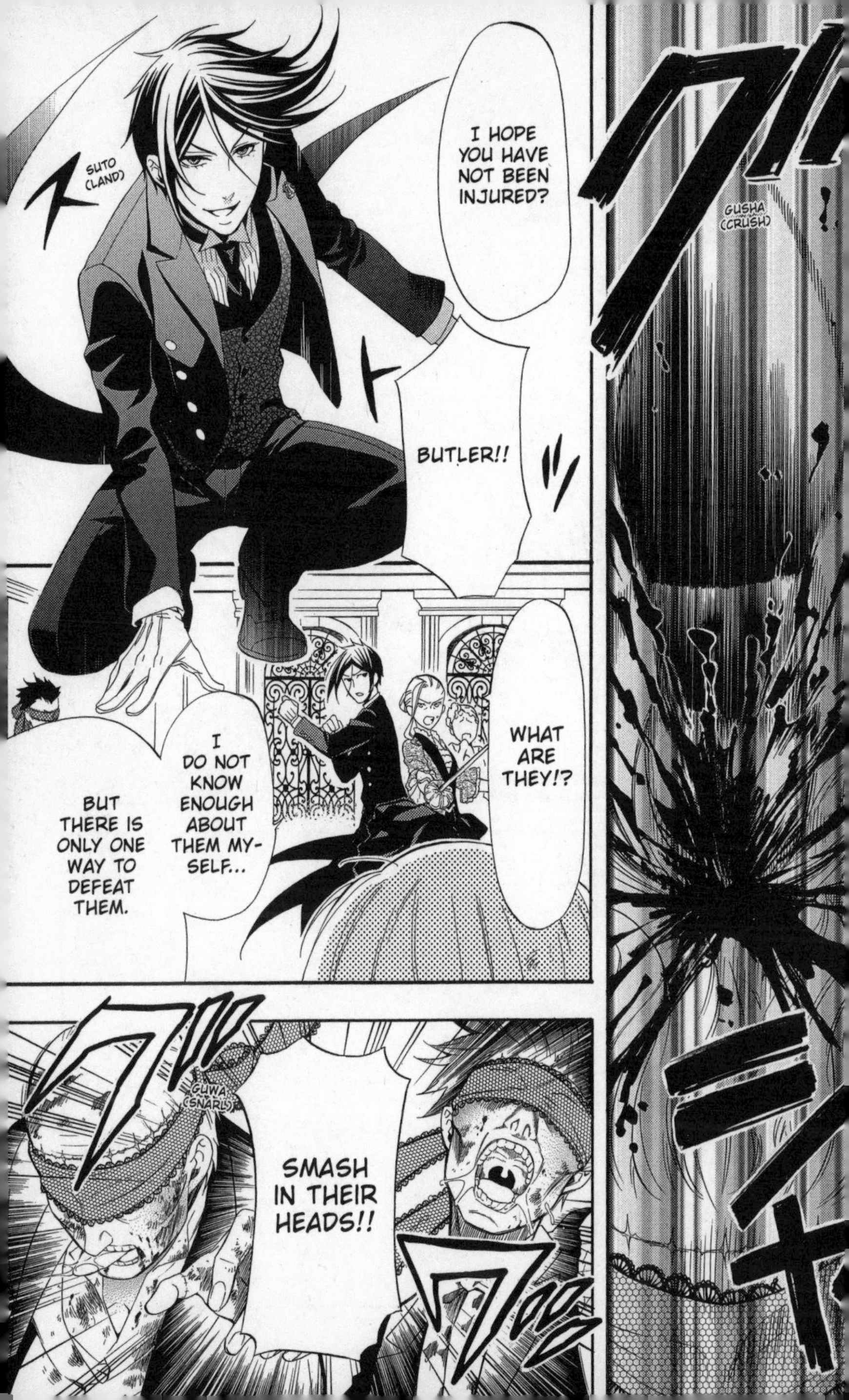
GUSHA (CRUSH)
I HOPE YOU HAVE NOT BEEN INJURED?
SUTO (LAND)
BUTLER!!
WHAT ARE THEY!?
I DO NOT KNOW ENOUGH ABOUT THEM MY-SELF...
BUT THERE IS ONLY ONE WAY TO DEFEAT THEM.
GUWA (SNARL)
SMASH IN THEIR HEADS!!

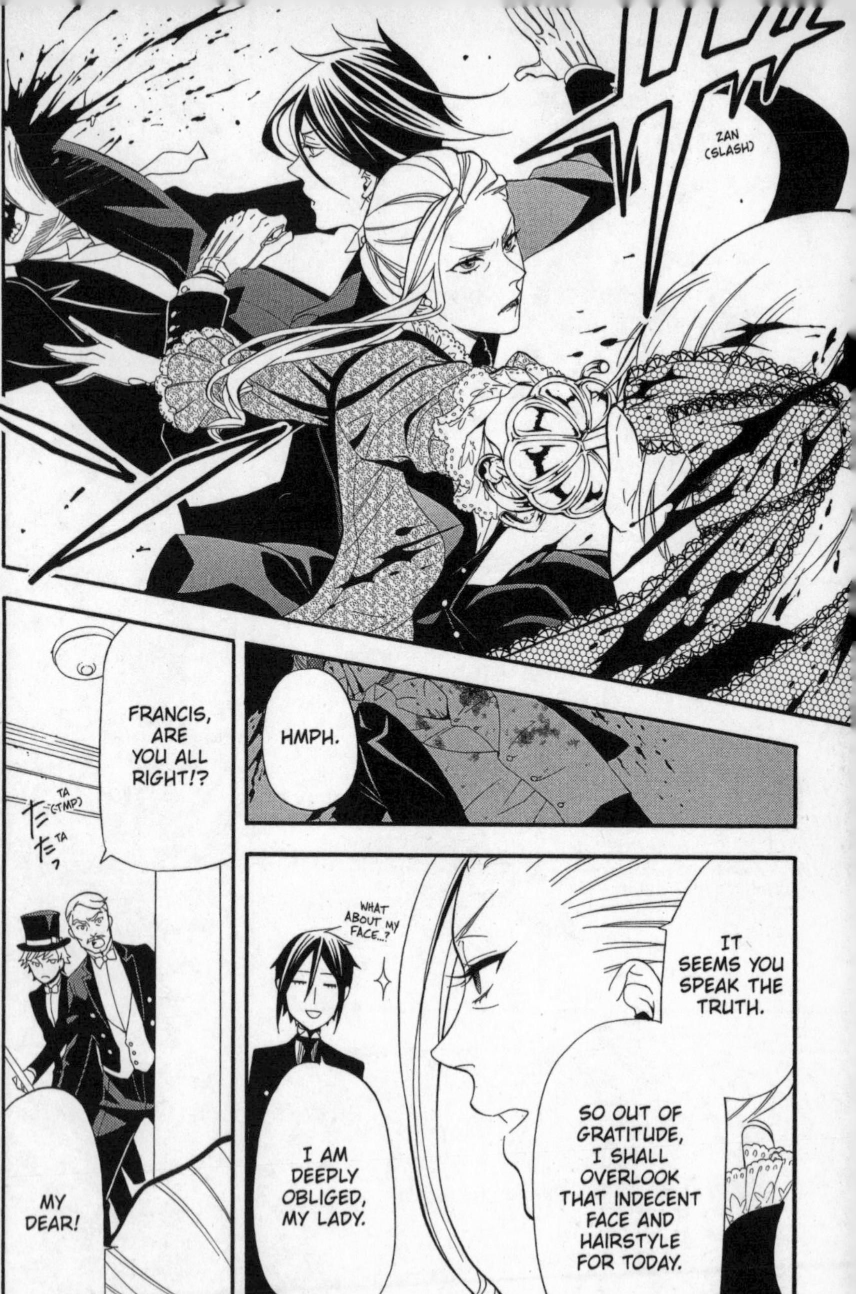
ZAN (SLASH)
HMPH.
IT SEEMS YOU SPEAK THE TRUTH.
SO OUT OF GRATITUDE, I SHALL OVERLOOK THAT INDECENT FACE AND HAIRSTYLE FOR TODAY.
WHAT ABOUT MY FACE...?
I AM DEEPLY OBLIGED, MY LADY.
FRANCIS, ARE YOU ALL RIGHT!?
TA TA (TMP)
MY DEAR!

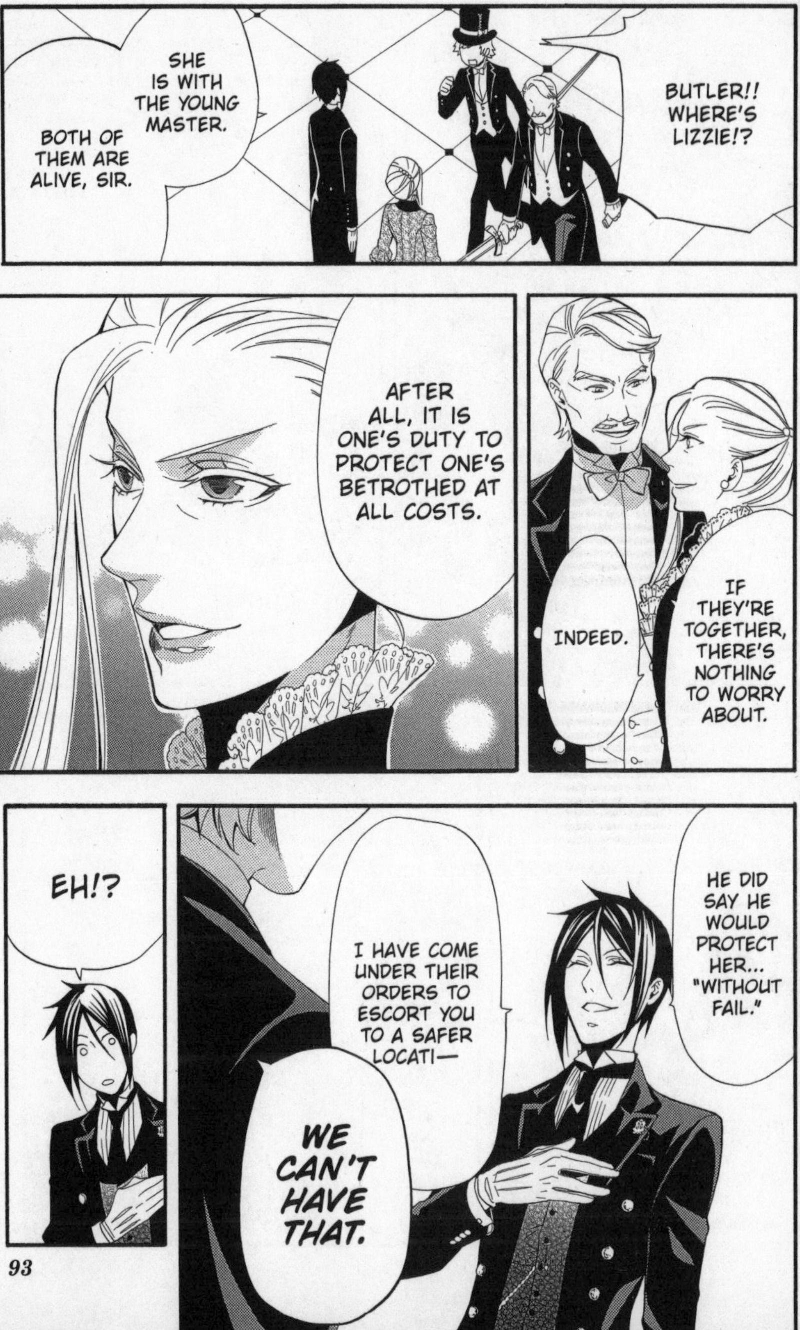
BUTLER!! WHERE'S LIZZIE!?
SHE IS WITH THE YOUNG MASTER.
BOTH OF THEM ARE ALIVE, SIR.
IF THEY'RE TOGETHER, THERE'S NOTHING TO WORRY ABOUT.
INDEED.
AFTER ALL, IT IS ONE'S DUTY TO PROTECT ONE'S BETROTHED AT ALL COSTS.
HE DID SAY HE WOULD PROTECT HER... "WITHOUT FAIL."
I HAVE COME UNDER THEIR ORDERS TO ESCORT YOU TO A SAFER LOCATI—
WE CAN'T HAVE THAT.
EH!?

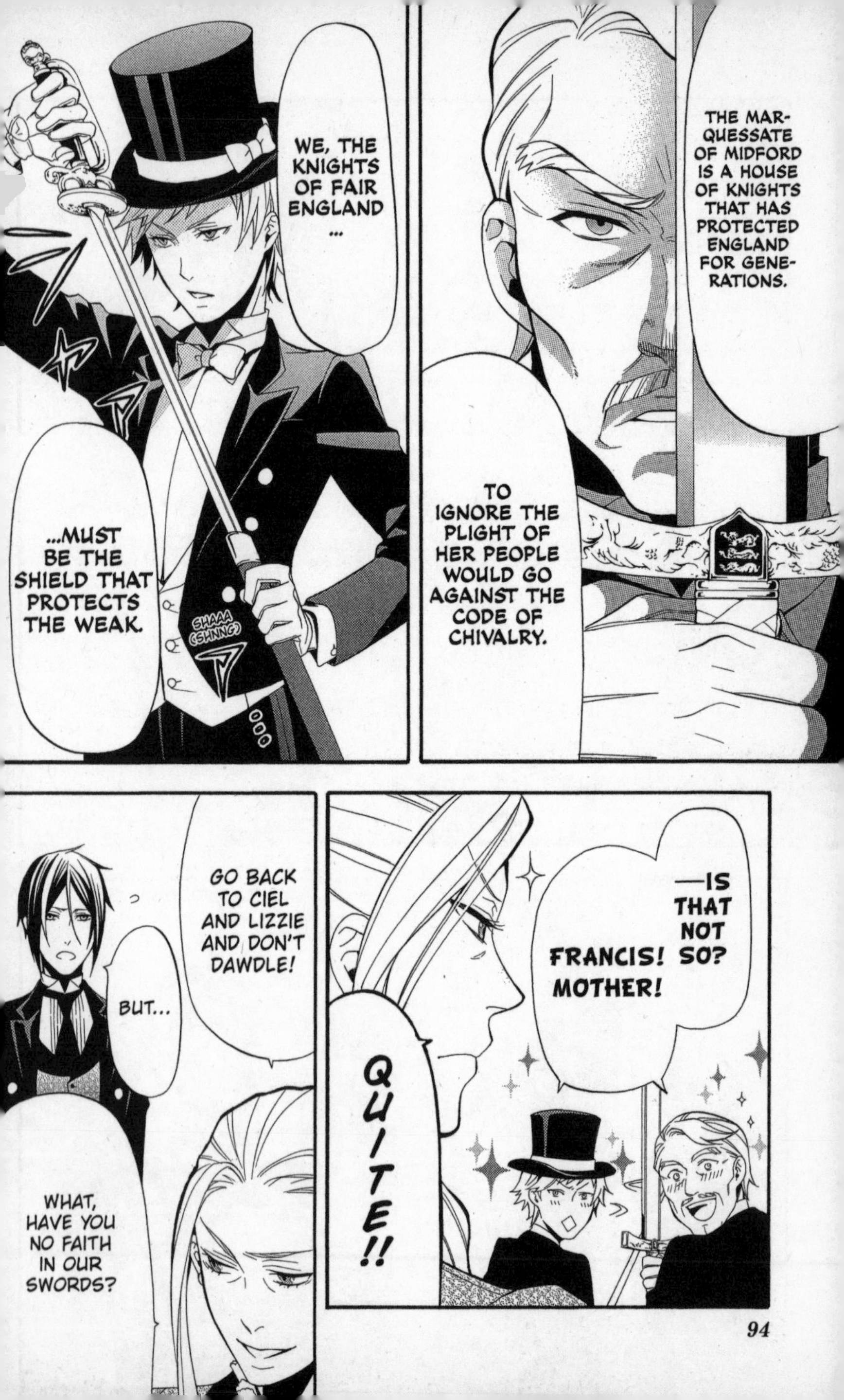
THE MARQUESSATE OF MIDFORD IS A HOUSE OF KNIGHTS THAT HAS PROTECTED ENGLAND FOR GENERATIONS.
TO IGNORE THE PLIGHT OF HER PEOPLE WOULD GO AGAINST THE CODE OF CHIVALRY.
WE, THE KNIGHTS OF FAIR ENGLAND...
...MUST BE THE SHIELD THAT PROTECTS THE WEAK.
SHAAA (SHNNG)
—IS THAT NOT SO?
FRANCIS! MOTHER!
QUITE!!
GO BACK TO CIEL AND LIZZIE AND DON'T DAWDLE!
BUT...
WHAT, HAVE YOU NO FAITH IN OUR SWORDS?

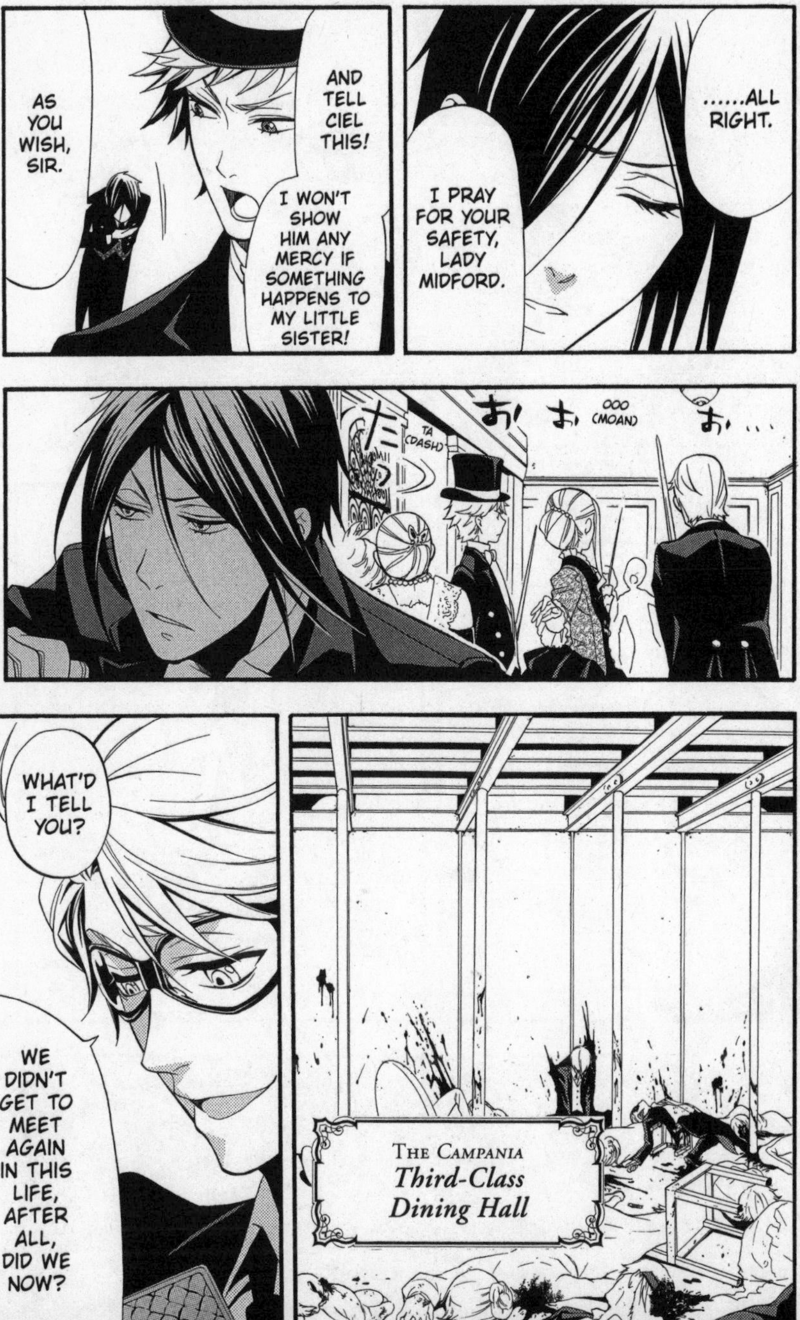
......ALL RIGHT.
I PRAY FOR YOUR SAFETY, LADY MIDFORD.
AND TELL CIEL THIS!
I WON'T SHOW HIM ANY MERCY IF SOMETHING HAPPENS TO MY LITTLE SISTER!
AS YOU WISH, SIR.
OOO (MOAN)
TA (DASH)
THE CAMPANIA Third-Class Dining Hall
WHAT'D I TELL YOU?
WE DIDN'T GET TO MEET AGAIN IN THIS LIFE, AFTER ALL, DID WE NOW?

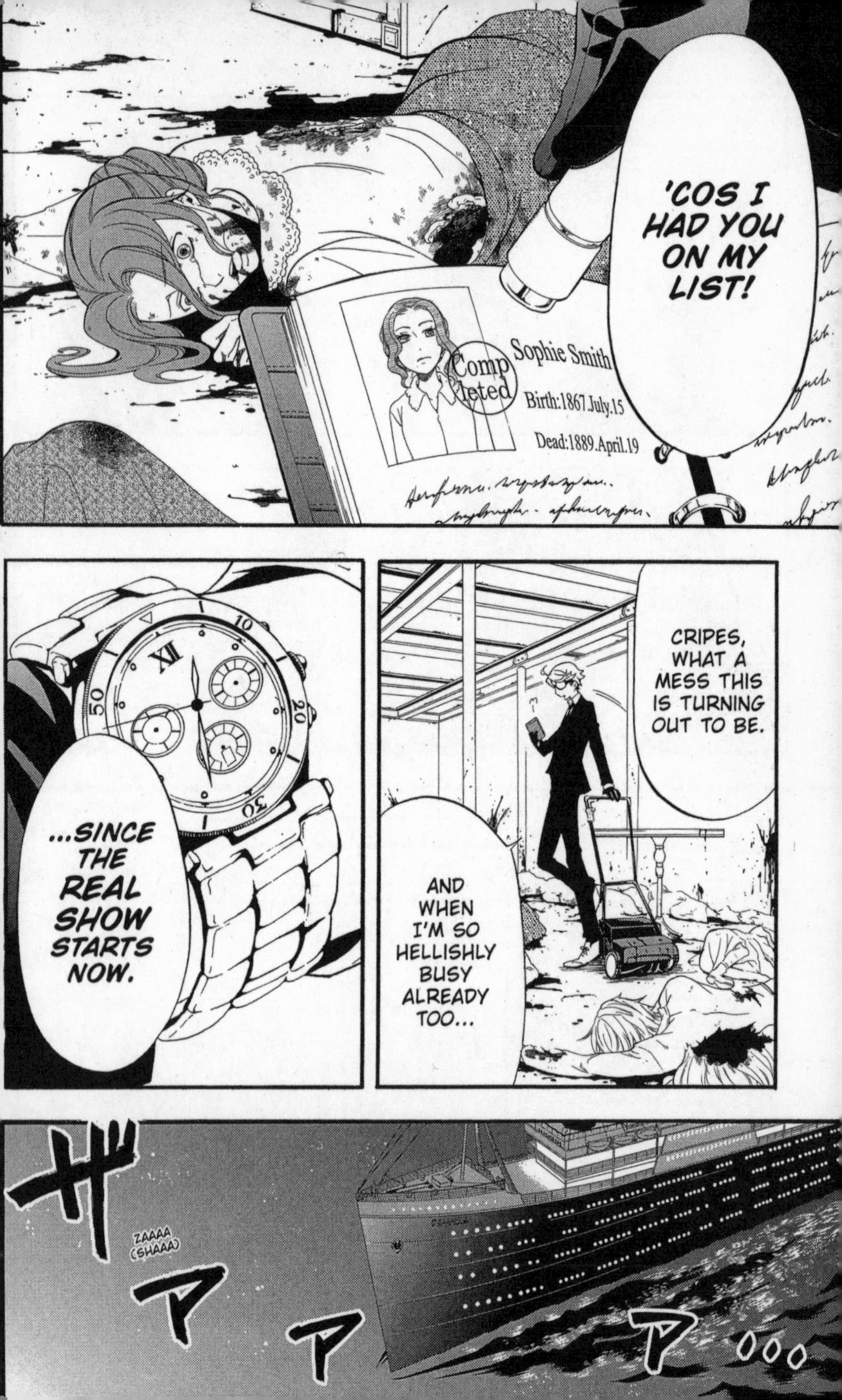
'COS I HAD YOU ON MY LIST!
Sophie Smith
Completed
Birth:1867.July.15
Dead:1889.April.19
CRIPES, WHAT A MESS THIS IS TURNING OUT TO BE.
AND WHEN I'M SO HELLISHLY BUSY ALREADY TOO...
...SINCE THE REAL SHOW STARTS NOW.
ZAAAA (SHAAA)

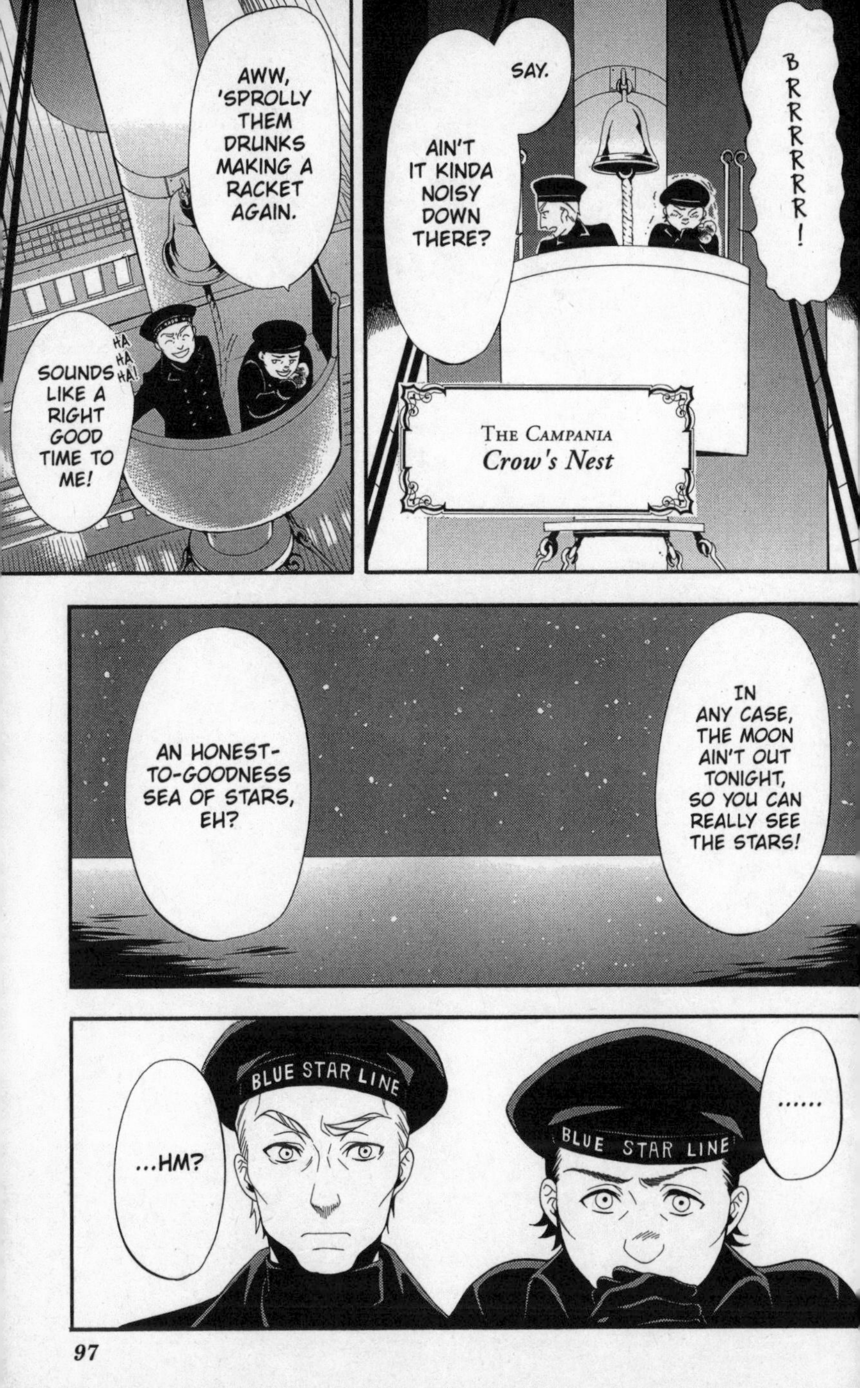

BRRRRRR!
SAY.
AIN'T IT KINDA NOISY DOWN THERE?
THE CAMPANIA Crow's Nest
AWW, 'SPROLLY THEM DRUNKS MAKING A RACKET AGAIN.
HA HA HA!
SOUNDS LIKE A RIGHT GOOD TIME TO ME!
IN ANY CASE, THE MOON AIN'T OUT TONIGHT, SO YOU CAN REALLY SEE THE STARS!
AN HONEST-TO-GOODNESS SEA OF STARS, EH?
BLUE STAR LINE
BLUE STAR LINE
......
...HM?

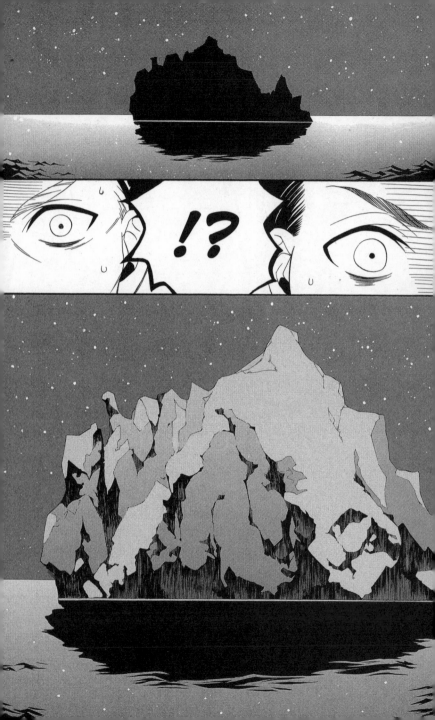

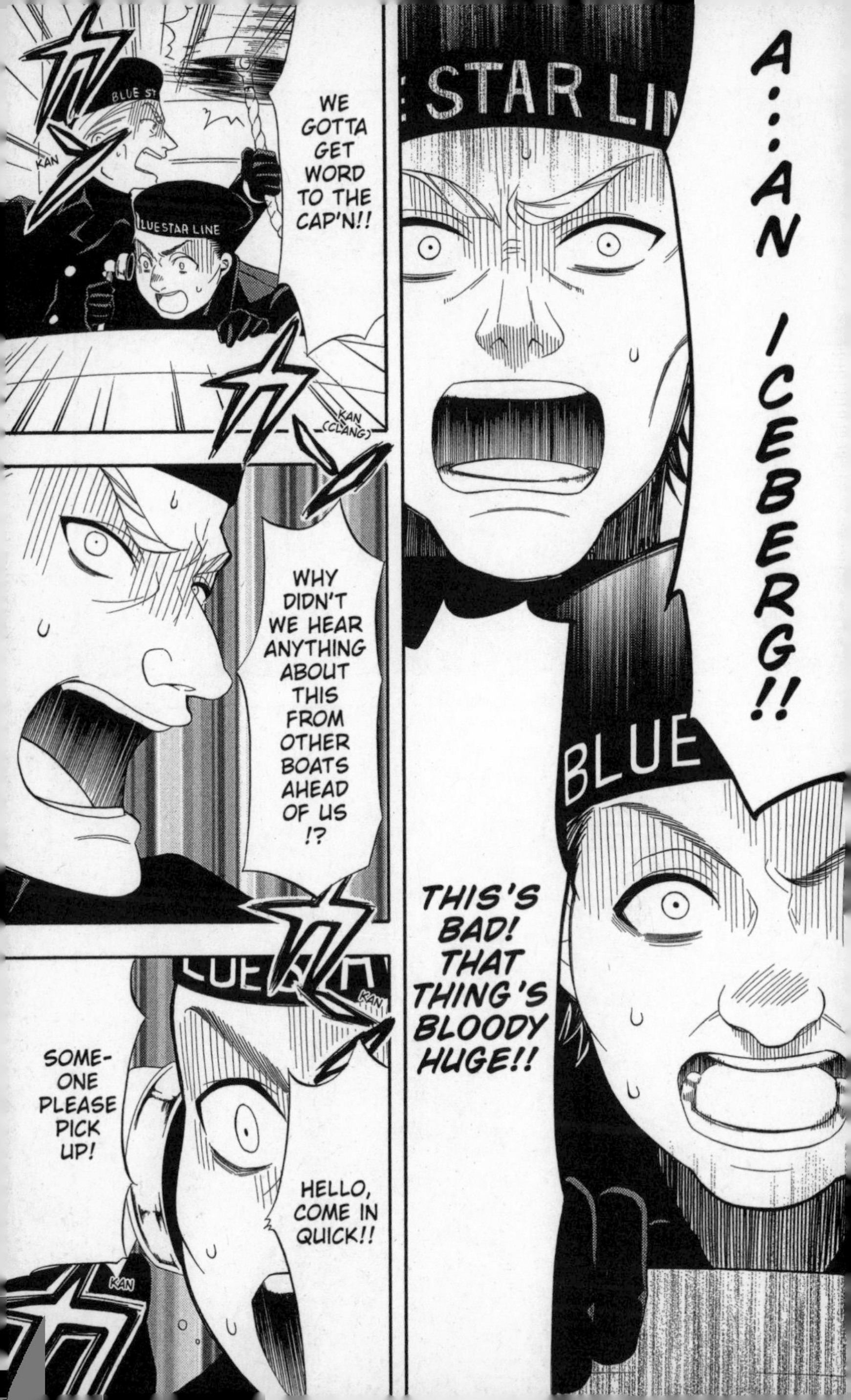
A...AN ICEBERG!!
BLUE
THIS'S BAD! THAT THING'S BLOODY HUGE!!
WE GOTTA GET WORD TO THE CAP'N!!
BLUE ST
BLUESTAR LINE
KAN
KAN (CLANG)
WHY DIDN'T WE HEAR ANYTHING ABOUT THIS FROM OTHER BOATS AHEAD OF US !?
KAN
HELLO, COME IN QUICK!!
SOME-ONE PLEASE PICK UP!
KAN

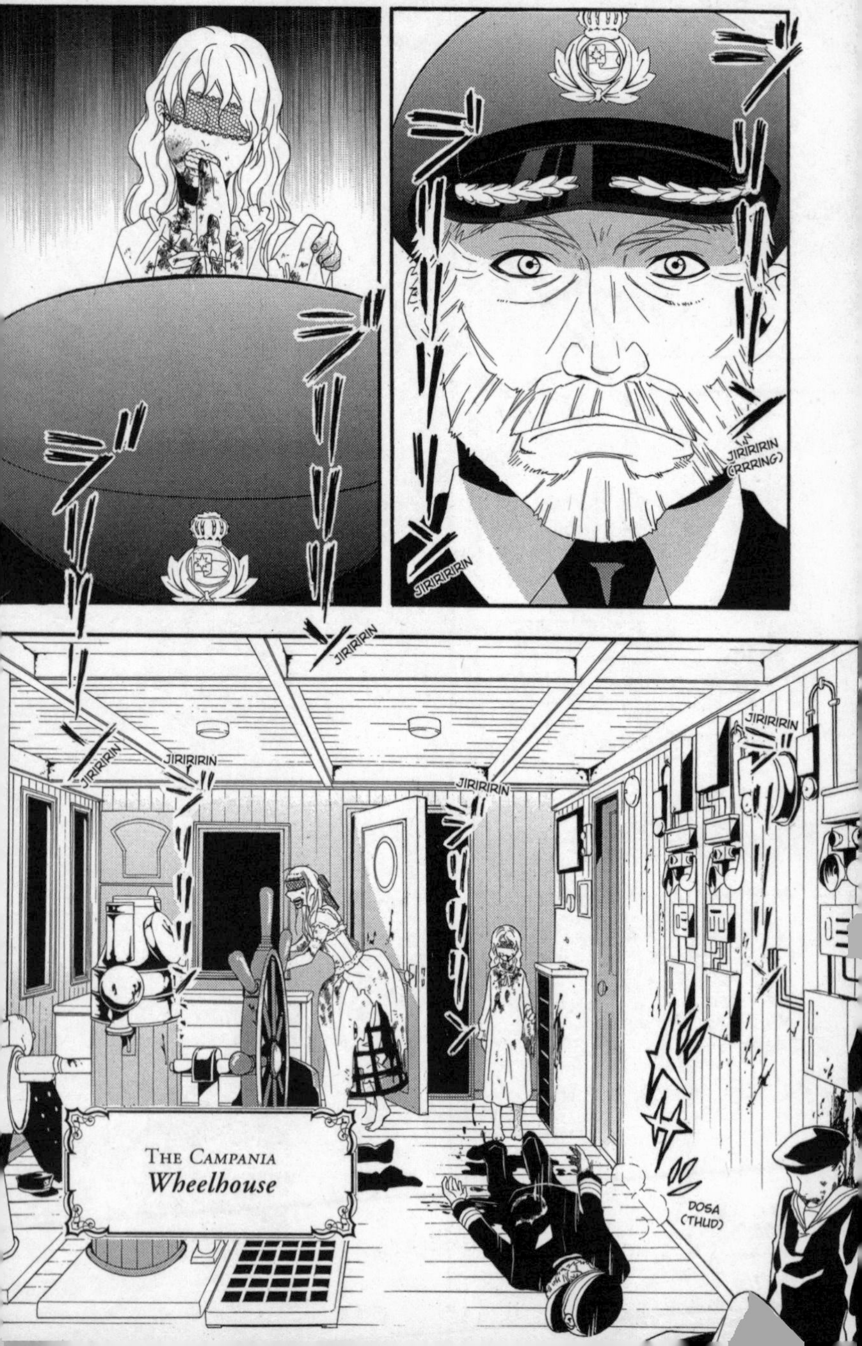
JIRIRIRIN
(RRRING)
JIRIRIRIN
JIRIRIRIN
JIRIRIRIN
JIRIRIRIN
JIRIRIRIN
JIRIRIRIN
THE CAMPANIA
Wheelhouse
DOSA
(THUD)

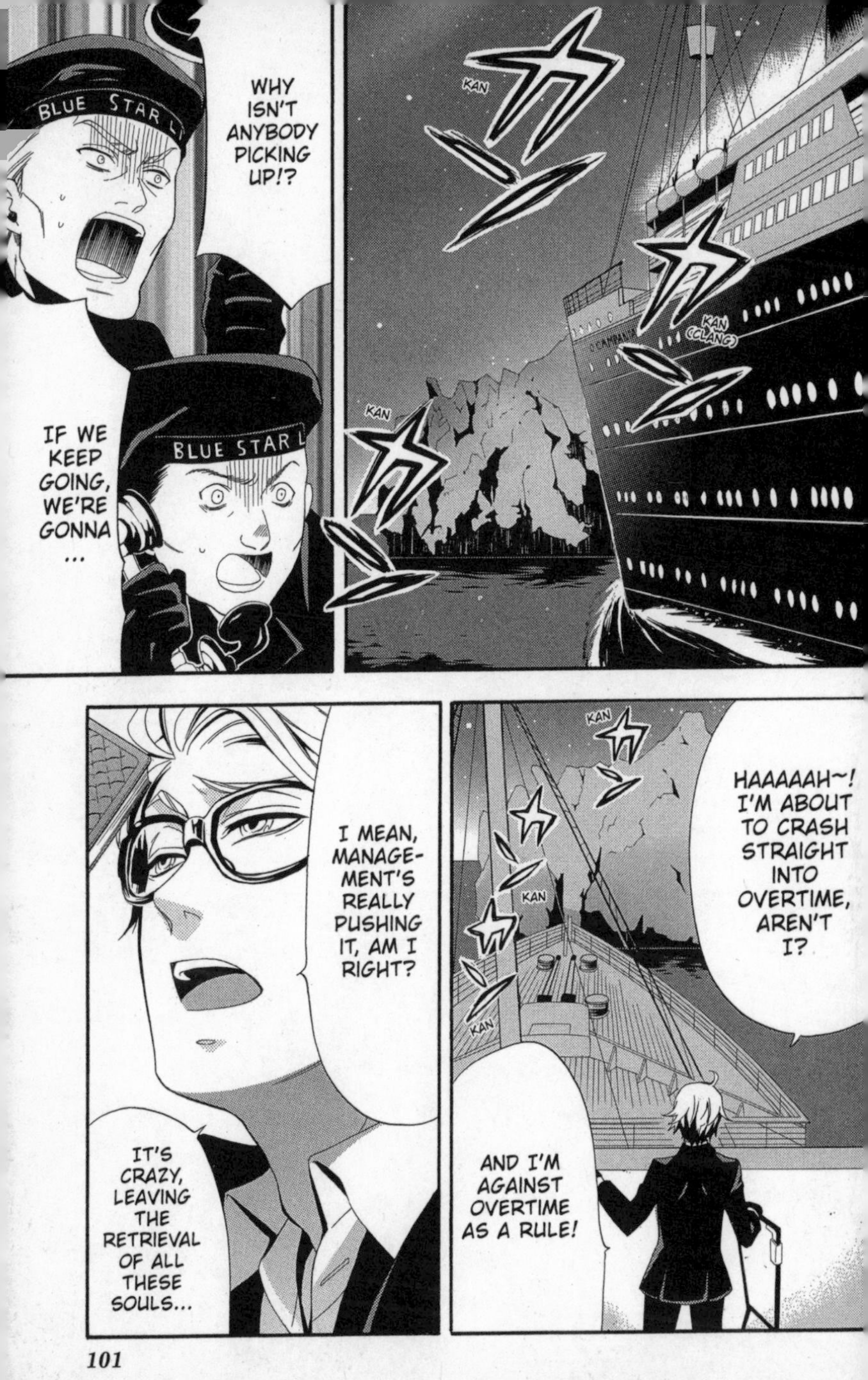
KAN
KAN (CLANG)
KAN
WHY ISN'T ANYBODY PICKING UP!?
IF WE KEEP GOING, WE'RE GONNA ...
KAN
KAN
KAN
HAAAAAH~! I'M ABOUT TO CRASH STRAIGHT INTO OVERTIME, AREN'T I?
AND I'M AGAINST OVERTIME AS A RULE!
I MEAN, MANAGEMENT'S REALLY PUSHING IT, AM I RIGHT?
IT'S CRAZY, LEAVING THE RETRIEVAL OF ALL THESE SOULS...

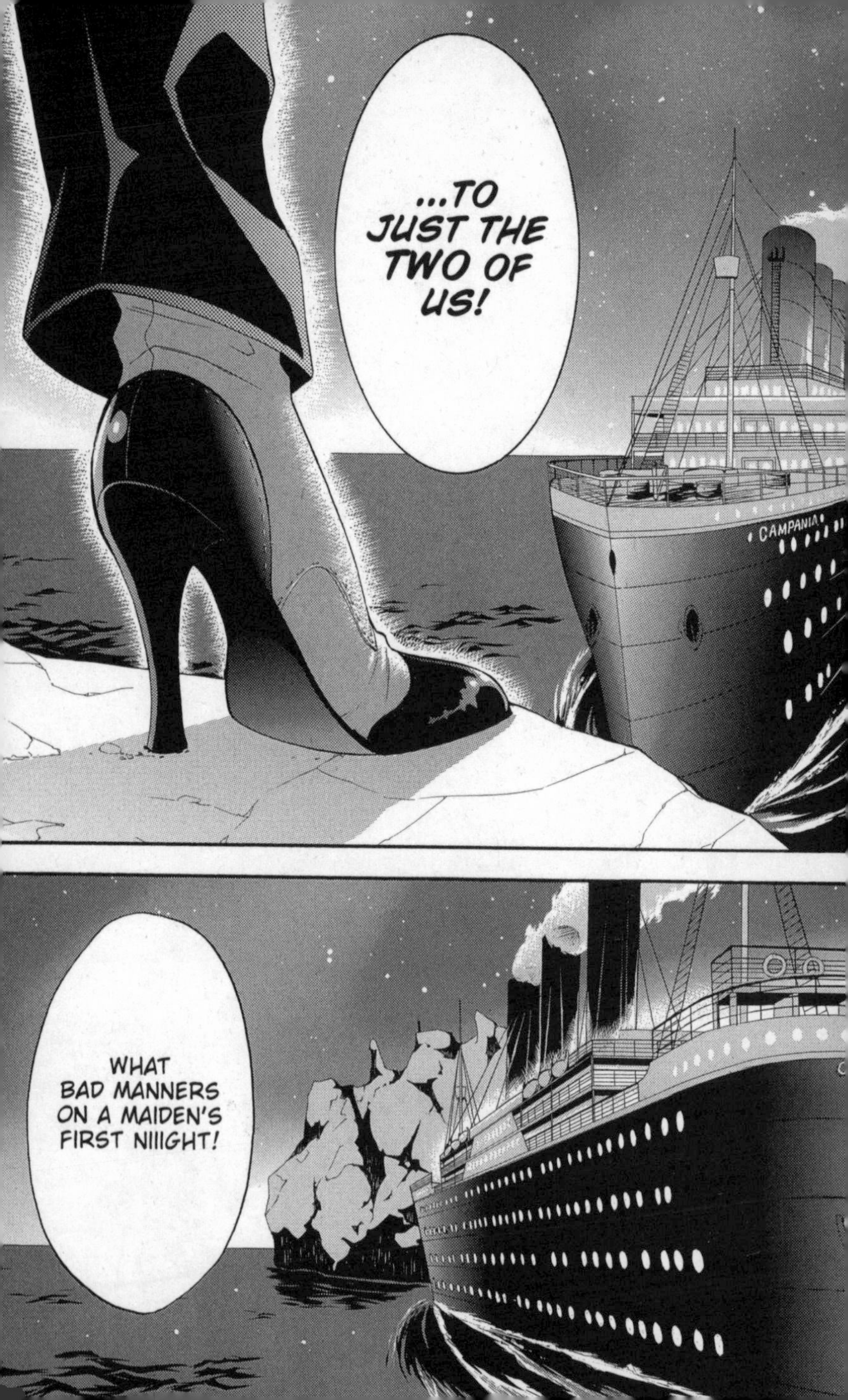
...TO JUST THE TWO OF US!
CAMPANIA
WHAT BAD MANNERS ON A MAIDEN'S FIRST NIIIGHT!

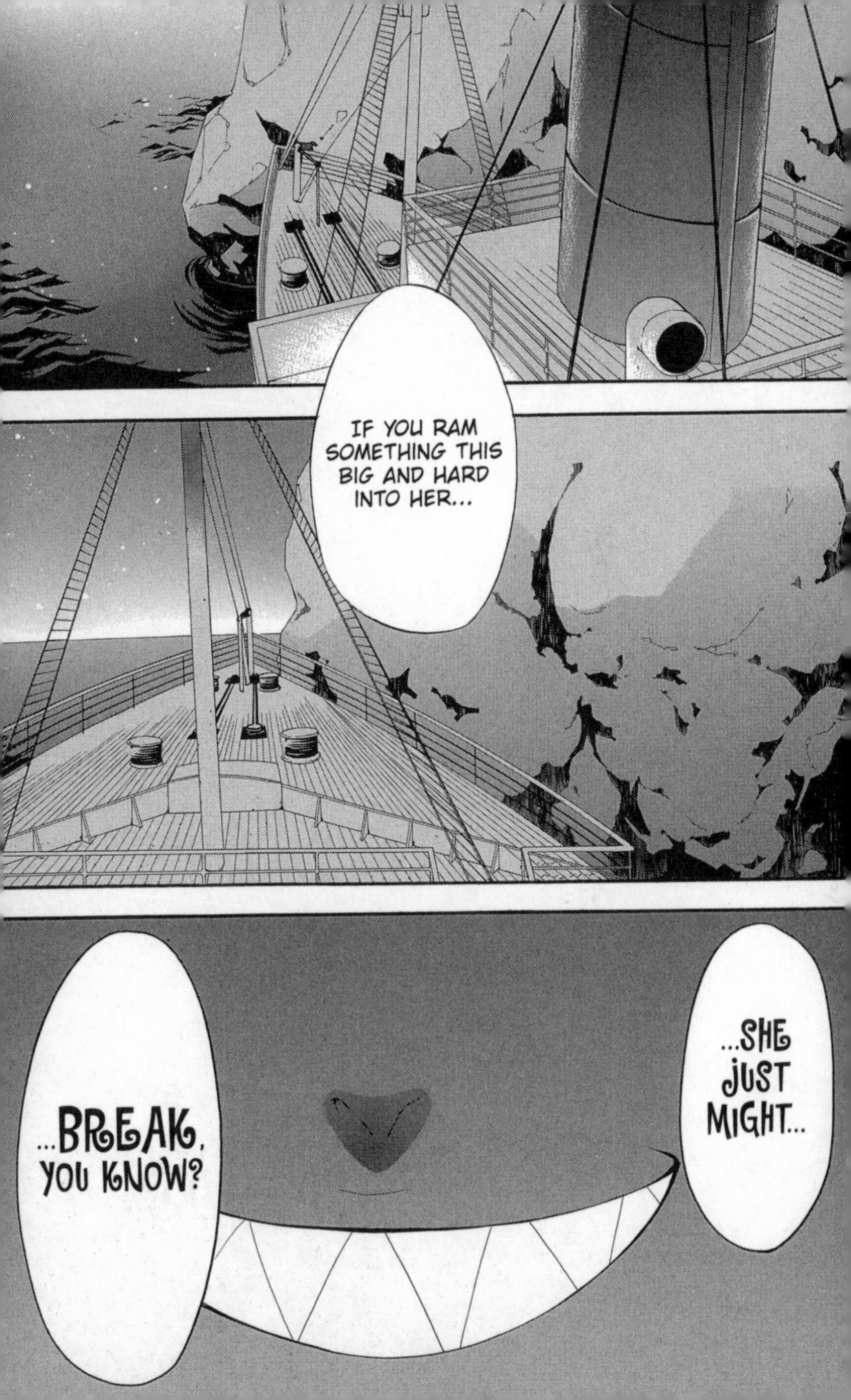
IF YOU RAM SOMETHING THIS BIG AND HARD INTO HER...
...SHE JUST MIGHT...
...BREAK, YOU KNOW?

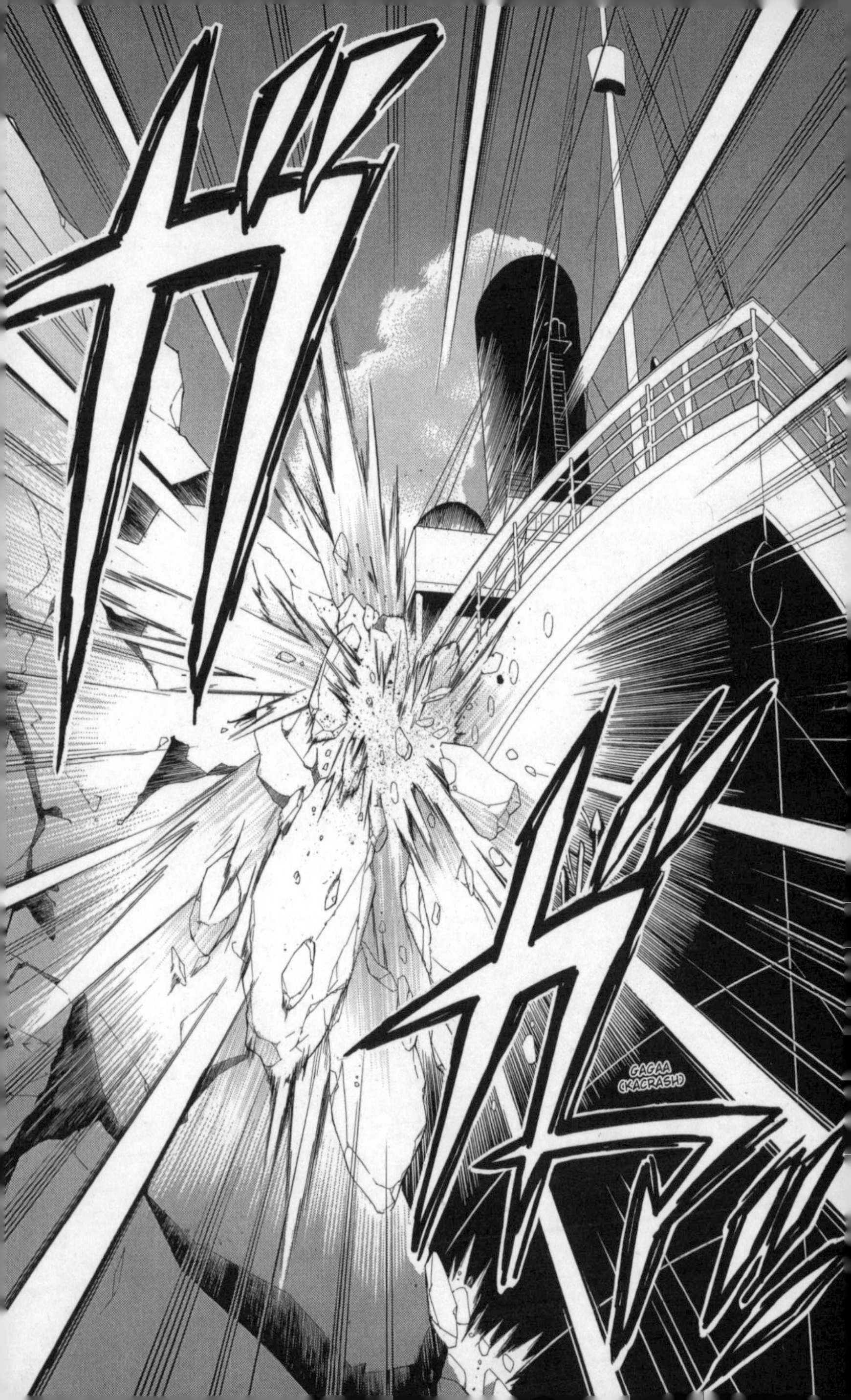
GAGAA
(KACRASH)

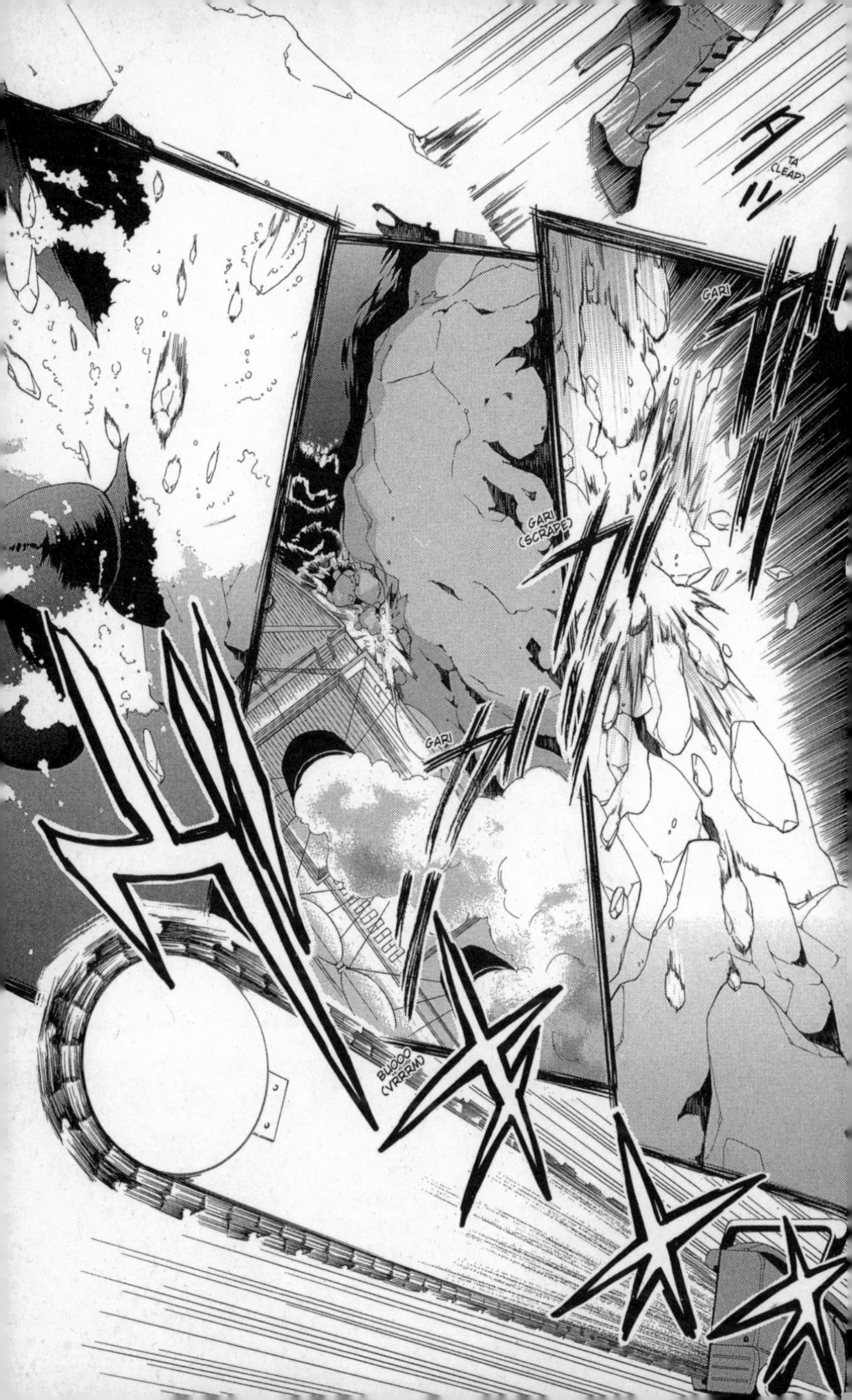
TA (LEAP)
GARI
GARI (SCRAPE)
GARI
BUOOO (VRRRM)

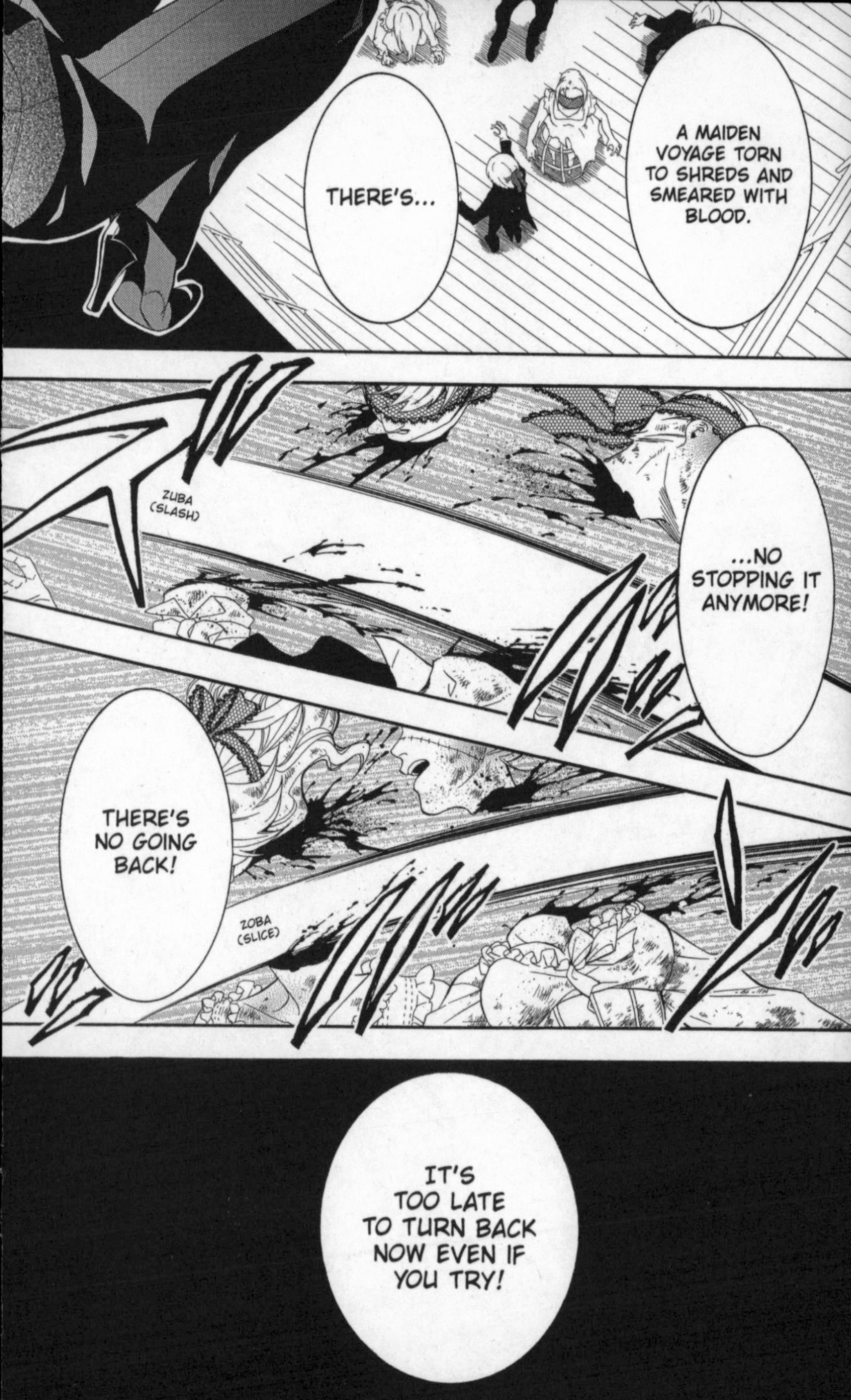
A MAIDEN VOYAGE TORN TO SHREDS AND SMEARED WITH BLOOD.
THERE'S...
...NO STOPPING IT ANYMORE!
ZUBA (SLASH)
THERE'S NO GOING BACK!
ZOBA (SLICE)
IT'S TOO LATE TO TURN BACK NOW EVEN IF YOU TRY!

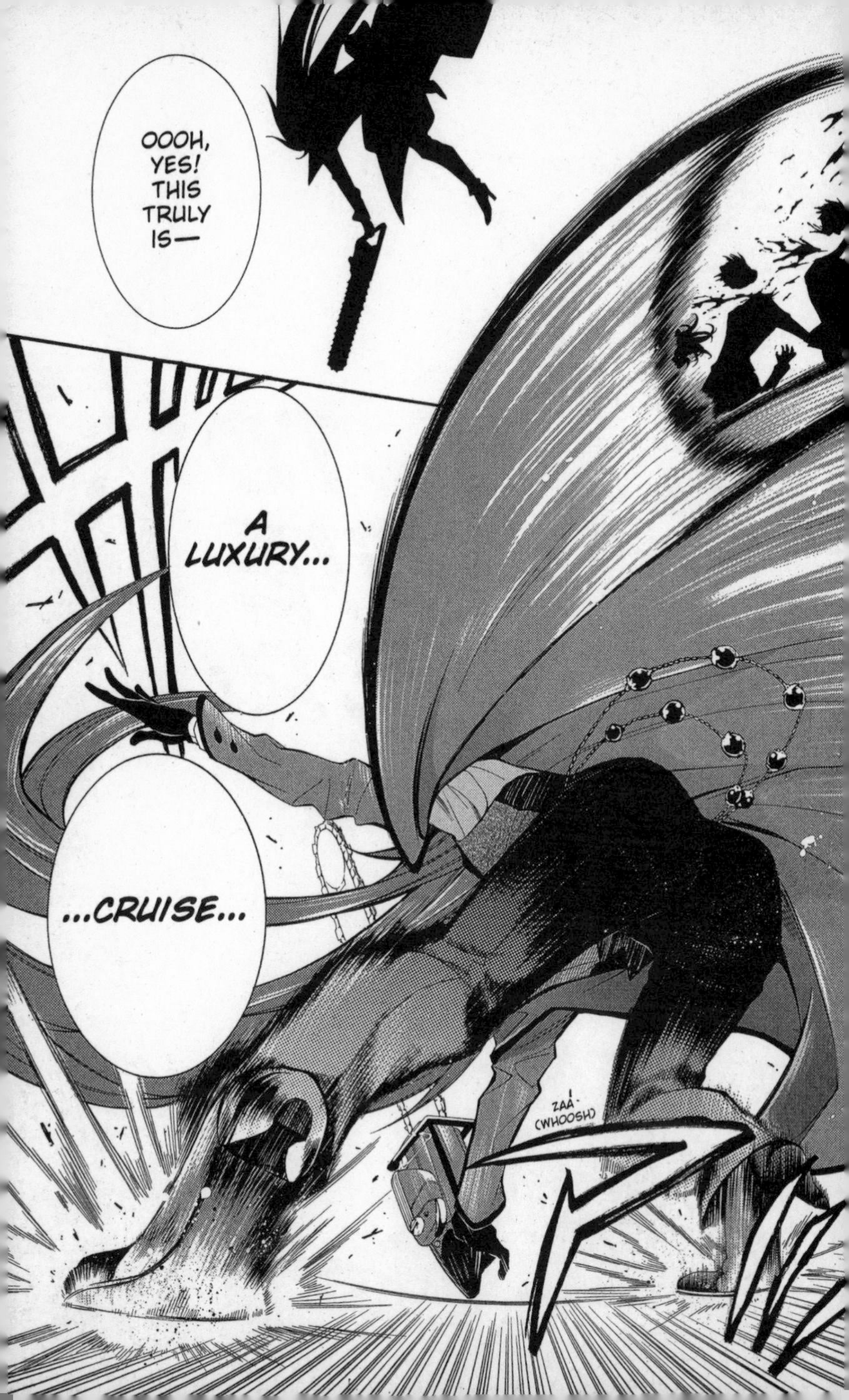
OOOH, YES! THIS TRULY IS—
A LUXURY...
...CRUISE...
ZAA (WHOOSH)

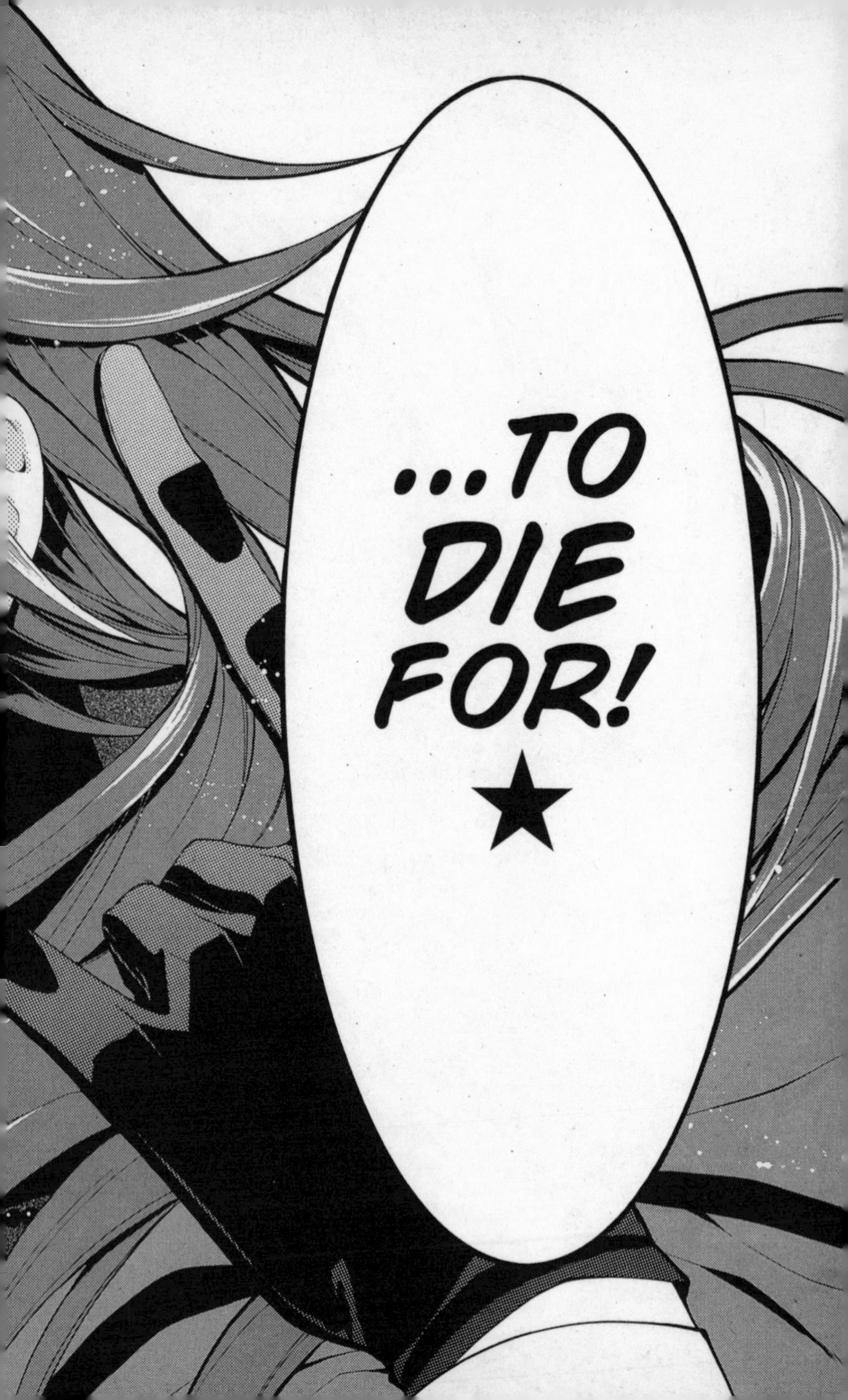
...TO DIE FOR! ★

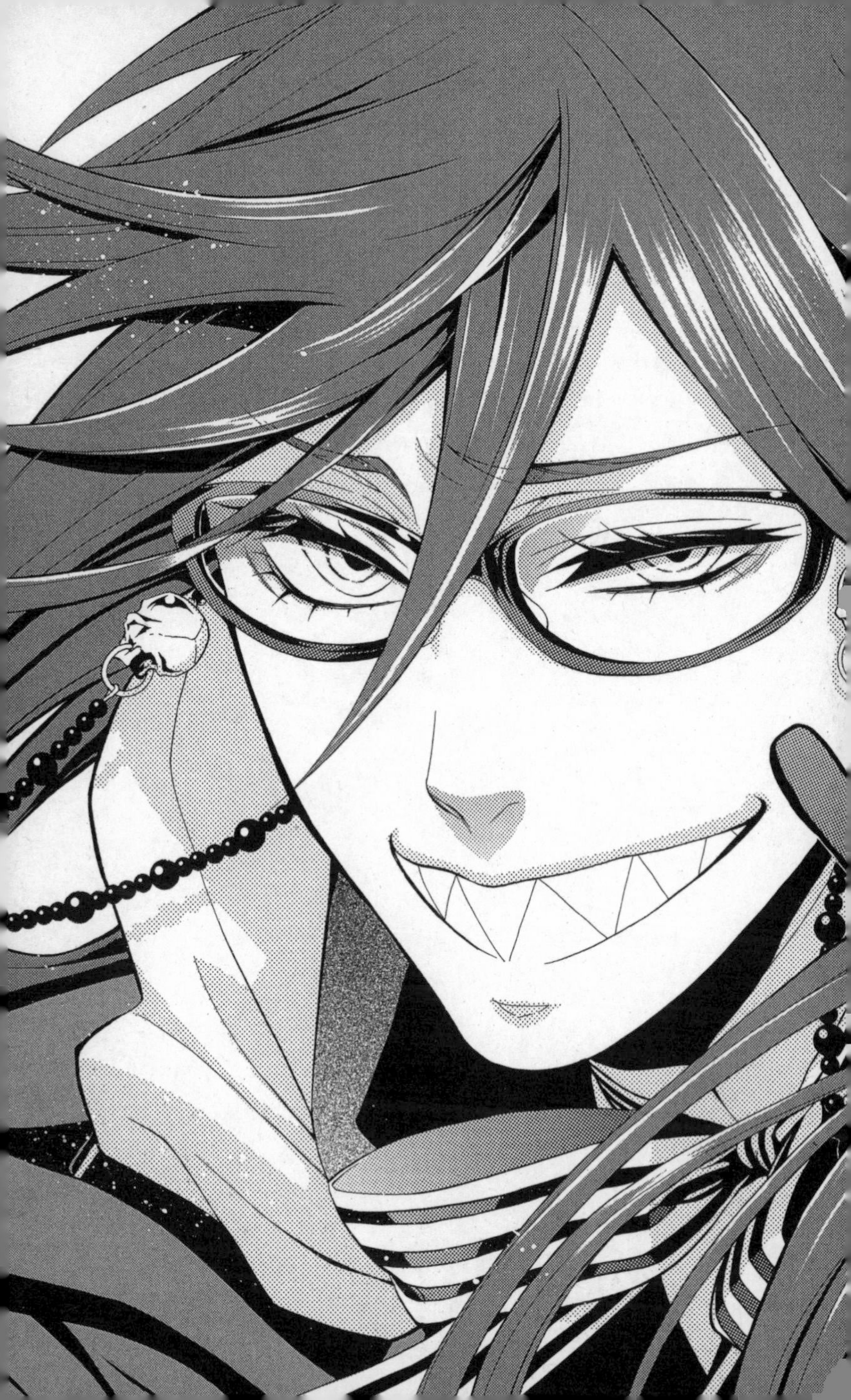

Black Butler

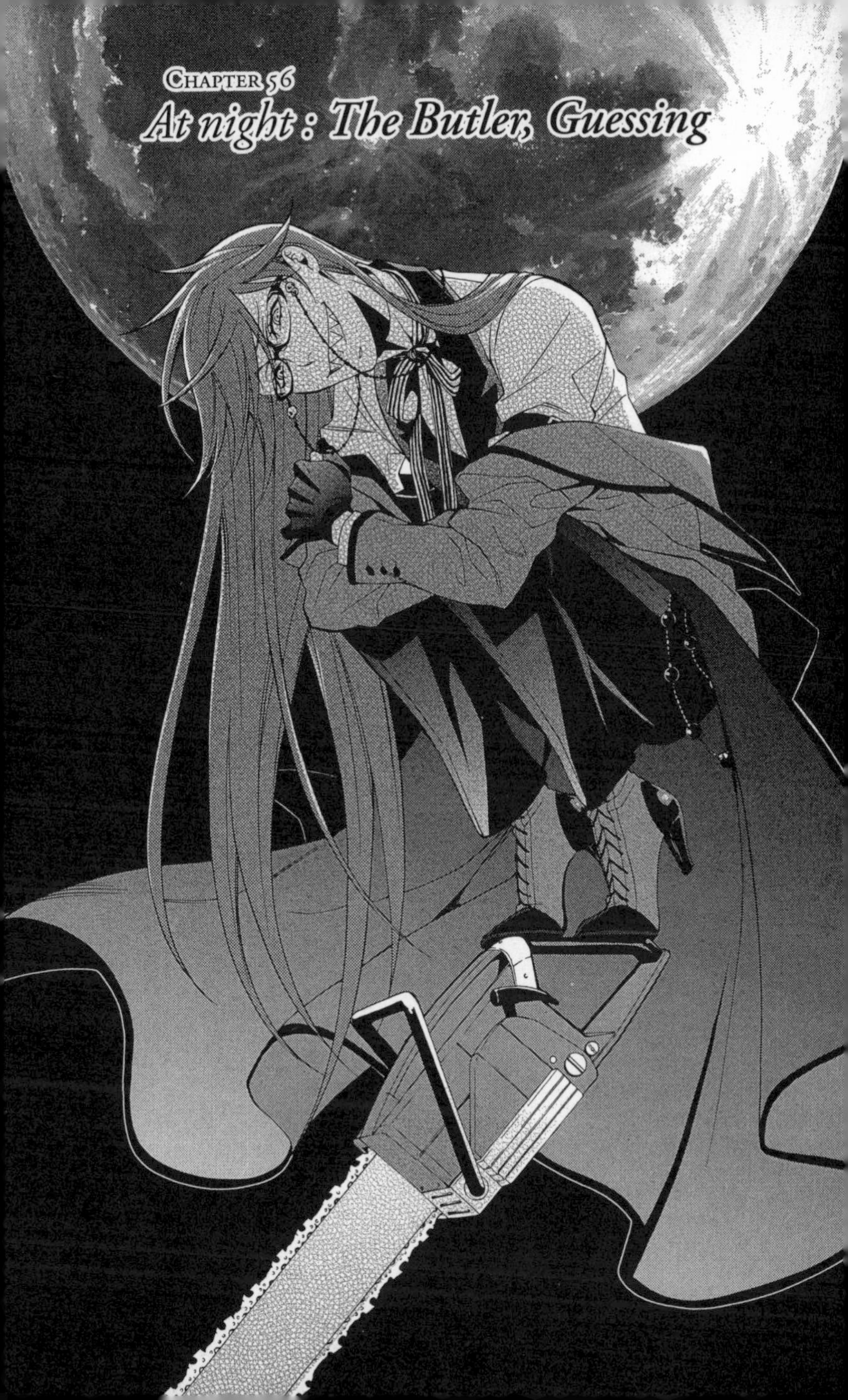
CHAPTER 56
At night : The Butler, Guessing

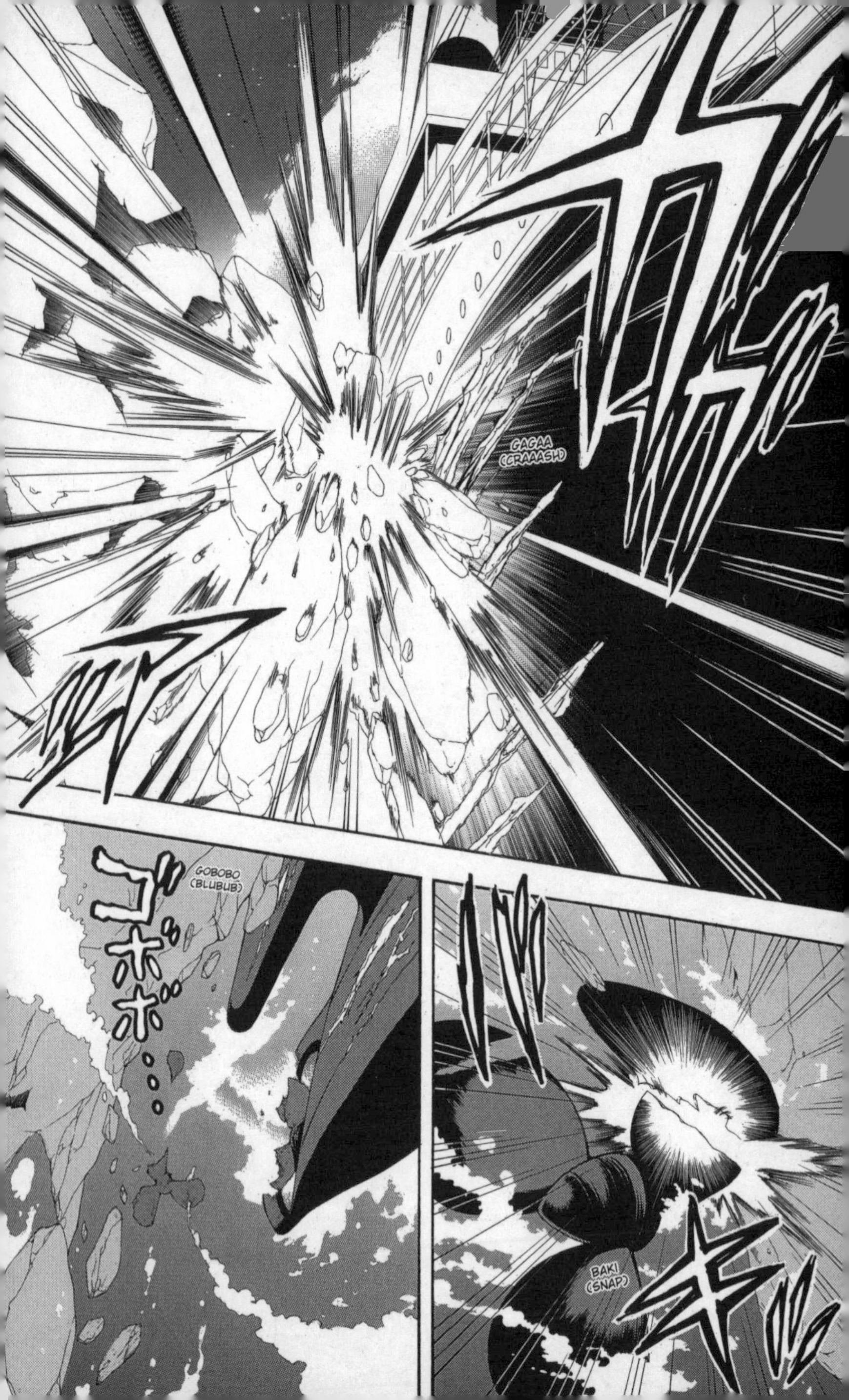
GAGAA (CRAAASH)
BAKI (SNAP)
GOBOBO (BLUBUB)

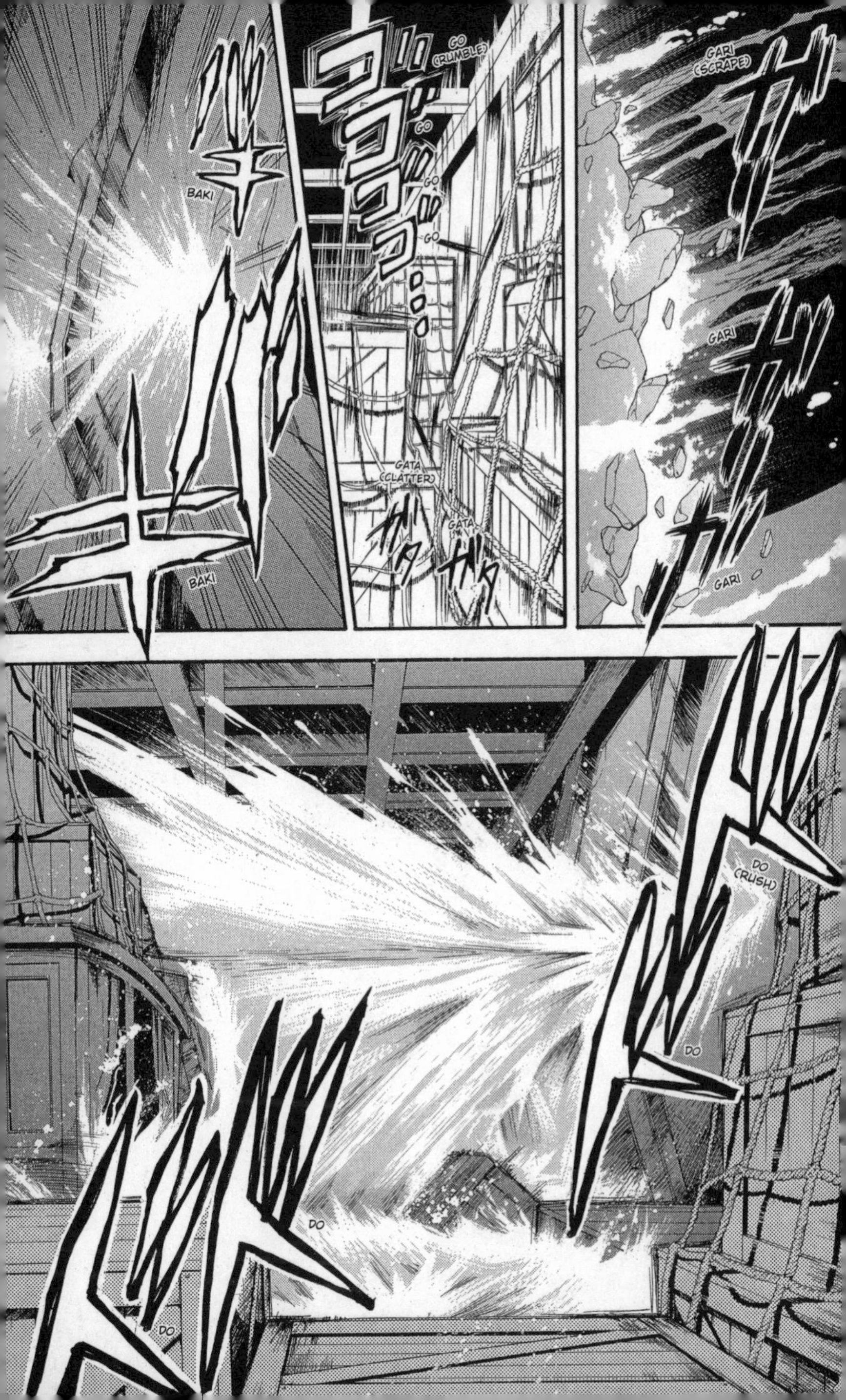
GARI (SCRAPE)
GARI
GARI
GO (RUMBLE)
GO
GO
GO
GATA (CLATTER)
GATA
BAKI
BAKI
DO (RUSH)
DO
DO
DO

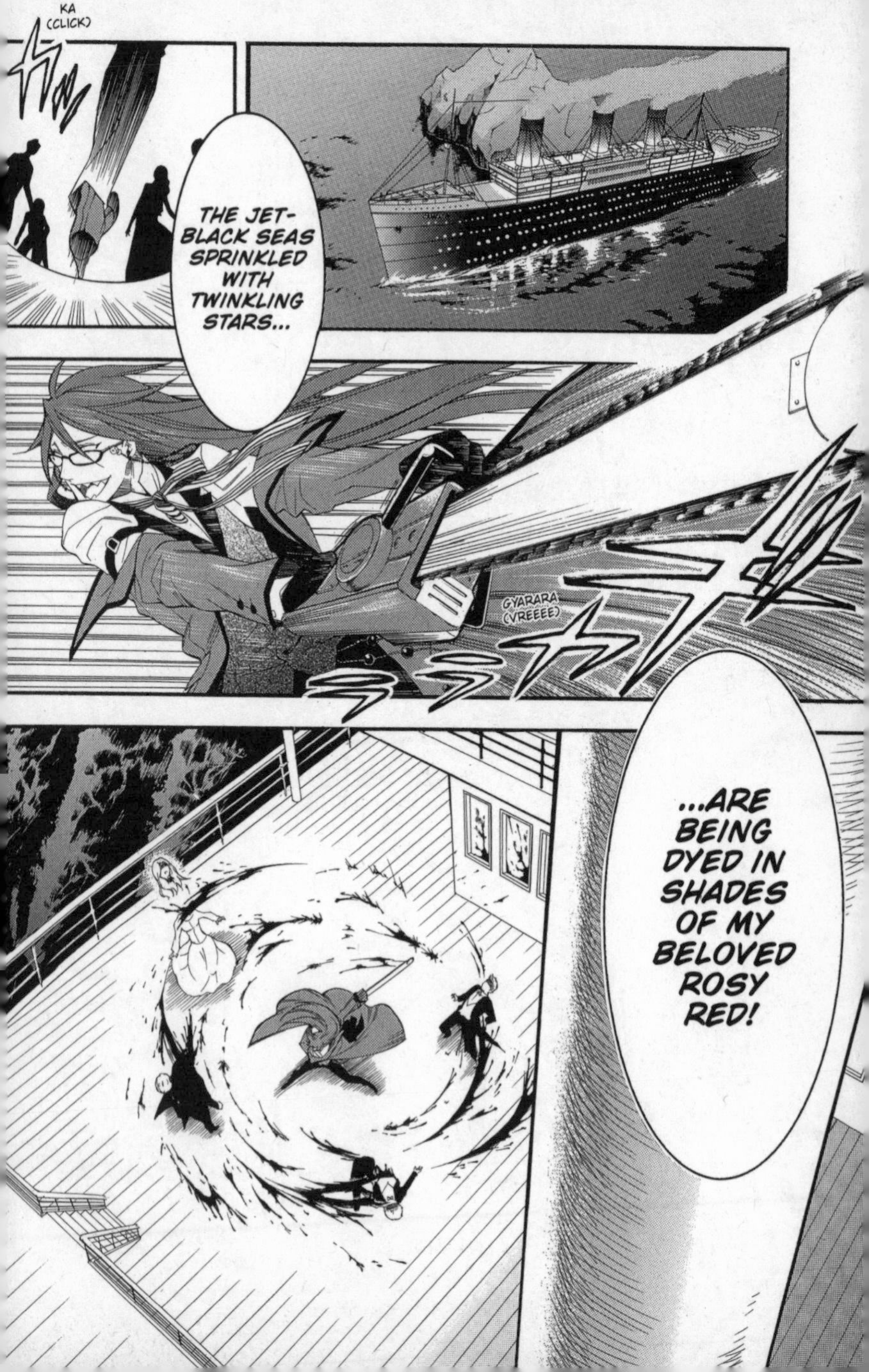
THE JET-BLACK SEAS SPRINKLED WITH TWINKLING STARS...
KA (CLICK)
GYARARA (VREEEE)
...ARE BEING DYED IN SHADES OF MY BELOVED ROSY RED!

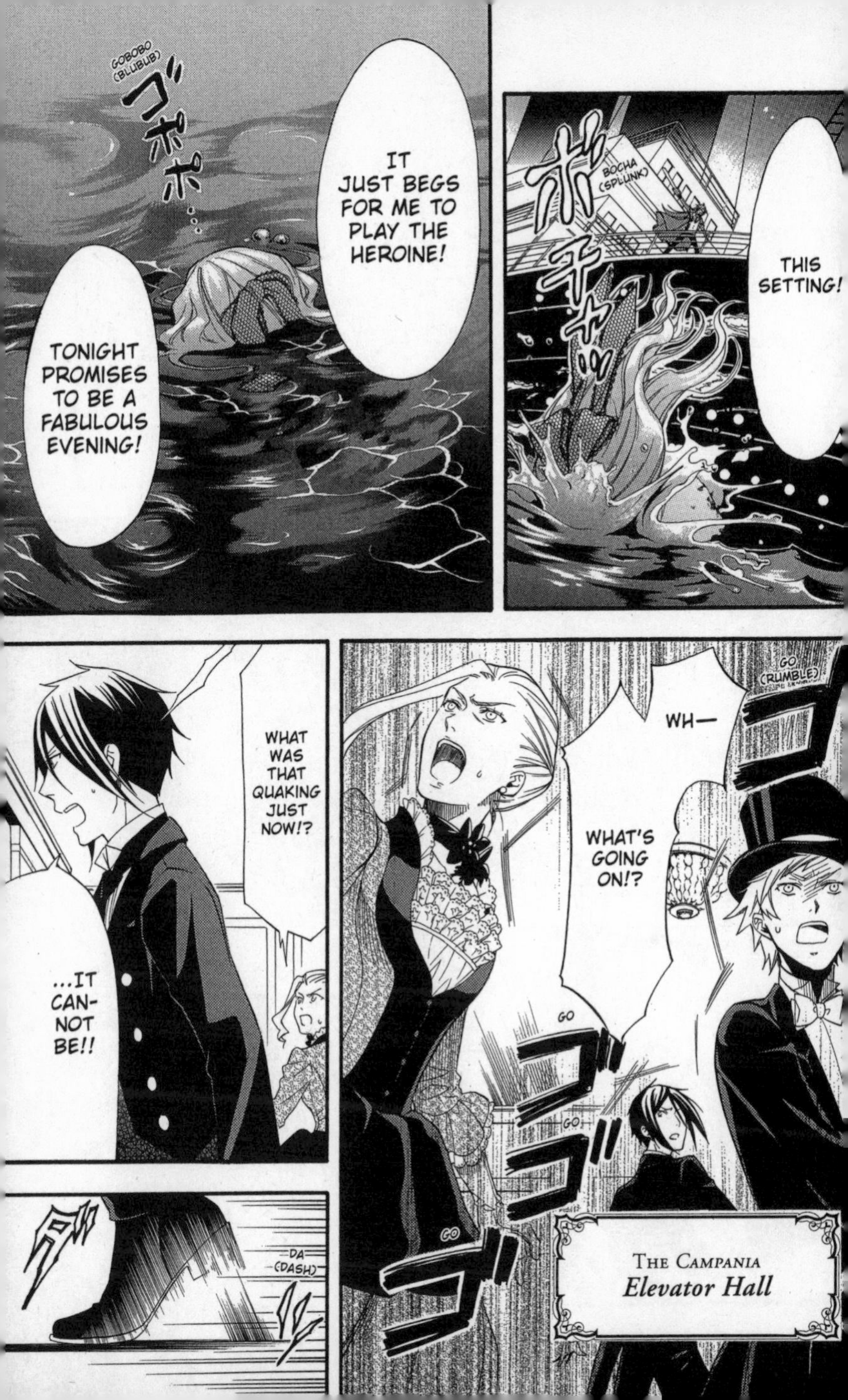
THIS SETTING!
BOCHA (SPLUNK)
IT JUST BEGS FOR ME TO PLAY THE HEROINE!
GOBOBO (BLUBUB)
TONIGHT PROMISES TO BE A FABULOUS EVENING!
GO (RUMBLE)
WH—
WHAT'S GOING ON!?
GO
GO
GO
THE CAMPANIA
Elevator Hall
WHAT WAS THAT QUAKING JUST NOW!?
...IT CAN-NOT BE!!
DA (DASH)

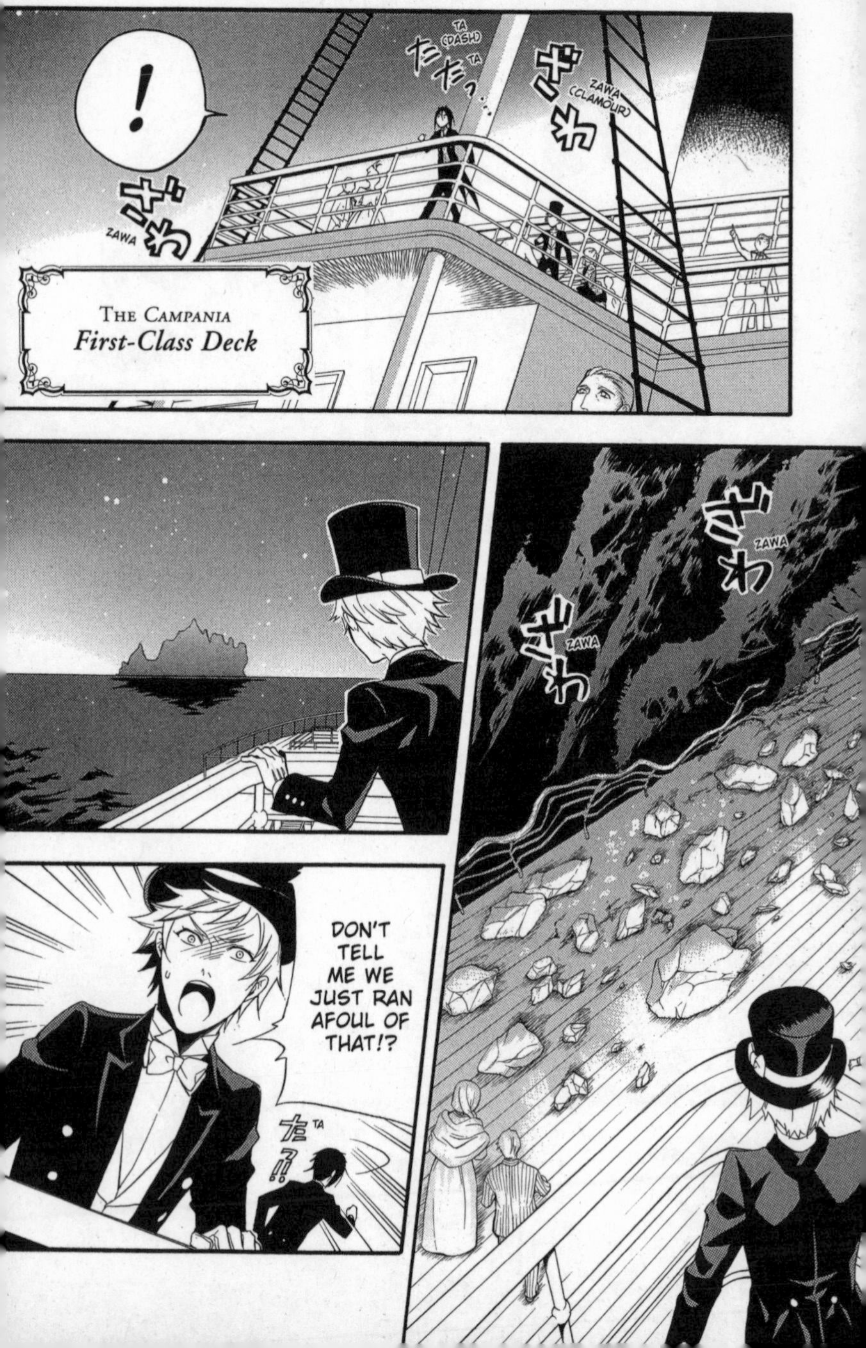
ざわ
ZAWA (CLAMOUR)
たたっ
TA (DASH) TA
!
ざわ
ZAWA
THE CAMPANIA
First-Class Deck
ざわ
ZAWA
ざわ
ZAWA
DON'T TELL ME WE JUST RAN AFOUL OF THAT!?
た
TA

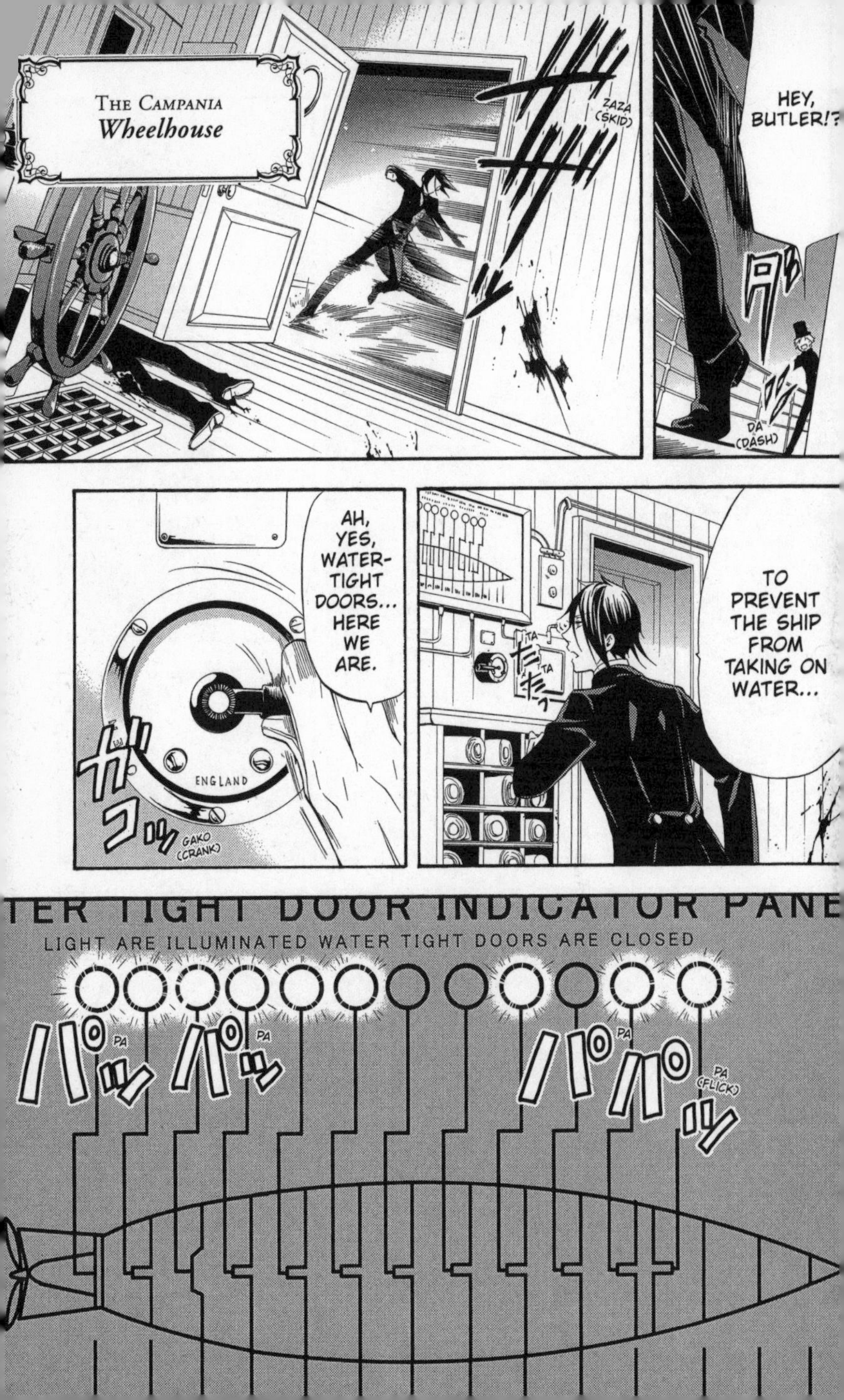

HEY, BUTLER!?
DA (DASH)
ZAZA (SKID)
The Campania Wheelhouse
TO PREVENT THE SHIP FROM TAKING ON WATER...
TA
TA
AH, YES, WATER-TIGHT DOORS... HERE WE ARE.
ENGLAND
GAKO (CRANK)
TER TIGHT DOOR INDICATOR PANE
LIGHT ARE ILLUMINATED WATER TIGHT DOORS ARE CLOSED
PA
PA
PA
PA (FLICK)

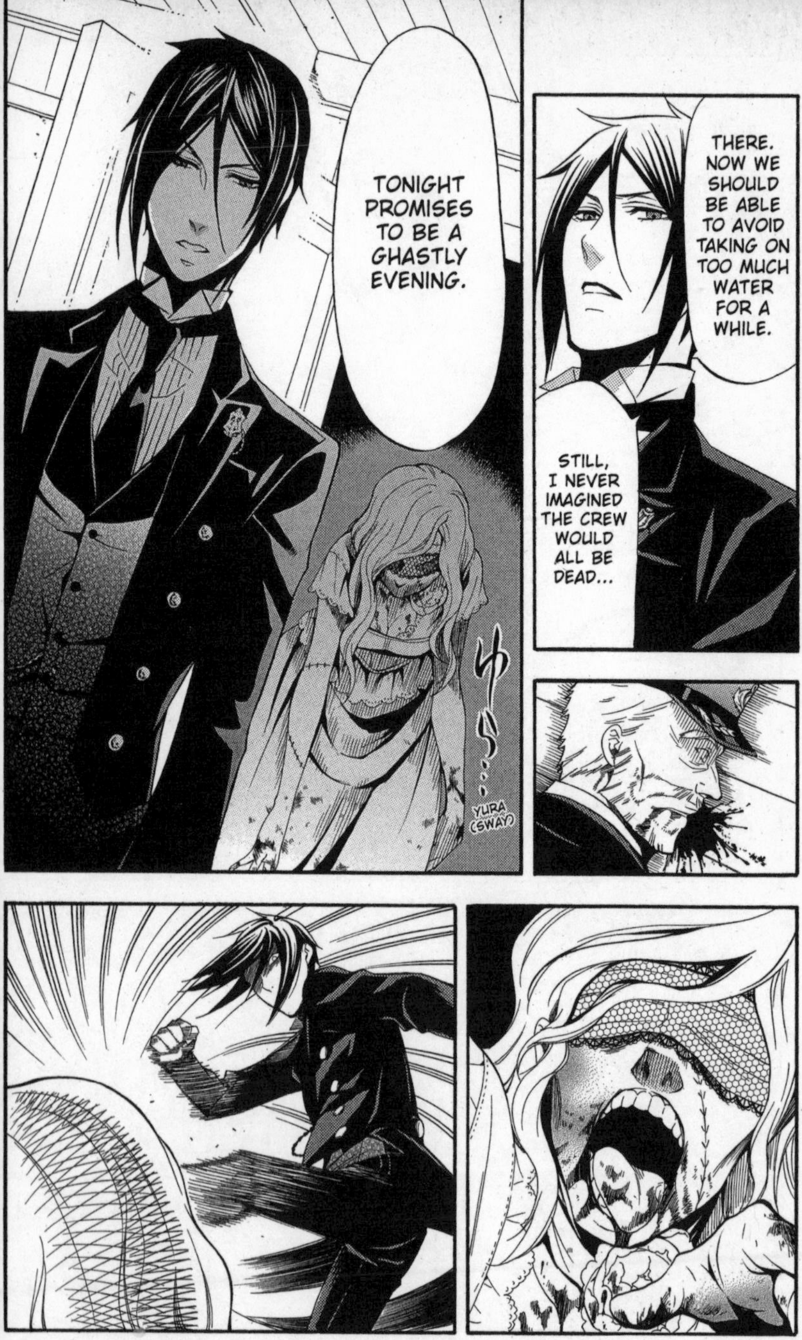
THERE. NOW WE SHOULD BE ABLE TO AVOID TAKING ON TOO MUCH WATER FOR A WHILE.
STILL, I NEVER IMAGINED THE CREW WOULD ALL BE DEAD...
TONIGHT PROMISES TO BE A GHASTLY EVENING.
ゆら…
YURA (SWAY)

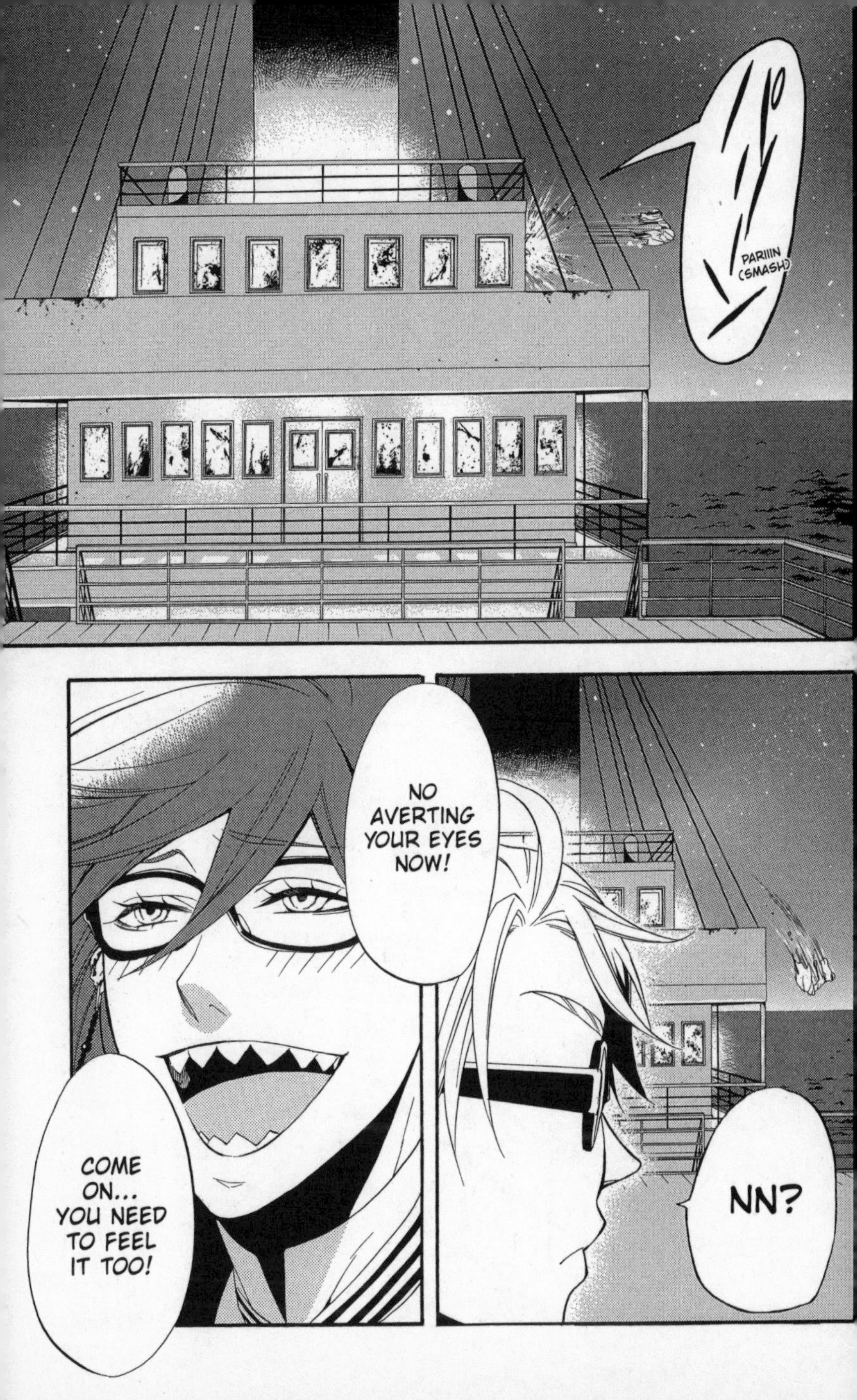
PARIIIN (SMASH)
NN?
NO AVERTING YOUR EYES NOW!
COME ON... YOU NEED TO FEEL IT TOO!

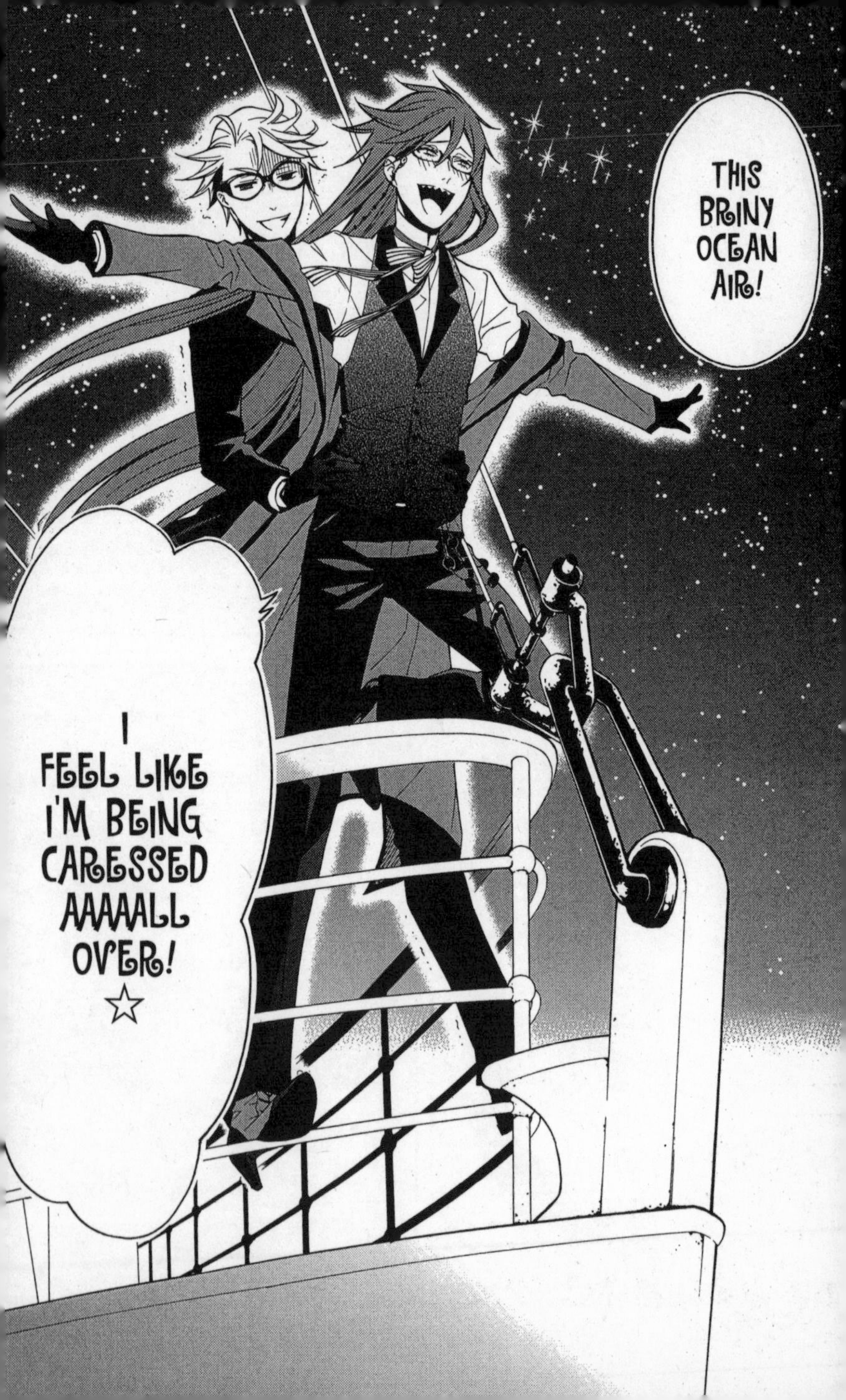
THIS BRINY OCEAN AIR!
I FEEL LIKE I'M BEING CARESSED AAAAALL OVER! ☆

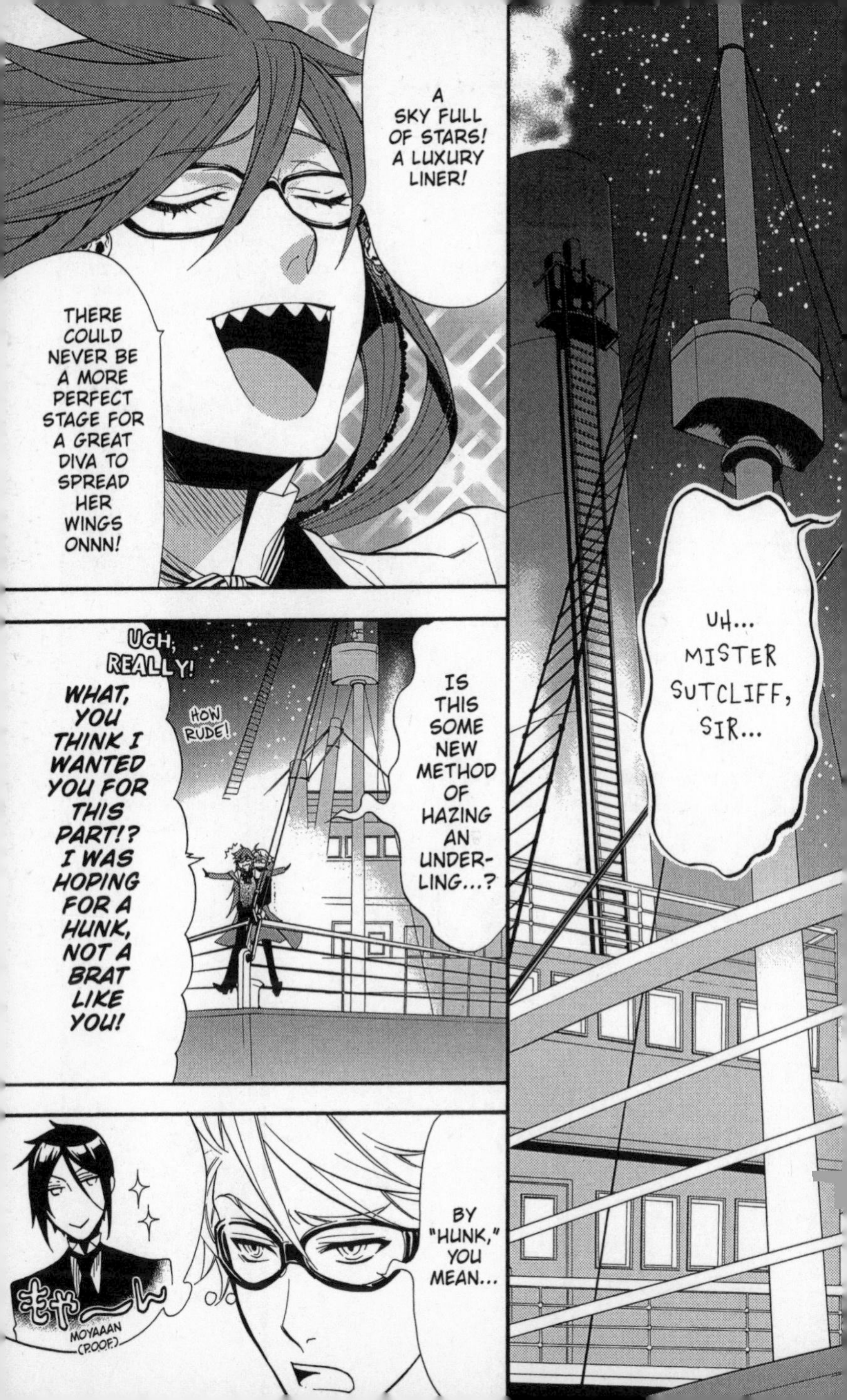
UH... MISTER SUTCLIFF, SIR...
A SKY FULL OF STARS! A LUXURY LINER!
THERE COULD NEVER BE A MORE PERFECT STAGE FOR A GREAT DIVA TO SPREAD HER WINGS ONNN!
IS THIS SOME NEW METHOD OF HAZING AN UNDER-LING...?
UGH, REALLY!
HOW RUDE!
WHAT, YOU THINK I WANTED YOU FOR THIS PART!? I WAS HOPING FOR A HUNK, NOT A BRAT LIKE YOU!
BY "HUNK," YOU MEAN...
もや〜ん
MOYAAAN (POOF)

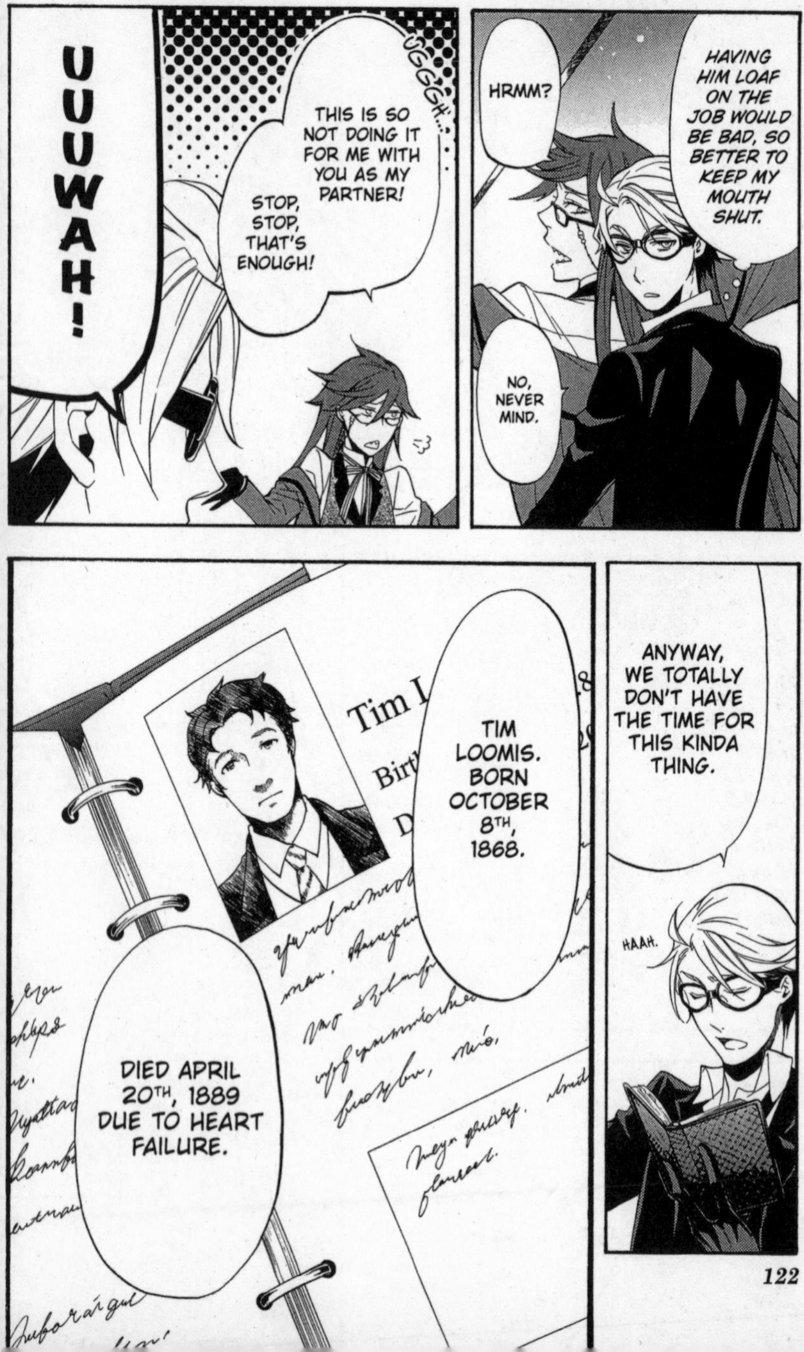
HRMM?
HAVING HIM LOAF ON THE JOB WOULD BE BAD, SO BETTER TO KEEP MY MOUTH SHUT.
NO, NEVER MIND.
UGGGH...
THIS IS SO NOT DOING IT FOR ME WITH YOU AS MY PARTNER!
STOP, STOP, THAT'S ENOUGH!
UUUWAH!
ANYWAY, WE TOTALLY DON'T HAVE THE TIME FOR THIS KINDA THING.
HAAH.
TIM LOOMIS. BORN OCTOBER 8TH, 1868.
DIED APRIL 20TH, 1889 DUE TO HEART FAILURE.

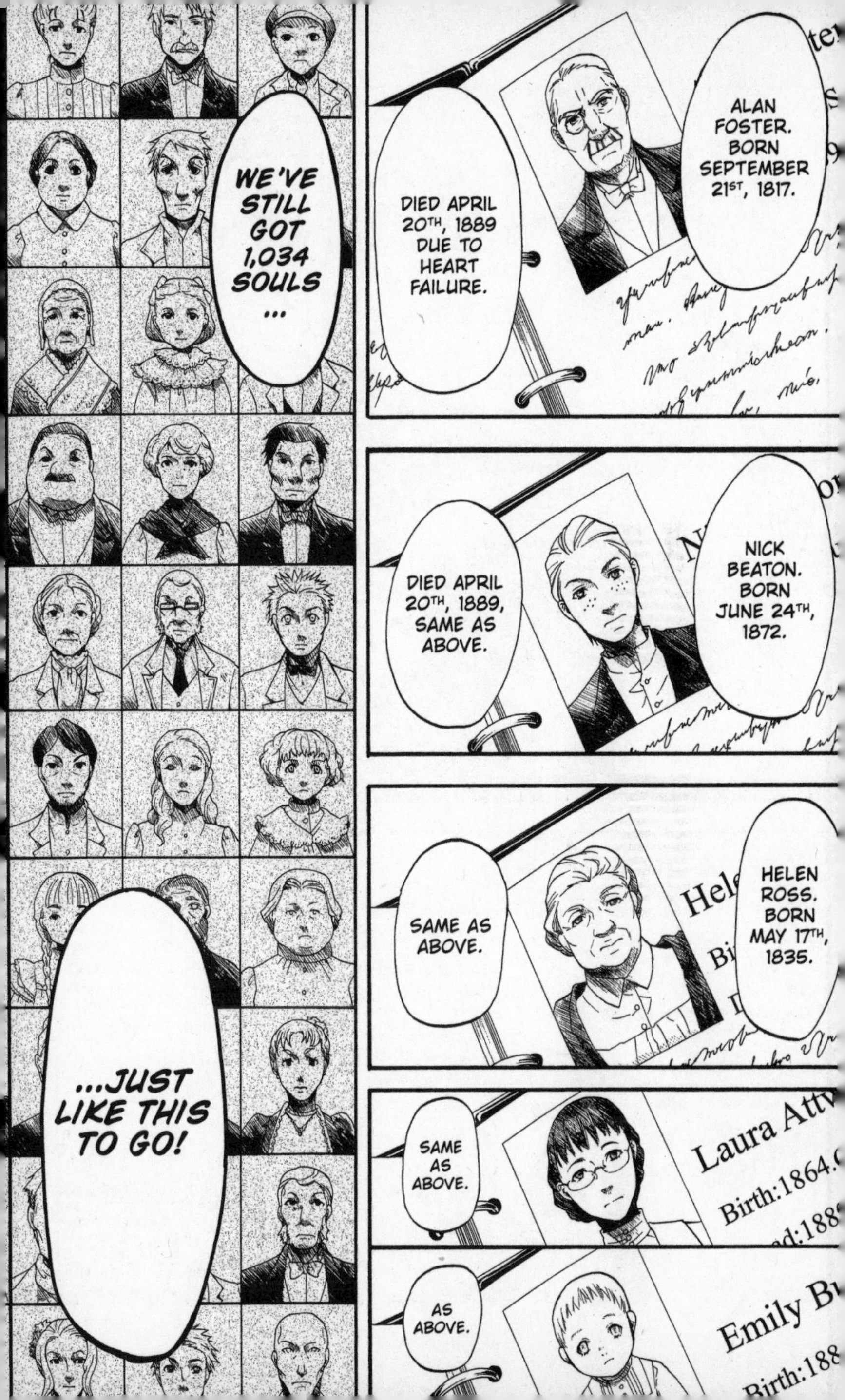
ALAN FOSTER. BORN SEPTEMBER 21ST, 1817.
DIED APRIL 20TH, 1889 DUE TO HEART FAILURE.
NICK BEATON. BORN JUNE 24TH, 1872.
DIED APRIL 20TH, 1889, SAME AS ABOVE.
HELEN ROSS. BORN MAY 17TH, 1835.
SAME AS ABOVE.
SAME AS ABOVE.
AS ABOVE.
WE'VE STILL GOT 1,034 SOULS...
...JUST LIKE THIS TO GO!

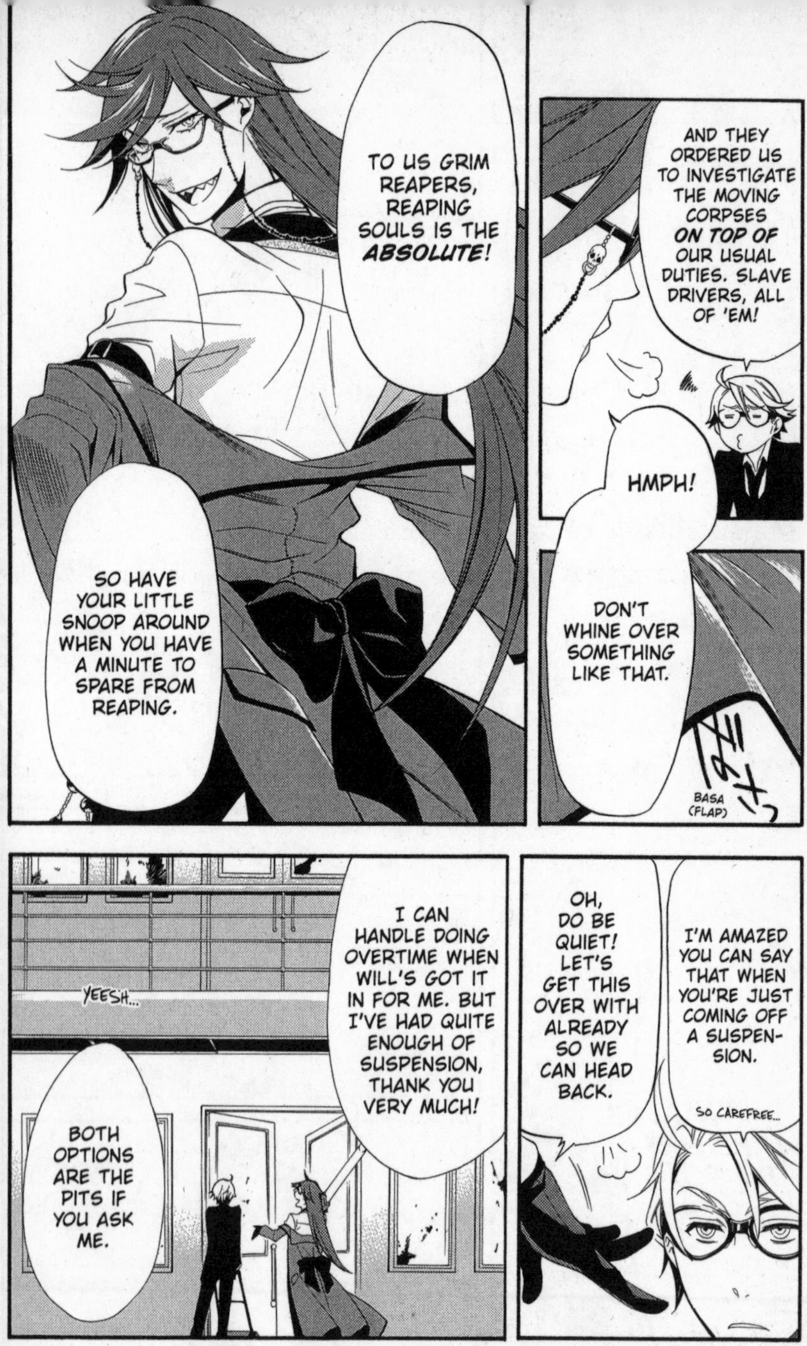
AND THEY ORDERED US TO INVESTIGATE THE MOVING CORPSES **ON TOP OF** OUR USUAL DUTIES. SLAVE DRIVERS, ALL OF 'EM!
HMPH!
DON'T WHINE OVER SOMETHING LIKE THAT.
BASA (FLAP)
TO US GRIM REAPERS, REAPING SOULS IS THE ***ABSOLUTE***!
SO HAVE YOUR LITTLE SNOOP AROUND WHEN YOU HAVE A MINUTE TO SPARE FROM REAPING.
I'M AMAZED YOU CAN SAY THAT WHEN YOU'RE JUST COMING OFF A SUSPENSION.
SO CAREFREE...
OH, DO BE QUIET! LET'S GET THIS OVER WITH ALREADY SO WE CAN HEAD BACK.
I CAN HANDLE DOING OVERTIME WHEN WILL'S GOT IT IN FOR ME. BUT I'VE HAD QUITE ENOUGH OF SUSPENSION, THANK YOU VERY MUCH!
YEESH...
BOTH OPTIONS ARE THE PITS IF YOU ASK ME.

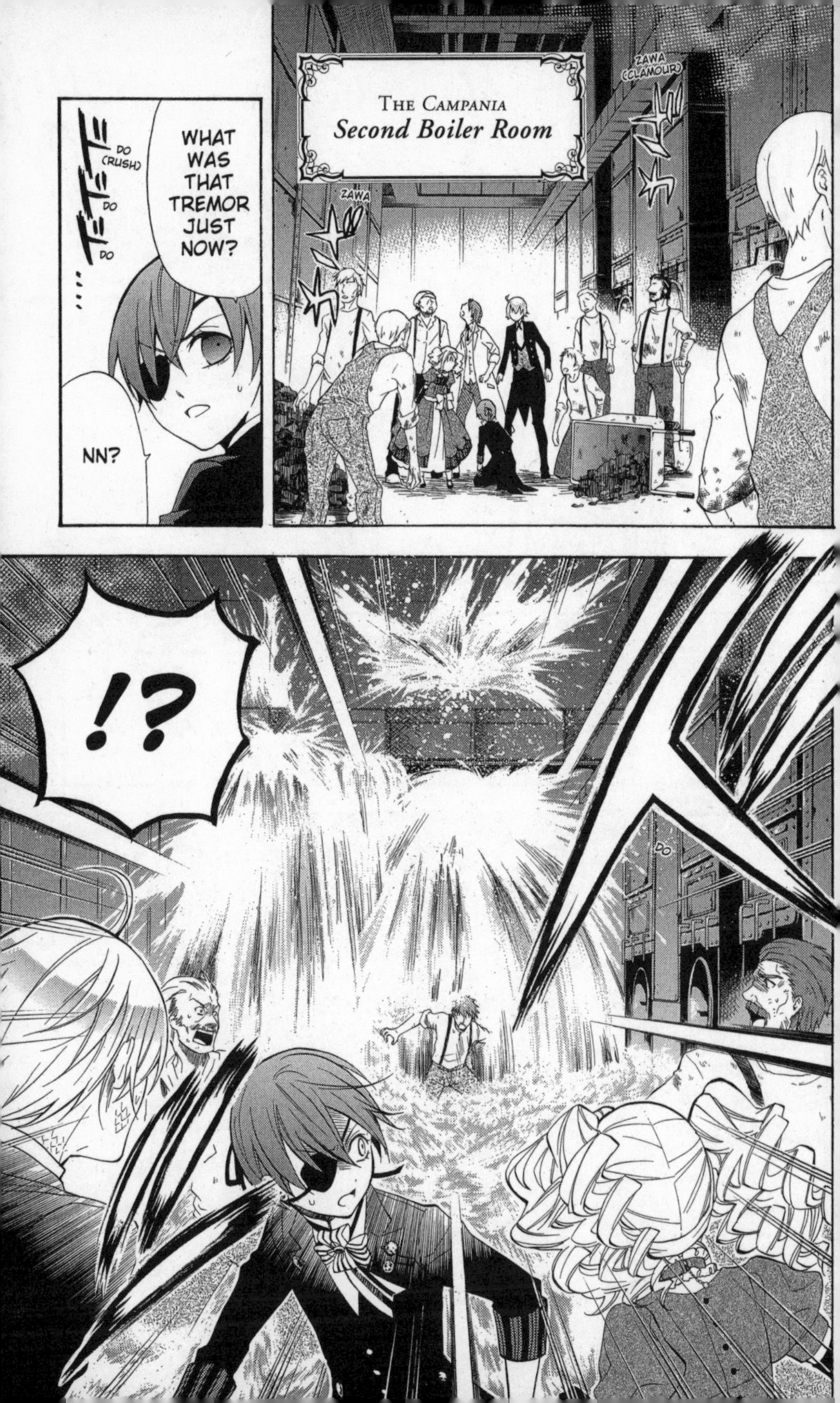
THE CAMPANIA
Second Boiler Room
ZAWA (CLAMOUR)
ZAWA
DO (RUSH) DO DO
WHAT WAS THAT TREMOR JUST NOW?
....
NN?
!?
DO

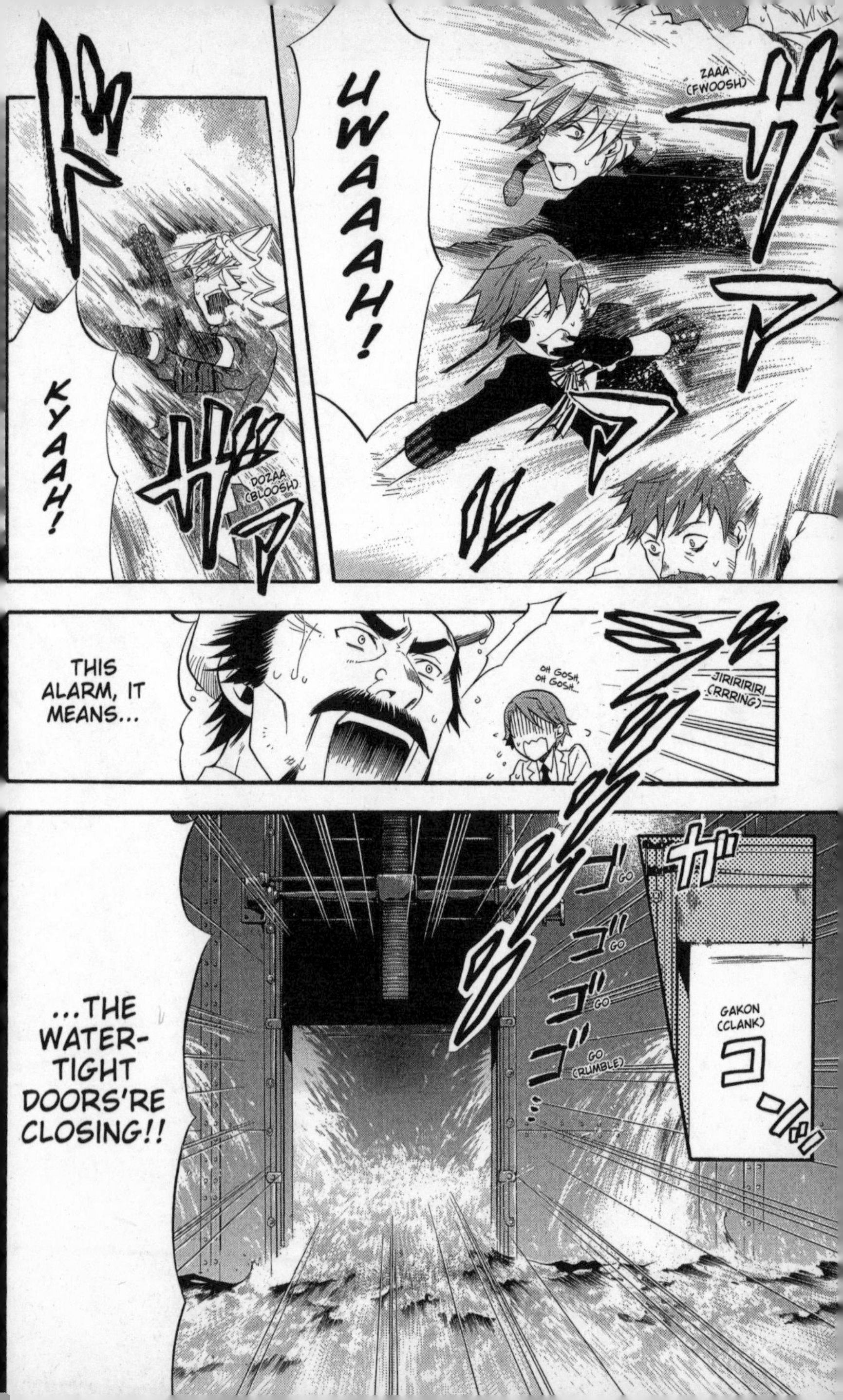
ZAAA (FWOOSH)
UWAAAAH!
DOZAA (BLOOSH)
KYAAAH!
JIRIRIRIRI (RRRING)
OH GOSH, OH GOSH...
THIS ALARM, IT MEANS...
GAKON (CLANK)
GO GO GO GO (RUMBLE)
...THE WATER-TIGHT DOORS'RE CLOSING!!

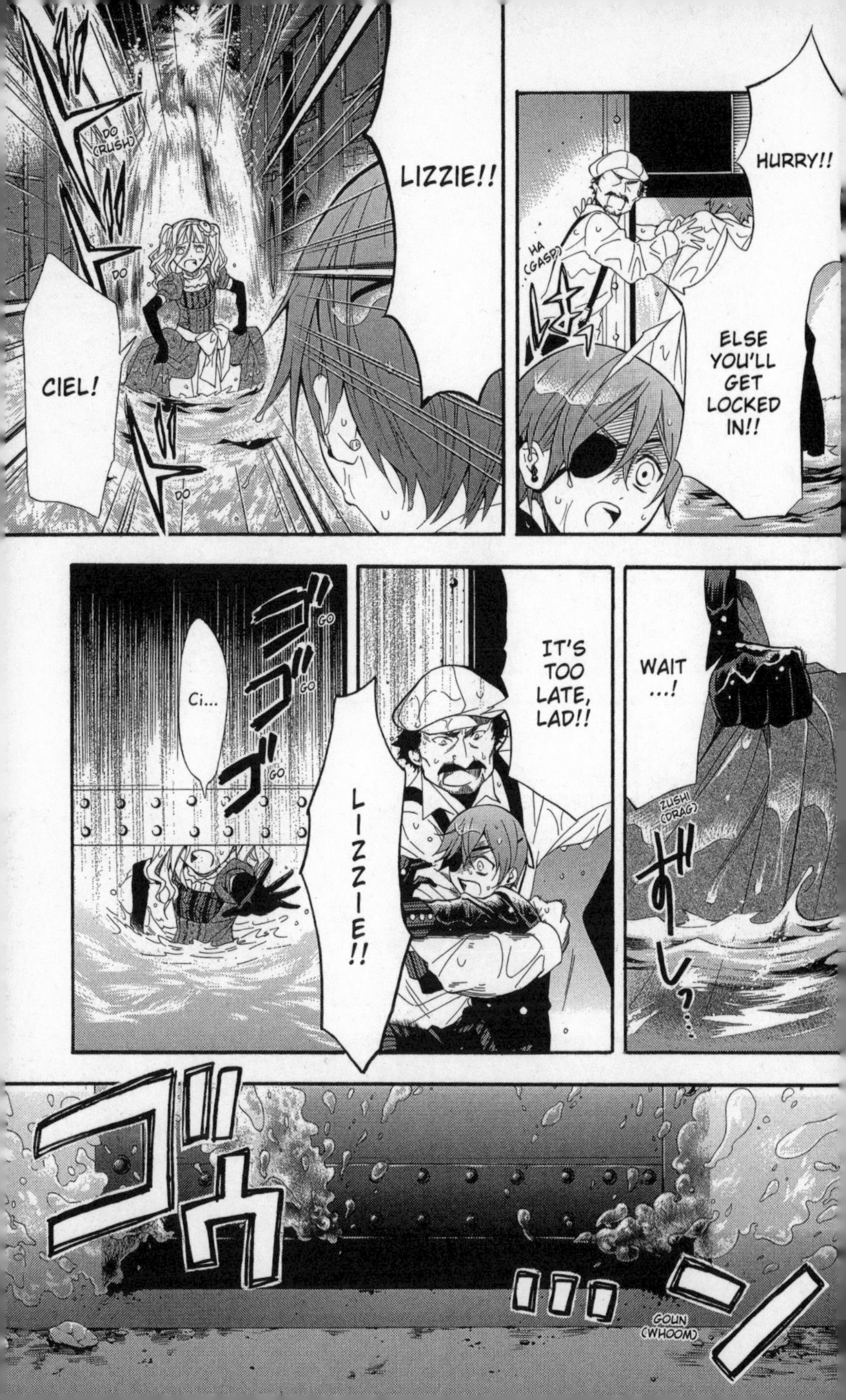
HURRY!!
HA (GASP)
ELSE YOU'LL GET LOCKED IN!!
LIZZIE!!
DO (RUSH)
DO
CIEL!
DO
WAIT ...!
ZUSHI (DRAG)
IT'S TOO LATE, LAD!!
LIZZIE!!
GO
GO
GO
Ci...
GOUN (WHOOM)

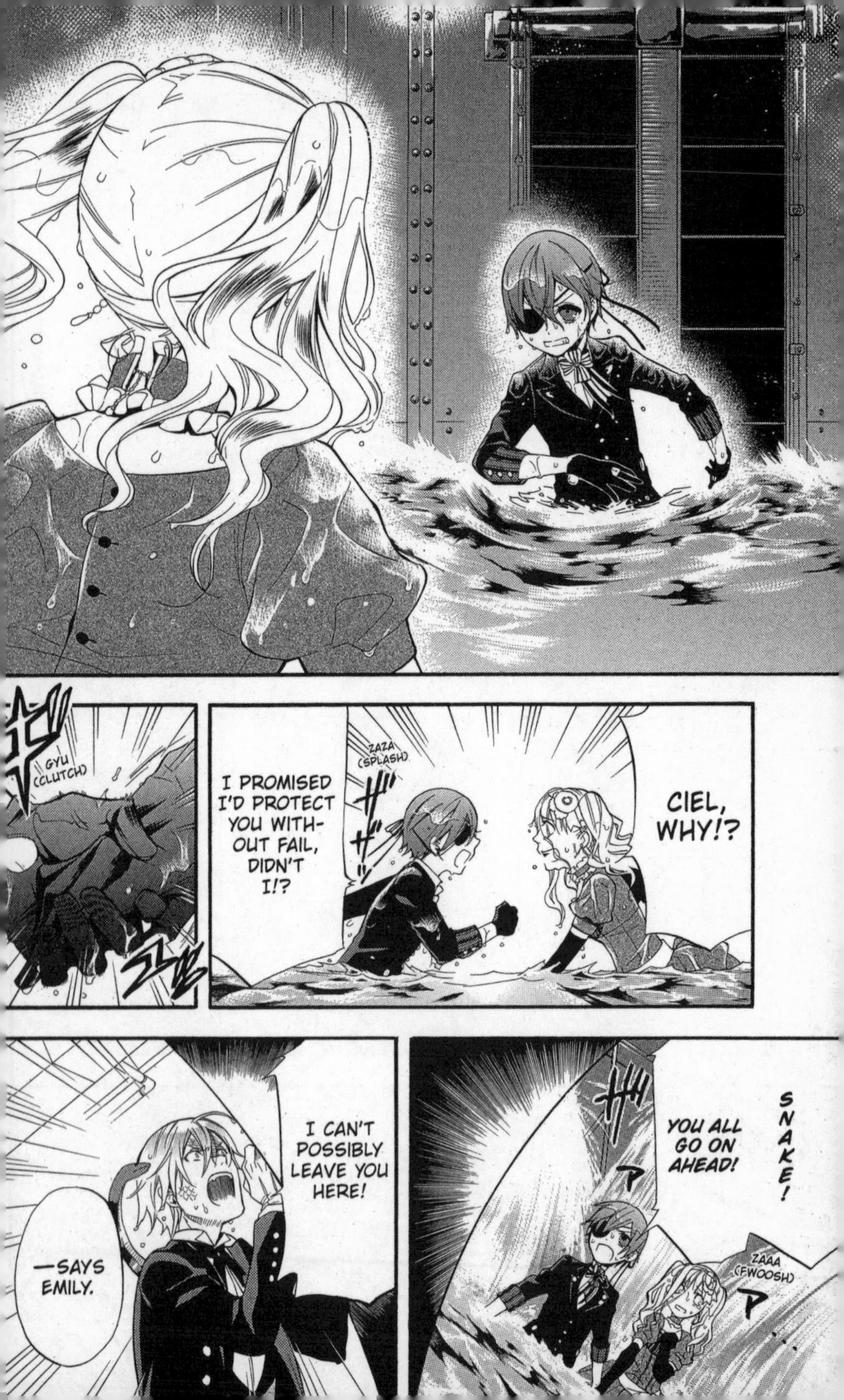
CIEL, WHY!?
ZAZA (SPLASH)
I PROMISED I'D PROTECT YOU WITHOUT FAIL, DIDN'T I!?
GYU (CLUTCH)
SNAKE!
YOU ALL GO ON AHEAD!
ZAAA (FWOOSH)
I CAN'T POSSIBLY LEAVE YOU HERE!
—SAYS EMILY.

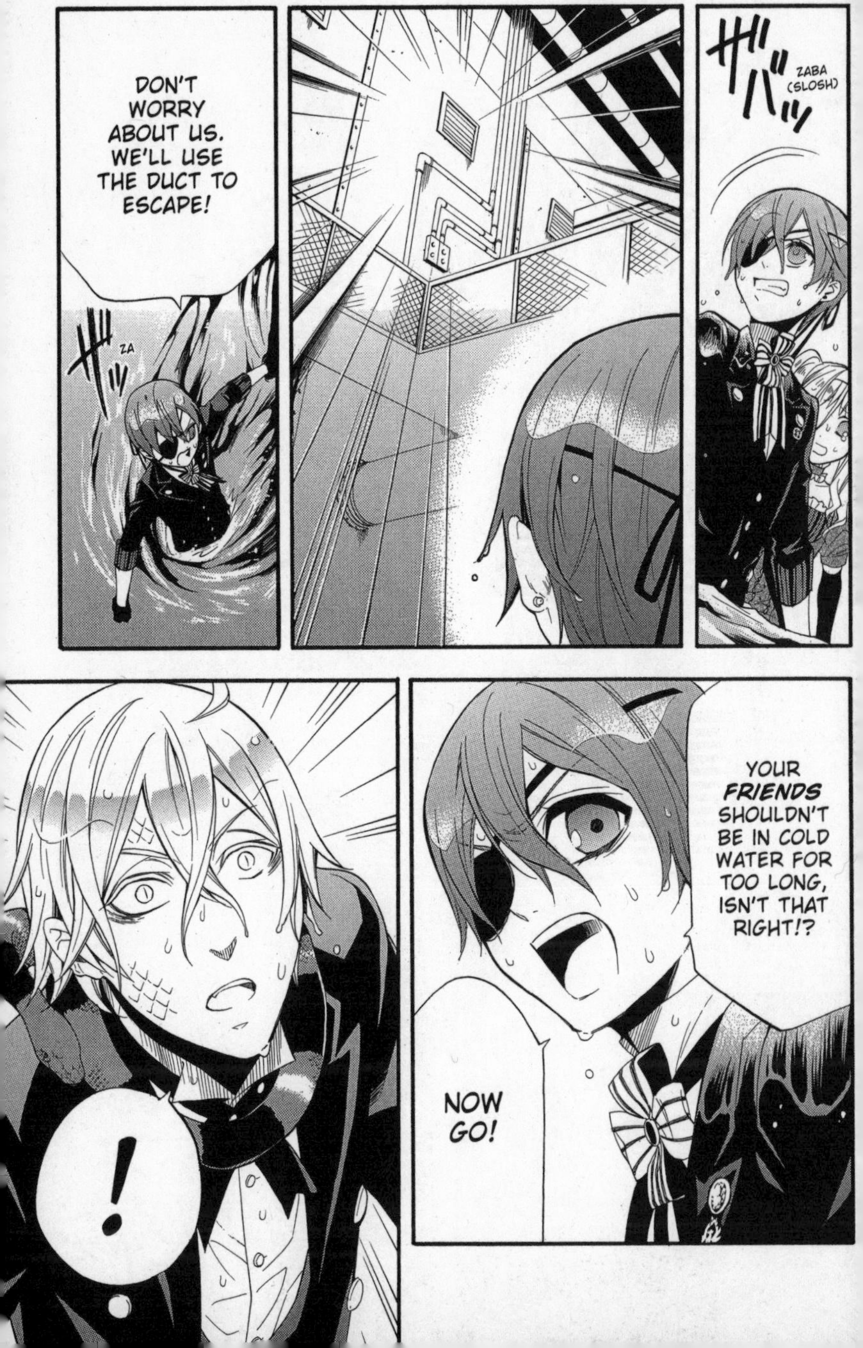
ザバッ
ZABA (SLOSH)
ザッ
ZA
DON'T WORRY ABOUT US. WE'LL USE THE DUCT TO ESCAPE!
YOUR *FRIENDS* SHOULDN'T BE IN COLD WATER FOR TOO LONG, ISN'T THAT RIGHT!?
NOW GO!
!

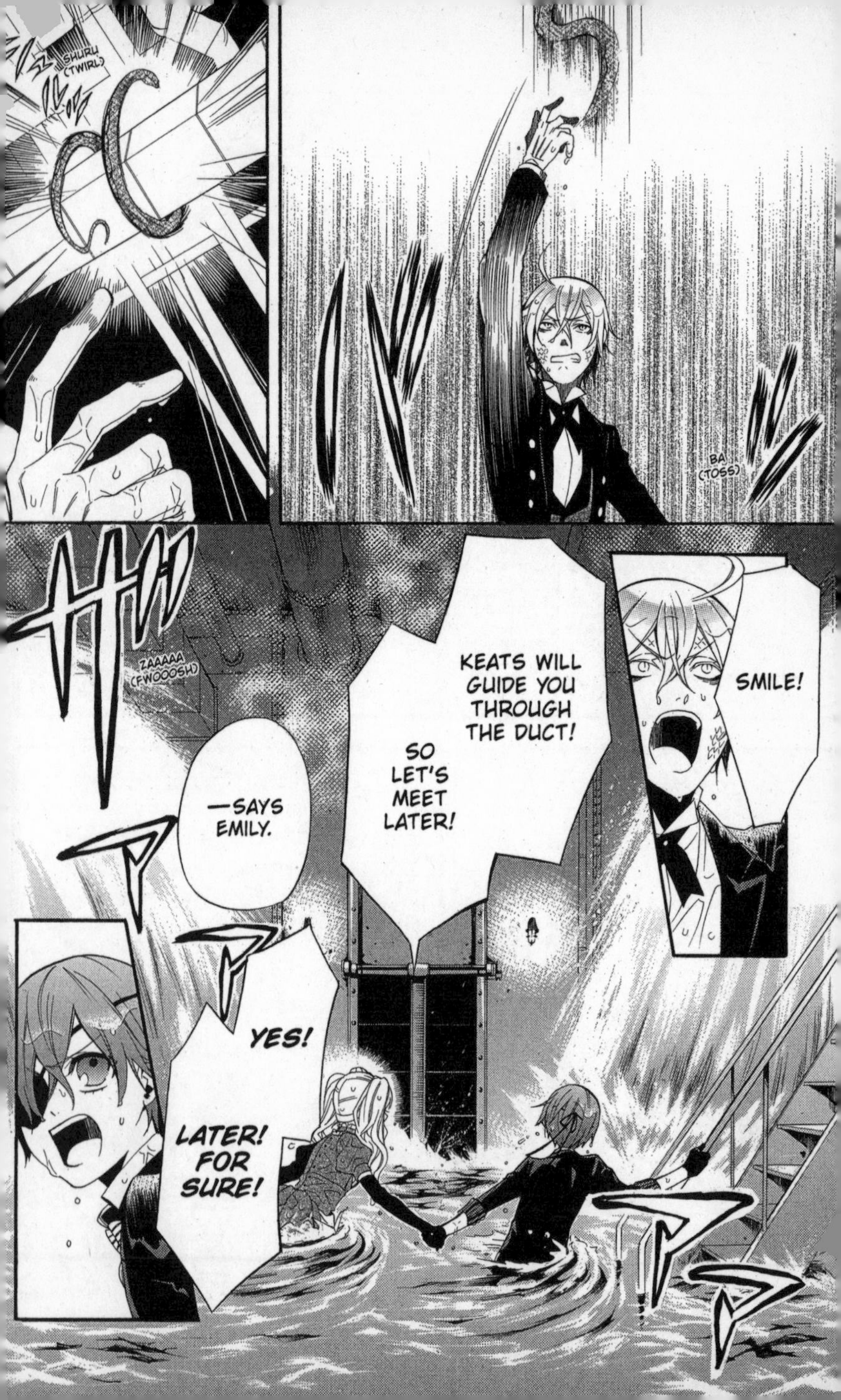
BA
(TOSS)
SHURU
(TWIRL)
SMILE!
KEATS WILL GUIDE YOU THROUGH THE DUCT!
SO LET'S MEET LATER!
—SAYS EMILY.
ZAAAAA
(FWOOOSH)
YES!
LATER! FOR SURE!

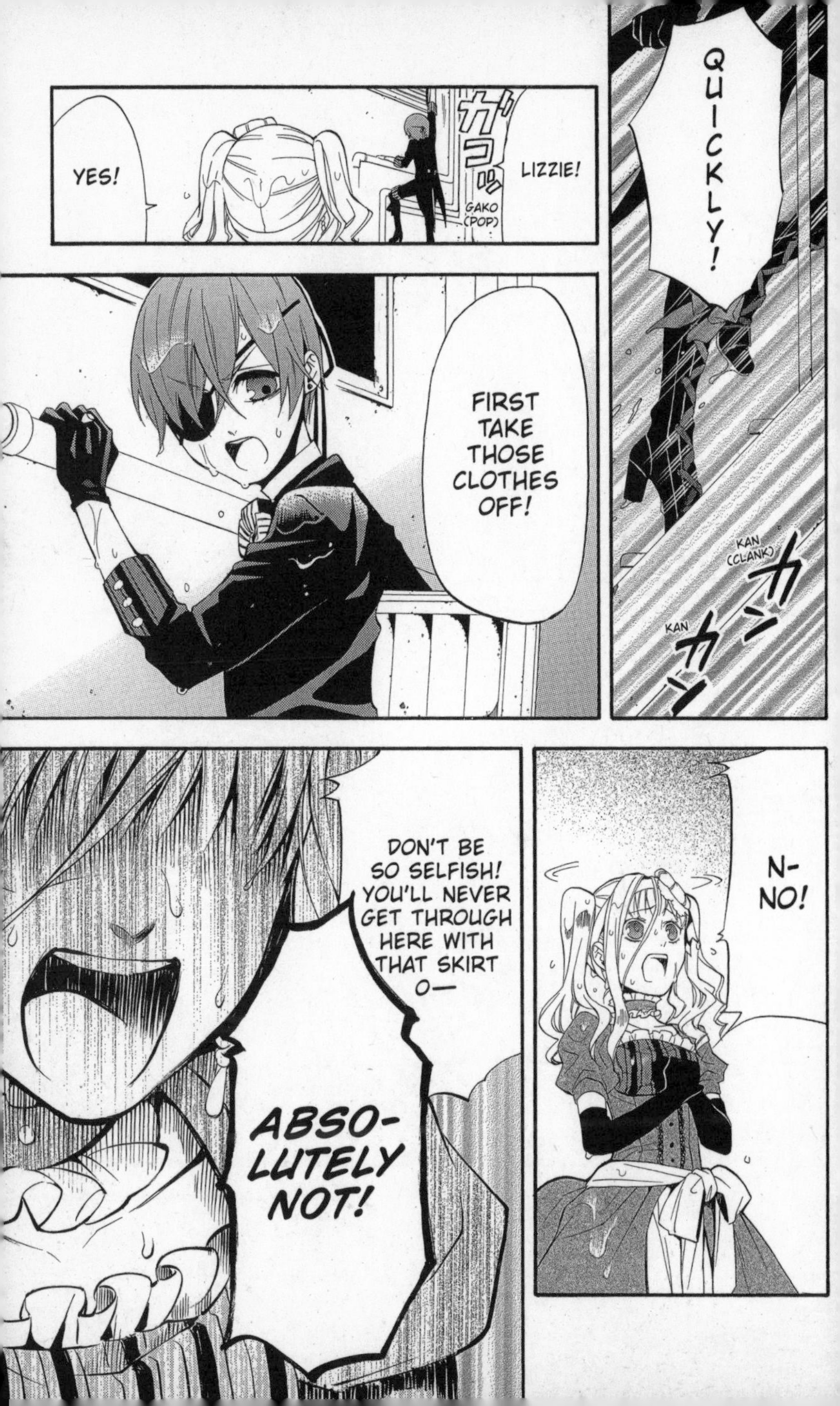
QUICKLY!
KAN (CLANK)
KAN
LIZZIE!
GAKO (POP)
YES!
FIRST TAKE THOSE CLOTHES OFF!
N-NO!
DON'T BE SO SELFISH! YOU'LL NEVER GET THROUGH HERE WITH THAT SKIRT O—
ABSOLUTELY NOT!

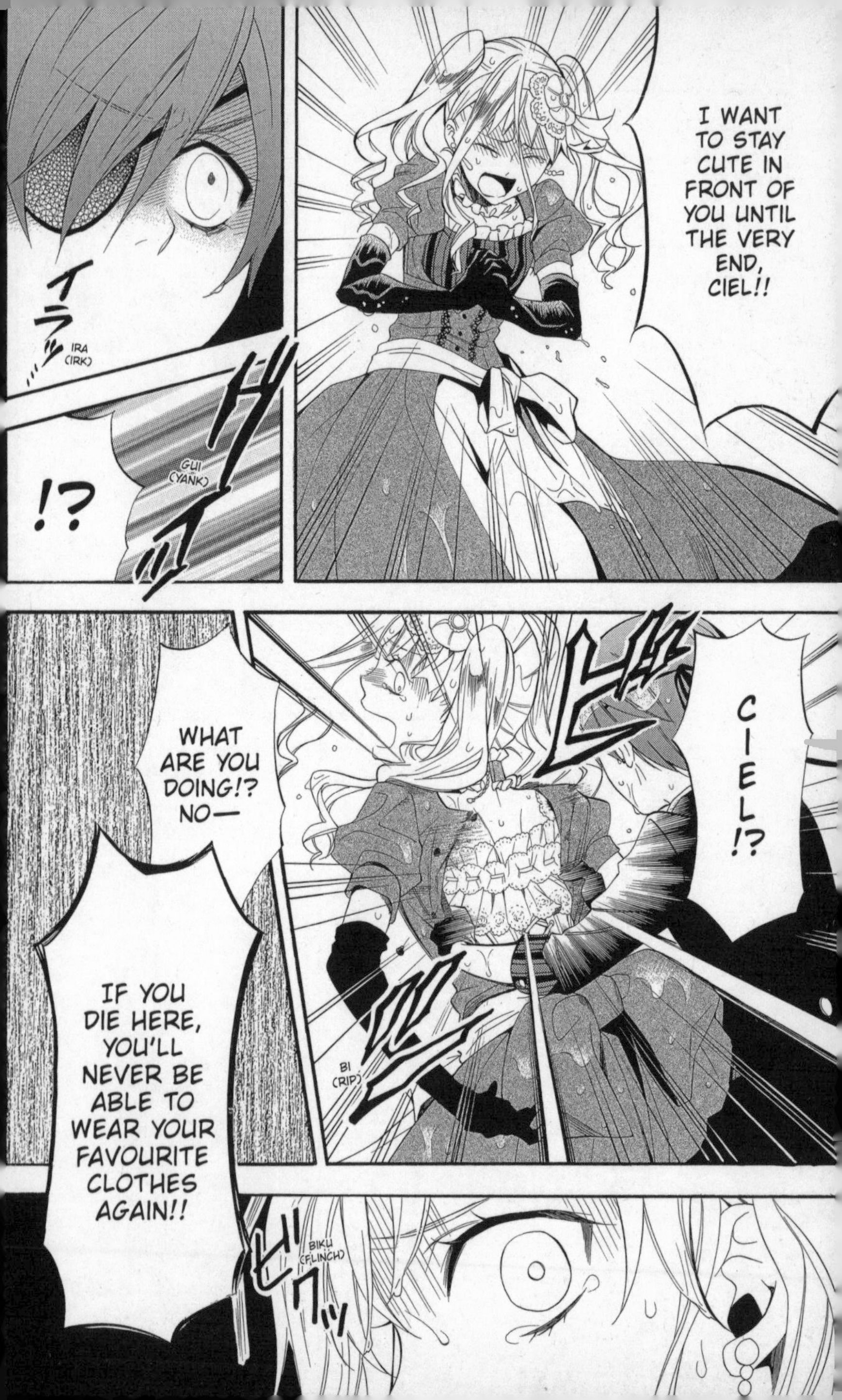
I WANT TO STAY CUTE IN FRONT OF YOU UNTIL THE VERY END, CIEL!!
IRA (IRK)
GUI (YANK)
!?
CIEL!?
WHAT ARE YOU DOING!? NO—
BI (RIP)
IF YOU DIE HERE, YOU'LL NEVER BE ABLE TO WEAR YOUR FAVOURITE CLOTHES AGAIN!!
BIKU (FLINCH)

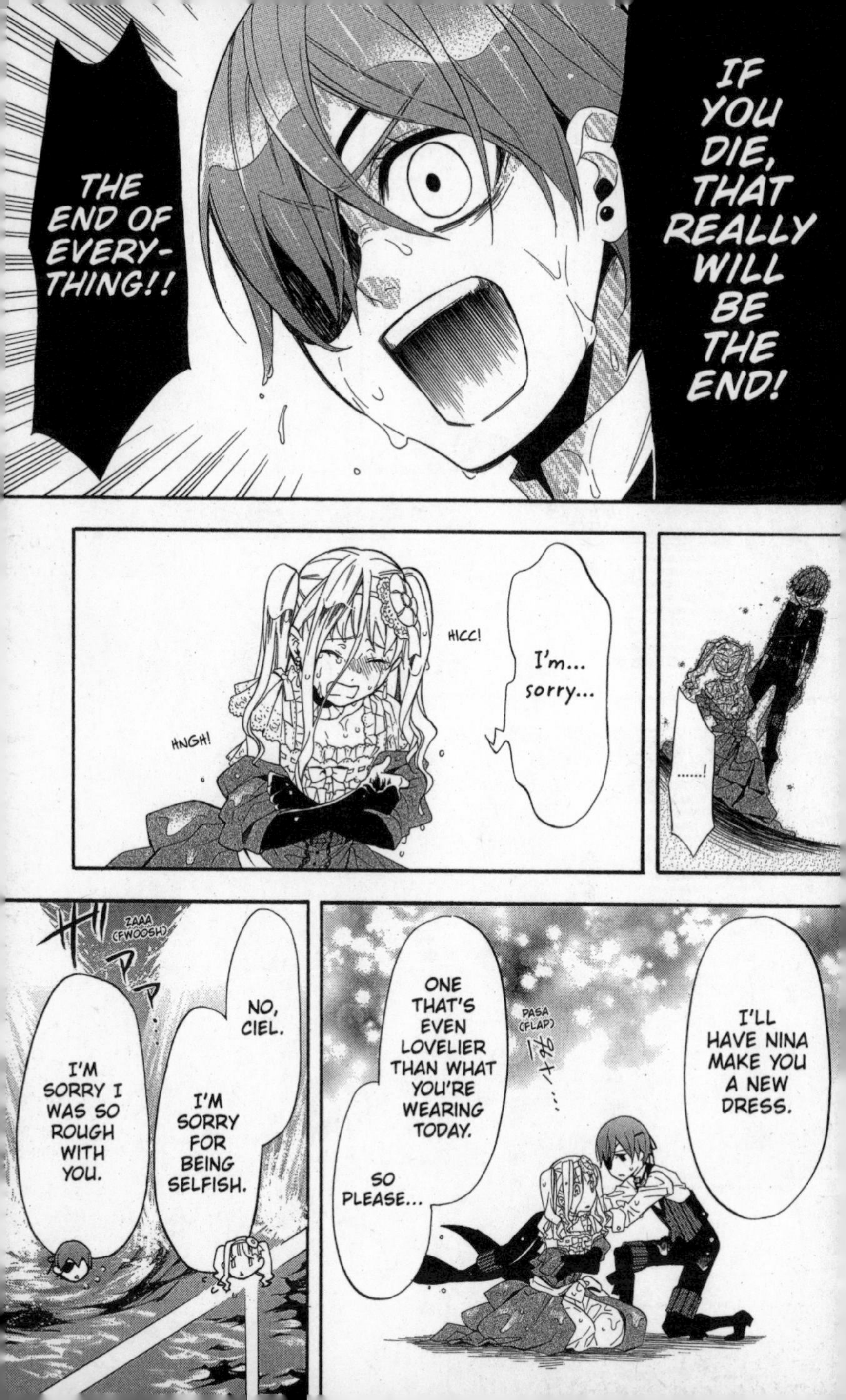
IF YOU DIE, THAT REALLY WILL BE THE END!
THE END OF EVERY-THING!!
......!
HICC!
I'm... sorry...
HNGH!
I'LL HAVE NINA MAKE YOU A NEW DRESS.
PASA (FLAP)
ONE THAT'S EVEN LOVELIER THAN WHAT YOU'RE WEARING TODAY.
SO PLEASE...
ZAAA (FWOOSH)
NO, CIEL.
I'M SORRY FOR BEING SELFISH.
I'M SORRY I WAS SO ROUGH WITH YOU.

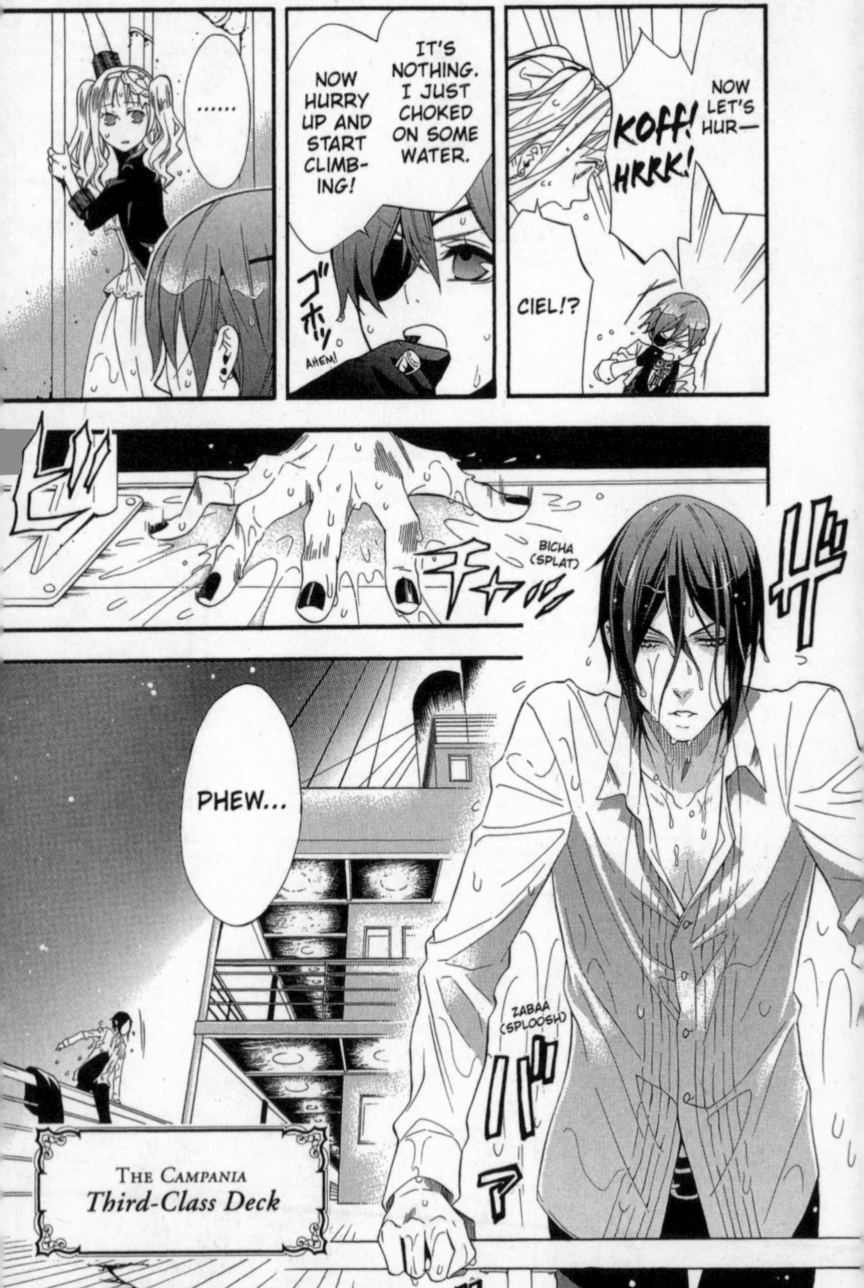
NOW LET'S HUR—
KOFF! HRRK!
CIEL!?
IT'S NOTHING. I JUST CHOKED ON SOME WATER.
NOW HURRY UP AND START CLIMBING!
AHEM!
......
BICHA (SPLAT)
PHEW...
ZABAA (SPLOOSH)
THE CAMPANIA
Third-Class Deck

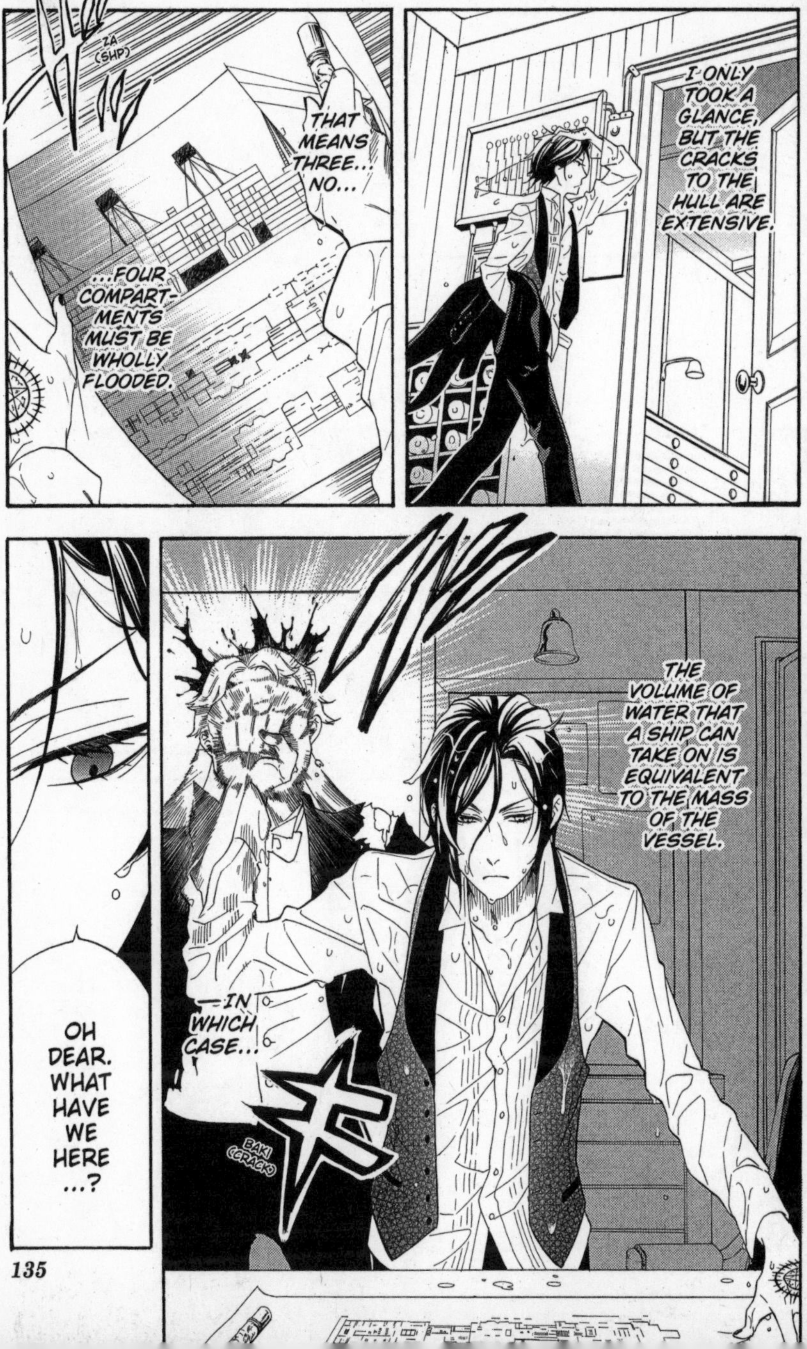
I ONLY TOOK A GLANCE, BUT THE CRACKS TO THE HULL ARE EXTENSIVE.
ZA (SHP)
THAT MEANS THREE... NO...
...FOUR COMPART-MENTS MUST BE WHOLLY FLOODED.
THE VOLUME OF WATER THAT A SHIP CAN TAKE ON IS EQUIVALENT TO THE MASS OF THE VESSEL.
—IN WHICH CASE...
BAKI (CRACK)
OH DEAR. WHAT HAVE WE HERE ...?

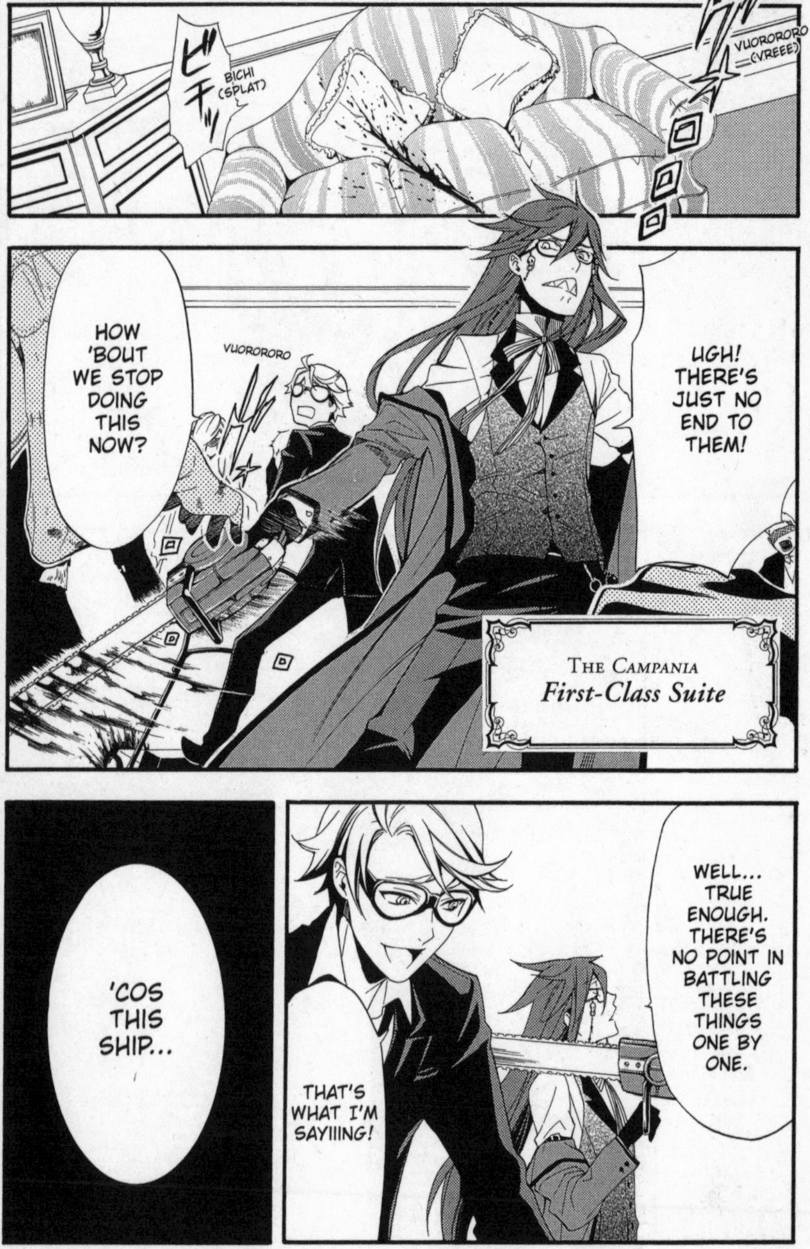
VUORORORO (VREEE)
BICHI (SPLAT)
UGH! THERE'S JUST NO END TO THEM!
THE CAMPANIA First-Class Suite
VUORORORO
HOW 'BOUT WE STOP DOING THIS NOW?
WELL... TRUE ENOUGH. THERE'S NO POINT IN BATTLING THESE THINGS ONE BY ONE.
THAT'S WHAT I'M SAYIIING!
'COS THIS SHIP...

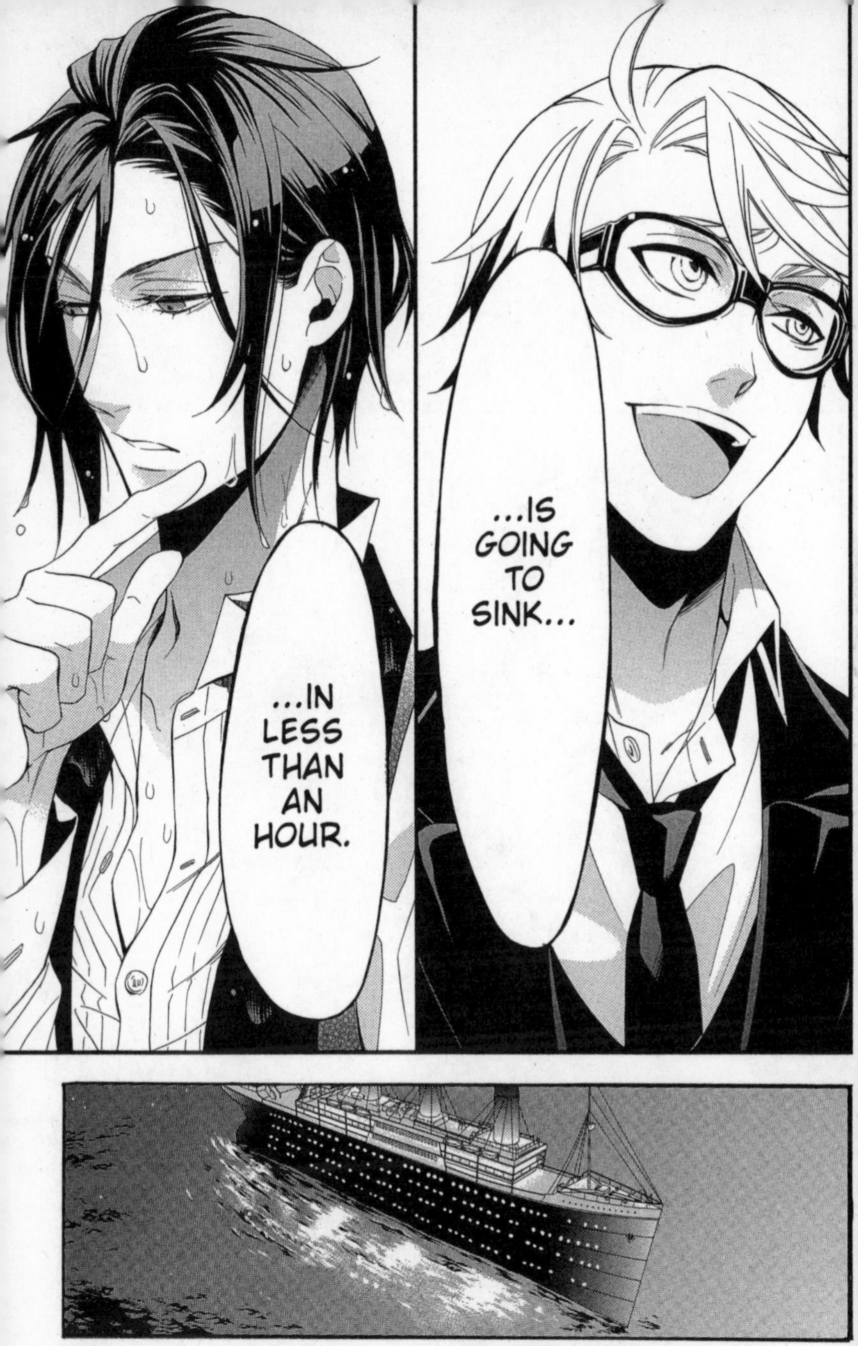
...IS GOING TO SINK...
...IN LESS THAN AN HOUR.

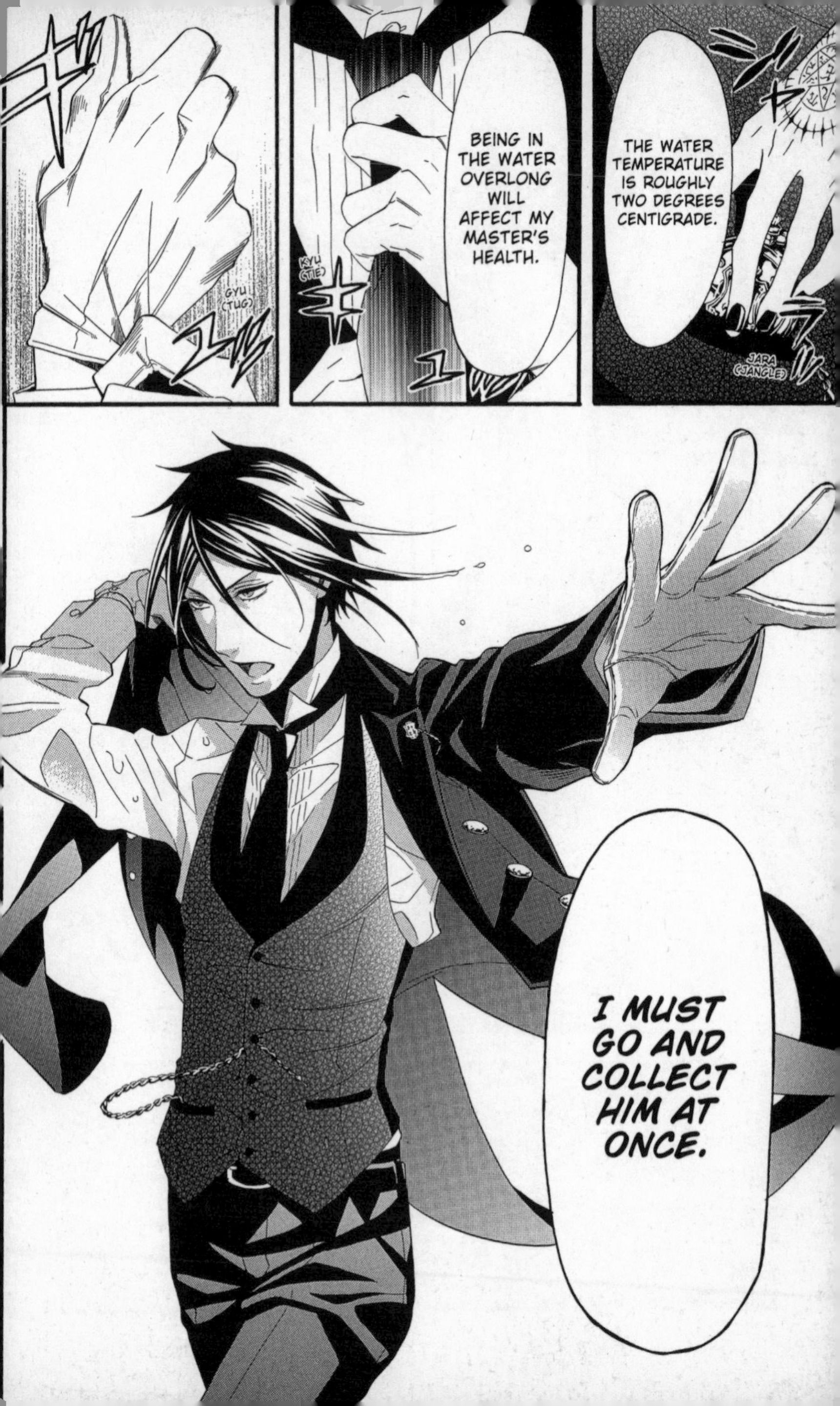
THE WATER TEMPERATURE IS ROUGHLY TWO DEGREES CENTIGRADE.
JARA (JANGLE)
BEING IN THE WATER OVERLONG WILL AFFECT MY MASTER'S HEALTH.
KYU (TIE)
GYU (TUG)
I MUST GO AND COLLECT HIM AT ONCE.

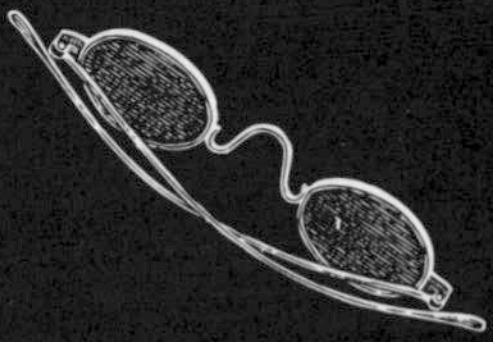

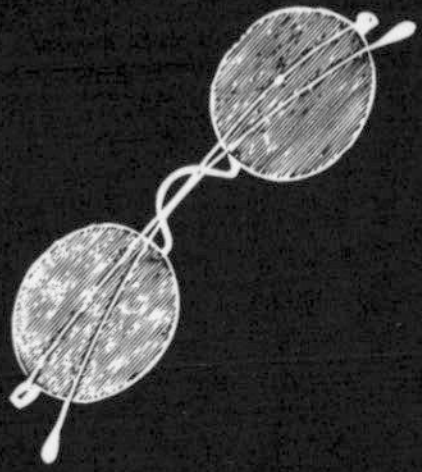

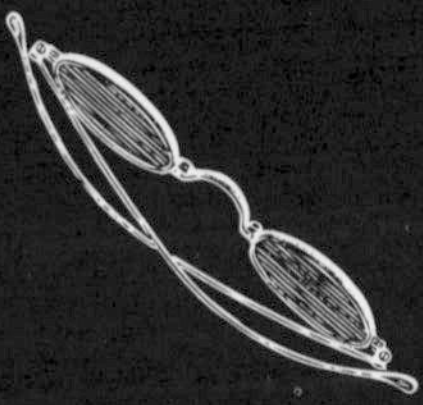

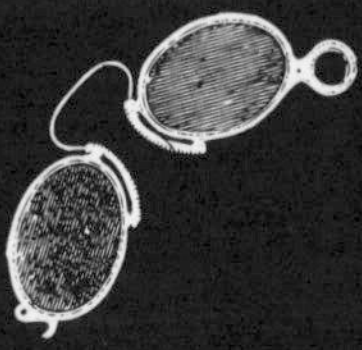

Black Butler

Chapter 57
At midnight : The Butler, Struggling

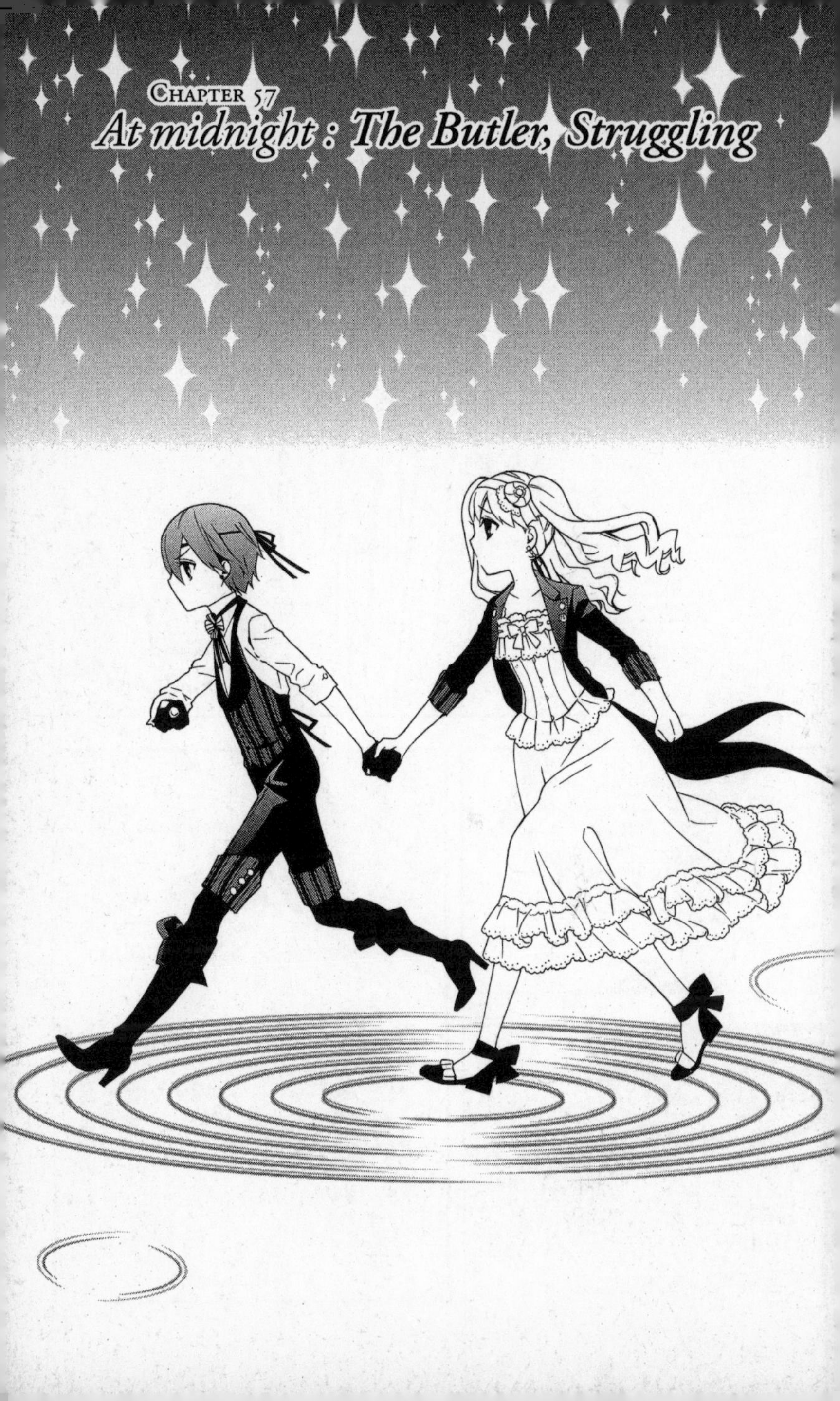

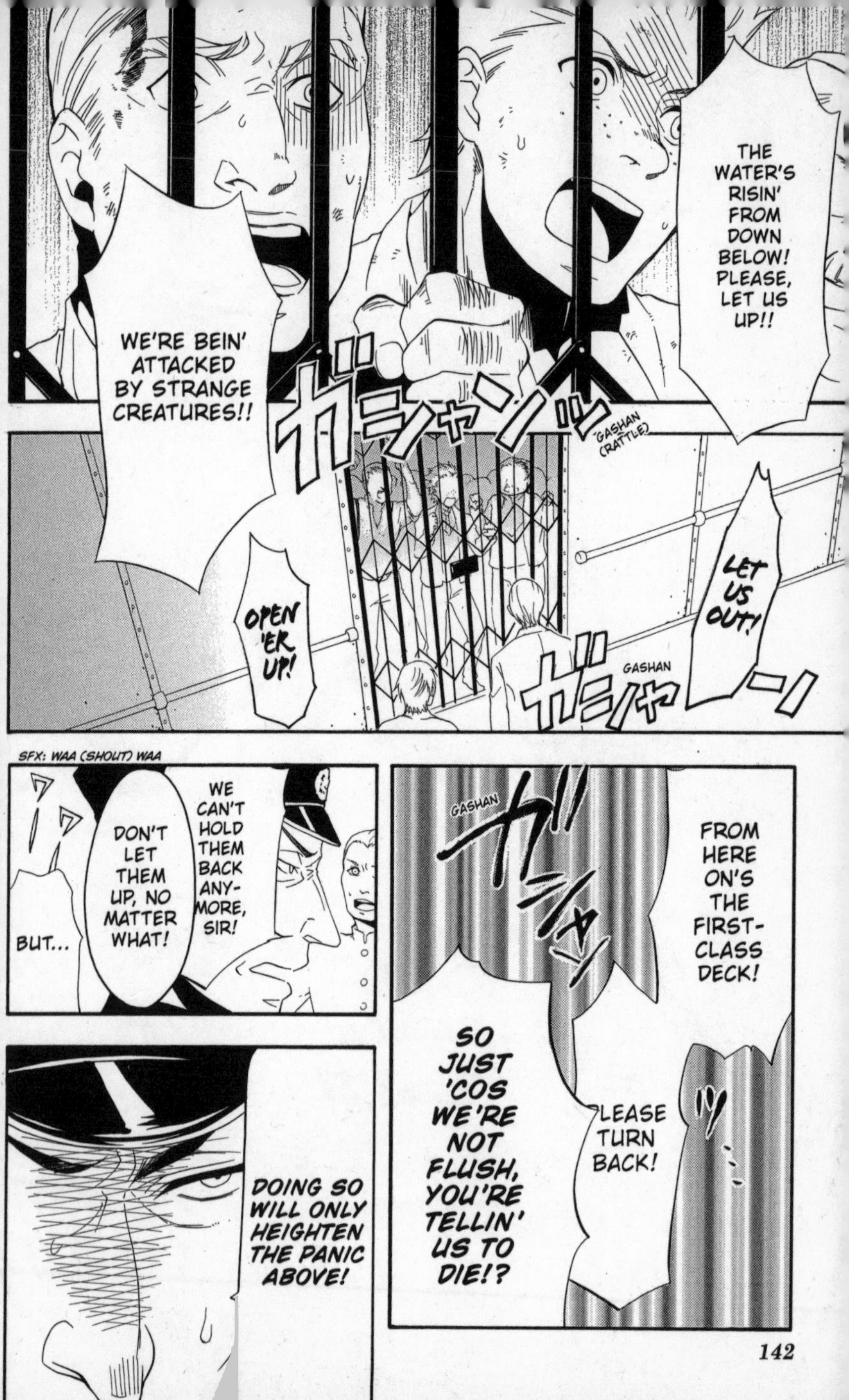
THE WATER'S RISIN' FROM DOWN BELOW! PLEASE, LET US UP!!
WE'RE BEIN' ATTACKED BY STRANGE CREATURES!!
GASHAN (RATTLE)
LET US OUT!
GASHAN
OPEN 'ER UP!
SFX: WAA (SHOUT) WAA
GASHAN
FROM HERE ON'S THE FIRST-CLASS DECK!
LEASE TURN BACK!
SO JUST 'COS WE'RE NOT FLUSH, YOU'RE TELLIN' US TO DIE!?
WE CAN'T HOLD THEM BACK ANYMORE, SIR!
DON'T LET THEM UP, NO MATTER WHAT!
BUT...
DOING SO WILL ONLY HEIGHTEN THE PANIC ABOVE!

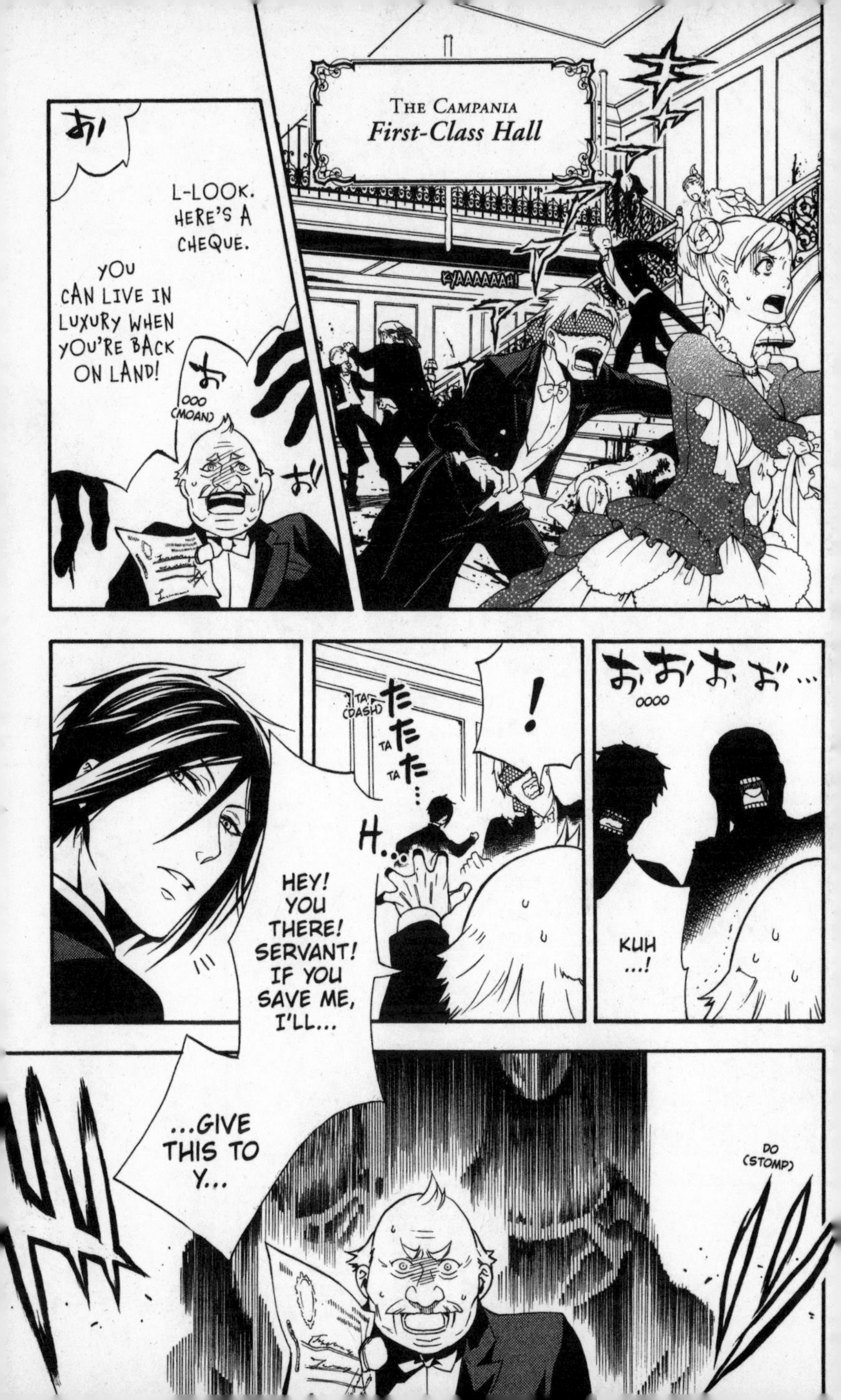

THE CAMPANIA
First-Class Hall
KYAAAAAAH!
あ!
L-LOOK. HERE'S A CHEQUE.
YOU CAN LIVE IN LUXURY WHEN YOU'RE BACK ON LAND!
お
OOO (MOAN)
お
おおおお…
OOOO
KUH …!
!
TA (DASH)
たたた…
TA
TA
H…
HEY! YOU THERE! SERVANT! IF YOU SAVE ME, I'LL…
…GIVE THIS TO Y…
DO (STOMP)

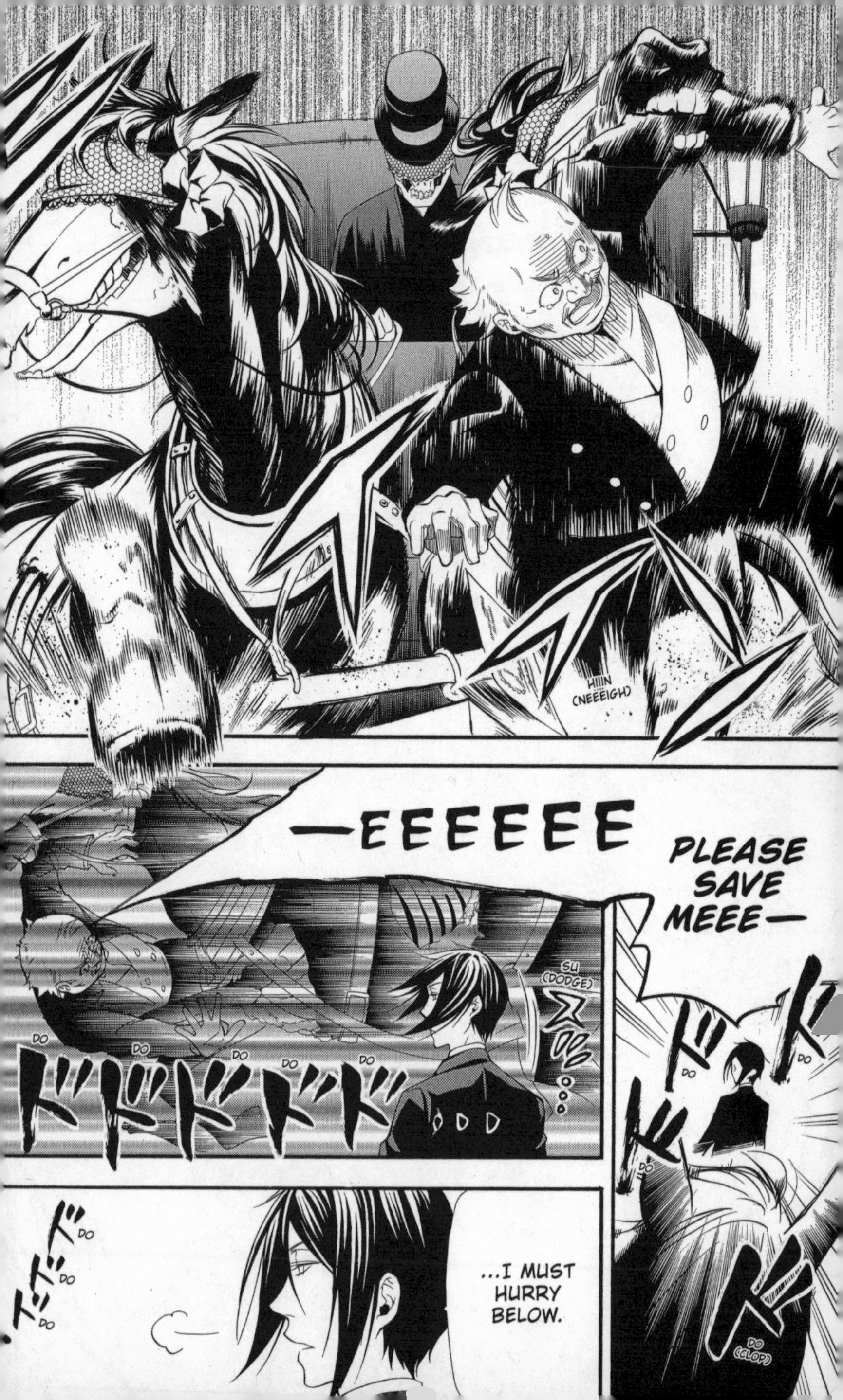
HIIIN
(NEEEIGH)
PLEASE SAVE MEEE—
DO DO DO DO
ドドドド
DO
(CLOP)
—EEEEEE
SU
(DODGE)
DO DO DO DO DO
ドドドドドド
DO DO DO
ドドド
...I MUST HURRY BELOW.

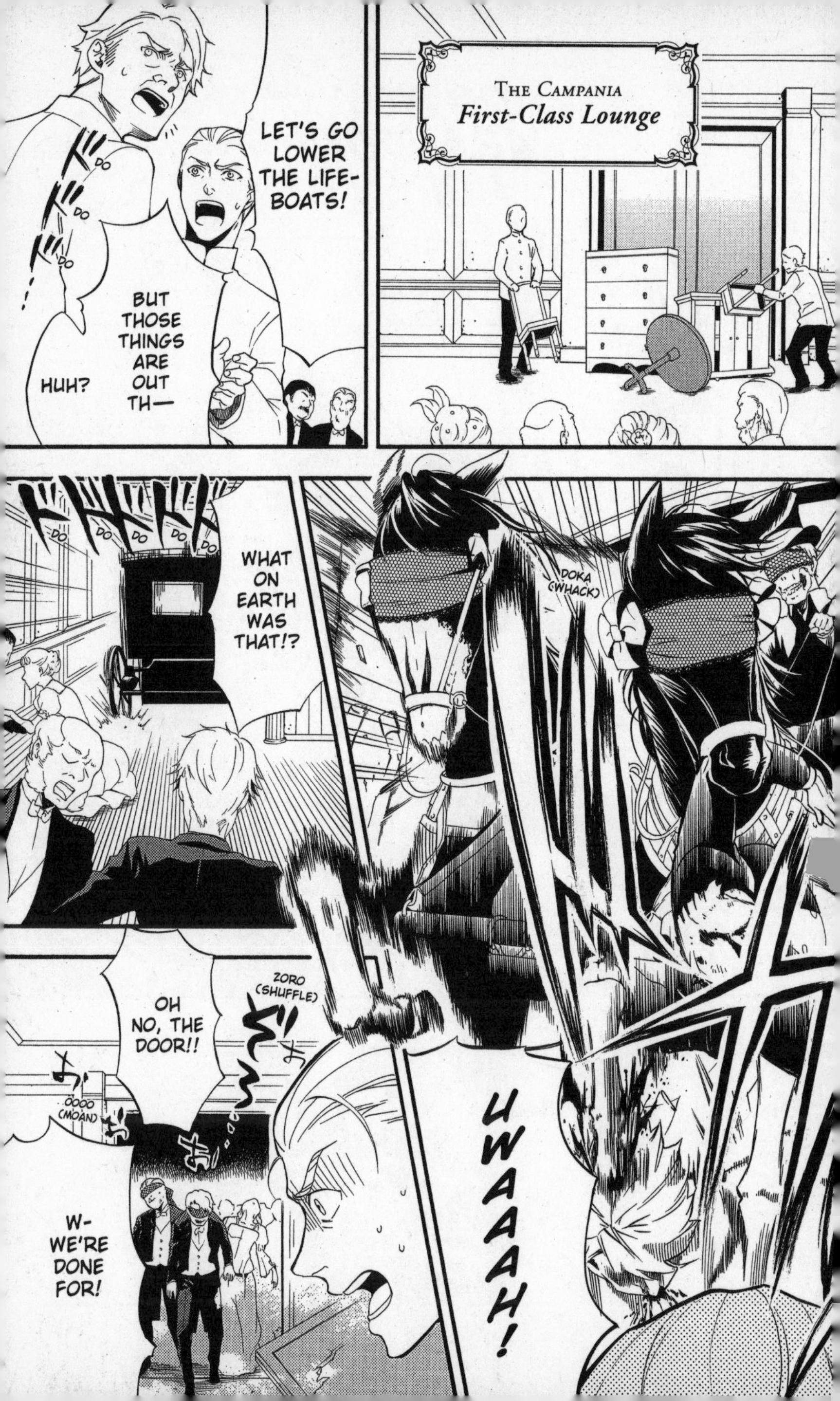

THE CAMPANIA
First-Class Lounge
LET'S GO LOWER THE LIFE-BOATS!
DO DO DO
BUT THOSE THINGS ARE OUT TH—
HUH?
DOKA (WHACK)
UWAAAH!
DO DO DO DO DO DO
WHAT ON EARTH WAS THAT!?
ZORO (SHUFFLE)
OH NO, THE DOOR!!
OOOO (MOAN)
W-WE'RE DONE FOR!

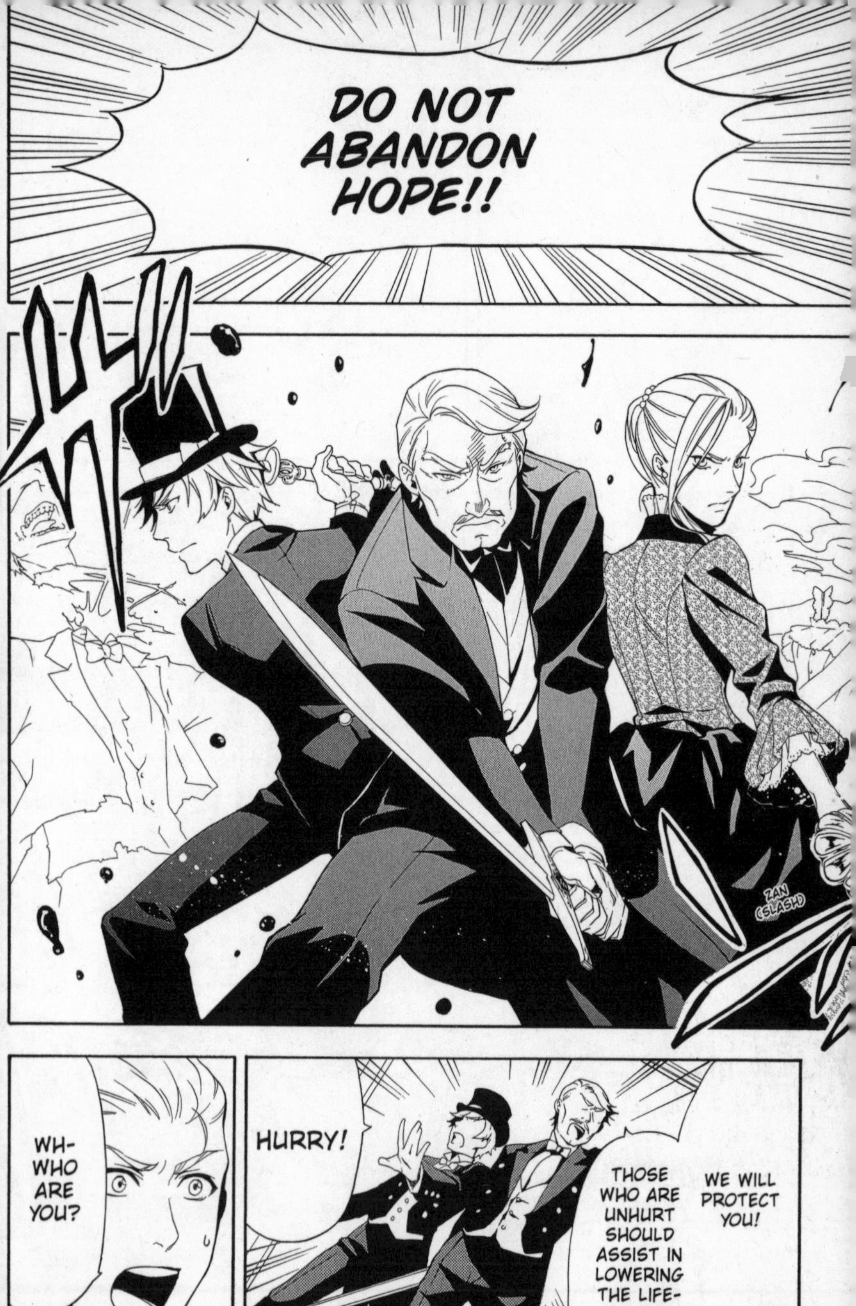
DO NOT ABANDON HOPE!!
ZAN (SLASH)
WE WILL PROTECT YOU!
THOSE WHO ARE UNHURT SHOULD ASSIST IN LOWERING THE LIFE-BOATS!
HURRY!
WH-WHO ARE YOU?

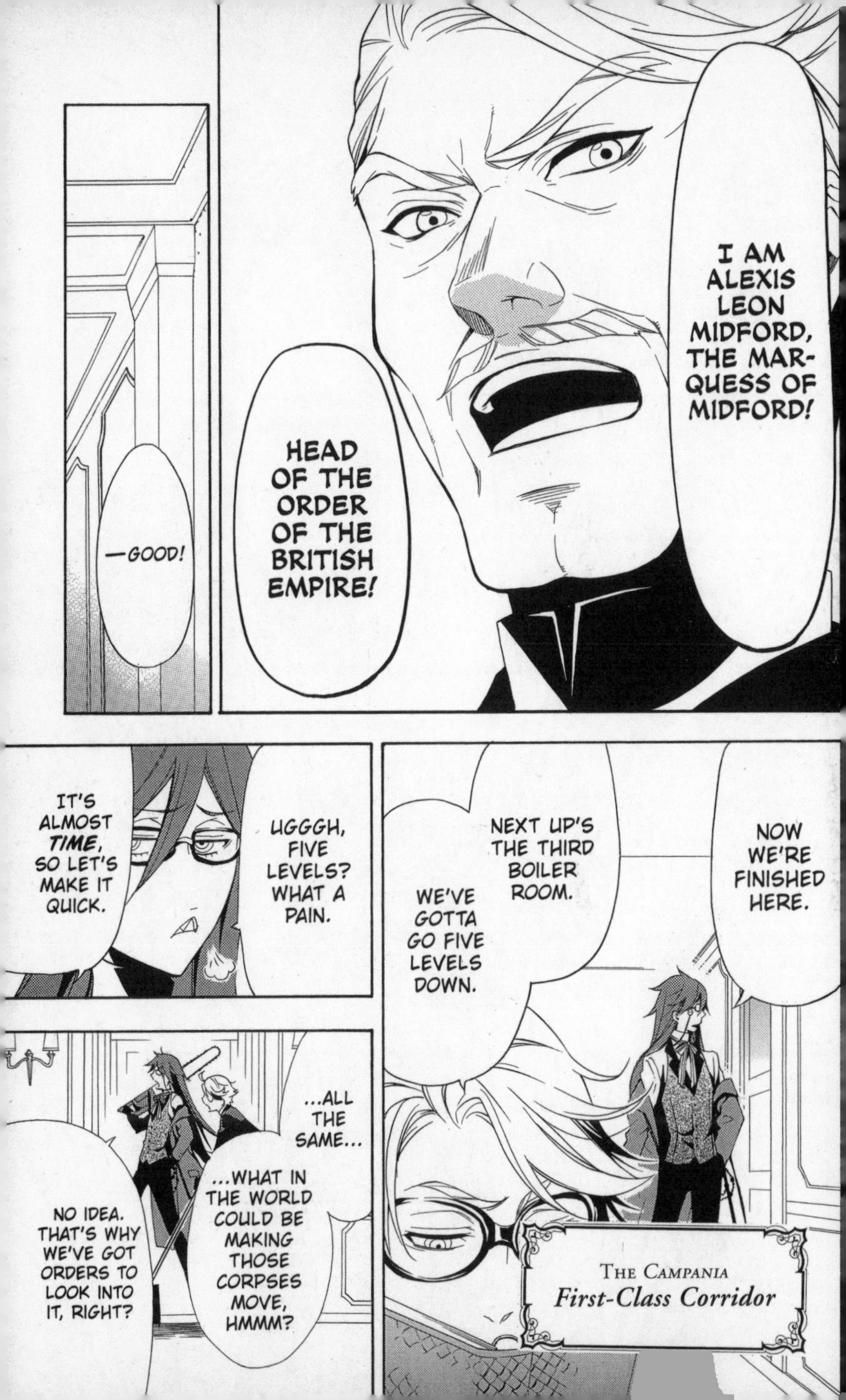
I AM ALEXIS LEON MIDFORD, THE MARQUESS OF MIDFORD!
HEAD OF THE ORDER OF THE BRITISH EMPIRE!
—GOOD!
NOW WE'RE FINISHED HERE.
NEXT UP'S THE THIRD BOILER ROOM.
WE'VE GOTTA GO FIVE LEVELS DOWN.
THE CAMPANIA
First-Class Corridor
UGGGH, FIVE LEVELS? WHAT A PAIN.
IT'S ALMOST *TIME*, SO LET'S MAKE IT QUICK.
...ALL THE SAME...
...WHAT IN THE WORLD COULD BE MAKING THOSE CORPSES MOVE, HMMM?
NO IDEA. THAT'S WHY WE'VE GOT ORDERS TO LOOK INTO IT, RIGHT?

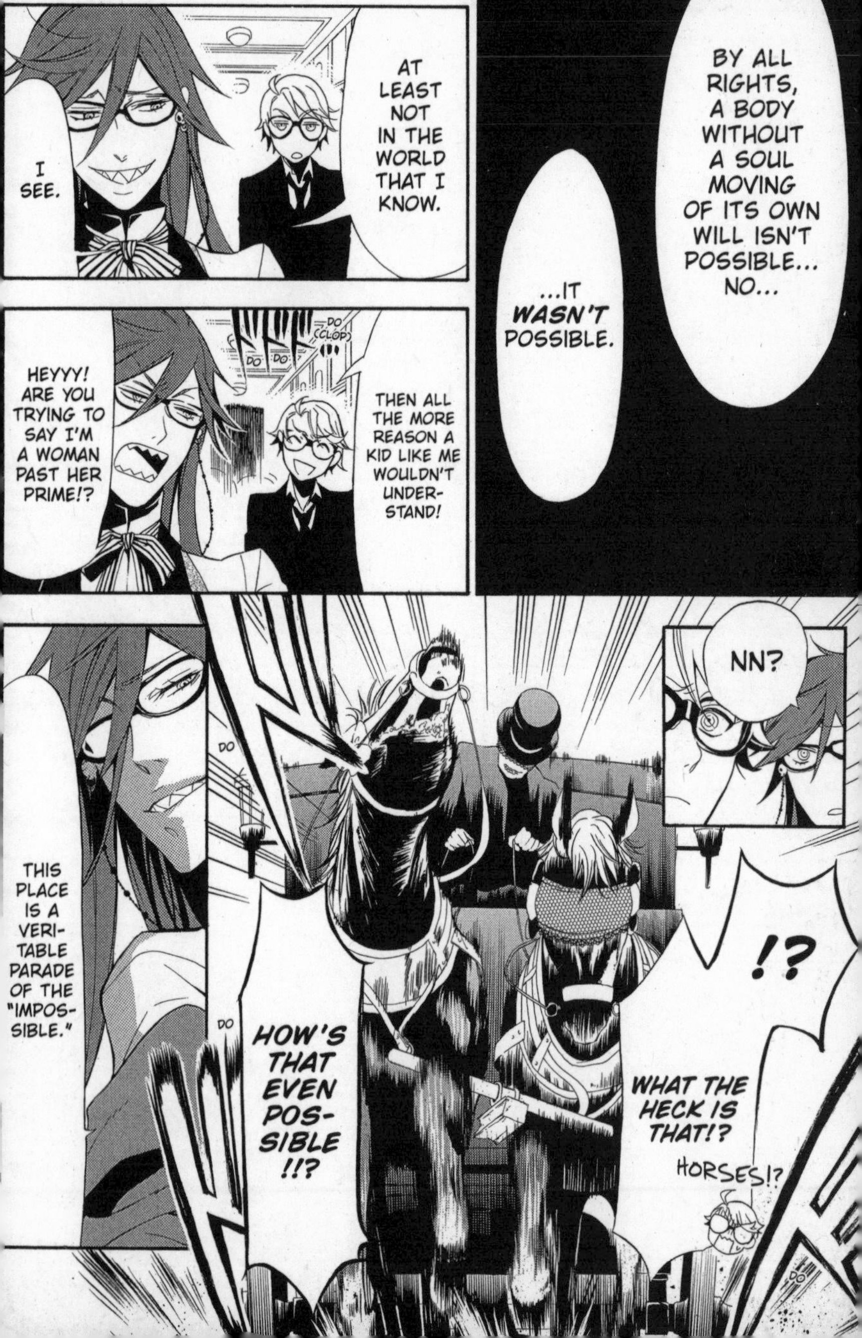
BY ALL RIGHTS, A BODY WITHOUT A SOUL MOVING OF ITS OWN WILL ISN'T POSSIBLE... NO...
...IT *WASN'T* POSSIBLE.
AT LEAST NOT IN THE WORLD THAT I KNOW.
I SEE.
DO (CLOP)
DO DO
THEN ALL THE MORE REASON A KID LIKE ME WOULDN'T UNDERSTAND!
HEYYY! ARE YOU TRYING TO SAY I'M A WOMAN PAST HER PRIME!?
NN?
!?
WHAT THE HECK IS THAT!?
HORSES!?
DO
HOW'S THAT EVEN POS-SIBLE!!?
DO
DO
THIS PLACE IS A VERI-TABLE PARADE OF THE "IMPOS-SIBLE."

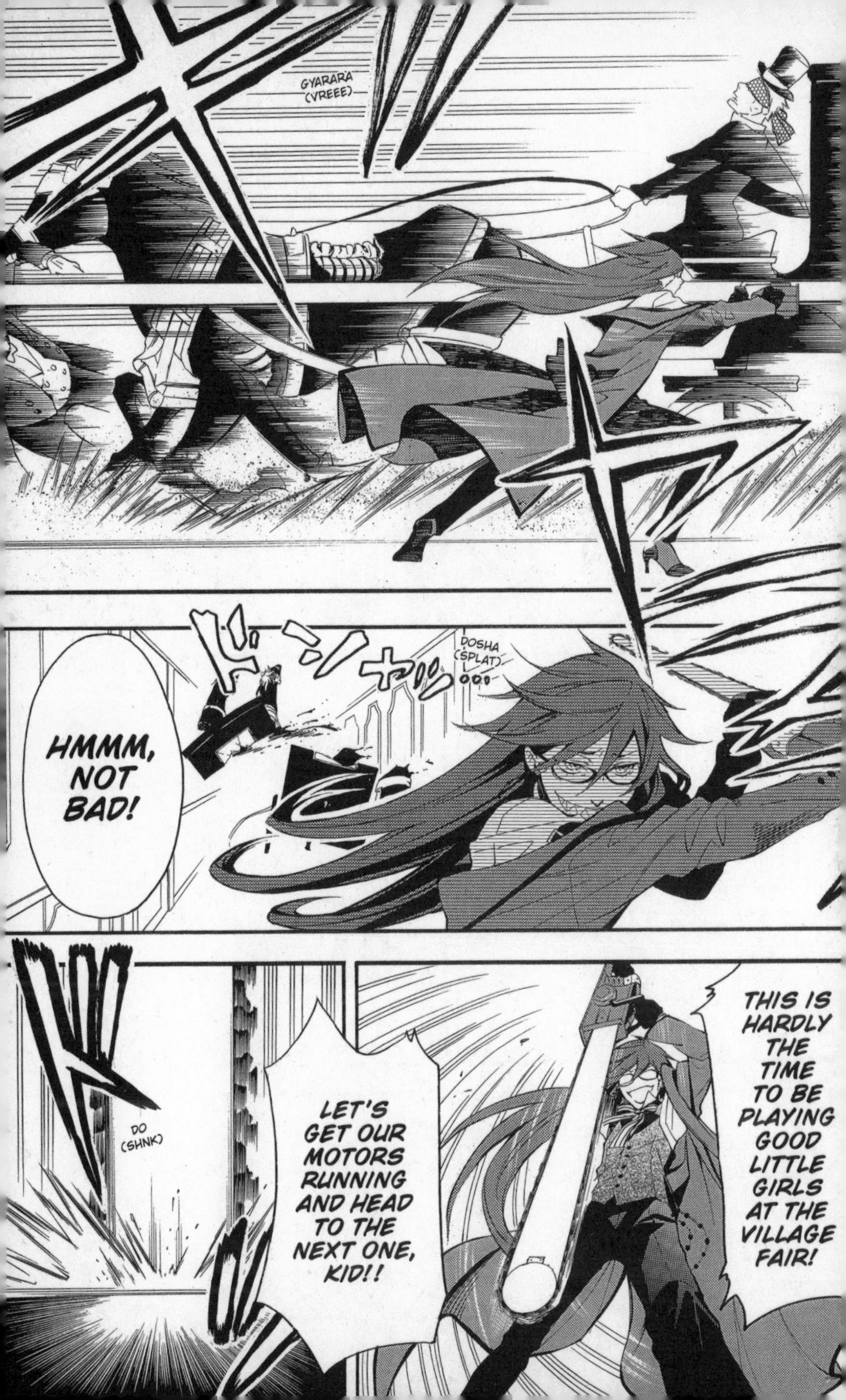
GYARARA (VREEE)
DOSHA (SPLAT)
HMMM, NOT BAD!
THIS IS HARDLY THE TIME TO BE PLAYING GOOD LITTLE GIRLS AT THE VILLAGE FAIR!
LET'S GET OUR MOTORS RUNNING AND HEAD TO THE NEXT ONE, KID!!
DO (SHNK)

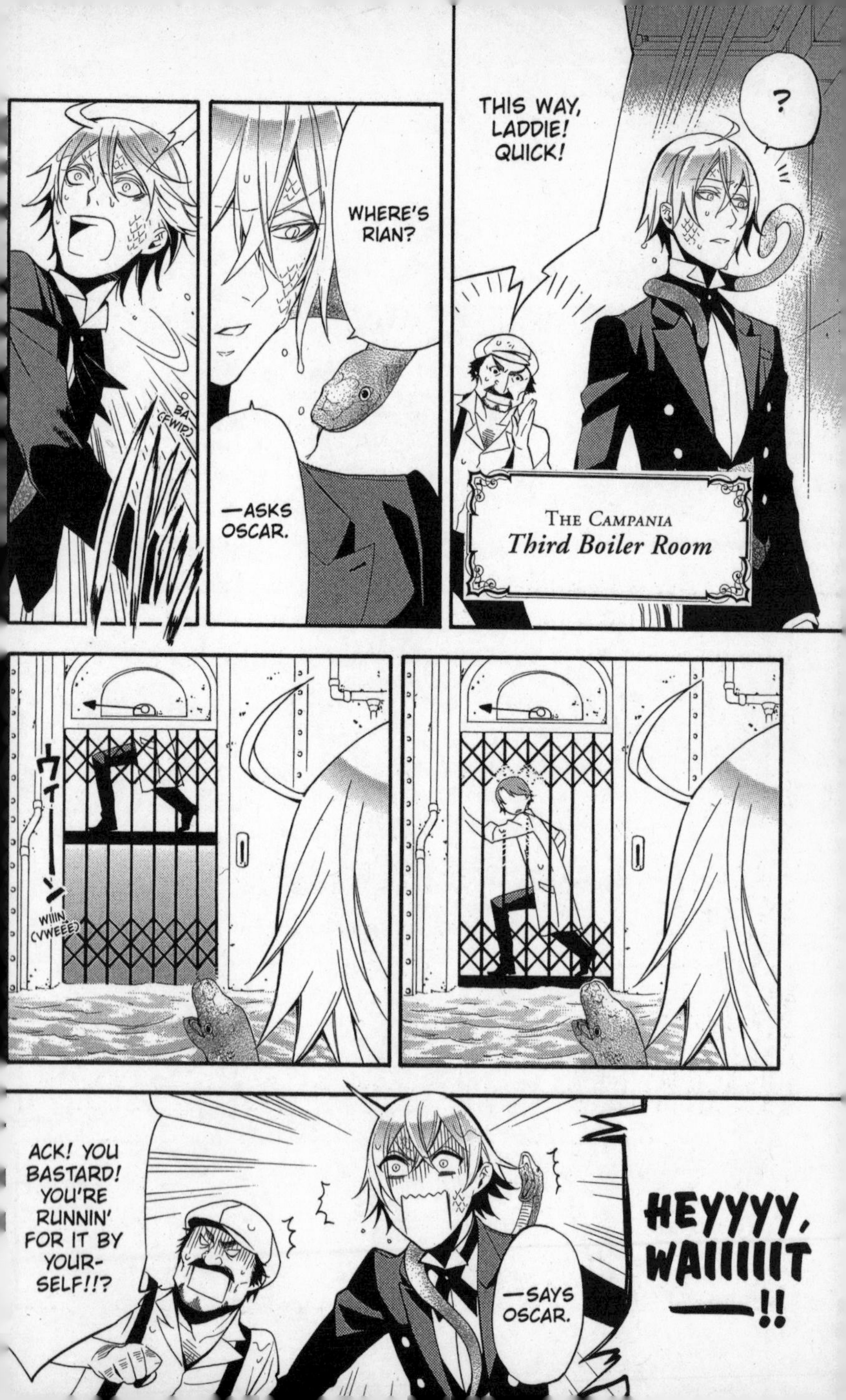
?
THIS WAY, LADDIE! QUICK!
THE CAMPANIA
Third Boiler Room
WHERE'S RIAN?
—ASKS OSCAR.
BA (FWIP)
ウィーン
WIIIN (VWEEE)
HEYYYY, WAIIIIIT——!!
—SAYS OSCAR.
ACK! YOU BASTARD! YOU'RE RUNNIN' FOR IT BY YOUR-SELF!!?

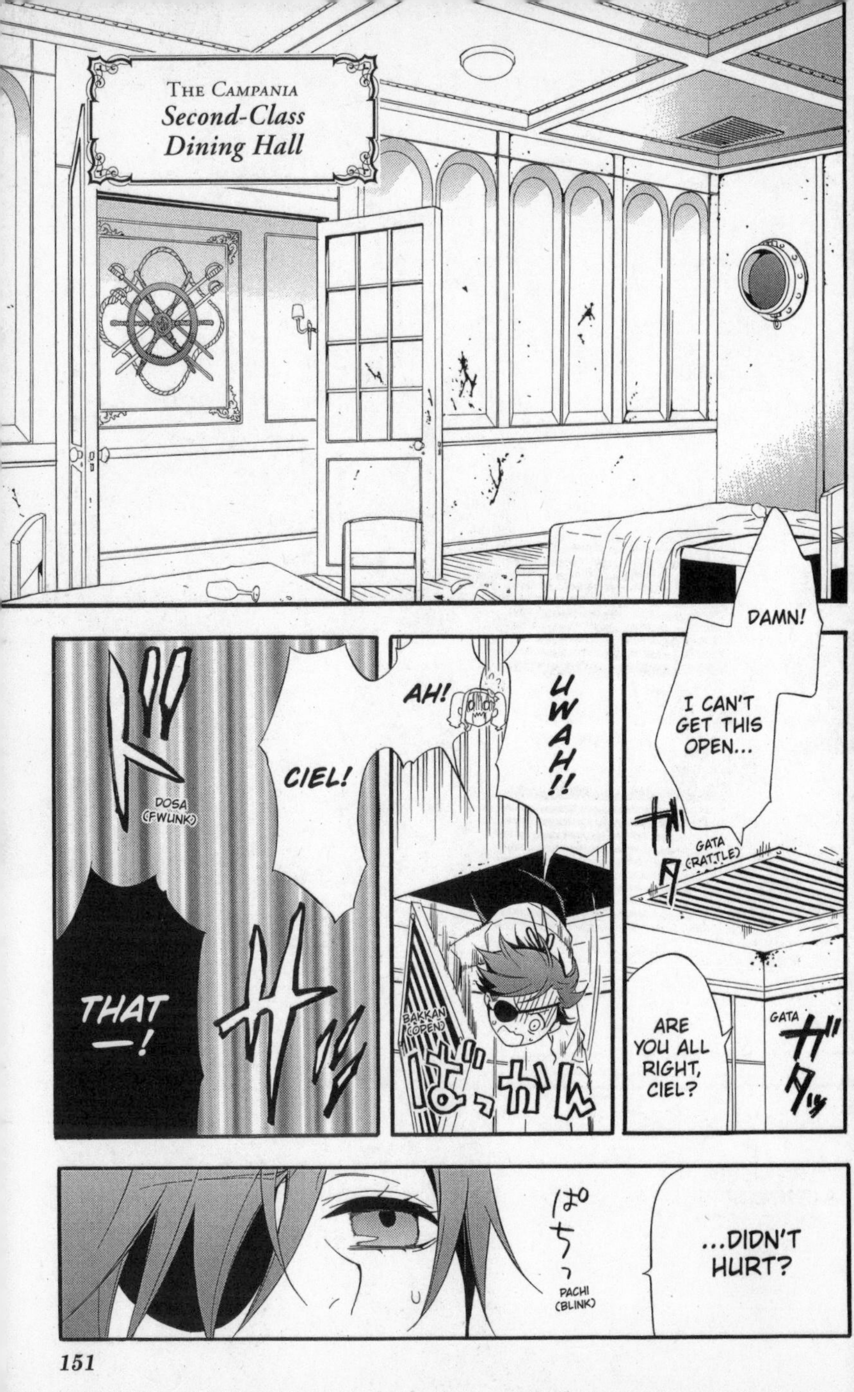
The Campania
Second-Class
Dining Hall
DAMN!
I CAN'T GET THIS OPEN...
GATA (RATTLE)
ARE YOU ALL RIGHT, CIEL?
GATA
UWAH!!
AH!
BAKKAN (OPEN)
CIEL!
DOSA (FWUNK)
THAT—!
PACHI (BLINK)
...DIDN'T HURT?

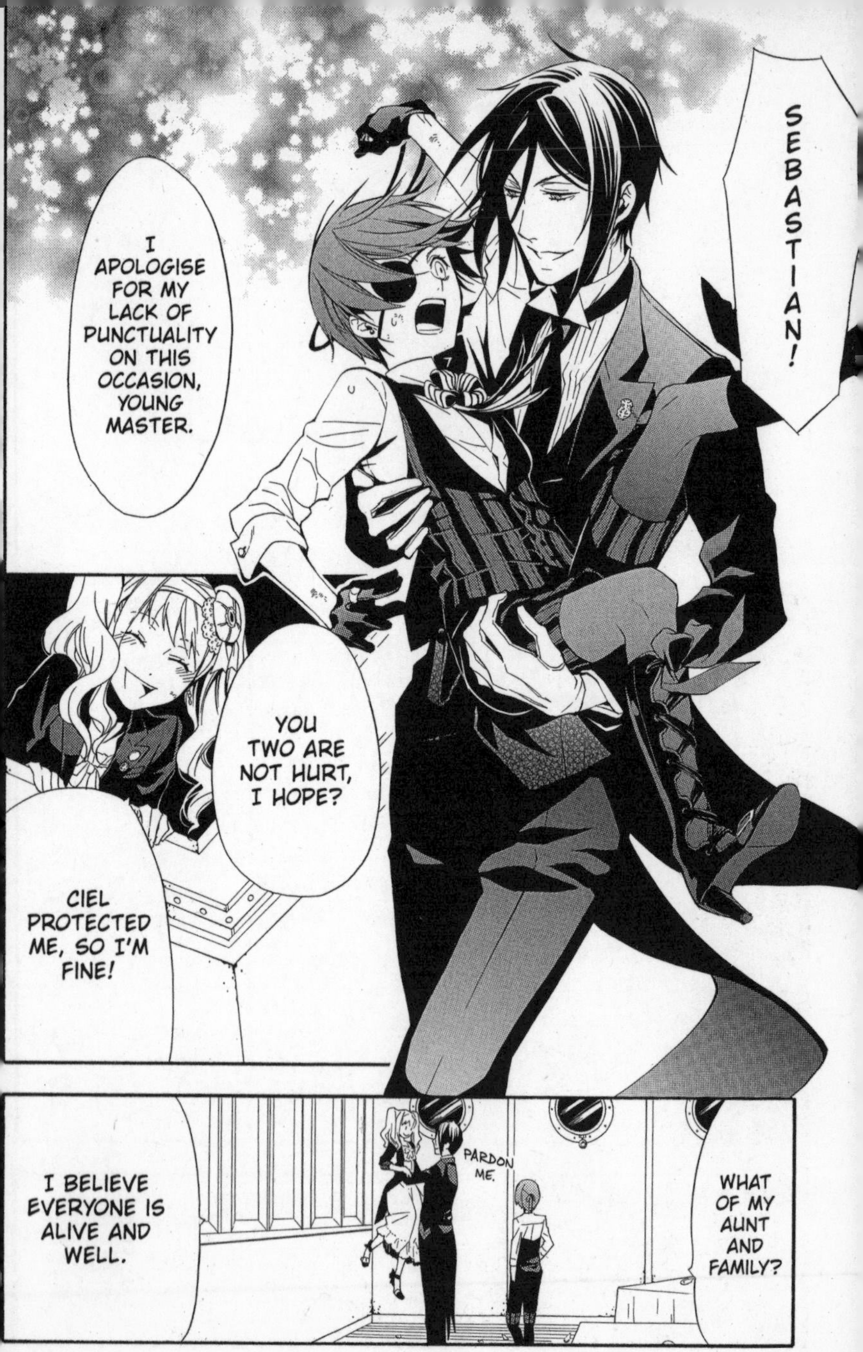
SEBASTIAN!
I APOLOGISE FOR MY LACK OF PUNCTUALITY ON THIS OCCASION, YOUNG MASTER.
YOU TWO ARE NOT HURT, I HOPE?
CIEL PROTECTED ME, SO I'M FINE!
WHAT OF MY AUNT AND FAMILY?
PARDON ME.
I BELIEVE EVERYONE IS ALIVE AND WELL.

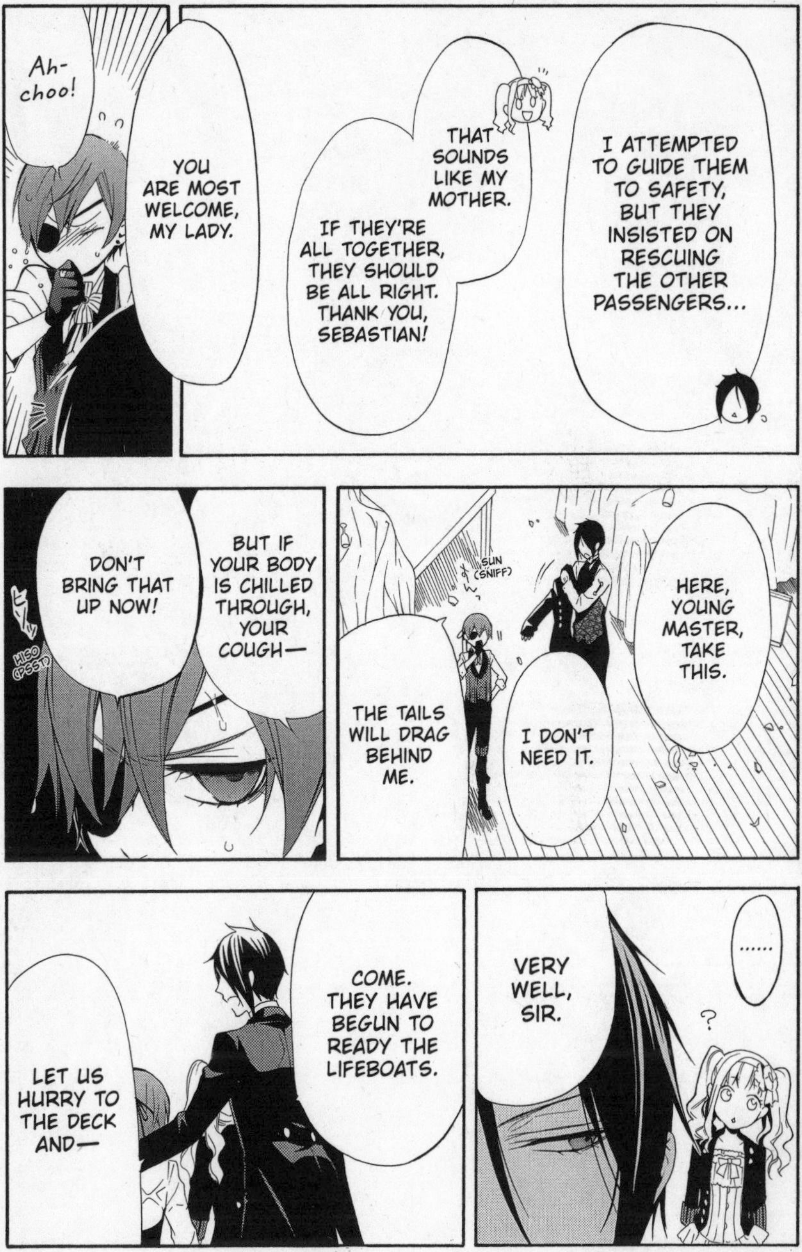
I ATTEMPTED TO GUIDE THEM TO SAFETY, BUT THEY INSISTED ON RESCUING THE OTHER PASSENGERS...
THAT SOUNDS LIKE MY MOTHER.
IF THEY'RE ALL TOGETHER, THEY SHOULD BE ALL RIGHT. THANK YOU, SEBASTIAN!
YOU ARE MOST WELCOME, MY LADY.
Ah-choo!
HERE, YOUNG MASTER, TAKE THIS.
SUN (SNIFF)
I DON'T NEED IT.
THE TAILS WILL DRAG BEHIND ME.
BUT IF YOUR BODY IS CHILLED THROUGH, YOUR COUGH—
DON'T BRING THAT UP NOW!
HISO (PSST)
......
VERY WELL, SIR.
?
COME. THEY HAVE BEGUN TO READY THE LIFEBOATS.
LET US HURRY TO THE DECK AND—

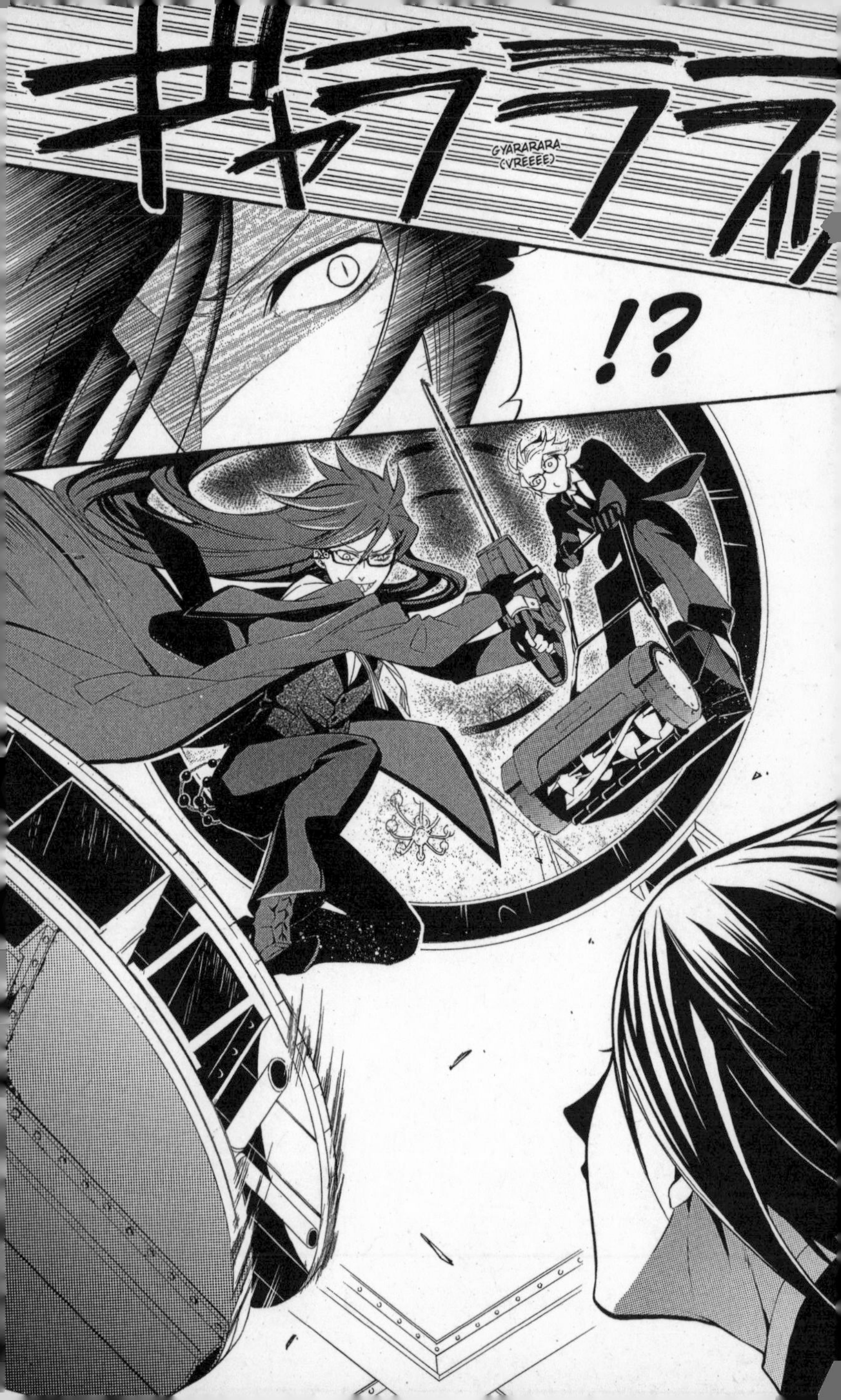
ギャラララ
GYARARARA
(VREEEE)
!?

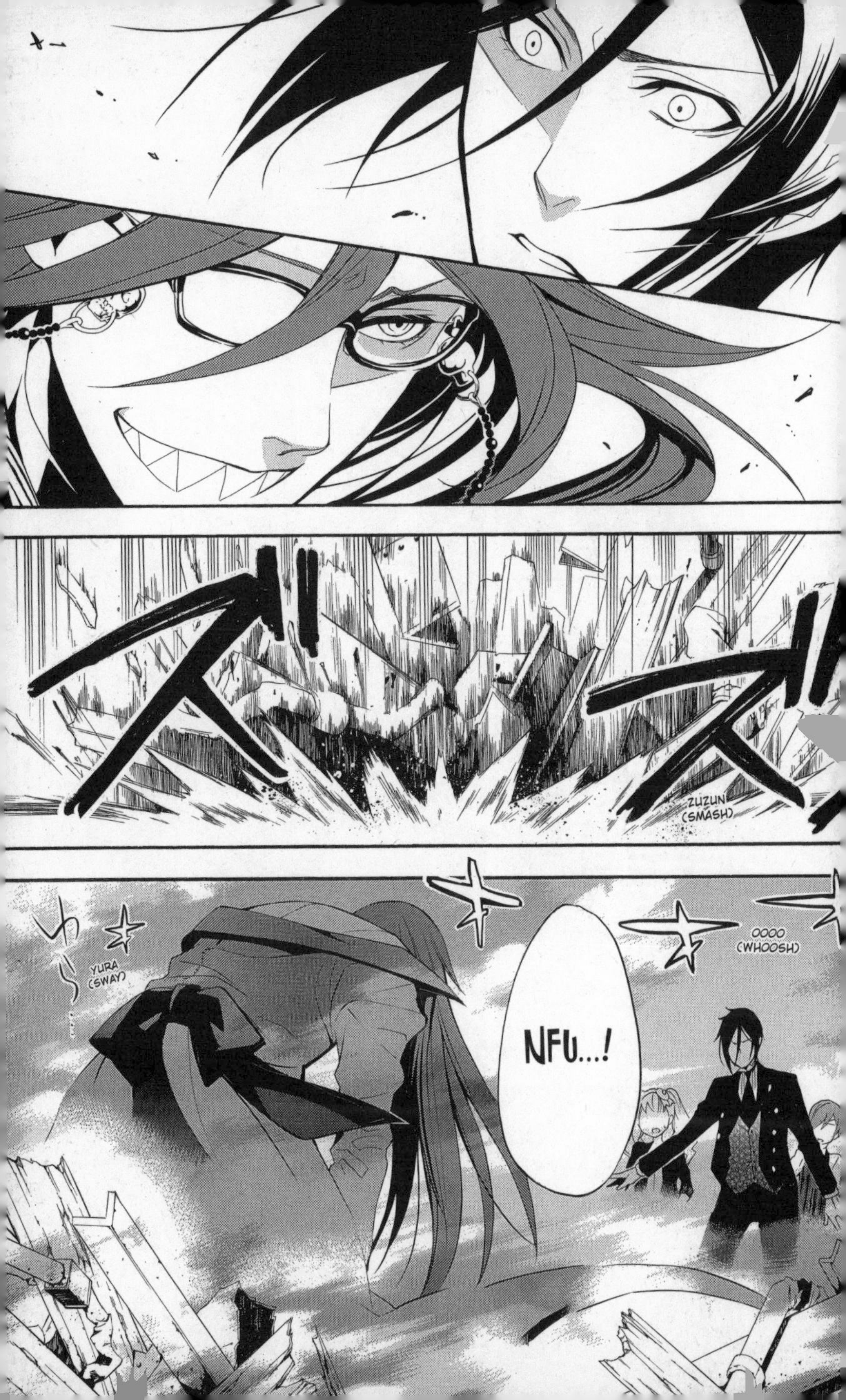
ZUZUN
(SMASH)
OOOO
(WHOOSH)
NFU...!
YURA
(SWAY)

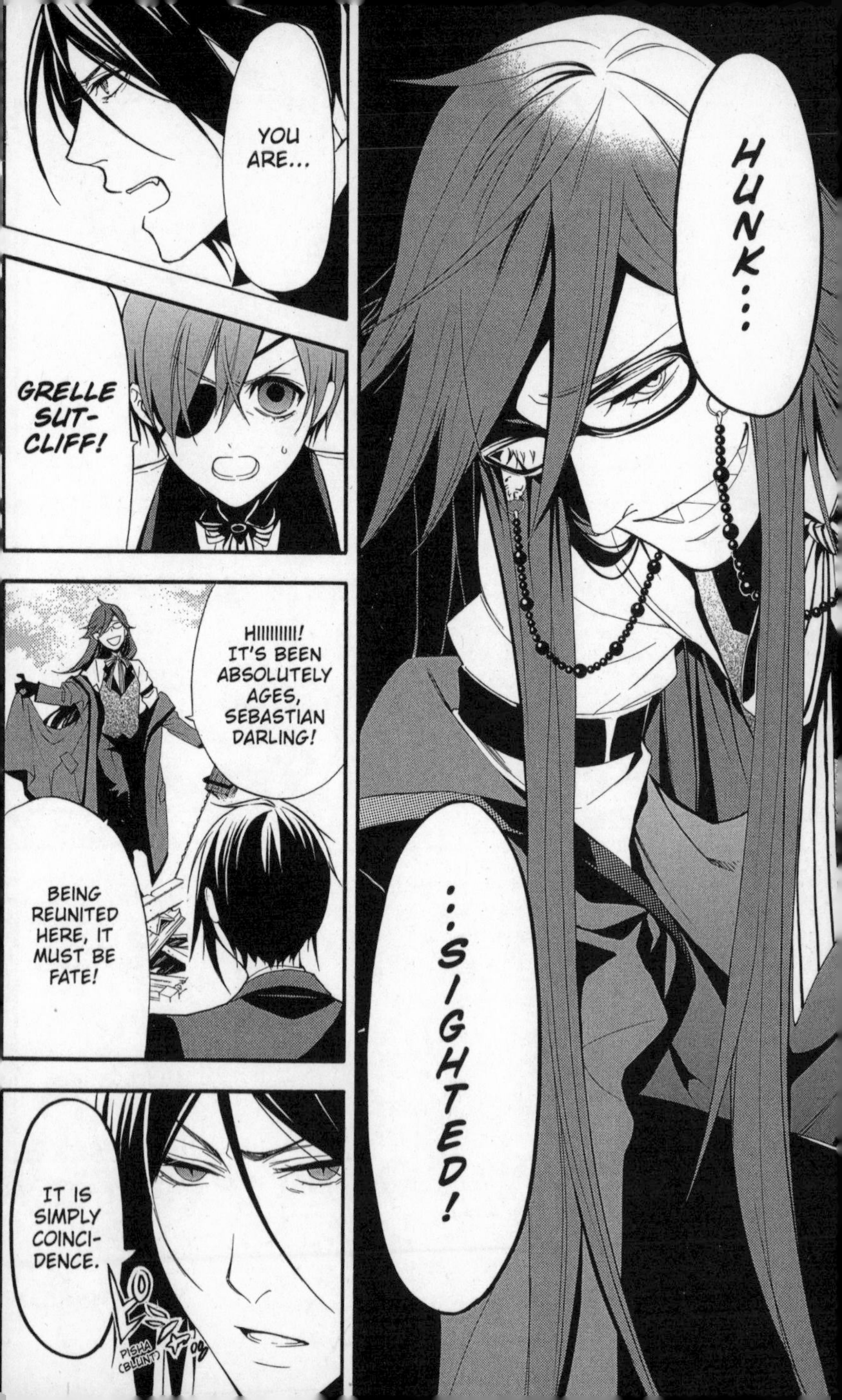
HUNK...
...SIGHTED!
YOU ARE...
GRELLE SUT-CLIFF!
HIIIIIIIIII! IT'S BEEN ABSOLUTELY AGES, SEBASTIAN DARLING!
BEING REUNITED HERE, IT MUST BE FATE!
IT IS SIMPLY COINCI-DENCE.
PISHA (BLUNT)

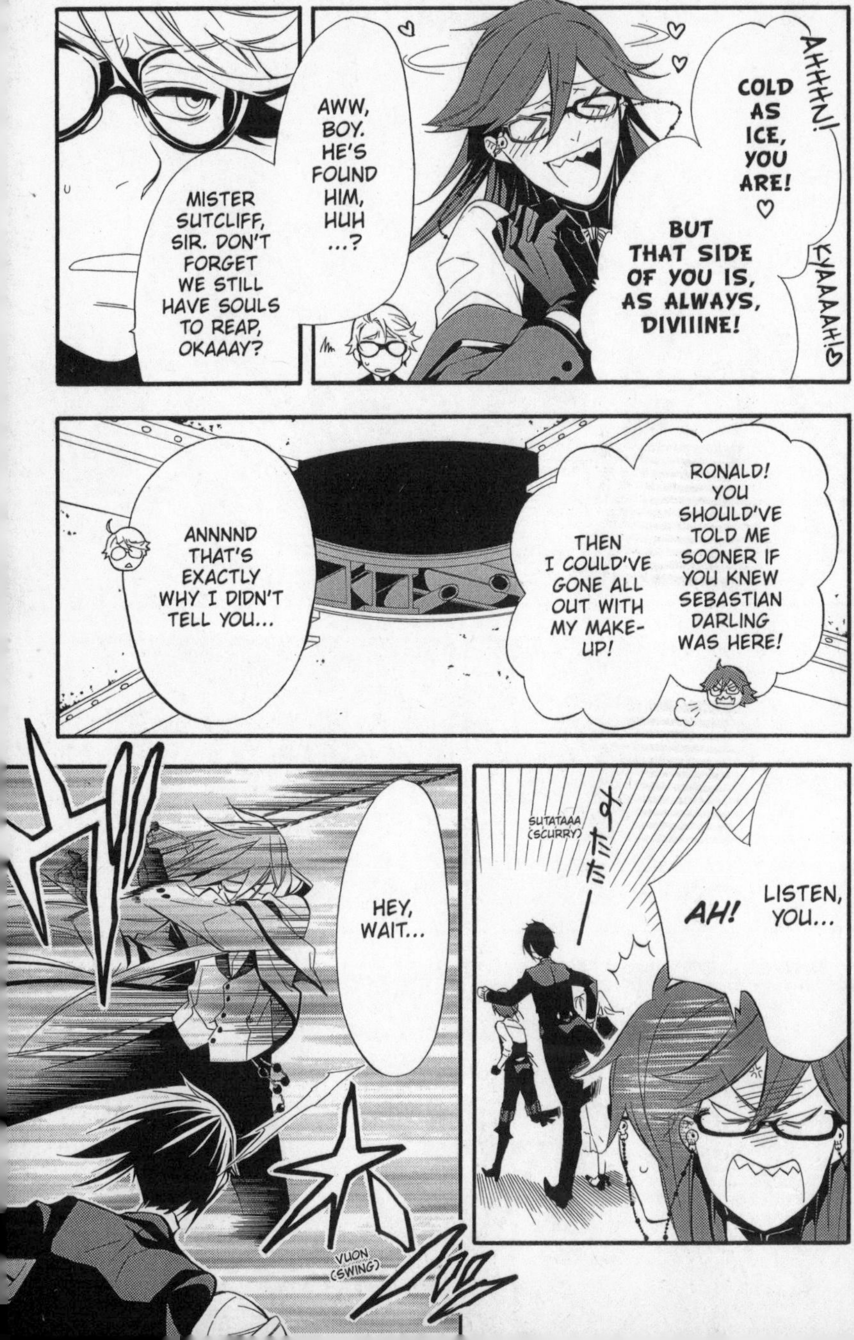
AHHHN!
COLD AS ICE, YOU ARE! ♡
BUT THAT SIDE OF YOU IS, AS ALWAYS, DIVIIINE!
KYAAAAAH!♡
AWW, BOY. HE'S FOUND HIM, HUH ...?
MISTER SUTCLIFF, SIR. DON'T FORGET WE STILL HAVE SOULS TO REAP, OKAAAY?
RONALD! YOU SHOULD'VE TOLD ME SOONER IF YOU KNEW SEBASTIAN DARLING WAS HERE!
THEN I COULD'VE GONE ALL OUT WITH MY MAKE-UP!
ANNNND THAT'S EXACTLY WHY I DIDN'T TELL YOU...
LISTEN, YOU...
AH!
SUTATAAA (SCURRY)
HEY, WAIT...
VUON (SWING)

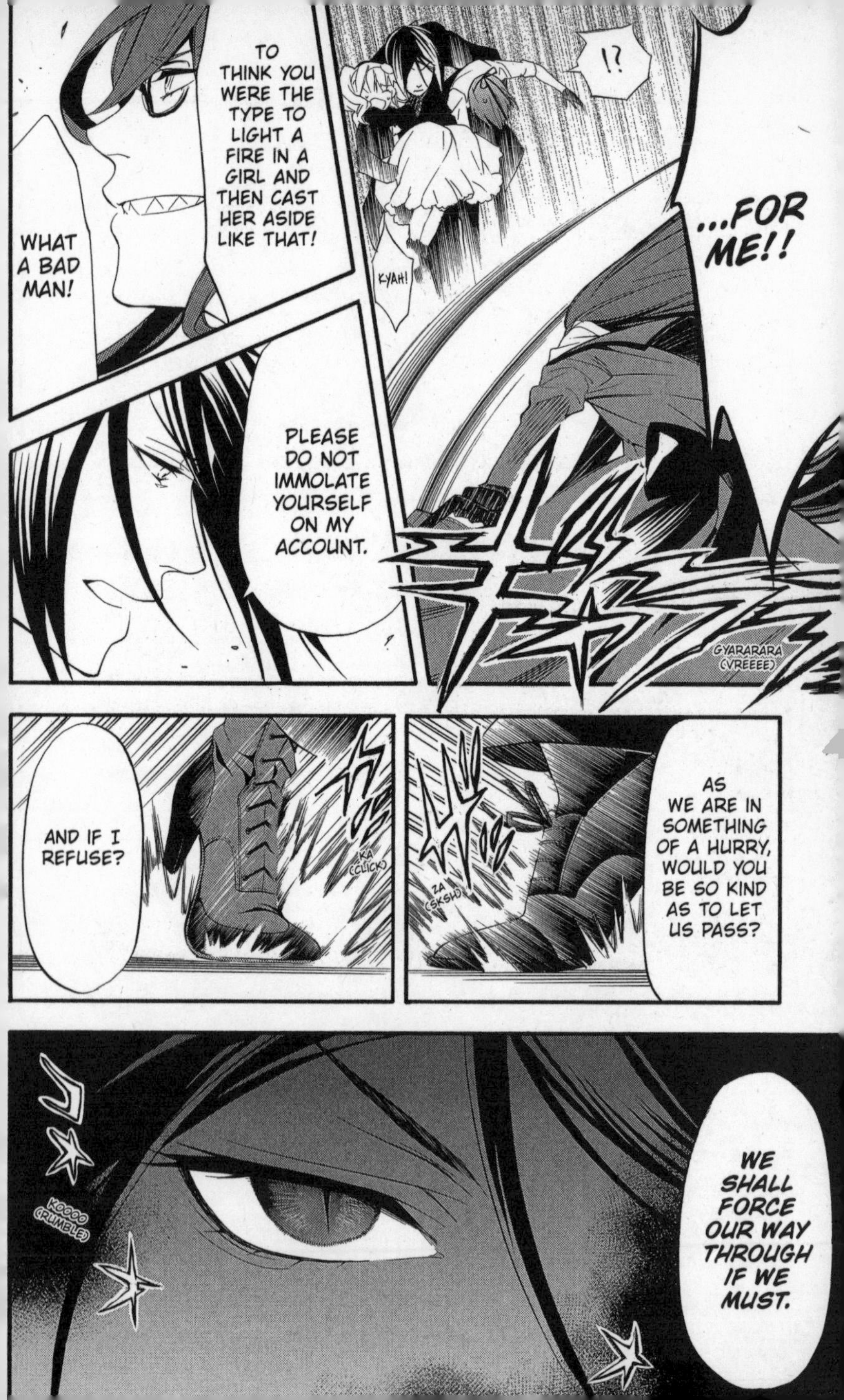
!?
KYAH!
...FOR ME!!
GYARARARA (VREEEE)
TO THINK YOU WERE THE TYPE TO LIGHT A FIRE IN A GIRL AND THEN CAST HER ASIDE LIKE THAT!
WHAT A BAD MAN!
PLEASE DO NOT IMMOLATE YOURSELF ON MY ACCOUNT.
AS WE ARE IN SOMETHING OF A HURRY, WOULD YOU BE SO KIND AS TO LET US PASS?
ZA (SKSH)
KA (CLICK)
AND IF I REFUSE?
WE SHALL FORCE OUR WAY THROUGH IF WE MUST.
KOOOO (RUMBLE)

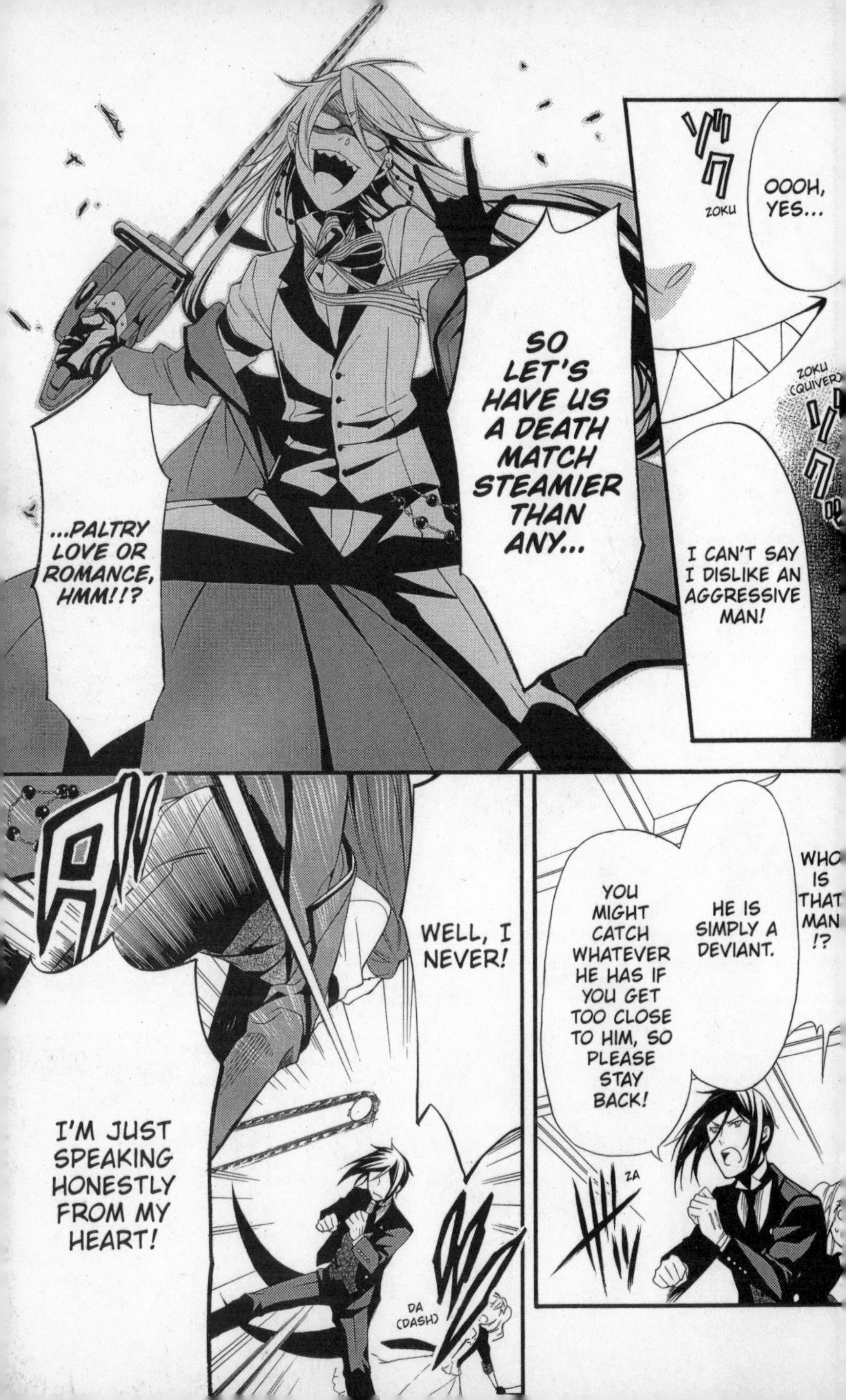
ZOKU
OOOH, YES...
ZOKU (QUIVER)
I CAN'T SAY I DISLIKE AN AGGRESSIVE MAN!
SO LET'S HAVE US A DEATH MATCH STEAMIER THAN ANY...
...PALTRY LOVE OR ROMANCE, HMM!!?
WHO IS THAT MAN!?
HE IS SIMPLY A DEVIANT.
YOU MIGHT CATCH WHATEVER HE HAS IF YOU GET TOO CLOSE TO HIM, SO PLEASE STAY BACK!
ZA
WELL, I NEVER!
I'M JUST SPEAKING HONESTLY FROM MY HEART!
DA (DASH)

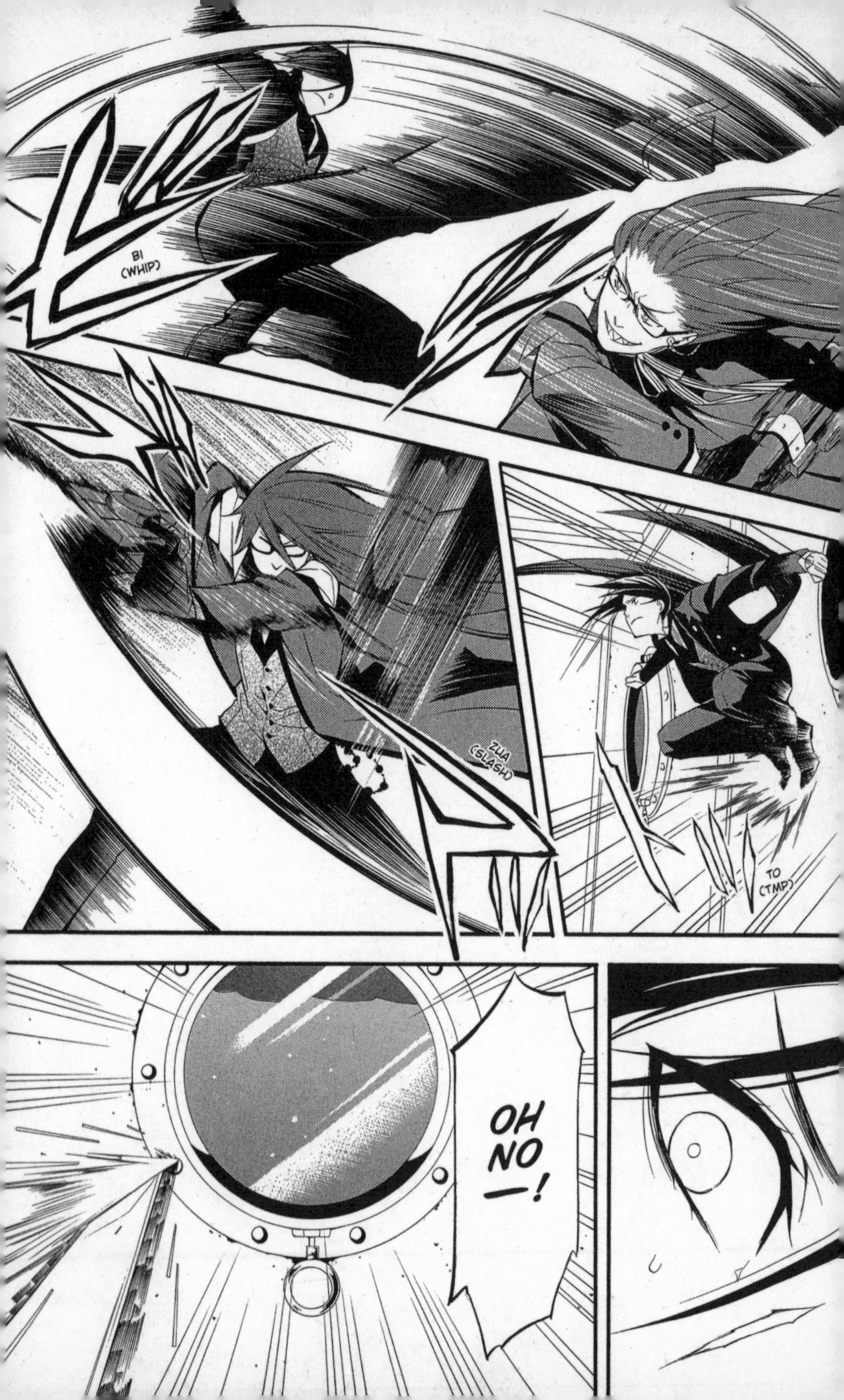
BI (WHIP)
TO (TMP)
ZUA (SLASH)
OH NO —!

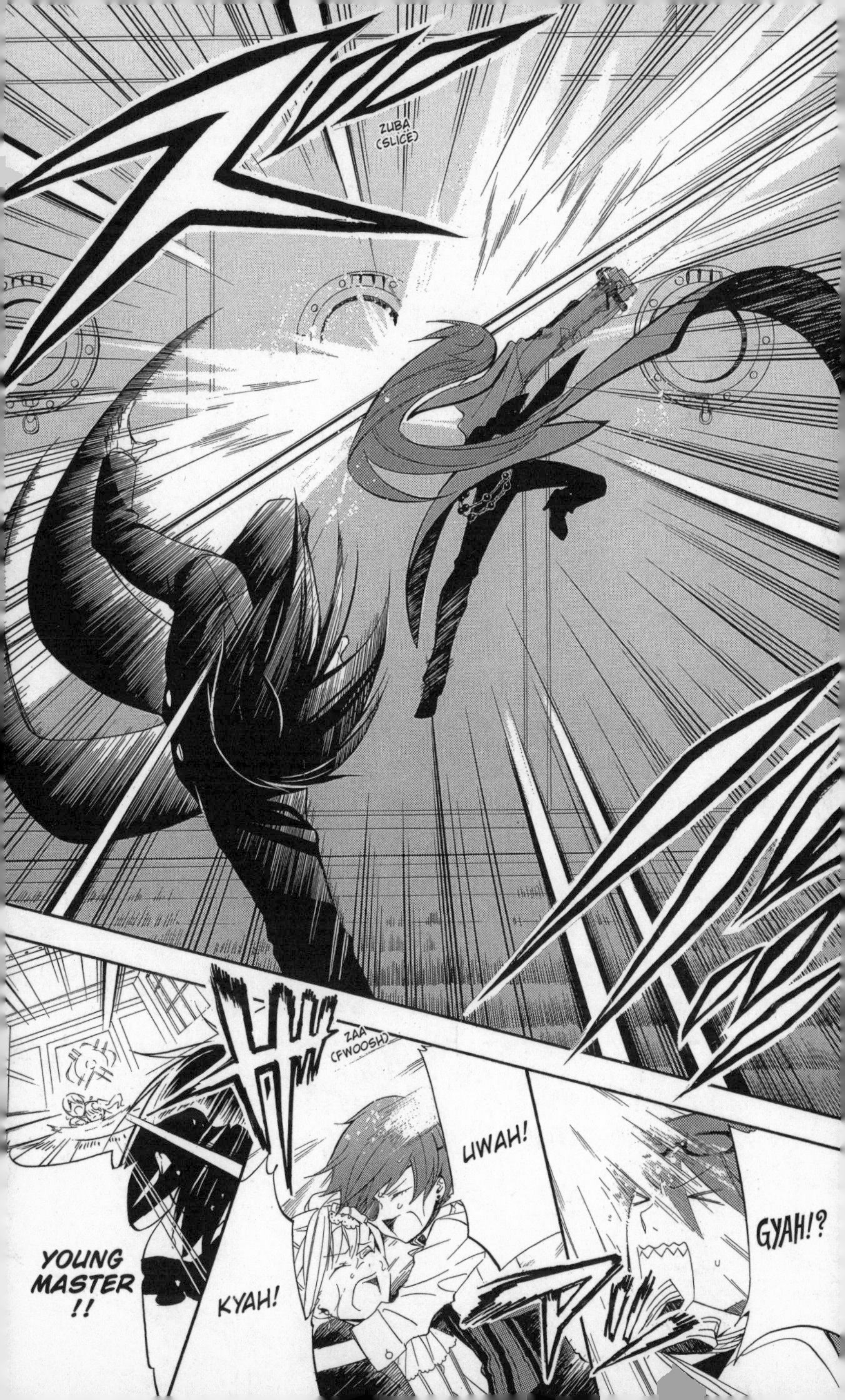
ZUBA
(SLICE)
GYAH!?
UWAH!
ZAA
(FWOOSH)
KYAH!
YOUNG
MASTER
!!

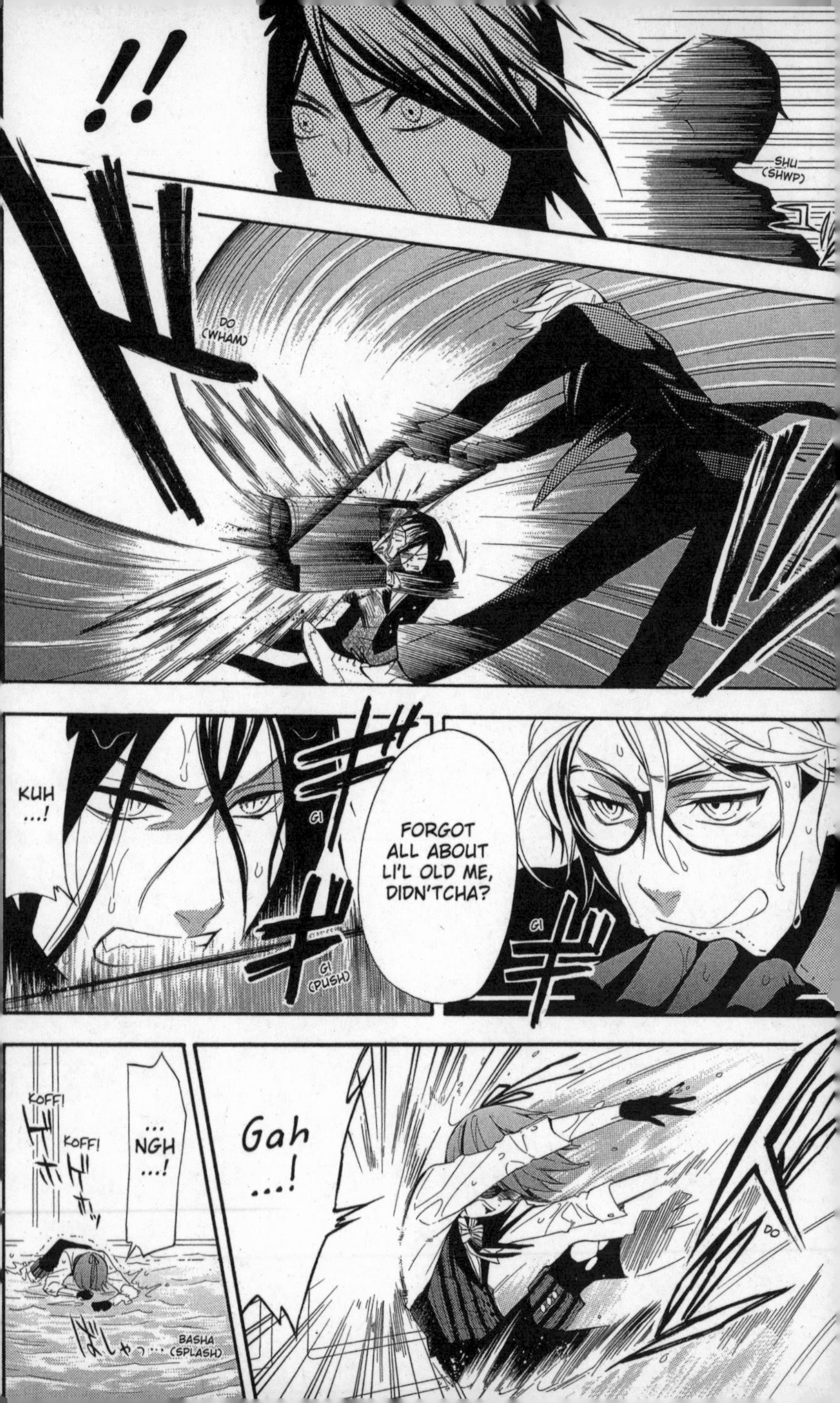
SHU (SHWP)
!!
DO (WHAM)
FORGOT ALL ABOUT LI'L OLD ME, DIDN'TCHA?
GI
KUH ...!
GI
GI (PUSH)
Gah ...!
DO
... NGH ...!
KOFF!
KOFF!
BASHA (SPLASH)

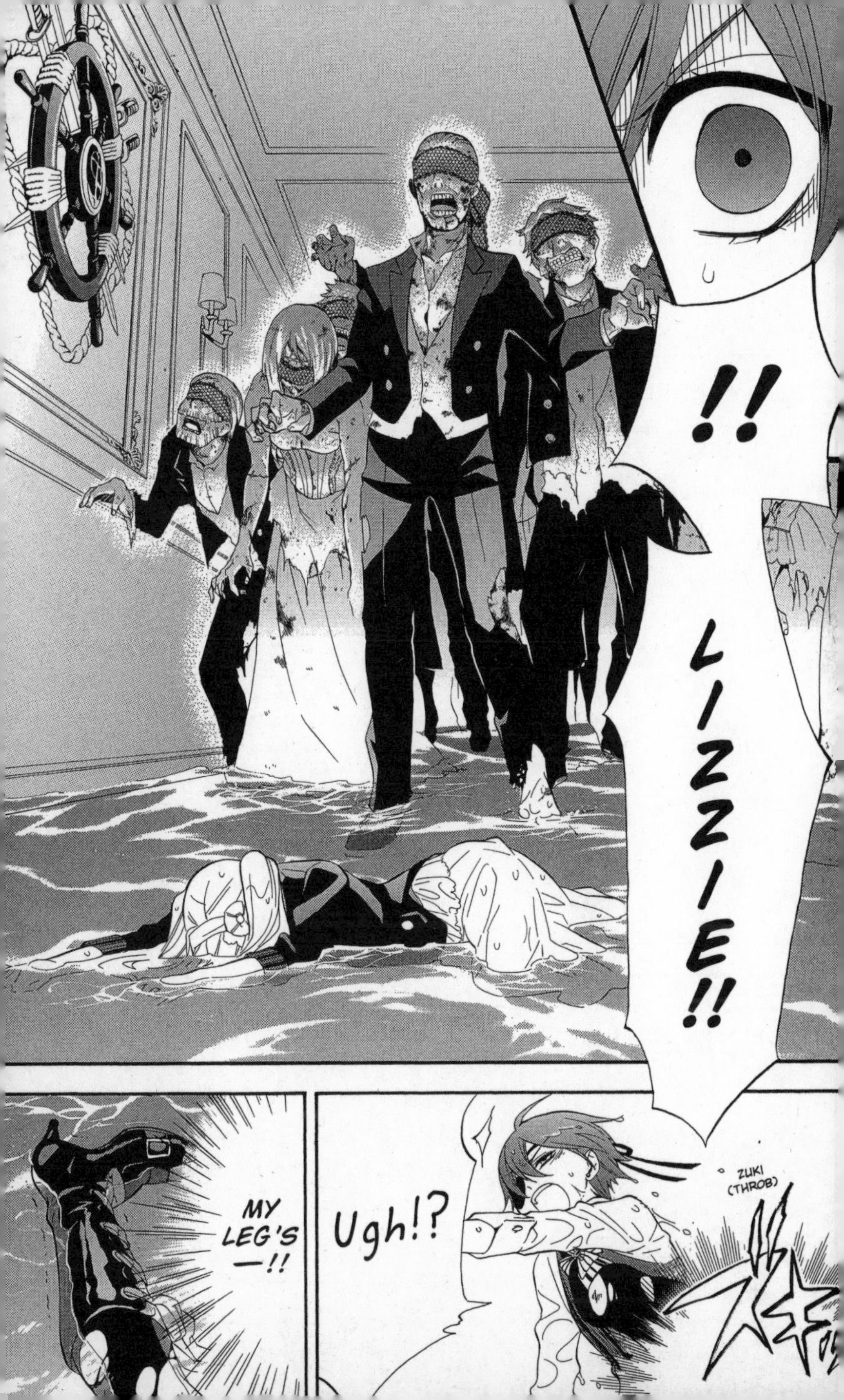
!! LIZZIE!!
ZUKI (THROB)
Ugh!?
MY LEG'S—!!

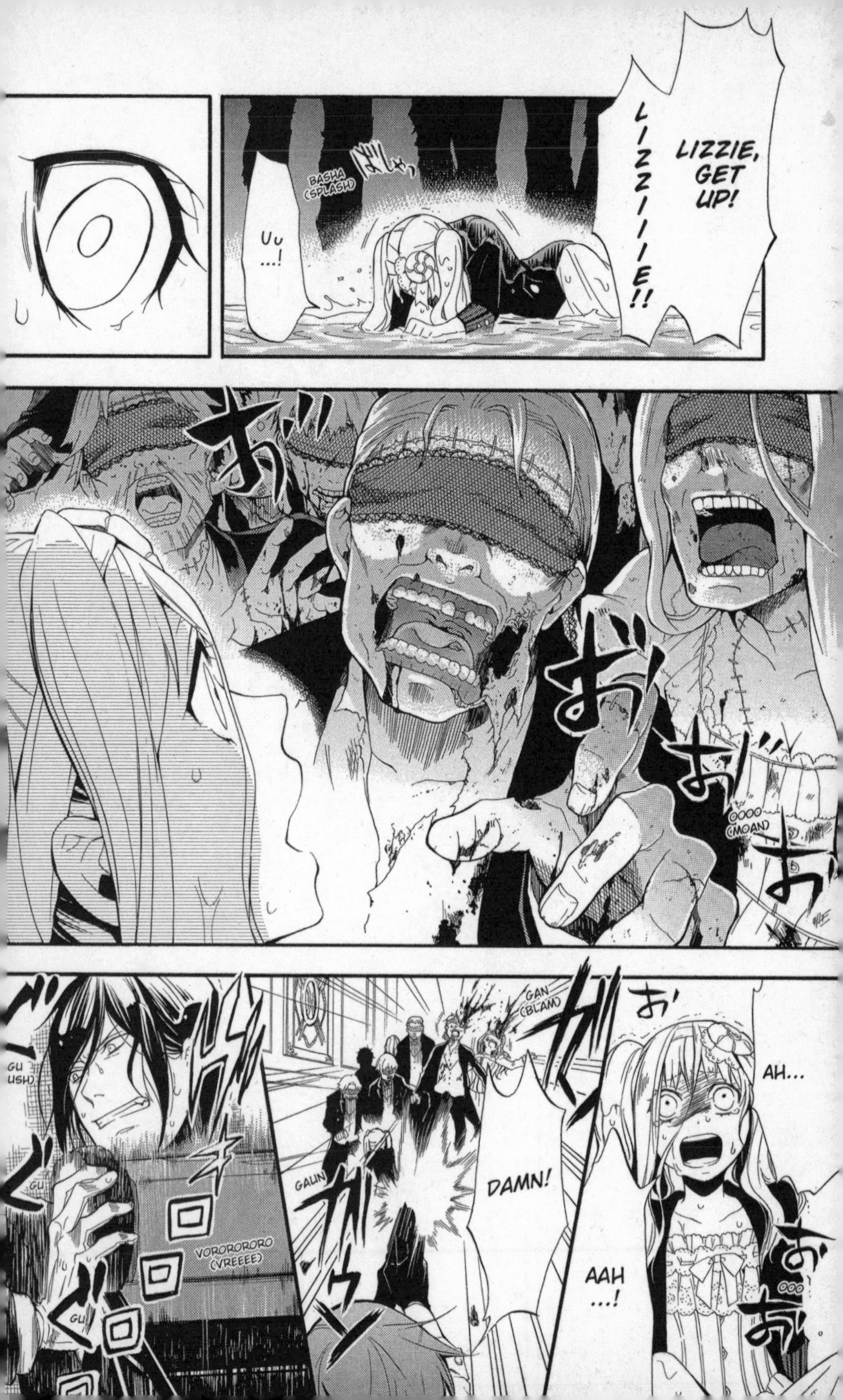

LIZZIE, GET UP!
LIZZIIIIE!!
BASHA (SPLASH)
Uu ...!
OOOO (MOAN)
AH...
GAN (BLAM)
AAH ...!
OOO
DAMN!
GAUN
GU
VORORORORO (VREEEE)
GU

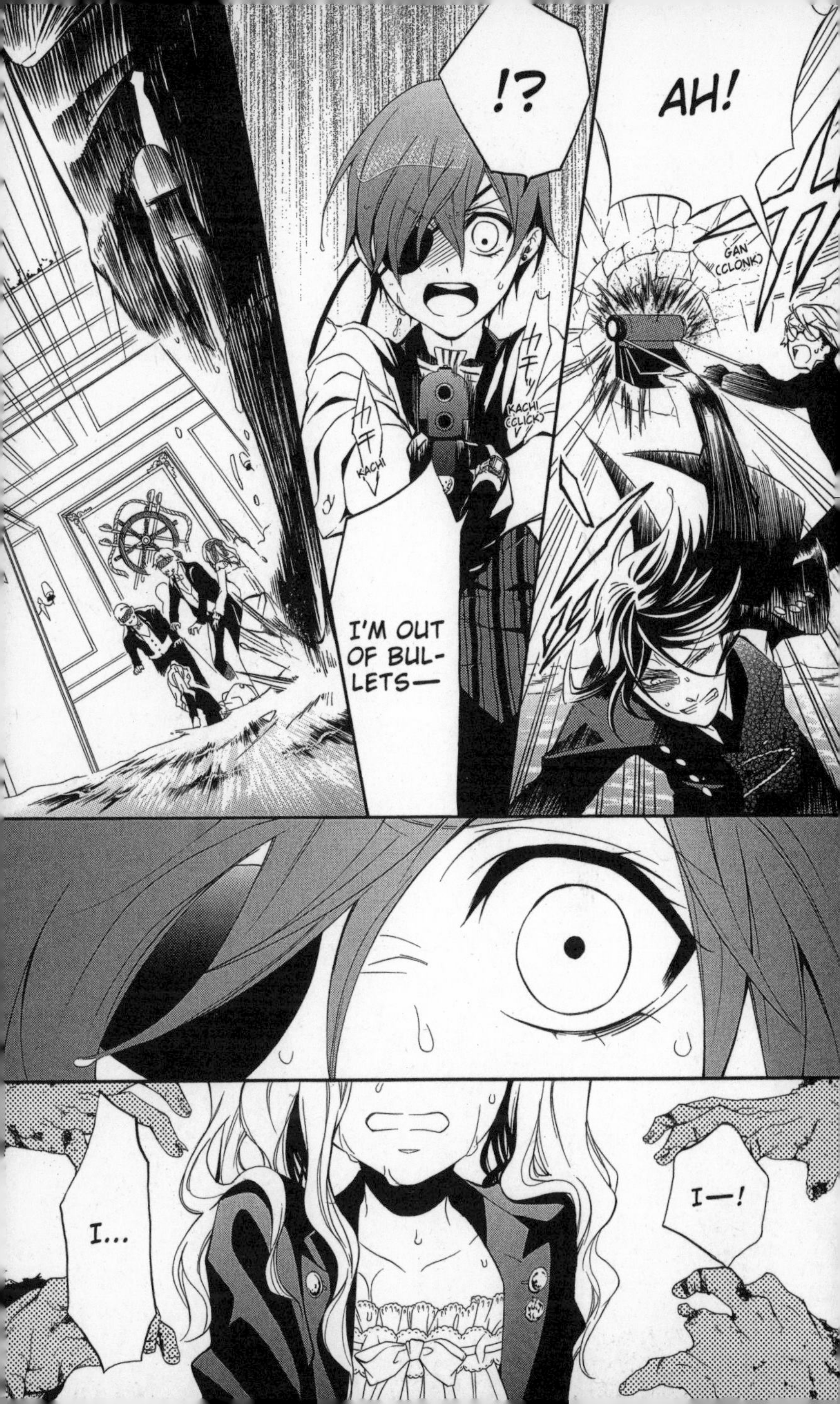
AH!
GAN (CLONK)
!?
KACHI (CLICK)
KACHI
I'M OUT OF BUL-LETS—
I—!
I...

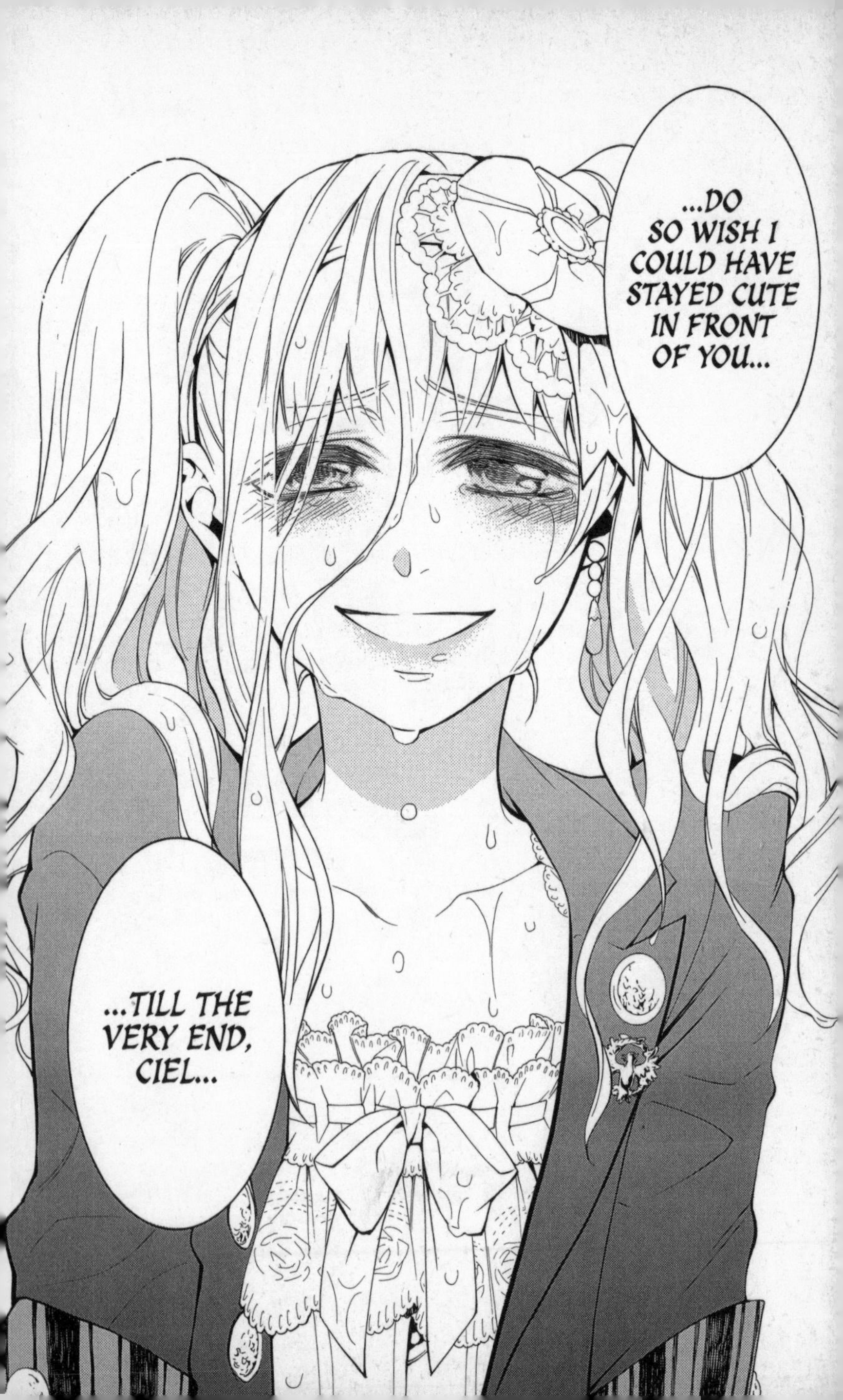
...DO SO WISH I COULD HAVE STAYED CUTE IN FRONT OF YOU...
...TILL THE VERY END, CIEL...

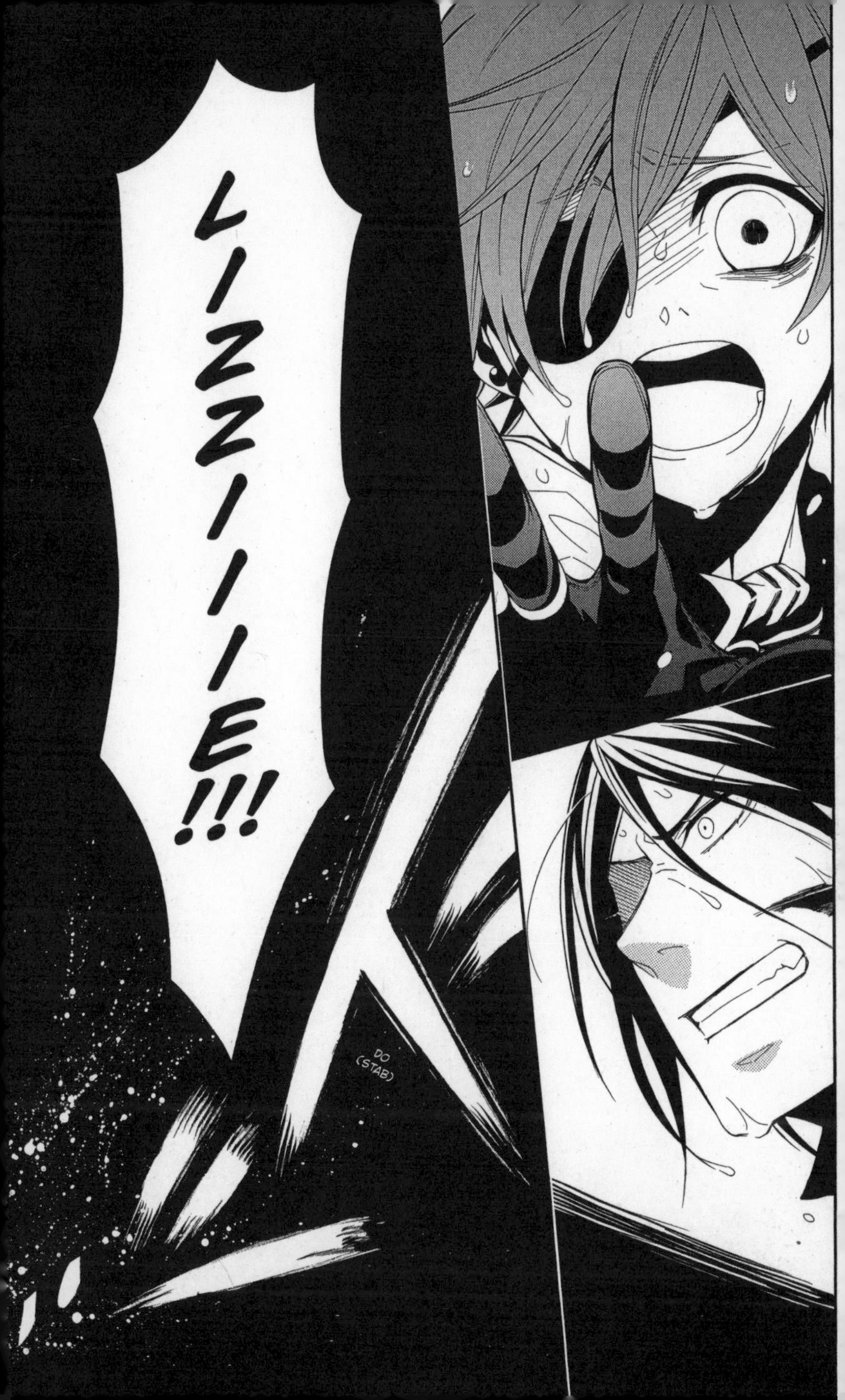
LIZZIIIE!!!
DO (STAB)

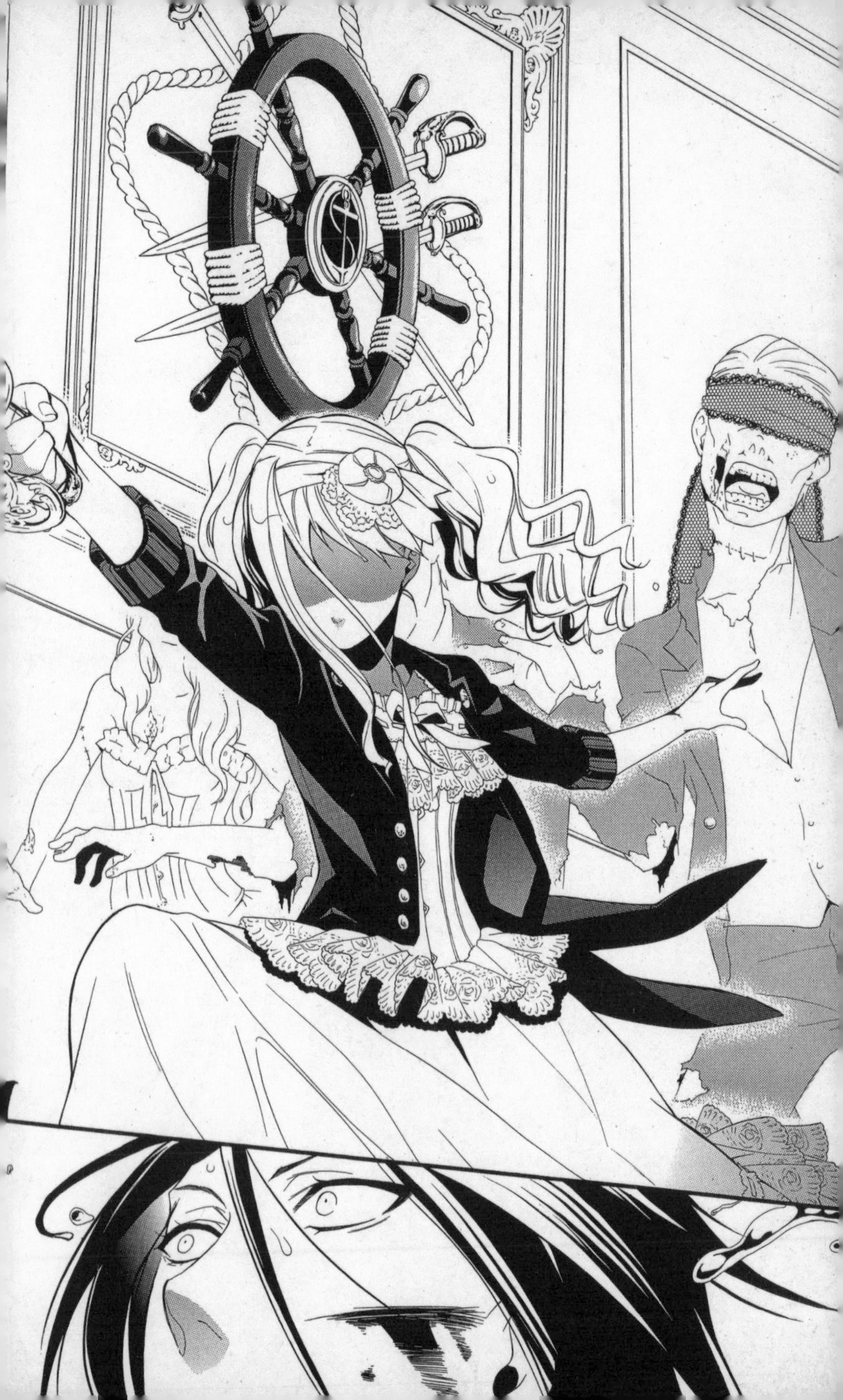

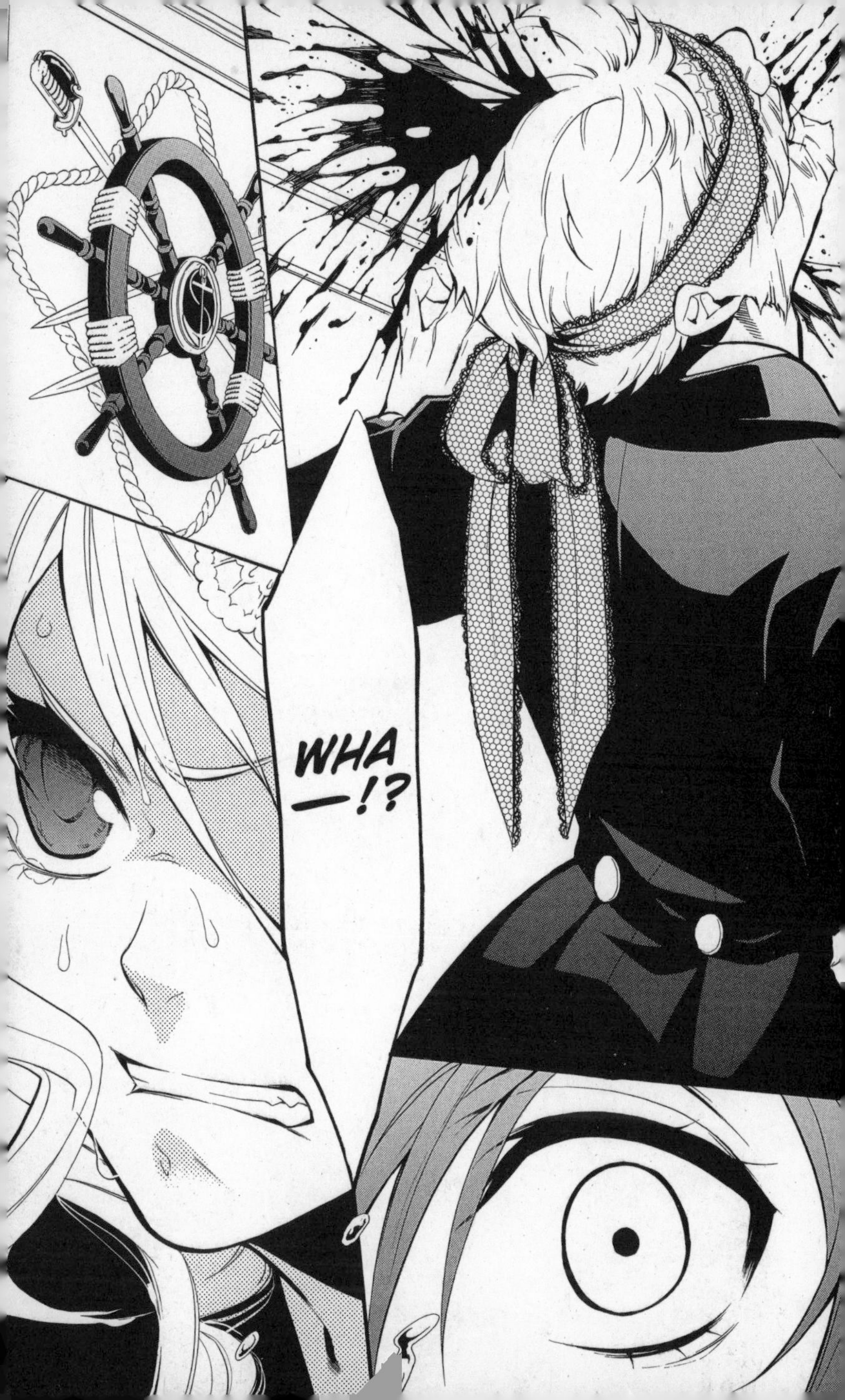
WHA—!?

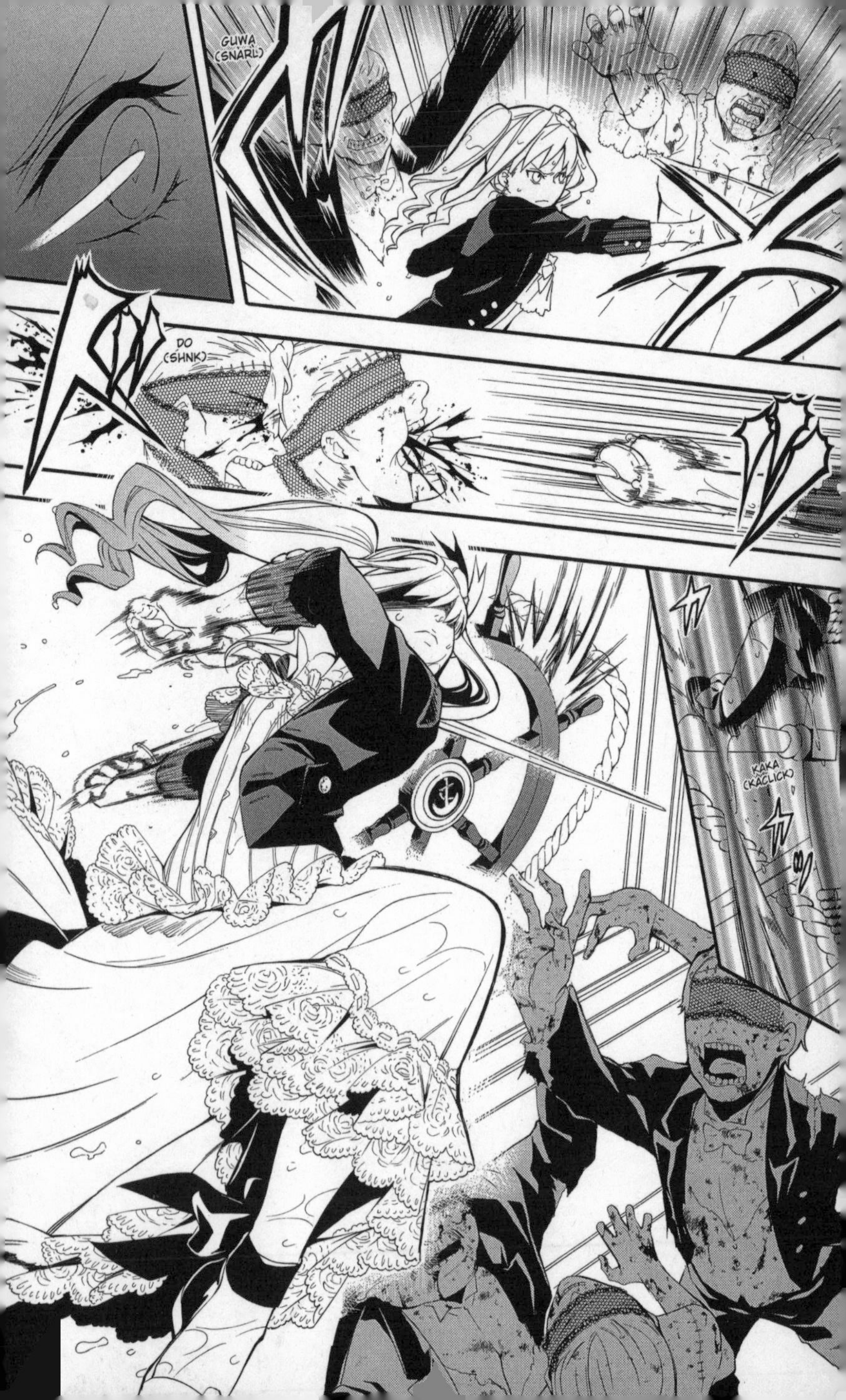
GUWA
(SNARL)
DO
(SHNK)
KAKA
(KACLICK)

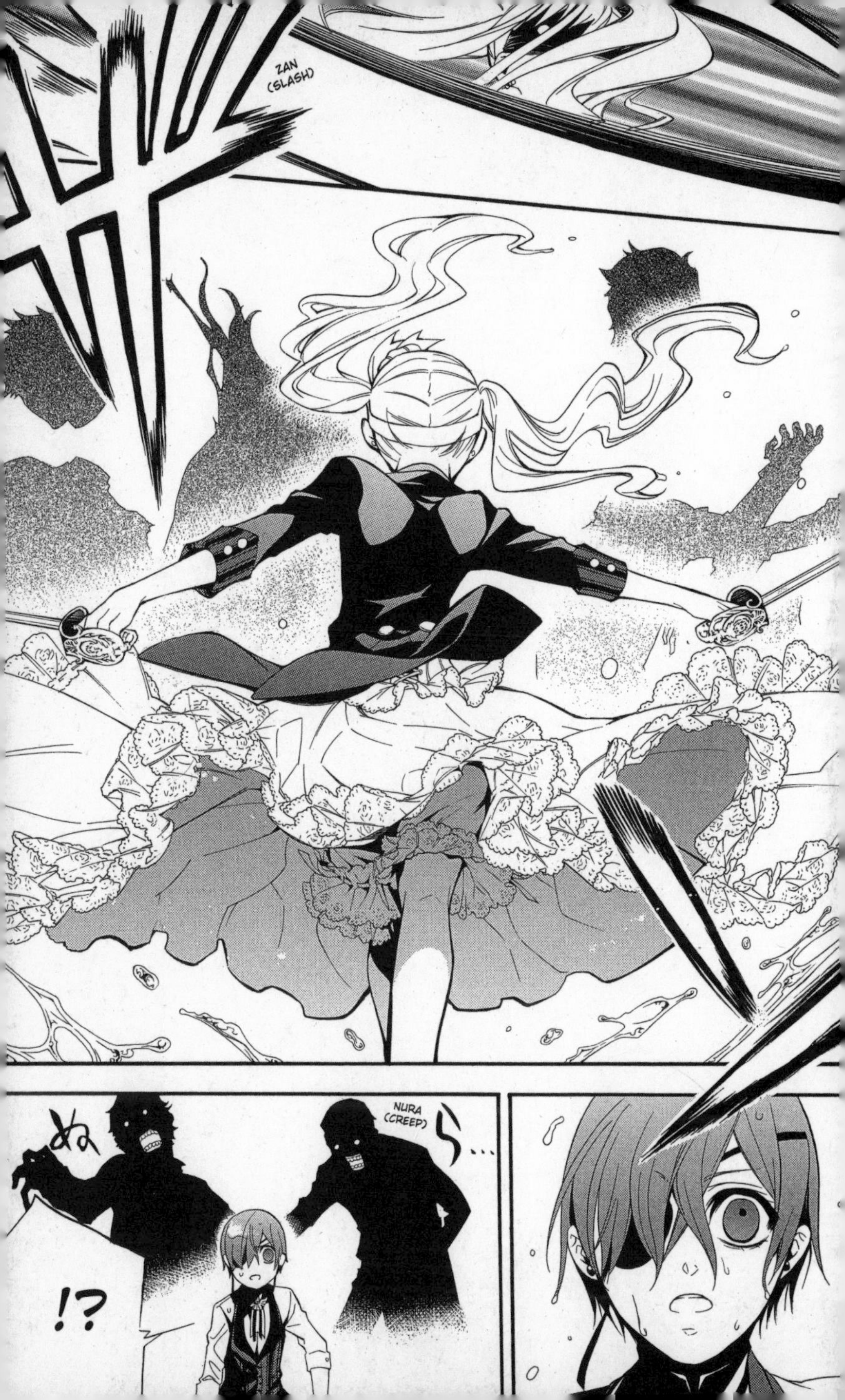
ZAN (SLASH)
NURA (CREEP)
ぬ
ら…
!?

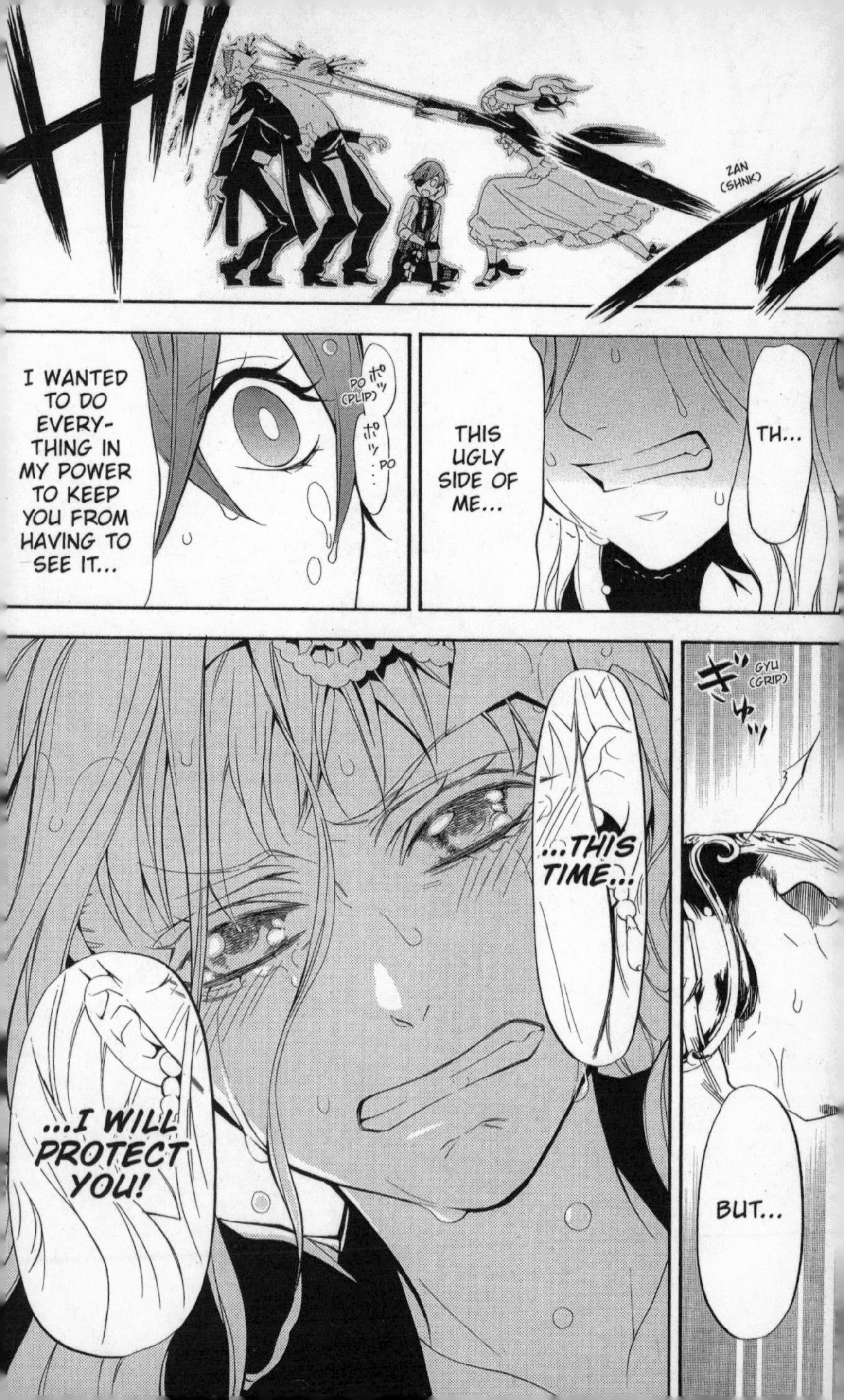
ZAN (SHNK)
TH...
THIS UGLY SIDE OF ME...
PO (PLIP)
PO
I WANTED TO DO EVERYTHING IN MY POWER TO KEEP YOU FROM HAVING TO SEE IT...
GYU (GRIP)
BUT...
...THIS TIME...
...I WILL PROTECT YOU!

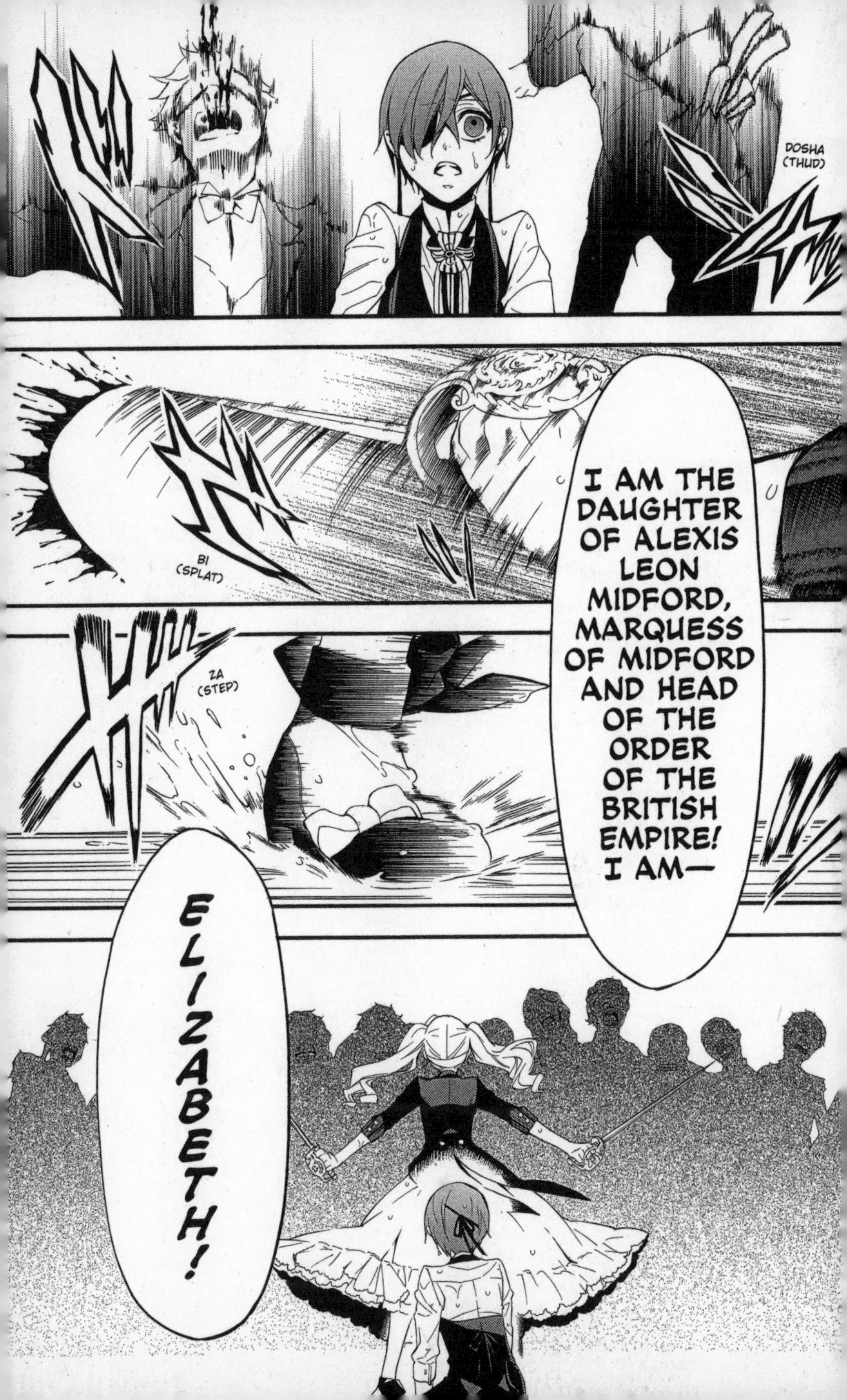
DOSHA (THUD)
BI (SPLAT)
I AM THE DAUGHTER OF ALEXIS LEON MIDFORD, MARQUESS OF MIDFORD AND HEAD OF THE ORDER OF THE BRITISH EMPIRE! I AM—
ZA (STEP)
ELIZABETH!

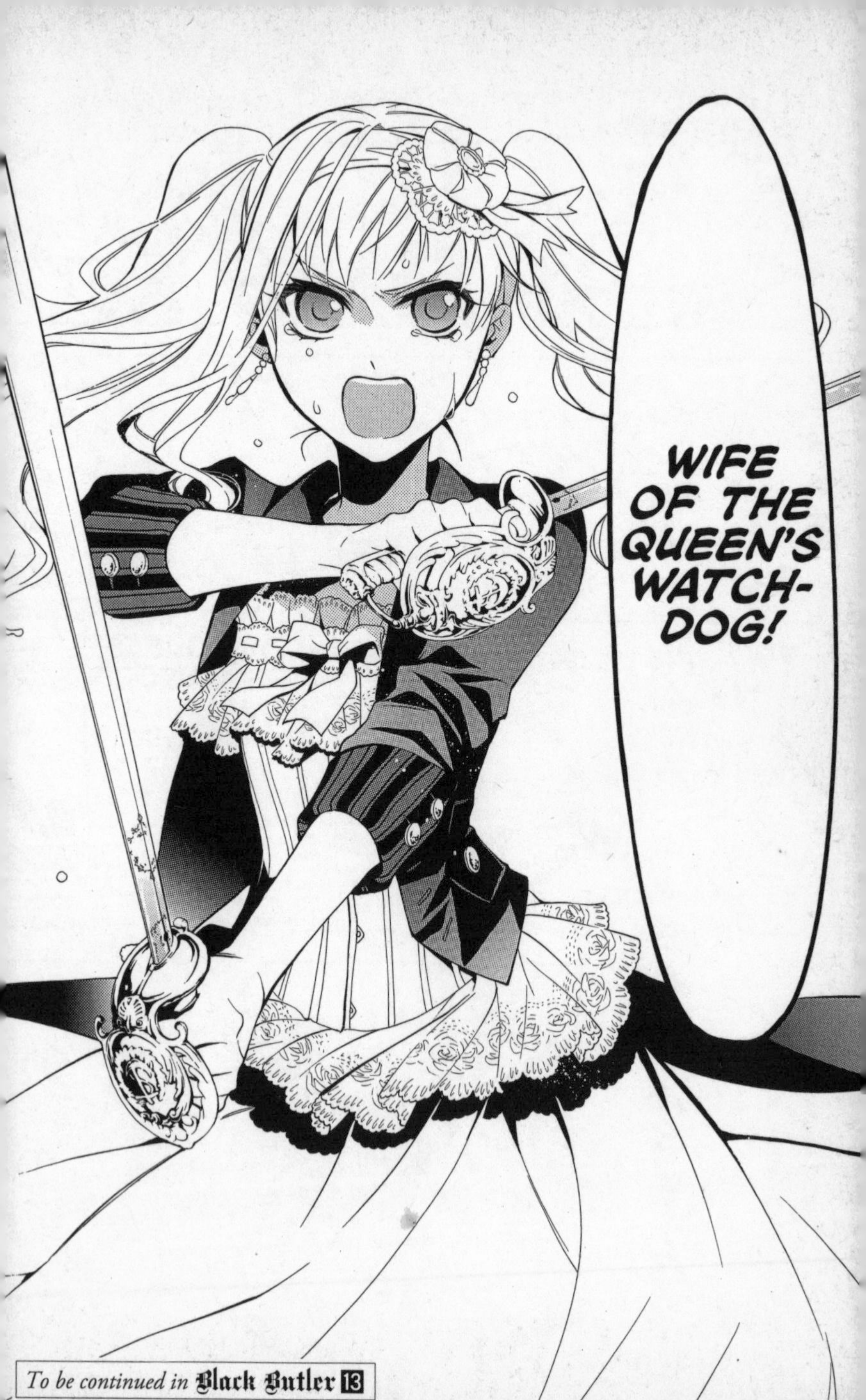
WIFE OF THE QUEEN'S WATCH-DOG!

To be continued in Black Butler 13

⇒ Black Butler ⇐

黒執事

❖

Downstairs

Wakana Haduki

SuKe

7

Saito Torino

*

Takeshi Kuma

*

Yana Toboso

❖

SpecialThanks

Yana' s Mother

Sakuya

for You!

Translation Notes

Inside Front and Back Covers
Black Idol
In Japan, there was an all-male pop idol group named Hikaru GENJI, whose gimmick was wearing roller skates. They were active in the late 1980s-early 1990s. One of their hits was "Paradise Galaxy," the lyrics of which are parodied here. Roughly translated, the song opens with the lyrics, "Welcome to this place / Let's play in paradise." Another of their hits was titled "The Glass Teens," which is also parodied here and includes the lyrics, "We collect nothing but fragile things / This sparkle's not for show, we're the glass teens."

Page 25
Orlop deck
Ships in the *Campania*'s class, like the *RMS Titanic* (which launched for its maiden voyage on April 10, 1912 from the port of Southampton bound for New York City), were built with ten decks, the second to last lowest of these was the orlop deck. This deck fell below the waterline and was used primarily for cargo.

Page 26
Donne
John Donne (1572-1631) was a famous English metaphysical poet and satirist active in the sixteenth century.

Page 67
Reciprocating steam engines
The *Titanic* was propelled by two massive reciprocating steam engines (the biggest of their kind at the time), each of which powered a propeller. Combined with a steam turbine, which fed off the steam from the engines, these mechanisms gave the *Titanic* her speed.

Page 80
Marconi wireless room
The Marconi wireless room on the *Titanic* was equipped with the most powerful equipment of its kind at the time and was manned around the clock by two operators who worked for the Marconi Company, a pioneer in the field of such technology. They sent and received passenger messages and also received communications from other vessels, including warnings about the conditions of the route ahead.

Page 86
Osiris
In Egyptian mythology, Osiris is the god of the dead, the underworld, and life after death. He is also said to judge the dead in the afterlife.

Page 97
Crow's nest
As on the *Campania*, the *Titanic*'s crow's nest was manned by two lookouts, who were the first to sight the iceberg that would seal the luxury liner's fate on the bitterly cold night of April 14, 1912.

Page 107
"A luxury cruise to DIE for!★"
In the original, Grelle says "*DIEkoukai DEATH*" here. Without the wordplay, "*daikoukai desu*" would translate to "It's a great voyage."

Page 130
Keats
John Keats (1795-1821) is one of the best known and loved English Romantic poets. He was active in the early nineteenth century but would not earn his reputation as one of the greats until after his death.

Yana Toboso

AUTHOR'S NOTE

Drawing manga is similar to a journey by sea. The wide ocean is the story. The *mangaka* is a vessel. The characters are the ship's crew. Characters who haven't appeared yet are like lovers waiting on land. If you don't see them for a while, your brain fools you into believing they're the very picture of beauty, but the reality is actually rather different...

That's my take anyway. And so I present to you Volume 12, rocked by rough waves.

MAR 0 3 2016

BLACK BUTLER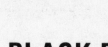

YANA TOBOSO

Translation: Tomo Kimura • Lettering: Alexis Eckerman

KUROSHITSUJI Vol. 12 © 2011 Yana Toboso / SQUARE ENIX CO., LTD. All rights reserved. First published in Japan in 2011 by SQUARE ENIX CO., LTD. English translation rights arranged with SQUARE ENIX CO., LTD. and Hachette Book Group through Tuttle-Mori Agency, Inc.

Translation © 2013 by SQUARE ENIX CO., LTD.

Yen Press
Hachette Book Group
1290 Avenue of the Americas, New York, NY 10104

www.HachetteBookGroup.com
www.YenPress.com

Yen Press is an imprint of Hachette Book Group, Inc. The Yen Press name and logo are trademarks of Hachette Book Group, Inc.

First Yen Press Edition: January 2013

ISBN: 978-0-316-22534-2

10 9 8 7

BVG

Printed in the United States of America